WITHDRAWN

# Safe Practice

in Physical Education and School Sport

association for
**Physical Education**

ISBN: 978-1-905540-54-9

**Authors:**

Peter Whitlam and Glen Beaumont

**Additional authors:**

Games – Anne Chapple, Brunel University
Individual and Special Needs – Dr Keith Gutteridge, Consultant
Health-related Exercise – Dr Jo Harris, Loughborough University
Outdoor and Adventure Activities – Andy Murphy, Lancashire Local Authority
Safeguarding Children and Young People – Keith Spencer, GK Partnership, and Steve Boocock, CPSU
Combat Sports – Janet Thorpe, Kirklees Local Authority

**afPE appreciates the contributions through review made by:**

Leverne Barber – University of Worcester
Susan Cooke – Lancashire Local Authority
Nigel Edwards – Stoke Local Authority
Martin Elliott – DCSF Pupil Well-being Health and Safety Unit
Denise Fountain – Calthorpe Special School and Sports College
Jon Glenn – Amateur Swimming Association
Jenny Gray – Oxford Brookes University
Madeline Haines – Early Years Consultant
Vanessa Incledon – University of Worcester
Angela James – Gloucestershire Local Authority
Steve Kibble – Devon Local Authority
David Maiden – SLANOPE
Eileen Marchant – afPE NCfCPD Lead Consultant

Wayne Marland – Lancashire Local Authority
Colette Maynard – Worcestershire Local Authority
Mark Perkins – Partnerships for Schools
Yasmin Purshouse – Swimming Teachers Association
Martin Radmore – Norfolk Local Authority
Carole Raymond – afPE NCfCPD Lead Consultant and former HMI
John Read – English Schools Football Association
Martin Reddin – British Gymnastics
Dr Lynne Spackman – DCELLS PE Officer
Peter Sutcliffe – UK Athletics
Glenn Swindlehurst – Lancashire Local Authority
Karen van Berlo – University of Worcester
Sue Wilkinson – afPE Business and Development Manager
Jes Woodhouse – afPE Project Manager
Carolyn Woolridge – NDTA Vice Chair

**afPE project lead officer:** Sue Wilkinson
**Coachwise editor:** Christopher Stanners
**Coachwise designer:** Saima Nazir
**Photographs** © Alan Edwards
**Indexer:** Glyn Sutcliffe

Published on behalf of afPE by

Room 117
Bredon
University of Worcester
Henwick Grove
Worcester
WR2 6AJ
Tel: 01905-855 584
Fax: 01905-855 594

Building 25
London Road
Reading
RG1 5AQ
Tel: 0118-378 6240
Fax: 0118-378 6242
Email: enquiries@afpe.org.uk
Website: www.afpe.org.uk

**Coachwise Business Solutions**
Chelsea Close
Off Amberley Road, Armley
Leeds LS12 4HP
Tel: 0113-231 1310 Fax: 0113-231 9606
Email:
enquiries@coachwisesolutions.co.uk
Website: www.coachwisesolutions.co.uk

070374

# Foreword

I am pleased to welcome this seventh edition of *Safe Practice in Physical Education and School Sport*, as published by the Association for Physical Education (afPE). It is a near-indispensable, and updated, compendium of advice and information. All school staff and others who organise or take charge of young people in curricular physical activity can learn from it.

The book shows how sensible and informed preparation will help young people fulfil their potential, in a range of sports, under expert instruction. It therefore assists the government's promotion, with the Health and Safety Executive (HSE), of sensible and enabling risk management.

I am pleased 85% of 5–16-year-olds in England are now taking at least two hours of high-quality physical education and school sport each week (we achieved this a year earlier than planned). In the longer term, we want to offer all 5–16-year-olds up to five hours of sport each week. This will be made up of the two hours within the school day together with a further three hours of sport beyond the school day. This will be delivered by a range of school, community and club providers. We also want to offer up to three hours of sport each week for 16–19-year-olds. *Safe Practice in Physical Education and School Sport* will underpin all this.

I also like the book's new feature of including some details of case studies. These help to focus schools and others away from less-sensible practice. They reinforce the message that the law protects our careful teachers and coaches.

afPE has agreed to make some sections of the new edition available on the public-domain page of its website. For this, I am grateful.

**Andrew Adonis, Parliamentary Under Secretary for Schools**

# Contents

# Appendices

⊙Also included on the accompanying CD

# Introduction

## About this Handbook

Welcome to the seventh edition of *Safe Practice in Physical Education and School Sport*. This edition, commissioned by afPE, succeeds previous editions written under the auspices of baalpe. It has been fully updated to reflect recent developments in statute, case law and current practice in the field of physical education, physical activity and school sport. It has also been extensively restructured and redesigned to ensure that it remains user-friendly.

The only publication of its kind, this handbook is essential reading for all those involved in the delivery of physical education, physical activity and school sport in all types of educational establishments. The aim of the handbook is to provide a sound framework against which readers may analyse and adjust their own practice, and to help readers make informed judgements about safety and risk management in relation to their own circumstances.

This handbook has been written by two highly qualified experts in the field of safety and risk management in physical education and school sport who have drawn, wherever necessary, upon a wider pool of recognised expertise. It has also been reviewed by a wide range of relevant individuals and organisations to ensure that the guidance provided is accurate and relevant across the whole of the United Kingdom and across the full range of activities and sports included in the handbook. Numerous national organisations commend the contents to school staff, parents and other adults working in an educational context. It is also used extensively by the legal profession.

The principles set out in this handbook are also relevant to other contexts, such as further and higher education, prison services and commercial providers and other countries. All those involved in the delivery of physical activity in such contexts should be able to apply the guidance provided to their own circumstances.

The handbook aims to provide guidance on good practice. However, it is recognised that school staff may work within a range of reasonable options (as per the Woodbridge School case [2002]) which can include the application of acceptable strategies other than those included here. The style also reflects contemporary interpretation of effective risk management, pursuing themes related to competence and responsibility.

It is important that those involved in the planning and delivery of physical activities understand and apply the generic principles of safe practice to their particular circumstances, rather than rely on simplistic checklists. To aid readers in developing or confirming such an understanding and application, this handbook has been written, wherever appropriate, to provide general principles in the first part of a chapter, which readers should then apply to their particular circumstances. Where relevant, these general principles are followed by activity-specific guidance. It is important that where recommendations to refer to earlier sections are made, this advice is followed in order to provide a comprehensive view of the issues involved.

Employers (local authorities, governors, trustees or proprietors) may impose local requirements and provide effective guidance relating to health and safety. Such requirements and guidance should be known and applied where relevant.

The term *must* is used only where the situation described relates to a statutory requirement. Otherwise, *should* and similar terminology are used to illustrate regular and approved practice.

The term *parents* is intended to include carers, guardians and other next-of-kin categories.

## Structure

This handbook is divided into three main parts:

- **Part 1** provides general guidance on the effective management of risk in physical education, school sport and physical activity.

- **Part 2** provides specific guidance on individual activities and sports.

- **The Appendices** provide readers with a wide range of additional and supplementary information clearly referenced in the text. The appendices with posters or forms you might want to print out are included on the CD. Those with lists of useful websites also appear on the CD, with hyperlinks to the sites in question.

The guidance provided in *Part 1* applies to each of the individual activities and sports included in *Part 2*. It is therefore essential to refer to the whole of *Part 1* in addition to the relevant chapter(s) in *Part 2*. Information in the *Appendices* supplements what is in the main text and should be accessed according to need.

Good practice in physical education and school sport reflects safe practice which, in turn, involves the effective management of risk. In this context, physical education may be defined as providing a balance between appropriate challenge and an acceptable level of risk.

Figure 1 below displays the three key dimensions that impact on this balance and the key considerations relating to them:

The **people** involved in
a physical-education activity

The **context** in which
the activity takes place

The **organisation**
of the activity

**Figure 1: The key dimensions in balancing appropriate challenge and acceptable risk**
(courtesy of Beaumont, Eve, Kirkby and Whitlam)

This triangular concept of risk assessment involving the three dimensions of **people**, **context** and **organisation** is central to this handbook (please refer to *Chapter 3: Risk Management* for additional explanation). The majority of chapters, and particularly those in *Part 2*, have incorporated this structure under the heading **What Staff Should Know**. However, some chapters in *Part 1* are predominantly focused on one dimension only and where this is the case, it is made clear in the chapter introduction. The table below lists these particular chapters under their appropriate heading.

| People | Context | Organisation |
|---|---|---|
| Chapter 11: Religious and Cultural Issues | Chapter 2: Physical Education and the Law | Chapter 3: Risk Management |
| | Chapter 8: Accident Procedures and First-aid Management | Chapter 5: Management of the Curriculum |
| | Chapter 12: Equipment in Physical Education | |
| | Chapter 13: Personal Protection | |
| | Chapter 14: Clothing and Personal Effects | |
| | Chapter 15: Buildings and Facilities | |
| | Chapter 16: Transporting Pupils | |

The full diagram in Figure 1 is set out in *Appendix 2F* (see page 303 and the CD) or can be downloaded from the afPE website: www.afpe.org.uk

All chapters adopt a common four-part format, beginning with a short **Introduction** that establishes the nature and particular demands of the issue, or activity, in question.

Following on from the introduction comes the section **What Staff Should Know**. This provides detailed guidance and recommendations, which staff need to consider in the context of safe practice.

It is important that all pupils are involved in the assessment and management of risk at a level appropriate to their age, ability, experience and behaviour. The importance of risk education for pupils is highlighted throughout the handbook and is reinforced in each chapter with a **What Pupils Should Know** section.

Finally, each chapter concludes with **Additional Information** about further contacts and support materials relevant to the activity/issue and, where possible, reference to existing case law for illustrative purposes. Further detail about many of the cases referred to can be found in *Case Law in Physical Education and School Sport: A Guide to Good Practice*[1].

Substantial **Appendices** are also provided, containing a wide range of materials, such as exemplar risk assessments, further guidance materials, relevant government department guidance, NGB statements and other helpful materials.

## Legislation

Health and safety legislation applies to all the home countries in the United Kingdom. However, other specific legislation may vary. Although the position in each of the home countries is broadly similar, those involved in the delivery of physical education and school sport in Northern Ireland, Scotland and Wales are recommended to visit the following websites for details of specific legislation and policy:

- www.opsi.gov.uk/legislation/northernireland/ni_legislation.htm

- www.opsi.gov.uk/legislation/scotland/about.htm

- www.opsi.gov.uk/legislation/wales/wales_legislation.htm

## Further Help

The aim of this handbook is to provide comprehensive guidance for all those involved in the delivery of physical education and school sport. Inevitably, it is impossible to account for all eventualities and readers may have specific issues or concerns that are not answered by the relevant chapter(s) of this handbook. In these circumstances, readers are encouraged to seek further clarification from appropriate sources (eg local authority support staff, higher education providers, other school staff) and/or afPE through:

- the Association's newsletter

- the Association's website

- direct access to the Association's Health and Safety Team (email, telephone, written correspondence)

- the Association's health and safety professional development programme

- the Association's National College for Continuing Professional Development (NCCPD) programme (contact cpdopportunities@afpe.org.uk).

Please refer to the relevant chapters for a list of useful contacts and website addresses for this purpose.

[1] Whitlam, P. (2004) *Case Law in Physical Education and School Sport: A Guide to Good Practice*. Leeds: Coachwise Business Solutions. ISBN: 978-1-902523-77-4

# Glossary of Terms

| | |
|---|---|
| Additional educational needs | Specific requirements relating to issues such as ability, cultural background, ethnicity and language, which may have safety implications and should be considered by those delivering physical education and school sport. |
| Adults | Occasionally used as a collective term for school staff, volunteers and paid coaches. |
| Adults supporting learning | See Support staff. |
| Coaches | All those who are not members of school staff who are contracted (ie paid) to deliver an agreed physical-education or school-sport programme. |
| Cover staff | Adults employed to supervise groups doing pre-prepared work. They may not have any expertise in physical education and, as such, should take groups for classroom-based lessons. |
| EAL pupils | Pupils with English as an additional language. |
| Employers | Includes local authorities, local authority children's services, departments of education and education service, education and library boards, school governing bodies, trustees, managers of other premises (including school grounds and outdoor centres) and self-employed people who employ others. |
| Foundation/Key Stage 1 | In Northern Ireland, pupils aged 5–7 years. |
| Head teachers | All those responsible for managing educational establishments (includes principals). |
| Helpers | Used specifically in the context of special educational needs. |
| Key Stage 1 | Pupils aged 5–7 years (now covered by the Foundation Phase in Wales, which includes pupils aged 3–7). |
| Key Stage 2 | Pupils aged 7–11 years. |
| Key Stage 3 | Pupils aged 11–14 years. |
| Key Stage 4 | Pupils aged 14–16 years. |
| Parents | Includes carers, guardians and other next-of-kin categories. |
| Physical education | Short for the term *physical education and school sport* – abbreviated to *physical education* or *PESS* for convenience. |
| Pupils | All young people attending any form of educational establishment. |
| School sport | All sessions which take place outside of lesson time (formerly known as *extra-curricular activities* or *out-of-school-hours learning*). |
| Subject leaders | All those responsible for managing physical education and school sport in any phase or educational establishment. |
| Staff | Any adult delivering physical education to pupils with the approval of the head teacher, including qualified teachers, volunteers and paid coaches, agency staff and those on a school staffing roll without qualified teacher status, such as learning mentors, classroom assistants and teaching assistants. |
| Support staff | Adults without qualified teacher status (QTS) who contribute to education programmes whether in a paid or voluntary capacity. (The term *practitioners* is used in Wales.) |

| | |
|---|---|
| Teachers | Used specifically in circumstances where qualified teachers have a particular responsibility (includes lecturers in further and higher education). |
| Volunteers | Adults (and young leaders under the age of 18 who are closely managed by school staff) who are not paid for their work within physical-education or school-sport programmes (includes trainee teachers). |

## Abbreviations

| | |
|---|---|
| AALS | Adventure Activities Licensing Service |
| ABA | Amateur Boxing Association |
| ABRS | Association of British Riding Schools |
| afPE | Association for Physical Education |
| AIDS | acquired immune deficiency syndrome |
| ARA | Amateur Rowing Association |
| ASA | Amateur Swimming Association |
| BAB | British Aikido Board |
| BCA | British Caving Association |
| BCU | British Canoe Union |
| BG | British Gymnastics |
| BHS | British Horse Society |
| BJA | British Judo Association |
| BMA | British Medical Association |
| BMG | British Association of Mountain Guides |
| BOF | British Orienteering Federation |
| BSA | British Surfing Association |
| BSAC | British Sub-Aqua Club |
| BSI | British Standards Institute |
| BS EN | British Standards European Norm |
| BWA | British Wrestling Association |
| BWLA | British Weightlifting Association |
| CE | Conformité Européene |
| CEOP | child exploitation and online protection |
| CPD | continuing professional development |
| CRB | Criminal Records Bureau (also Disclosure Scotland and AccessNI) |
| CYQ | Central YMCA Qualifications |
| DCSF | Department for Children, Schools and Families (formerly Department for Education and Skills [DfES]) |
| DCELLS | Department for Children, Education, Lifelong Learning and Skills (Wales) |
| EAL | English as an additional language |
| EU | European Union |
| FARS | Federation of Artistic Roller Skating |
| FILA | Fédération Internationale des Luttes Associées |
| FIT | Fields in Trust |
| GAA | Gaelic Athletic Association |
| GNAS | Grand National Archery Society |

| | |
|---|---|
| HASEE | *Health and Safety on Educational Excursions* |
| HASPEV | *Health and Safety for Pupils on Educational Visits* |
| HIV | human immunodeficiency virus |
| HSE | Health and Safety Executive |
| HSO | health and safety officer |
| HSWA | Health and Safety at Work Act 1974 |
| IEP | individual education plan |
| ILAM | Institute of Leisure and Amenity Management |
| IRB | International Rugby Board |
| ISA | Independent Safeguarding Authority |
| ISRM | Institute of Sport and Recreation Management |
| ITE | initial teacher education |
| ITT | initial teacher training |
| LA | local authority |
| LCMLA | Local Cave and Mine Leader Assessment Scheme |
| LOtC | *Learning Outside the Classroom* |
| MCA | Maritime and Coastguard Agency |
| MLTUK | Mountain Leader Training UK |
| NCSS | National Council for School Sport |
| NDTA | National Dance Teachers Association |
| NGB | national governing body |
| NISA | National Ice Skating Association |
| NQF | National Qualifications Framework |
| NQT | newly qualified teacher |
| NSSA | National School Sailing Association |
| OAA | outdoor and adventurous activities |
| OCR | Oxford, Cambridge and RSA Examinations |
| PADI | Professional Association of Diving Instructors |
| POCA | Protection of Children Act 1999 |
| QCA | Qualifications and Curriculum Authority |
| QTS | qualified teacher status |
| R | Regina |
| REPs | Register of Exercise Professionals |
| RFL | Rugby Football League |
| RFU | Rugby Football Union |
| RIDDOR | Reporting of Injuries, Diseases and Dangerous Occurrences Regulations 1995 |
| RLCEP | Rugby League Coach Education Programme |
| RLSS | Royal Life Saving Society UK |
| RNIB | Royal National Institute of Blind People |
| RoSPA | Royal Society for the Prevention of Accidents |
| RYA | Royal Yachting Association |
| SEN | special educational needs |
| SENCO | special educational needs coordinator |
| SLSA | Surf Life Saving Association |
| STA | Swimming Teachers' Association |

# Part one
## General Guidance

8

# Chapter one
## General and Common Principles

This chapter sets the scene for the remainder of the book by outlining and summarising elements of safe practice that permeate all physical activity within the context of physical education and school sport (PESS).

## 1.1 Introduction

1.1.1 This chapter summarises the key principles staff should consider in their safe and effective planning, delivery and evaluation of PESS.

1.1.2 Young people in today's society have access to a diverse and extremely wide range of physical activity. This extends from outdoor and adventurous pursuits to sports-hall activities such as basketball or trampolining; from activities that are based upon individual achievement, such as gymnastics and athletics, to those where a collective effort is required, as in team games; from sports that rely on significant self-regulation, such as golf, to those that need to be tightly controlled, such as combat sports or invasion games involving physical contact.

1.1.3 **Risk is inherent in all physical activity** and needs to be assessed and managed effectively. It is neither possible nor desirable to remove all risks from physical activity, but it is important that the different hazards and risks involved in different activities are recognised. Some activities are clearly more hazardous than others and involve a higher possibility of injury or harm than others. Sports involving a high degree of physical contact, for instance, record a greater number of injuries than activities in which contact is expressly forbidden or simply not part of the context. Whatever the activity, the generic safety principles listed below should be considered and, where appropriate, applied to, and integrated into, the risk-management process.

1.1.4 It is also important that young people are involved in learning to manage risks effectively as part of their education.

## 1.2 What Staff Should Know

### People

1.2.1 Staff should have a **sound knowledge** of any activity that they intend to teach or lead. Judgements about necessary competence will often be informed by formal qualifications, such as specialist physical-education training, post-training professional development and national governing body (NGB) coaching awards. However, **previous experience** in a particular activity should also count when assessing an adult's capability to lead an activity.

1.2.2 Additionally, all staff should be confident in working with children and young adults and know what kind of activity, level of physical challenge and organisational procedures are appropriate to a particular developmental stage. Staff should also demonstrate **an appropriate knowledge of the needs of individual pupils and pupil groups**. They should be deemed fit and proper persons to be working with young people, whether working independently with groups – in which case formal Criminal Records Bureau (CRB) disclosure certification will be required – or assisting a more qualified member of staff or coach.

1.2.3 **Qualifications in first aid** should match the requirements of the situation. Resuscitation technique, procedures for treating neck and spinal injuries and the arrest of bleeding constitute baseline knowledge for those responsible for supervising physical activities, particularly in remote situations. The **school's procedures for managing first aid and emergency situations** and how to implement these procedures are essential knowledge for all staff.

1.2.4 Pupils should demonstrate a **good understanding of rules and procedures** associated with safe participation, in terms of their own involvement and that of others, and, wherever possible, share in the risk-assessment process. It is important to remember that many rules and regulations found in games activities, for instance, are directly concerned with safety and should be respected accordingly.

## Context

1.2.5 Care should be taken to ensure that **working areas, equipment and storage** meet acceptable standards for reliable and safe usage. Regular maintenance and inspection by an appropriate agency are essential. Resources and equipment need to be compatible with the age, size, strength, ability and experience of the participating groups. Faulty equipment should never be used and should always be securely stored until made good or replaced.

1.2.6 Staff should exercise vigilance and systematically check that participants and staff present themselves in **appropriate attire** and in an acceptably safe manner. Clothing, personal protective equipment, where recommended, and footwear should be appropriate to the activity, fit well and provide secure traction, ensuring the well-being of the individual wearer and other participants alike. This would also include attention to long hair, personal effects and inappropriate manicure.

## Organisation

1.2.7 Clearly understood and well-communicated **risk-assessment and management procedures** are central to safe practice and constitute an ongoing process.

1.2.8 Group size, facility restrictions and pupil behaviour will influence teaching and organisation.

1.2.9 Staff should be aware of the risks associated with personal participation while teaching or coaching physical activities, particularly those involving physical contact or in which hard missiles (eg cricket/rounders balls) are used. **Staff participation** should be restricted to practical demonstrations in a controlled setting or to bring increased fluency into a game situation. Such involvement should not compromise any ability to retain acceptable control of the whole group.

1.2.10 It is essential that, in teaching situations, pupils are **well matched** in terms of size, weight, age, experience, confidence and ability wherever physical contact, weight bearing and hard missiles, such as rounders or cricket balls, are involved. Teaching of any physical activity should always follow a **carefully planned and graduated progression** based on a well-differentiated scheme of work. Pupils should be deemed competent and appropriately prepared before embarking on more complex and demanding physical tasks.

1.2.11    **Conditioned or modified versions** of activities encourage safe participation and are particularly effective with groups of beginners, groups of varying abilities, or where any lack of personal protective equipment has safety implications.

1.2.12    The nature and demands of different kinds of physical education and school sport (PESS) will inevitably require greater or lesser amounts of off-site activity. Consideration needs to be given to the **safe transportation** of pupils and appropriate standards of care ensured to match those found within the normal school environment.

1.2.13    National governing bodies (NGBs) issue directives concerning the safe management of their respective activities. It is generally accepted that, within the context of outdoor adventurous activities, such directives should be closely followed. Compliance will also be needed whenever a match or competition takes place under the auspices of an NGB. Activity undertaken as part of a prescribed curriculum, school sport, or involving friendly fixtures is not legally bound to such directives, but serious consideration should be given to them as good advice when compiling risk assessments.

## 1.3    What Pupils Should Know

1.3.1    The spirit of the activity should be considered as important as playing to the rules. A healthy attitude to competition and challenge should be encouraged and adopted by all participants. Loss of temper, dissent and overzealous play can have major safety implications.

1.3.2    Decisions made by officials, coaches and leaders merit respect and compliance.

1.3.3    Risk assessment is an inherent part of any involvement in physical activity. It informs safe practice and participation and should never be overlooked or ignored.

1.3.4    Personal responsibility needs to be taken for ensuring that conduct, personal effects, clothing, footwear and any necessary items of equipment appropriate to the activity meet safety expectations.

1.3.5    Behaviour should be such that it does not interfere with learning and safe practice.

## 1.4    Additional Information

*Appendix 2A: A Generic Risk-assessment Prompt Sheet,* pages 296–297, supports this summary.

# Chapter two
## Physical Education and the Law

**2**

This chapter deals with a **contextual** aspect of risk management. It seeks to equip staff with a working knowledge about those elements of the law and legal processes that are most likely to affect and determine their duty-of-care obligations within the context of physical education and school sport (PESS).

## 2.1 Introduction

2.1.1 The aim of this chapter is to raise the awareness of all those who work or help in schools of their legal duties and responsibilities in relation to safe practice.

2.1.2 All adults who contribute to the delivery of physical education, school sport and physical-activity programmes operate within a complex legal framework involving both criminal and civil law. The relevant elements considered here include the standard of care expected, negligence, health and safety, disability discrimination, violent conduct in sport, and safeguarding children and young people.

2.1.3 English and Welsh law are common, but the legal systems in Scotland and Northern Ireland are distinct in some ways from that in England and Wales. However, the principles of good practice as safe practice are universal.

## 2.2 What Staff Should Know

### Civil law

2.2.1 Civil law is a combination of common law and a few Acts of Parliament applicable to private claims for compensation. Common law is that law that has evolved through custom and practice and over time as individuals resorted to the courts for compensation because of some harm or damage caused by the acts of omission or commission by another person. In PESS, the damage is usually in the form of injury. The claimant sues the other person, the defendant, for damages in the form of compensation. If the action is successful then the defendant is found liable. Where compensation is awarded as a result of a successful action, it is assessed on the basis that it is to compensate the claimant for the injury, rather than to punish the defendant for the careless act.

2.2.2 Unless personal accident insurance is taken out, which normally covers injury with longer-term or permanent effects, the only compensation available to an injured person is through a civil-court claim for damages.

2.2.3 This search for compensation has led to an apparent increase in litigation in PESS over recent years. However, in relation to the amount of PESS taught, claims for negligence are actually rare. Concern is sometimes expressed by school staff when claims are settled out of court. Such settlements may often be made on an economic basis, in that a settlement is cheaper than fighting the claim in court, and with no admittance of liability. In such instances, staff should not assume that a claim for negligence has been accepted by their employer.

### a. Duty of care

2.2.4    Everyone has a duty of care not to cause harm to others.

2.2.5    The standard of care expected of the public is that of 'a reasonably competent person'. The standard of care expected of school staff originally applied only to teachers and was described as being *'in loco parentis'*, in place of a prudent parent. This standard has been modified and updated to the context of a school rather than a home because a teacher clearly has responsibility for more children at any one time and in a different environment. Modernisation of the school workforce has broadened the scope of this level of professional responsibility even further to include all adults who work with young people.

2.2.6    As school staff are deemed to possess specialist skills in the profession of teaching, they are not judged using the general 'reasonably competent person' criteria, but judged as whether some people in the same profession would have done the same action (ie it is regular and approved practice in the profession). This is known as the **Bolam test**, in which '…a man is not negligent if he is acting in accordance with such a practice merely because there is a body of opinion who would take a contrary view'.

> For a reference to the case that established the Bolam test, see *2.5.3*, page 21, in this chapter.

2.2.7    Within this recognition of whether accepted practice is applied, the courts have also recognised that there is no single answer to a situation. Staff are expected to operate 'within a range of reasonable options', as established in the case of Woodbridge School v Chittock (2002). This supports the Bolam principle, in that the teaching profession is judged according to what it would be common to see across the profession, with no single remedy deemed to be the answer to an issue.

2.2.8    The standard of care has thus been set as that of a reasonably competent person working at an acceptable level of expertise and in the same area of activity. A member of staff, coach or volunteer who is inexperienced would be judged by the same standard as more experienced colleagues to avoid inexperience being frequently used as a defence against an allegation of negligence.

2.2.9    A fair and realistic view of responsibility is usually taken as not expecting perfection, but requiring a standard appropriate to a competent professional person. There is no distinction in the standard of care expected between teachers and others working with pupils, other than that set by the level of expertise the individual offers and the circumstances within which he/she works.

2.2.10   School staff have a duty to work within a system that anticipates and manages risks. Head teachers must ensure that such a system is operable, even by recently appointed staff.

2.2.11   School staff continue to exercise a duty of care for pupils aged 18 when under school regulations. This duty of care applies to any school pupil until he/she has reached the age of 19, at which stage a young person ceases to have the legal status of being a registered school pupil.

2.2.12   The duty and standard of care is continuous and cannot be diluted or removed by any association with the terms *holiday, abroad, weekend* or similar terms. Whatever the school organises, the school retains a responsibility for.

**b.        Higher duty of care**

2.2.13    Where an adult has knowledge and experience which is higher than that to be expected of a reasonably competent person acting in his/her position or capacity then he/she is judged by that enhanced standard of foresight. This defines a **higher duty of care**, in that an adult with specialist expertise, qualifications or responsibility is expected to have a greater insight and awareness of the consequences of his/her actions. Thus, 'specialists' in a particular area, or adults leading higher-risk activities, or adults responsible for very young children or young people with limited abilities are deemed to have a higher duty of care, that is a higher level of responsibility, for those in their care and will be judged as having a greater degree of insight relating to the consequences of their actions.

**c. Negligence**

2.2.14    Compensation for injury caused by the careless, unintentional actions of staff, officials or participants in PESS is usually obtained through a claim of negligence.

2.2.15    Negligence may arise when an individual's actions fall below the standard of care expected in the particular circumstances to protect others from the unreasonable risk of harm.

2.2.16    An allegation of negligence needs four requirements:

i.   A duty of care is owed to the other person (ie the defendant has some responsibility for the claimant).

ii.  That duty is breached in some way (ie the defendant is careless by act or omission).

iii. Damage arises from the breach (ie injury occurs to the claimant due to the defendant's carelessness).

iv.  The harm was foreseeable (ie the act or omission could have been anticipated, was unreasonable and fell below the expected level of care).

If all four requirements are present then negligence may be evident.

2.2.17    Injuries will occur in PESS simply because of its active nature. These are **'no-fault' accidents**. It is the element of carelessness that may impose a liability of negligence. The use of reasonable foresight, anticipation and forward planning is expected, set at the level of guarding against the probable consequences of a failure to take care, to avoid acts or omissions that could be reasonably foreseen as likely to cause injury to other people.

2.2.18    Claims for negligence are normally made against employers. Significant levels of protection exist against allegations of negligence by staff as individuals.

**d. Defences against a charge of negligence**

2.2.19    **Vicarious liability:** An employer is responsible for the acts of an employee when he/she is acting in the proper course of his/her employment. This would apply to anything undertaken as part of any contractual or sanctioned voluntary duty. For this reason, those working in PESS are expected to:

• work within guidelines and policies laid down by the employer

• gain permission for particular activities

• follow regular and approved practice

• maintain an up-to-date awareness of the subject through continuing professional development (CPD).

Where someone is not competent to undertake the responsibility placed on him/her, but has been placed in that situation by the employer, or the employer's representative, such as a head teacher, the employer may be directly liable for the negligence. A head teacher, as the manager technically deploying staff, must ensure individual staff have the competence to fulfil the demands of any tasks to which they have been deployed.

2.2.20 **Contributory negligence:** Any act or omission by the injured party seeking compensation that contributes to the injury may be taken into account when compensation is determined. The level of compensation may then be reduced according to the claimant's percentage of responsibility for contributing to the injury. The younger the person injured, the less likely he/she is to be considered to have an awareness of his/her contribution to the situation. A similar decision is likely to be made for those with some form of learning difficulty.

2.2.21 **Voluntary assumption of risk:** This principle allows the court to provide no compensation to a claimant whatsoever. It is based on the premise that the participant knowingly accepts the possibility of injury through taking part in an activity within the laws, spirit or common practice of that activity. It does not allow for the infliction of harm outside the laws and spirit of a game so any intentional or reckless infliction of injury cannot be defended under this principle. It is a concept that would apply to adult participation in sport or to voluntary participation by young people only in very specific circumstances. It would be difficult to apply this defence to a pupil in physical-education lessons that require participation as part of a prescribed curriculum. It would also be difficult to show that young people, particularly, were fully cognisant of the risks involved and were legally competent to accept them. The only consent to injury that parents have to accept on behalf of their children is that which arises as a result of an unforeseeable accident.

2.2.22 **Good practice defences** against allegations of negligence would include the following:

i. **A portfolio of records:** Evidence of the following can be of great value in refuting allegations of negligence:

- policies and guidelines

- schemes of work

- registers of attendance

- assessment records

- medical information

- risk assessments

- accident logs and analysis of these

- equipment maintenance reports

- minutes of meetings

- evidence of professional development

- training records.

ii. **Regular and approved practice:** Practice that is typical of that seen nationally, rather than only locally, is deemed to be widely used because it is safe. Such practice is typical of that evident in local authority (LA) and NGB or national association guidelines.

16

iii. **Using equipment only for the purpose it was designed for:** Equipment needs to be fit for purpose. Improvisation of equipment or teaching situations should proceed only with very careful forethought in order to avoid the possibility of injury arising from makeshift arrangements.

iv. **Progression:** Progressive practices enable young people to develop or proceed in competence and confidence in more complex movement and skills application over time.

v. **Comparable size, ability, experience and confidence:** Matching these considerations when young people are weight bearing or when physical contact or an accelerating projectile, such as a cricket ball, form part of a teaching situation provides a context in which young people may practise and improve safely.

vi. **Effective officiating:** Knowing and applying the rules of a game knowledgably provides a safe and consistent context in which pupils may learn.

vii. **The adult's role in playing a game:** Adults should avoid playing a full part as a participant in a game with young people due to the differences in strength and experience. It is good practice to take a limited role in a game periodically to set up situations that enable the pupils to learn from that participation. This would exclude adult involvement in activities such as tackling, shooting with power and bowling or pitching with pace.

viii. **Codes of conduct:** These set out the expectations placed on a pupil and are useful documents to make clear to pupils and parents the standards expected of those taking part. In extreme circumstances, a code of conduct could be used as the basis for the early return of an individual from an event, such as an adventure holiday, if his/her behaviour causes concerns and the parents are aware of acceptable behaviour being a condition of taking part.

> For a code of conduct, see *Appendix 12: Code of Conduct for Pupils on Educational Visits,* page 358 and the CD.

### e. Consent forms

2.2.23　It is a common misconception that consent forms signed by parents indemnify the teacher against any claim for negligence. This is not so. **Such disclaimers have no standing in law.** The courts would not recognise anyone being absolved of his or her responsibility before an event takes place. Also, under the principles of the Unfair Contract Terms Act 1977, minors have three years after reaching the age of consent (18 years old) to retrospectively file a claim in their own right for any injury suffered as a minor. This clearly sets a parental consent form as a participation agreement only. Such an agreement does not absolve responsibility. It is a signed statement indicating that the parent has been informed of, and understands, the risks involved in an activity and agrees to comply with the conditions stated.

2.2.24　As a form of consent, participation agreements apply to optional activities and not to mandatory educational experiences such as the school's duty to deliver a prescribed curriculum.

**Statute within civil law**

2.2.25    Judicial decisions and custom and practice are the main bases for claims of civil wrong. Only a few Acts of Parliament are relevant to civil claims. These include the following:

- The Occupiers' Liability Acts 1957 and 1984, which introduced a duty of care to all lawful visitors to a site or facility. The occupier, owner or manager is required to take reasonable precautions to ensure that visitors, be they pupils or adults, will be reasonably safe in using the premises for the purposes they were invited to be there for. A claim could be made when an occupier, owner or manager is shown to have, or is expected to have, an awareness of some defect in the premises that could lead to injury. The standard expected relates to that of negligence and includes an awareness that children are likely to be less careful than adults – an obvious implication for school and leisure facilities. School leadership teams are therefore responsible for ensuring that school premises are safe to use.

- The Special Educational Needs and Disability Act 2001, together with the Disability Discrimination Act 2005 (which amended the Disability Discrimination Act 1995) set LAs and school governing bodies a duty not to treat disabled pupils less favourably, without justification, than their non-disabled peers (**the less favourable treatment duty**) and to make reasonable adjustments to ensure that disabled pupils are not put at a substantial disadvantage compared to non-disabled pupils (the **reasonable adjustments duty**). The reasonable adjustments duty requires schools to think ahead, anticipate the barriers that disabled pupils may face and remove or minimise them before a disabled pupil is placed at a substantial disadvantage. This planning should include consideration of health and safety issues in physical education.

## Criminal law

2.2.26    Criminal law addresses offences that are serious enough to be deemed against society, rather than an individual. A successful prosecution requires a level of proof **beyond reasonable doubt**. This is higher than the level of **probability** in civil cases. A guilty verdict results in a conviction, with the penalty consisting of imprisonment, a fine, prohibition, probation or community service. The punishment provides no direct benefit to the injured party.

2.2.27    Criminal prosecutions in education are much less common than civil claims for negligence, but there are occasions, particularly under health and safety law, when criminal prosecutions are made.

## Health and safety

2.2.28    Schools have been fully included in health and safety legislation since the enactment of the Health and Safety at Work Act 1974. This Act moved the emphasis from compensation of the injured to the proactive prevention of injury. The Act seeks to secure the health, safety and welfare of those at work and to protect others visiting and using the premises against risks to their health and safety arising out of the activities of those at work.

2.2.29    By law, employers are responsible for health and safety. Employers must provide a safe work environment, in terms of a safe workplace and safe systems of work. This includes a requirement for a written policy, the identification of personnel with responsibility for the organisation of health and safety and the arrangements for effective implementation of the policy. Schools should develop and apply their own policy for health and safety, including consideration of PESS, based on the employer's policy.

2.2.30    Health and safety is integral to good management. Head teachers have responsibility for everything over which they have control. This includes all day-to-day health-and-safety issues, whether to do with sessions organised in curriculum time, out of hours, at weekends or even during holidays. Where they do not have direct control, such as in aspects of capital finance, they are expected to take all reasonable measures to minimise a problem. Subject leaders are responsible for health-and-safety issues within a subject area. Teachers and support staff are expected to know and apply the school policy, report any shortcomings to senior management and to take reasonable steps to control any existing risks.

2.2.31    Employers cannot transfer their responsibility for health and safety, but may delegate, where appropriate, the tasks necessary to discharge the responsibility. It is at this level that teachers of physical education are involved in matters of health and safety – in carrying out risk assessments, interpreting the policy within PESS, informing others of the risks and taking part in any appropriate professional development.

2.2.32    The health and safety of employees and non-employees, such as pupils and other visitors, must be safeguarded so far as is **'reasonably practicable'**. This means that the level of risk should be balanced against the cost of reducing that risk. Measures to manage the risk (ie reduce or eliminate it) must be taken unless the cost of doing so is obviously unreasonable compared to the degree of risk, but the balance must be firmly on the side of health and safety.

2.2.33    The legal duties in health and safety are similar to those related to negligence (ie responsibility, carelessness and foreseeability) with the essential difference that injury must be evident for liability in negligence, but exposure to the risk is sufficient for action under health-and-safety statute.

2.2.34    The Management of Health and Safety Regulations 1999 require that risk assessments be carried out and that these be recorded where there are more than five employees. Risk assessments are central to any health-and-safety system. Assessments must be made of the risks to which employees, pupils and others who visit the school premises are exposed so that appropriate action can be taken to protect their health and safety.

2.2.35    Risk assessments are simply systematic general examinations of environmental factors, workplace activities and the people involved, which will enable those responsible to identify the risks posed by competence, working methods, processes, equipment and environmental influences. Having identified the hazards and determined the degree of risk, then action may be required to reduce a high level of risk to a reasonable one.

> For more information on this issue, see *Chapter 3: Risk Management*, pages 23–30.

## Violence in sport

2.2.36    Injuries occur in sport because of bad luck, careless acts or unacceptable violence on the pitch. Violence in sport may cause injury inflicted outside the laws and spirit of the game. This is assault: the fear of or actual infliction of force. **Dangerous play in sport represents unacceptable risk.**

2.2.37      Violence in sport is not confined to adult participation. It is thus relevant to school staff, coaches and managers in school situations because they have a **secondary, vicarious liability** for the actions and behaviour of the pupils on the pitch as they are the final adult to place the pupils in a competitive situation.

2.2.38      There is, as yet, no reported case of such criminal vicarious liability in PESS in the UK, but it could occur where a team manager has knowledge of a pupil's proven violent sporting offences and fails to apply sanctions such that encouragement to persist is evident through continued selection.

2.2.39      Staff who teach, encourage or accept over-aggressive play may be held liable if their players go beyond the rules and spirit of the game. Failure to exercise control of a team is the responsibility of the team manager, a responsibility the manager cannot afford to ignore.

## Safeguarding children in PESS

2.2.40      Adults working with children are in positions of great moral and legal responsibility. Occasionally, this responsibility is transgressed by the adult's actions. The most serious is when children are abused, particularly in a physical or sexual form. Supervising pupils in PESS provides access to changing rooms and the opportunity of seeing children partially clothed, creating the possibility of physical contact and inappropriate photography.

2.2.41      Approved and recognised systems and procedures exist in schools to provide effective protection for young people. NGBs, the National Society for the Prevention of Cruelty to Children Child Protection in Sport Unit (NSPCC – CPSU), Children 1st, sports coach UK, the Department for Children, Schools and Families (DCSF) and, in Wales, the Department for Children, Education, Lifelong Learning and Skills (DCELLS) have all produced helpful literature. Schools need to be aware of child-protection requirements and have effective safeguarding systems in place. All staff who have unrestricted access to young people should have been vetted by the Independent Safeguarding Authority (ISA) and have obtained an enhanced disclosure certificate from the Criminal Records Bureau (CRB), Disclosure Scotland or AccessNI before being allowed to work in any position that provides them with sole access.

> **Note:** Where the abbreviation CRB is used in the text, it refers to the Criminal Records Bureau, Disclosure Scotland and AccessNI.

2.2.42      The Children Act 2004 and the Safeguarding Vulnerable Groups Act 2006 place a statutory duty on key people and bodies to make arrangements to safeguard and promote the welfare of children. Statutory guidance setting out the duty has been published and may be accessed at the DCSF website: www.dcsf.gov.uk

2.2.43      These arrangements require a commitment to the importance of safeguarding and promoting children's welfare, making available to all staff a clear statement of the school's responsibilities towards children, a clear line of accountability within the school for safeguarding and promoting the welfare of children, and training on safeguarding and promoting the welfare of children for all staff working with, or in contact with, children and families.

2.2.44      Safe recruitment procedures must be in place to ensure that inappropriate adults cannot work with pupils.

## 2.3    What Pupils Should Know

2.3.1    Pupils should know:

- how to apply the risk-assessment process at their own level

- the importance of following guidance and instruction about how to participate responsibly.


## 2.4    Additional Information

A summary of relevant statute, regulations and guidance is set out in *Appendix 1: Relevant Statute, Regulations and Guidance*, pages 287–295.


## 2.5    Case Law Examples

2.5.1    Williams versus Eady (1893):
*This described the expected standard of care as that of a careful parent.*

2.5.2    Lyes versus Middlesex County Council (1962):
*This case determined that the application of the careful parent test should be in the context of a school rather than a home because a teacher clearly has responsibility for more children at any one time and in a different environment than the home.*

2.5.3    Bolam versus Friern Hospital Management Committee (1957):
*This established that a person who possesses specialist skills in a profession is not judged by the standard of the reasonable man, but by the standard of people within the same profession.*

2.5.4    Gower versus LB of Bromley (1999):
*This ruling broadened the scope of a teacher's standard of care to encompass a 'reasonable member of the teaching profession', thus expanding the standard of 'in loco parentis' to all adults involved in teaching young people.*

2.5.5    Stokes versus Guest, Keen and Nettleford (Bolts and Nuts) Limited (1968):
*This case determined that, where a defendant has knowledge and experience which is higher than that to be expected of a reasonable person acting in his/her position or capacity, he/she is judged by that enhanced standard of foresight, in other words a higher duty of care.*

2.5.6    Woodbridge School versus Chittock (2002):
*This established the principle of a 'reasonable range of options', recognising that no single response was the correct way in which to deal with an issue, rather that some degree of flexibility according to the circumstances was a more appropriate professional response.*

# Chapter three
## Risk Management

This chapter deals with an **organisational** aspect of risk. It explains the process of risk management within the context of the school and PESS and clarifies the risk-management roles and responsibilities of those involved in the delivery of physical education and related activity.

## 3.1 Introduction

3.1.1 Risk management is central to safe practice. It involves managing the risk (or possibility) of injury by:

- assessing what could cause harm

- judging whether the risk of harm is significant

- controlling or reducing any significant risk of harm (injury) to an acceptable and reasonable level by some form of corrective action or **control measure**.

3.1.2 In the context of PESS, risk management should assist staff in providing appropriate challenges. It should always be remembered that all physical activity involves risk. Staff should not seek to eliminate risk. Overcaution can result in sterile and meaningless activity. **Risk aversion** – seeking to minimise or even remove any potential hazard, rather than effectively manage it – can limit participants' ability to benefit from a physical activity, in terms of learning, motivation and ultimate fulfilment, or deprive them of it altogether.

3.1.3 Three dimensions need to be considered when making a balanced decision to proceed with, modify or cancel an activity or event:

- the **people** involved in the activity (eg pupils or staff)

- the **context** in which the activity takes place (eg the working area, equipment or procedures used)

- the **organisation** of the activity (eg group management, teaching approach or preparation for the activity).

3.1.4 The risk-management model below illustrates the link between these three elements and may be flexibly applied across the full provision of physical activity and organised sport (see *Appendices 2F–J,* pages 303–307, and the CD).

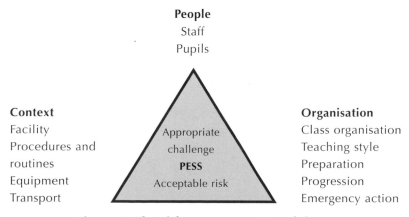

**People**
Staff
Pupils

**Context**
Facility
Procedures and routines
Equipment
Transport

Appropriate challenge
**PESS**
Acceptable risk

**Organisation**
Class organisation
Teaching style
Preparation
Progression
Emergency action

**Figure 2: The risk-management model**
(courtesy of Beaumont, Eve, Kirkby and Whitlam)

## 3.2 What Staff Should Know

### The importance of assessing and managing risk

3.2.1 Everyone has a right to be educated in a safe and healthy environment. However, PESS cannot be totally free from the possibility of injury because it involves practical activity that frequently includes moving at speed, changing direction, often in a confined space, and making rapid decisions.

3.2.2 The purpose of developing risk management in physical education is to:

- offer physical education within a well-managed and safe educational context
- establish common and well-understood codes of practice
- provide consistent administrative and organisational procedures
- ensure that statutory and local requirements are understood and complied with.

3.2.3 Staff have a legal duty to take proactive and positive steps to ensure the health and well-being of their pupils. The standard of care is expected to be reasonable, informed by professional training and guided by common sense.

3.2.4 There are three main types of risk assessment:

a. **Generic risk assessment** – general principles that might apply to an activity wherever it may take place. This will usually be the starting point and is usually provided in written form from the employer, national governing body (NGB) or similar organisation.

b. **Site- or activity-specific risk assessment** – usually carried out for each activity or facility with **specific consideration** of the people involved, the context and the organisation of the activity. This is usually in a written form and reviewed periodically.

c. **Ongoing risk assessment** – (sometimes referred to as **dynamic risk assessment**) carried out while an activity or event is taking place, taking into account and responding to unforeseen issues, such as sudden illness, changes in climatic conditions or ineffective officiating. This is not in written form, but is the expertise that evolves over time and is used during the activity, in forward planning and also to inform future risk assessments.

3.2.5 The Health and Safety Executive (HSE) has the power to confirm that risk assessments are carried out and instigate action against those organisations that fail to do so.

3.2.6 Under the terms of the Management of Health and Safety at Work Regulations 1999, employers have a duty to ensure that periodic formal, activity- or site-specific risk assessments are carried out in the establishments for which they are responsible. In the context of community and voluntary controlled schools, the employer is the local authority (LA). In the case of foundation, trust, voluntary aided, academy and independent schools, governors are the employer. In practice, the majority of voluntary aided schools 'buy in' to LA insurance provision and consequently comply with LA health-and-safety regulation, but this does not abnegate their responsibility for maintaining up-to-date policies. Responsibility for health and safety is usually delegated to head teachers and governors on a day-to-day basis. Under these arrangements, a careful examination must be carried out of what might cause harm to pupils, staff and visitors during all activities organised by the school. Systems need to be put in place to mitigate and manage the potential for such harm.

3.2.7    Under the terms of the Regulatory Reform (Fire Safety) Order 2005, schools are obliged to include a specific, written fire risk assessment within their overall risk-management provision. In the context of physical education, this should involve:

- the identification of escape routes from designated working areas
- safety procedures relating to enclosed areas from which there is no escape (eg storerooms)
- the safe storage of flammable items (eg mats)
- the clear display of and easy access to fire extinguishers
- contingency planning for any emergency evacuation in cold or inclement weather.

3.2.8    School staff should constantly assess risk (ie the likelihood of something causing injury) every working day by applying logic, common sense and specialist knowledge. Forward planning, judgements made during the session and post-session evaluation all contribute to ongoing risk assessment and ultimately inform more formal, written, site-specific risk assessments. Different staff, however, will have differing duties and responsibilities, as summarised below.

3.2.9    The **head teacher** should:

- ensure that regular equipment inspections and risk assessments are carried out
- submit safety reports to governors
- ensure that health-and-safety information is effectively communicated
- maintain overall day-to-day management of health and safety.

3.2.10   The **subject leader** for physical education should:

- establish systematic review procedures to encourage safe practice
- carry out risk assessments
- inspect apparatus and equipment on a regular basis
- ensure appropriate safeguarding provision is made
- inform senior management of any safety concerns
- lead on professional development relating to safe practice
- communicate relevant safety information to all staff
- maintain an up-to-date staff safety handbook/policy
- manage and oversee the use of volunteers and coaches.

3.2.11   **Other staff** should:

- follow school and LA safety guidelines and policies
- ensure a safe working environment
- participate in safety reviews and risk assessments
- take action to reduce risk to acceptable levels
- report any safety concerns as soon as possible to their supervisor/line manager.

3.2.12   Wherever practicable, pupils should be encouraged to complete their own risk assessment of an activity in order that they may share in the risk-assessment process. As key participants, they should always be party to – in a form that they are able to comprehend and make sense of – the definitive risk assessments undertaken by staff. It is also essential that all adults, voluntary or otherwise, concerned with supervision of the activity or event are made suitably aware of any risk assessment.

3.2.13   **Risk assessments** are most effectively carried out:

- as a team exercise using collective expertise

- in or around the facility/location in which the activity is planned to take place

- using the **people, context, organisation** model

- when based upon existing documentation, procedures and practice, establishing whether any additional precautions are necessary over and above those currently in place

- by thinking sequentially through a planned session from start to finish (ie assembly, changing, moving to the working area, activity, return).

## The risk assessment process

3.2.14   The table below illustrates a typical range of generic risk-assessment aspects that might be helpful in compiling activity- or site-specific risk assessments.

**Table 1: Typical generic risk assessment aspects to consider**

| People | Context | Organisation |
|---|---|---|
| **Staff:** <br> • Qualifications/ experience/confidence <br> • Whether continuing professional development (CPD) is needed to improve expertise <br> • Whether supervision is required at all times <br> • Knowledge of individuals and group <br> • Knowledge of the curriculum <br> • Effective observation and analysis skills <br> • Effective control and discipline <br> • Clothing/personal effects appropriate for teaching PESS <br> • Teaching position in relation to pupils <br> • Assistants know limits of their role/responsibility <br> • Effective communication between teacher and support staff <br> • Insurance cover where needed <br> • Disclosure certificates seen by appropriate designated personnel | **Facility:** <br> • Changing rooms safe <br> • Work area hazard free – no obstructions <br> • Clean, non-slip floor/ water clarity <br> • Sufficient space for group size/activity <br> • Any shared-use issues <br> • Access issues for those with disabilities <br> • Operating procedures known and applied <br> • Fire regulations applied <br> • Safety signs in place <br> • Secured when not in use <br><br> **Procedures/routines:** <br> • Orderly movement to work area <br> • Access to facility <br> • First-aid equipment/ procedures/responsibilities known and in place <br> • Notices in place providing essential safety information | **Class:** <br> • Numbers known/register checked <br> • Regular scanning/head counts <br> • Group-organisation/ management procedures in place <br> • Warm-up/preparation/ safe-exercise principles applied <br> • Demonstrations accurate <br> • Involvement of pupils with visual, hearing, motor or cognitive impairment <br><br> **Teaching style:** <br> • Planned sessions providing continuity and progression <br> • Appropriate teaching style used <br> • Rules consistently applied <br> • Regular and approved practice used <br> • Support techniques known and applied <br> • Intervention appropriate <br> • Tasks differentiated |

| People | Context | Organisation |
|---|---|---|
| • Parents informed and involved as necessary<br><br>**Pupils/performers:**<br>• Group sizes<br>• Adult:pupil ratio<br>• Whether additional supervision is required<br>• Control/discipline/behaviour<br>• Individual and group abilities<br>• The demands of the activity need to match pupils<br>• Clothing/personal effects<br>• Clothing appropriate for the activity<br>• Jewellery<br>• Safety equipment/ personal protection<br>• Medical conditions known<br>• Policy on physical contact/substantial access applied<br>• Disability Act requirements about access and involvement in PESS for those with cognitive, visual, hearing or motor impairment<br>• Pupils/performers know routines and procedures | **Equipment:**<br>• Used for purpose it was designed for<br>• Suitable for the activity<br>• Handling/carrying/siting issues<br>• Accessibility/storage<br>• Safety/rescue equipment present<br>• Annual/periodic inspection check<br>• Checked before use by performers<br>• No improvisation<br>• Routines for collection/ retrieval/changing<br><br>**Transport:**<br>• Roadworthiness<br>• Safe embarkation<br>• Seat belts used<br>• Driver requirements/ responsibilities<br>• Passenger lists | **Preparation:**<br>• Written scheme of work sets out safety guidelines to be followed<br>• Equipment – size/type/quality/suitability<br>• Carrying/moving/ placing equipment<br>• Storage<br>• Safety policy applied<br><br>**Progression:**<br>• Progressive practices understood and applied<br>• Appropriate activities<br><br>**Emergency action:**<br>• Emergency/accident procedures/contingency plans known and applied |

For further information on these issues, see *Appendix 2: Risk Assessment Models and Examples,* pages 296–309, and the CD.

## Activity- and site-specific risk assessments

3.2.15    It is recommended that staff assess risk on a facility, activity or event basis using the model and generic aspects outlined above. For example, this may take the form of a risk assessment of a hall while considering the implications of the activities taught in that facility, activity areas of a curriculum, after-school clubs and the procedures for away matches, taking into account the:

- people involved

- facility/location to be used

- equipment

- procedures employed

- nature of the activity

- manner in which the activity will be taught.

3.2.16    Those at risk should then be identified. In the context of schools, risk management will be undertaken predominantly on behalf of **pupils**, but, on occasions, other groups will also merit consideration, such as **staff, visitors and, in rarer cases, members of the public.**

3.2.17 **All risks should be evaluated.** This involves making an informed judgement about whether an identified hazard is capable of causing injury or harm in some way. Generally, risks are categorised as **high, medium or low**. With experience, it is possible to arrive at a category of risk directly using professional judgement, but a matrix approach, as suggested by the HSE, is considered helpful by some. This involves evaluating the hazard's severity combined with probability to determine a risk rating.

3.2.18 However the judgement about risk rating is made, it is strongly advised that those in the education sector, and particularly generalist staff working in primary and special schools, operate within well-managed risk situations where the likelihood of injury is low. The management of high-risk environments requires considerable skill and experience from supervising staff, allied to extensive, rigorous and progressive preparation on the part of pupils. Risk management can only be effective when undertaken by staff deemed competent to do so at the level at which they operate.

3.2.19 The level of hazard in a particular environment or setting is determined by a number of contextual and organisational features, including the:

- extent of unpredictability in the task, event or activity

- speed of decision making required to stay safe

- complexity of the task or activity

- severity of any potential injury should things go wrong.

3.2.20 Human involvement is equally important in judgements about risk level and consideration should focus upon aspects relating to the qualifications and experience of staff in addition to the capabilities of individuals and the group.

## Recording risk

3.2.21 Findings should be recorded as the risk assessment is carried out. There is no set format for a formal written risk assessment. The statutory requirements are that it should:

- demonstrate that the assessment has been carried out

- identify any significant risks and who is affected by them

- identify what action is to be taken to reduce risk to an acceptable level

- record the assessment if there are more than five employees.

Sample risk assessment formats, together with some completed examples, are provided in *Appendix 2: Risk Assessment Models and Examples,* pages 296–309, and the CD.

3.2.22 Local requirements must always be complied with and staff should always check with their employers whether a particular format for recording risk is required.

3.2.23 Whenever health-and-safety procedures or practices are amended, the school or organisation has a duty to inform all those affected. This may be done verbally, in writing or diagrammatically.

3.2.24 Written risk assessments should be reviewed on a regular basis, typically annually or when circumstances change. The date of review should be indicated and the report signed off by the person(s) responsible.

## Ongoing risk assessment

3.2.25    Ongoing risk assessment is unwritten and represents a dynamic process.

3.2.26    During any activity or event, staff need to remain vigilant and should constantly reassess the precautions they have put in place. They should respond to any changes to the anticipated situation that might impact on pupil safety and well-being by modifying the activity in order to eliminate unacceptable risk.

3.2.27    Near misses – occurrences in which a group member could have suffered harm, but fortuitously did not – should be noted and used to inform future risk assessment.

## Risk control

3.2.28    Once a significant risk has been identified, an action plan or **control measure** is required to manage the risk(s) involved. Control measures may be provided through supervision, protection or training.

3.2.29    The following principles, procedures and expectations, using the **people, context, organisation** model, will assist staff in effectively controlling risk.

### Table 2: Effective risk management

| People | Context | Organisation |
|---|---|---|
| It is essential that all those involved in PESS sport are able to work safely.<br>• Ensure that school staff, volunteers and coaches are well qualified, competent and experienced.<br>• Devise and implement suitable working programmes and procedures.<br>• Maintain effective discipline and control.<br>• Provide appropriate supervision.<br>• Ensure compliance with directives concerning protective equipment and clothing. | It is essential that PESS is delivered in a safe environment.<br>• Inspect, repair and service facilities and equipment on a systematic basis.<br>• Display warning signs and notices where risks persist.<br>• Use good-quality equipment that meets British and European safety standards, where available.<br>• Use equipment that is compatible with the pupils' stage of development.<br>• Teach pupils how to manage equipment safely.<br>• Ensure compliance with established procedures. | It is essential that PESS is delivered in a safe and organised manner.<br>• Work to comprehensive, progressive and well-differentiated schemes of work.<br>• Match pupils in terms of strength, experience, ability and confidence where physical contact and competition are involved.<br>• Give clear instructions.<br>• Know when and how to use physical support.<br>• Use observational skills to determine pace, progress and challenge.<br>• Apply regular and approved practice. |

## 3.3    What Pupils Should Know

3.3.1    Pupils should know:

- PESS involves risk and requires a responsible attitude

- risk management applies in some form to **all** areas of physical activity and sport

- advice relating to safe practice, whether verbal or written, should never be ignored

- potential hazards should be reported to a responsible adult and **not** dealt with by pupils

- safe practice involves thinking ahead, wherever possible, about potential hazards and having a plan to keep everybody safe

- how to apply the risk-assessment process at their particular level

- how to recognise hazards and make decisions about how to control risks to themselves and others.

## 3.4      Additional Information

For a range of models and completed risk assessments, see *Appendix 2: Risk Assessment Models and Examples*, pages 296–309, and the CD.

### Resources

Beaumont, G. (2007) 'Health and Safety', *PE Matters*, 2 (1): 31.

Department for Communities and Local Government (DCLG) Publications (2006) *Fire Safety Risk Assessment: Educational Premises*. London: DCLG. ISBN: 978-1-851128-19-8.

HSE (2006) *Five Steps to Risk Assessment* (leaflet).

Whitlam, P. (2007) 'Health and Safety', *PE Matters*, 2 (2): 32.

## 3.5      Case Law Examples

3.5.1      R versus Kite, Court of Appeal (1996):
*Known as the Lyme Bay canoeing tragedy, a managing director of the adventure company was convicted of manslaughter on the basis that he had not established proper safety standards, including a failure to appoint staff with adequate experience for the demands of the activity.*

3.5.2      R versus Ellis, Manchester Crown Court (2003):
*A teacher was convicted of manslaughter and a failure to provide adequate care for the rest of the group when a pupil died during a pool plunging activity where the prevailing conditions required the activity to be cancelled and adequate contingency planning to be in place.*

3.5.3      Taylor versus Corby Borough Council, Northampton County Court (2000):
*The council was held liable for not carrying out adequate risk assessments of the state of some playing fields. The established system was reactive, in that faults were dealt with if noticed, rather than proactive through regular and adequate risk assessments.*

# Chapter four

## Competence to Teach Physical Education and School Sport

4

This chapter identifies and illustrates the meaning and relevance of competence for all those concerned with the delivery of PESS and physical activity.

## 4.1 Introduction

4.1.1 This chapter considers the implications for initial training and continuing professional development (CPD) for all adults who lead or assist in the delivery of PESS. It sets out a baseline of competence that all who work alone with pupils should meet in order to provide a safe learning environment.

4.1.2 **Competence to teach physical education** may be defined as having the skills, knowledge, understanding and expertise necessary to plan, deliver and evaluate a physical-education programme.

4.1.3 The Health and Safety Executive (HSE) highlights four means of demonstrating competence:

- to hold a relevant qualification
- to hold an equivalent qualification
- to have received appropriate in-house training
- to be competent through experience.

These are not totally discrete alternatives. Qualification, experience and training overlap to produce expertise in a particular field or aspect of PESS.

4.1.4 Staff are not legally required to hold a specific award in order to teach a physical-education activity unless their employer requires such qualification. However, it is wise for them to be able to demonstrate that they are suitably trained, experienced and qualified to undertake the activities in which they engage with pupils.

## 4.2 What Staff Should Know

### People

4.2.1 Head teachers should recognise that it is unwise for staff to work in areas in which they lack the appropriate experience and expertise. They and the employer may be held liable if anyone is deployed in a teaching situation for which they do not have the necessary competence to fulfil the demands of the role.

4.2.2 **Primary school teachers** may be required to teach all of the areas of activity in physical education. They should have satisfactorily completed an initial teacher education (ITE) course, which covered all the activities they will be required to teach. ITE institutes accredit new teachers as being competent in all aspects of the Standard for Initial Teacher Education. This implies that the individual teacher has experience and has been assessed against the framework criteria in all aspects of physical education. Where such accreditation is given and the new teacher's lack of experience and competence contribute to a foreseeable injury, then the Institute may be deemed liable for the erroneous accreditation.

4.2.3   Those primary teachers with little or no ITE in physical education may be at risk unless further training opportunities are provided. Such teachers should undertake appropriate professional development before being allowed to teach a full range of activities. Head teachers must be satisfied that all those who are required to teach physical education are able to do so in a safe manner, with a sound understanding of the needs and stages of development of all the pupils in their charge.

4.2.4   Teachers who are responsible for the planning, delivery and evaluation of physical-education programmes in **secondary schools** should have satisfactorily completed appropriate ITE and/or professional development courses that cover all the activities they will be required to teach.

4.2.5   Changes and developments in practice mean that those involved in physical education need to undertake professional development in order to keep abreast of what is acceptable and safe. **Professional-development** courses can provide additional training opportunities for deliverers of physical education. Such development opportunities may be necessary to compensate for omissions in ITE courses.

4.2.6   Some national governing bodies (NGBs) and other awarding bodies require qualifications to be revalidated periodically. This is not simply to endorse previous requirements, but to inform candidates of changes and developments that may have occurred in the interim period. Guidance should be obtained from the relevant NGB, awarding body or local authority (LA), education and library board in Northern Ireland, or an expert consultant.

4.2.7   The standards of expertise, discipline, relationships and risk management expected of all adults working with pupils need to be consistent with providing a safe working environment. This applies at all times and to all on- and off-site school-related activities.

4.2.8   The modernisation of school workforces and ever-broadening opportunities in programmes offered to pupils, both on- and off-site, have led to supervision and teaching responsibilities being given to adults who may not hold a teaching qualification. In these circumstances, the class teacher always maintains overall responsibility for what is taught and for the conduct, health and well-being of the pupils involved.

4.2.9   Adults without qualified teacher status (QTS) working in schools may be on the school staffing roll as **support staff** or contracted for services, often through an agency. In physical education, all adults in this category must work under the direction and supervision of a nominated teacher, but may, subject to their competence and the school's policy, work alongside or remotely from the class teacher and work with groups or whole classes. Head teachers should, on behalf of their employer, ensure that support staff are appropriately managed at all times.

In this handbook, the term *staff* refers to any adult – teacher, support staff, coach or volunteer – working with pupils in physical education or school sport.

The term *support staff* refers to adults without QTS who contribute to education programmes whether in a paid or voluntary capacity. (The term *practitioners* is used in Wales.)

# Context

4.2.10    LAs and school governing bodies may establish their own policies and insist on certain minimum qualifications before staff are allowed to teach some aspects of physical education, particularly those that involve potentially greater risk. Staff should be aware of these local requirements and ensure that they meet the criteria before teaching the activities concerned.

4.2.11    Initially, it is good practice for class teachers to **directly supervise support staff at all times** in order to evaluate their competence. Direct supervision involves support staff working alongside a class teacher so the teacher can intervene at any time, if necessary.

4.2.12    At a later stage, **distant supervision may be appropriate for support staff**, according to their competence and the level of responsibility assigned to them. This would allow them to work at some distance from a class teacher, possibly out of sight, in a different facility or even off site. However, frequent monitoring by the teacher would be part of good management.

4.2.13    It is good practice for schools to keep a register of any support staff used who are not on the school roll, including contact details and work undertaken, for future reference.

4.2.14    **Support staff who are competent to work at a distance from the class teacher** are defined by afPE as having:

- expertise in the range of activities to be taught, ie:
  - technical knowledge
  - knowledge of progression
  - awareness of safety and accident issues
  - knowledge and application of rules
- knowledge of the group – their abilities, confidence and particular needs
- familiarity with the aspects of learning within any prescribed curriculum process model
- the observation and analytical skills to ensure that what is going on is safe and to amend anything that is deemed unsafe
- effective class control.

4.2.15    The level of supervision required for support staff should be determined by a thorough risk assessment. Support staff should be judged on the national standards for Higher Level Teaching Assistants (HLTAs) or, alternatively, on the competences specific to physical education to determine the eventual level of direct, distant or remote supervision required, as described overleaf in Table 3.

**Table 3: Competences to determine the level of supervision required by support staff**

| Quality of Relationships | Knowledge of the Pupils | Pupil Management | Knowledge of the Activities |
|---|---|---|---|
| • Value, care for and respect all children.<br>• Present an appropriate role model (eg use of language, dress, fair play, equality).<br>• Seek to promote the ethos of the school.<br>• Work well with the school staff. | • Identify and respond to individual:<br> ▪ levels of confidence<br> ▪ ability<br> ▪ special educational needs<br> ▪ medical needs<br> ▪ behaviour<br> ▪ age/development stage. | • Use regular and approved practice.<br>• Match pupils' confidence, strength and ability in pair and group tasks.<br>• Maximise participation.<br>• Have strategies for effective pupil control and motivation.<br>• Apply the school's standard procedures and routines (eg child protection, emergency action, personal effects, handling and carrying equipment). | • Understand where and how their work fulfils or complements any relevant prescribed curriculum, programme of study and/or wider curriculum activity.<br>• Demonstrate the appropriate level of expertise to enable learning to take place in the activities being delivered.<br>• Demonstrate an understanding of the overall needs of the age group with whom they are working.<br>• Use:<br> ▪ suitable space for the group<br> ▪ differentiated equipment<br> ▪ differentiated practice<br> ▪ effective progression.<br>• Know and apply rules.<br>• Observation and analytical skills:<br> ▪ Provide a safe working and learning environment.<br> ▪ Identify faults and establish strategies for improvement. |

4.2.16    Careful thought should be given before **cover staff** are allowed to supervise practical lessons for absent physical-education staff. Where the competences set out above are not evident, the lesson should take place in a classroom with preset study materials. Where physical-education staff choose to combine classes to provide some form of physical activity for classes whose usual teacher is absent, they should carry out a risk analysis to determine that it is safe to proceed in the circumstances.

## Organisation

4.2.17    Staff may wish to introduce into a physical-education programme new, emergent activities for which codes of safe practice are still under development. In these circumstances, head teachers should be vigilant and proceed with caution. They need to contact their LA advisory service, a relevant consultant, expert staff in other schools, their insurer, or the relevant NGB or awarding body to obtain the best advice available as to whether to proceed.

4.2.18    Examples of potentially hazardous activities include swimming, trampolining, gymnastics, rugby football and outdoor and adventurous activities. Those teaching these activities should hold **recognised and current qualifications** (eg NGB and other awarding-body qualifications) to demonstrate their suitability to teach or coach the activities safely.

4.2.19    Evidence of accreditation can help head teachers when considering requests from staff to introduce potentially hazardous activities into the physical-education programme.

4.2.20    Some employers do not recommend the use of certain items of equipment in primary schools. Examples include rebound jumping equipment (eg trampettes and trampolines), which require very specialised knowledge and teaching to be used safely. Head teachers should be aware of, implement and monitor all such policies.

4.2.21    Staff should obtain the permission of their head teacher before introducing any new physical-education activity into their school, whether during curriculum time or in school-sport sessions. This is particularly important if the activity is potentially hazardous.

4.2.22    There is no statutory requirement for pupils to be supervised at all times. However, analysis of case law provides a clear indication that **the incidence of injury is much higher during unsupervised activities** than supervised ones.

4.2.23    Direct supervision of pupils enables the adult in charge to intervene at any time. Decisions to supervise less directly should not be taken lightly.

4.2.24    Where a degree of independence is required, progress towards remote supervision should be developed over time. The member of staff involved maintains responsibility for the pupils, regardless of whether he/she is present.

4.2.25    Direct supervision by staff is always required when minors (eg junior sports leaders) assist with the delivery of activities. Regardless of their experience and qualifications, **minors cannot be legally responsible for a group of children** and should therefore always work alongside a member of staff who is able to monitor them and intervene immediately, if necessary.

## 4.3    What Pupils Should Know

4.3.1    Pupils working independently or in a leadership context need to understand that they always remain under the care of an identified member of staff responsible in law for their supervision.

## 4.4 Additional Information

For more information on workforce planning, see *Appendix 2I: Safe Practice in Workforce Planning Poster*, page 306 and the CD.

*Appendix 3* contains:

- *Appendix 3A: Developing a Policy Statement and Guidelines for Workforce Planning in PESS*, pages 310–312

- *Appendix 3B: Best-practice Guidance on the Effective Use of Individual and Agency Coaches in PESS*, pages 313–316

- *Appendix 3C: Potential Roles and Responsibilities when Support Staff Lead Groups Off Site*, pages 317–318.

## 4.5 Case Law Examples

4.5.1 Jones versus Manchester Corporation (1958):
*This case established that where someone is not qualified or competent to undertake the responsibility placed on him/her, but has been placed in that situation by the employer, or the employer's representative such as a head teacher, then the employer may be directly liable for negligence.*

4.5.2 Viasystems (Tyneside) Ltd versus Thermal Transfer (Northern) Ltd, Court of Appeal (2005):
*This case established that two employers can be vicariously liable for the negligence of an employee. The implication from this is that a school, LA or other education employer utilising an external agency to deliver part or all of a physical-education programme could be held liable, along with the agency involved, should any member of the agency staff be negligent in carrying out his/her delegated role. This has a significant management implication for head teachers.*

4.5.3 Porter versus City of Bradford MBC, Court of Appeal (1985):
*A pupil was injured during a field-studies event when two pupils threw rocks from a bridge onto the rest of the group. The teacher, who had not previously taught the group, could not control or organise the group adequately. The LA, as employer, was held responsible for the teacher being deployed in that situation without the skills and training to provide adequate supervision and control.*

# Chapter five
## Management of the Curriculum

5

This chapter deals with an **organisational** aspect of risk management. It establishes the close relationship between good practice and safe practice and identifies a range of strategies to assist effective pupil learning within a safe teaching environment.

## 5.1 Introduction

5.1.1 Health and safety is a whole-school issue. As a practical subject based on a premise of appropriate challenge within an acceptable level of risk, physical education is particularly well placed to make a significant contribution to school provision for educating pupils in the essential area of learning about health and safety.

5.1.2 The English National Curriculum together with the outcomes of Every Child Matters place an obligation on school staff in England to plan for, and implement, learning experiences specifically designed to make children and young adults **more aware of the safety implications**, in terms of their own and others' participation in physical activity. The Qualifications and Curriculum Authority (QCA), for example, in outlining the aims of the Key Stage 3 curriculum, refers to all young people becoming 'confident individuals who...take managed risks and stay safe'. The 2008 national curriculum in Wales contains a section that clarifies learner entitlement and schools' responsibilities within the context of health and safety.

5.1.3 Whatever the choice of curriculum activities or sets of experiences that schools decide meet the needs of their pupils, certain **principles** will need to be adopted in order to sustain safe practice. It is universally accepted that good practice is safe practice, reflecting the close relationship between learning outcomes associated with skill, knowledge and understanding and acceptably safe participation. However, the converse is not necessarily true. Safe practice may not always be good practice, in that overcaution can compromise meaningful, challenging, and formative activity.

5.1.4 This chapter seeks to identify those key principles and procedures that contribute to the acceptably safe organisation and delivery of physical activity within the context of educational settings.

## 5.2 What Staff Should Know

5.2.1 The close relationship between good practice and safe practice is most obvious when the planning and delivery of the curriculum is guided by a number of characteristics:

a. There is clear **consistency** among staff in the implementation of policies and procedures. Pupils need a secure and reasonably predictable environment in order to learn effectively. This is not to say that staff cannot bring individuality to their teaching, but that agreed safety principles need to be applied unambiguously. A coherent and well-laid-out staff/departmental written policy and guidelines are essential to this process.

(see *Appendix 9: Framework for a Policy and Guidelines on Health and Safety in PESS* for a suggested format, pages 343–345).

b. All staff demonstrate an appropriate **understanding of pupil need** when applied to both groups and individuals. The key to this lies in effective assessment, record keeping and communication. It is critical that staff remain fully informed about pupils with physical and learning conditions that might place them at unnecessary risk through physical participation. Staff should be particularly aware of any medical condition that would affect their participation and any medical treatment that a particular pupil may be receiving and take into account its possible effects upon sensory perception, motor control and coordination. Similarly, prolonged absence from school may compromise the progress and performance of some pupils, whereas 'growth spurts' experienced as normal physical maturation can sometimes cause a temporary regression of psychomotor skill, strength, and endurance.

c. Opportunities are provided for **pupils to become involved in the assessment and management of risk** associated with the activities in which they participate. The definitive, formal risk assessment will always be undertaken by staff, but pupils should be expected to contribute at their own level wherever possible.

d. Staff work to well-structured **schemes of work and pupil records**. In many cases involving negligence, the issue of whether pupils have experienced appropriate preparation for a particular physical task is frequently raised. Devising suitable challenge and matching pupil capability to task is enhanced when founded upon progressive and structured learning experiences, enabled through a comprehensive scheme of work and systematic recording and assessment procedures. Planning should be directed at all levels of provision to ensure effective, meaningful and relevant content, including alternative lessons in case of wet weather.

e. **Levels of supervision** are appropriate to the nature of the activity and the pupils in the group. It is frequently difficult to define pupil:staff ratios for school-organised activities because of their highly contextual nature. The same activity would merit more generous staffing levels, for instance, if it was known that the teaching groups concerned presented challenging behaviour. In some areas of the curriculum, such as swimming or outdoor/adventurous activities, the type of environment may determine recommended ratios. A rigorous risk assessment of the activity in question should indicate suitable staffing arrangements in terms of both competence and number.

f. Staff demonstrate **well-developed observation skills**. The ability to analyse and evaluate pupil response to particular tasks is essential to safe teaching, as well as improving performance. Staff should be able to confidently establish, for instance:

- when the onset of fatigue begins to impact upon concentration levels; this is particularly important in activities such as swimming, gymnastics, trampolining and sustained running

- which teaching position offers the optimum position for ensuring safe performance of tasks by individuals and groups

- the frequency of head counts where an activity involves the movement of groups of pupils from one place to another.

g. **Regular communication with parents/carers**, informing them of school and departmental procedures associated with the safe delivery of curricular and school-sport programmes. This might include:

- the school's policy relating to the wearing of personal protective equipment (PPE)

- the management of pupil changing on and off site (swimming pools, leisure centres etc)

- arrangements for ensuring the safety of pupils when travelling to away fixtures.

h. **Lessons are seen to be orderly and well organised**. Poor discipline on the part of staff and reckless behaviour from pupils elevate risk beyond an acceptable level and can needlessly contribute to injury and harm. Lack of concentration and application cannot be tolerated within the context of physical activity, requiring staff to intervene rapidly to secure an appropriate focus on, and attention to, the task in hand.

> These considerations will form part of the risk-assessment process as set out in *Chapter 2: Physical Education and the Law,* pages 13–21.

## 5.3     What Pupils Should Know

5.3.1     Pupils should know:

- concentration is the key to improvement in performance and safe participation

- when and how fatigue can impair performance and put individuals at risk

- it is appropriate to express anxiety about a particular activity and not to be influenced by inappropriate peer pressure to attempt a task that they genuinely feel to be beyond their own capability

- repetition and consolidation are a necessary part of the skill-learning process and not to become impatient and frustrated when progress appears to be slow.

## 5.4     Additional Information

### Useful websites

Council for the Curriculum, Examinations and Assessment, Northern Ireland: www.ccea.org.uk/

DCSF Public Enquiry Unit, England: www.teachernet.gov.uk/teachingandlearning/subjects/pe/

Learning and Teaching Scotland: www.ltscotland.org.uk/physicaleducation/index.asp www.teachers.tv/video/browser/1003

Physical Education and Sport Strategy for Young People (PESSYP): www.teachernet.gov.uk/teachingandlearning/subjects/pe

PESS Project in Wales:
http://new.wales.gov.uk/topics/educationandskills/publications/guidance/33653511
11111?lang=en
http://new.wales.gov.uk/topics/educationandskills/publications/reports-estyn/estyn-
pess?lang=en
www.sports-council-wales.org.uk/getactiveinthecommunity/active-young-
people/pess
www.sports-council-wales.org.uk/links/physical-education

## 5.5   Case Law Examples

5.5.1   Hippolyte versus Bexley London Borough, Court of Appeal (1994):
*An established asthmatic pupil in a secondary school suffered a degree of brain damage subsequent to an attack developing during a lesson. She refused the teacher's request to report to the first-aider until the teacher's concern was so great that she then took the pupil to the school office for attention and expert support. The Court of Appeal dismissed the claim for negligence because the school had clear and detailed procedures and the teacher followed the procedures fully. It was also determined that the 16-year-old pupil, as an established asthmatic, would be fully aware of the implications of her refusal to follow the teacher's request for her to visit the first-aider.*

5.5.2   Moore versus Hampshire County Council, Court of Appeal (1981):
*A pupil missed physical-education lessons for a significant period of time due to a medical problem. Her parents had informed the school that she was not to take part in physical education until they had informed the school in writing that she could recommence activity. The head teacher had informed the physical-education staff of this. The girl wanted to take part after a while so she took her kit and told the teacher that she could now participate. The staff allowed this. During the lesson, she fell from an inverted gymnastic balance and was injured. The judges determined that the physical-education staff had ignored the directive from the head teacher in accepting the girl's version of being allowed to take part. They also judged that the teacher had paid insufficient attention to the pupil and should have monitored her work more closely because of the long layoff.*

5.5.3   Simmonds versus Isle of Wight Council, High Court (2003):
*A young pupil had a picnic with his parents prior to a school's sports day. He left his parents to go to his teacher for the beginning of the event. On his way, he strayed into a play area with swings, played on the swings and fell, breaking his arm. The parents blamed the school, but the claim was dismissed, partly on the basis that the school had not begun their duty of care for the child and emphasised the importance of the school making parents aware of when its staff assumed responsibility for the pupils and when their responsibility ended and parents reassumed the duty of care for their child.*

# Chapter six
## Extended Services and the Implications for PESS

6

This chapter identifies a number of procedures and recommendations designed to ensure the safety and well-being of children and young people involved in activities beyond the formal curriculum.

## 6.1 Introduction

6.1.1    Schools are now required to provide access or signposting to a range of **extended services available to the community** through the Education Act 2002. Access to services, facilities and activities may be provided directly by the school or through partner arrangements with independent agencies. Signposting to where extended services are available in the community will also be acceptable as some schools will not have provision and duplication is a waste of resources. Clusters of schools may arrange provision together.

6.1.2    Sport may form part of the provision in at least four elements that schools are required to provide or signpost:

   a. All-year-round childcare – from 8am to 6pm – may include sport, dance and similar activities.

   b. A varied menu of activities may include typical school sport, dance and other special-interest clubs.

   c. Parenting support could include family sporting activities.

   d. Community access is likely to involve the opening of sport and dance facilities to community groups.

   These will often be provided beyond the school day, but not necessarily by school staff or on the school site.

6.1.3    **Delivery** can be made **directly by the school** where the governing body designates school staff to establish a programme, employs any necessary additional staff and carries out any administration. Alternatively, schools can work in **partnership** with existing local private- and voluntary-sector providers, such as sports clubs in the locality. Clusters of schools may make collective arrangements as an education improvement partnership. Also, governing bodies may elect to establish a school company to provide and manage the extended services. Such a company becomes a legal entity separate from the school. This variation in provision thus may establish several issues that impact on health and safety.

6.1.4    Relevant issues **impacting on health and safety** are addressed in other chapters of this handbook. The guidance offered in the relevant chapters should be checked before commencing the organisation of sport- or dance-related activities as part of extended services. These issues include:

   • who employs the staff delivering any sport or dance courses in the extended provision (see *Chapter 2: Physical Education and the Law*, pages 13–21)

   • the coach/leader/teacher's competence to deliver the activity at the appropriate level (see *Chapter 4: Competence to Teach Physical Education and School Sport*, pages 31–36)

- the safe recruitment, vetting, management and monitoring of those delivering sessions, particularly with young people (see *Chapter 4: Competence to Teach Physical Education and School Sport,* pages 31–36)

- first-aid procedures (see *Chapter 8: Accident Procedures and First-aid Management,* pages 49–54)

- insurance cover provided or needed (see *Chapter 7: Insurance Issues,* pages 45–48)

- the security of the premises

- fire safety (see *Chapter 3: Risk Management,* pages 23–30, and *Appendix 1: Relevant Statute, Regulations and Guidance,* pages 287–295)

- driving minibuses (see *Chapter 16: Transporting Pupils,* pages 111–117)

- lettings policies.

## 6.2 What Staff Should Know

### People

6.2.1   The **school governing body** controls the use of school premises during and outside school hours. It may delegate tasks relating to extended services, but retains ultimate responsibility for extended services other than where a trust deed or transfer of control agreement (TOCA) exists. In these instances, other bodies control the occupation and use of the school premises at specified times.

6.2.2   Schools will need to consider the impact extended services will have on health and safety. Under the Health and Safety at Work Act 1974, and associated regulations, the employer is responsible for the health and safety of its employees, as well as non-employees who are on the work premises or who are affected by the employee's undertakings, such as those visiting the premises to participate in some activity.

6.2.3   It is important that whoever is managing any sport provision within extended services knows who his/her **employer** is, the **conditions** within which he/she is to work and the **insurance cover** provided.

6.2.4   The competence of anyone leading activities within extended services will need to be checked as part of the risk assessment. Any local requirements will need to be met.

6.2.5   **Safe recruitment principles** will need to be known and stringently applied. Where some other agency assumes responsibility for the organisation, management and delivery of the services, then it needs to be fully aware of any set standards and requirements.

### Context

6.2.6   The school **health-and-safety policy** needs to take account of the range of extended services and responsibility for the management of them.

6.2.7   **New risk assessments** should be carried out when additional activities and services are offered that may affect the health and safety of staff and visitors. These should assess the likely risks to staff, pupils, visitors and users of the premises. Although the employer is primarily responsible for risk assessments, this function can be devolved to somebody else.

6.2.8    **First-aid arrangements** may also need revision. Where schools permit others to use the premises, such as in a TOCA arrangement, they should set out the health-and-safety duties of those concerned, advise them of any specific health-and-safety issues (such as particular hazards) and of first-aid arrangements. It is essential that some form of direct communication with the emergency services is guaranteed when a school facility is used outside school hours.

6.2.9    The school's **insurance policy** should include external providers' liability. Where this is not the case, the commercial agencies as providers need to arrange their own insurance. Governing bodies should ensure that their insurance cover, and that arranged by external providers, is adequate and up to date.

6.2.10   **Site security** is another key consideration. Governing bodies should ensure they have a clear policy and procedures that set out their requirements, including access, use of equipment, use of resources, opening up and closing down and the safety of other users of the site. All managers of extended services should have a copy of the policy and procedures and should be told about any particular concerns. It is a governors' decision as to whether responsibility for locking and unlocking the school premises can be delegated to other individuals who are using particular facilities. This allows for more flexibility in the use of the premises and avoids undue pressure on the workload of existing staff, but the responsibility of occupiers of the site must be clearly established before any agreement is in place.

6.2.11   During the setting-up of extended services, schools need to ensure key **fire-safety procedures** are followed. When only parts of the school are open for evening or weekend use, schools and organisers of the extended provision should make sure that the necessary escape routes are open, with exits clearly signed. Where community groups bring their own equipment to the school, this needs to be checked to ensure it is compatible with school equipment and electrical services and complies with safety requirements.

6.2.12   Where public performances take place, existing regulations and procedures should be known by the organisers, followed and any audience limits complied with.

6.2.13   Practices specific to the school or agency managing the extended services need to be known and applied by all those delivering sport-related activities. For example, maintaining a register of attendees, clarity about when responsibility for the group commences and ends, required levels of supervision and required behaviour standards are all important issues.


## 6.3    What Pupils Should Know

6.3.1    Pupils should know:

• whether the activity offered is organised by the school or by another agency so that they know with whom to communicate

• the emergency evacuation procedures for the facility.


## 6.4    Additional Information

> For further information on health-and-safety issues in club links, see *Chapter 9: Safeguarding Children*, pages 55–72.

44

# Chapter seven
## Insurance Issues

Essentially, this chapter clarifies the type and nature of insurance provision needed by individuals, schools and organisations in order to fulfil legal and accepted practice requirements.

## 7.1    Introduction

7.1.1    Guidance about insurance can be of a general nature only as each employer, sport organisation and self-employed coach will have their own specific requirements.

7.1.2    Insurance policies are legal documents that define the **range and level of cover** provided. They usually contain conditions and exclusions. School staff should be aware of the detail set out in the policies or seek clarification where necessary. Insurance companies will apply the small-print conditions of the agreed cover and may nullify claims that are outside the specific requirements of the conditions set within the agreement. They also have the option to amend the range of cover at their discretion. For example, it is only recently that personal-injury cover in school rugby has been restricted to the level of tag rugby by many insurance brokers.

7.1.3    **Insurable interest** is the principle on which claims are made and met. This requires that the person to be covered by insurance must stand to lose financially, such as in the need to replace damaged property or cover a claim from a third party for compensation. This may be determined by the status and conditions of employment of those involved in the claim.

7.1.4    Taking out insurance cover creates benefits for individuals and organisations. These include:

- covering large losses that could not be afforded by the individual, school or other employer

- smoothing the impact of losses over time

- the provision of expert advice on the reduction and general management of risk.

7.1.5    It is important that **adequate risk assessment of activities and events** is made so that appropriate insurance cover can be arranged where necessary.

7.1.6    This chapter sets out the different types of insurance that all staff, whatever their qualification and employment status, need to check as to whether it is needed and who is responsible for its provision.

## 7.2    What Staff Should Know

### People

7.2.1    School status and whether or not a local authority (LA) retains insurance costs centrally will determine whether the school should make its own insurance arrangements.

7.2.2    Staff should check with their head teacher and/or employer to **clarify precisely what insurance cover is provided, under what circumstances the cover applies and whether it is advisable to initiate additional cover** for themselves or for any volunteer or visiting staff who may be self-employed. This information needs to be shared with any such volunteers or visiting staff.

7.2.3    Some employers may insure staff for any extension in the range of their **work outside their normal school role**, such as coaching or managing regional representative teams; others may not. Where this extension is not provided by the employer, then similar cover will need to be sought through the relevant national governing body (NGB) or established by the individual him/herself.

7.2.4    There are several aspects of insurance liability that may apply to any individual. This liability covers the legal obligation to compensate another person or agency injured or otherwise affected as a result of negligence on the part of an individual. This takes various forms:

a.  Under the **Employer's Liability** (Compulsory Insurance) Act 1969, employers must take out insurance to cover injuries to their employees that may occur while they work within the remit of their contract, whether they are permanent, temporary or contracted for specific services. LAs are exempt from this requirement, but the Department for Education and Employment (DfEE – now DCSF) Circular 2/94 *Local Management of Schools* established that LAs should either act as insurers or make other insurance arrangements to cover the potential liabilities of their employees. **Schools not maintained by an LA are not exempt** from the Employer's Liability (Compulsory Insurance) Act 1969 and must therefore comply with its requirements. Provision of this insurance does not apply to pupils in schools as they are visitors to school, rather than employees.

b.  **Public liability** cover is essential in order to address the legal responsibility for 'third party' claims made by others concerning the activities of the individual or group. This would include any negligent act by pupils within the scope of the school's provision for their education.

c.  **Professional liability** cover for staff is advisable. This provides cover against claims for breaches of professional duty by employees acting in the scope of their employment, such as giving poor professional advice. This type of cover is particularly important for anyone working in a self-employed capacity.

d.  **Personal injury** insurance for staff, against accidental bodily injury or deliberate assault by someone, is desirable. This may be arranged by the employer or may need to be provided by the individual. It is a parental responsibility to provide personal injury insurance for pupils. Some schools choose to make this facility available collectively to parents, but there is no requirement to do so.

There may also be a range of miscellaneous aspects that require insurance cover according to the particular role of the individual. These may be compulsory or merely advisable and may include travel or motor insurance. Individual staff will need to check whether personal exclusions and excesses apply and ensure that they report these to the employer if the employer provides the cover. Where not provided, it is the responsibility of the individual to ensure that adequate provision is made.

## Context

7.2.5    Insurance cover relating to the **use of facilities** should also be checked, along with who is financially responsible and under what circumstances, should any claim arise.

46

7.2.6    The relevant aspects of insurance include the following:

a.  The loss or damage to buildings, contents or other property.

b   **Public liability** cover is also essential for any 'third party' claims made by others against injury, loss or damage arising during legitimate occupation of premises, such as when lettings are made to other groups.

c   **Hirers' liability** covers individuals or agencies who hire premises against any claim for injury to others or damage to the property while they are using it. It is sensible for those hiring premises for activities to take out this type of insurance.

7.2.7    The provision and requirements for **transport insurance** vary. Staff need to take the following actions:

a.  Confirm that commercial transport companies have the appropriate range of insurance cover.

b.  Ensure that the school minibus insurance policy is appropriate for the journey being undertaken. There are additional insurance and licence requirements for travelling abroad. When travelling abroad, staff should be sure to take the insurance certificate (or a copy) on the journey.

c.  Check the employer's policy on the **use of private cars** to transport pupils. Local requirements vary considerably. Some employers do not allow it. Staff intending to use their own or others' private cars should enquire about the licensing, insurance and procedures required and obtain confirmation from other drivers that their insurance covers the risk involved.

## Organisation

7.2.8    The employer's insurance provision will cover all events organised by the school, whether on or off site, in lesson time or outside, in term time or during holidays, provided that the head teacher is fully aware of the events taking place. The head teacher will then determine whether the governors and LA (where appropriate as the employer) need to be informed. Staff should check what documentation needs to be completed and ensure that this is in place prior to the event.

7.2.9    All **special events** will need appropriate insurance. Staff should check with the head teacher and employer, if necessary, to clarify what provision is in place and what needs to be arranged specifically. Sports tours arranged wholly by the school are likely to be covered by some aspects of the employer's provision, but need some additional aspects to be arranged specifically.

7.2.10   Sports tours, ski trips and other events arranged as a package through a **commercial provider** usually have a full range of insurance cover built in. Staff need to check the detail carefully, particularly the levels of compensation offered and any particular exclusions to the cover. They also need to provide parents with full details of the cover so that parents can make additional arrangements should they wish.

7.2.11   Centrally organised events such as **sports festivals** in which pupils from a variety of schools take part will need appropriate insurance cover. It is important that the organiser for the managing agency, such as an NGB, schools association, schools partnership or LA, clarifies who the employer providing essential insurance is and what schools, or even individual parents, need to consider providing, then informing the relevant parties of this information.

## 7.3     What Pupils Should Know

7.3.1     Pupils need to be aware of all requirements needed to fulfil any personal insurance cover. For example, this may involve wearing mouth guards or some other protective equipment.

7.3.2     Pupils need to be aware of the importance of reporting any injury, damage or loss when it happens so that staff are fully aware of the situation, should parents make allegations, claims or enquiries at a later date. Such a requirement is most effective when it forms part of the whole-school policy on reporting injury, damage or loss.

7.3.3     Some schools arrange personal injury insurance cover for pupils. Such arrangements may contain particular restrictions and limited financial recompense. However, it is a parental responsibility to provide personal injury insurance cover for their children.

7.3.4     Staff should ensure that parents are made aware of what, if any, insurance cover is provided for pupils so that parents can then make their own decisions as to whether they need to make alternative arrangements. Precedent has been set that it is insufficient to simply request pupils to inform their parents. It is essential that effective communication is made to parents directly to inform them of what provision is made and what action they may wish to take themselves.

## 7.4     Additional Information

### Resources

DfES (2005) *Insurance: A Guide for Schools*. Nottingham: DfES Publications. ISBN: 978-1-841859-30-3. (Ref: DfES/0256/2003).

## 7.5     Case Law Examples

7.5.1     van Oppen versus The Clerk to the Bedford Charity Trustees (1988):
*The court established that it is the school's duty to insure against negligence and it is the parents' responsibility to consider personal injury insurance for their children because it is a matter of choice or discretion.*

7.5.2     G (a Child) versus Lancashire County Council (2000):
*A pupil received a serious mouth injury in hockey while not wearing a mouth guard. The judge determined that it is the responsibility of the school to ensure that parents receive critical information about personal protective equipment and that simply passing on the information via pupils is insufficient.*

7.5.3     Jones versus Northampton Borough Council, Court of Appeal (1990):
*A man hired a sports centre for a game of football, but failed to tell the other players that the floor was unsafe due to a leak in the roof. One player slipped on a wet patch and was injured. The hirer was held to be negligent for failing to inform the other players of the risk even though he was aware of it.*

# Chapter eight
## Accident Procedures and First-aid Management

This chapter is concerned with a **contextual** aspect of risk management. It clarifies the nature and scope of first-aid provision required within the context of PESS and recommends a range of procedures for the effective management of accidents and injuries.

## 8.1 Introduction

8.1.1 The Health and Safety (First Aid) Regulations 1981 require employers to provide **adequate and appropriate equipment, facilities and personnel** to enable first aid to be given to employees if they are injured or become ill at work. These statutory requirements for first-aid provision apply specifically to employees – the school staff – but the duty of care that is owed to pupils means, in practice, that provision is also made for pupils or any other visitor involved with and injured in any situation organised by school.

8.1.2 PESS involves movement, often in confined spaces, necessitating control in changing direction quickly, sometimes with the need to manipulate an object such as a ball, and, in some activities, physical contact. In such a context, injuries may occasionally occur. This alerts school staff to the need for appropriate first-aid expertise if teaching physical education or school sport.

## 8.2 What Staff Should Know

### Managing injury situations

8.2.1 All school staff should to be able to fulfil the requirements set out in the Approved Code of Practice and Guidance for the Health and Safety (First Aid) Regulations 1981, subsequently updated in 1997. The content of this guidance is basic common sense and is not threatening to anyone delivering physical education or school sport.

8.2.2 The guidance defines first aid as the initial management of any injury or illness suffered at work. It does not include the giving of tablets or medicines to treat illness, but the Regulations do not prevent staff specially trained beyond the initial management stage from doing so. No one is expected to give first aid beyond the level of his/her qualification or experience, but all are expected to **manage the initial situation**.

8.2.3 The **minimum requirements for first aid** in 'low-risk categories', such as schools, are as follows:

    a. To provide at least one suitably stocked, identifiable and easily accessible first-aid container. This would be augmented according to the particular circumstances of the school, such as a split-site arrangement or where the PESS facilities are somewhat distant from the centre of the school.

    b. For an 'appointed person' to take charge of first-aid arrangements and the management of first-aid situations and for there to be a qualified first-aider if there are more than 50 employees (ie staff, as pupils are visitors to the school) or if the school leadership deems it necessary to have trained first-aiders available.

c. To provide information, such as notices, for employees on first-aid arrangements.

d. To make provision for those working away from the main site by taking (as a minimum) a travelling first-aid kit.

e. To maintain records of incidents requiring first aid to be given.

8.2.4 Further arrangements should arise from a **risk assessment** of the needs of the particular establishment. The greater the risk, the more specialised the provision, such as more appointed persons, more first-aiders, more first-aid kits, a medical room, additional equipment or specialist equipment. In practice, this could be as straightforward as a large school needing to provide more first-aid kits. Records of past injuries and the range of provision for PESS should influence and inform the particular level of need.

8.2.5 The guidance thus expects the **school** to:

- assess the **needs for first aid** appropriate to the circumstances of the school

- **establish procedures** for dealing adequately with injuries sustained in any event organised by the school (on or off site, in lesson time or out of school hours)

- **inform the staff** of the procedures to be followed and **ensure that these are applied**; it is likely that the staff may be involved in determining the school procedures.

8.2.6 **Appointed persons** are not first-aiders. They should not give first-aid treatment for which they have not been trained. Appointed persons often decide to become trained in emergency aid, but this is not a requirement. They are responsible for taking charge when someone is injured or becomes ill. They look after the first-aid equipment, ensuring that it is regularly checked and replenished when needed. They also ensure that an ambulance or other professional medical expertise is called when deemed appropriate. They often then ensure that the parents of pupils are informed if their child has been unwell or injured while the school's responsibility. They also often collate the recording and reporting of necessary information.

8.2.7 **Staff must manage the initial injury situation** and summon the assistance of the appointed person for first aid. Contribution to dealing with the first-aid situation then depends on competence beyond the basic required level.

8.2.8 What does this mean for those teaching PESS? All involved in this specialist area should know the school accident/emergency procedures and the name and usual location of the appointed person. In the event of being involved in a situation where an injury occurs, this could require:

- sending for the appointed person to deal with the injury beyond the initial management stage

- ensuring the rest of the group is safe and free from the possibility of injury

- if the injured person is conscious, then calming, reassuring and checking for signs of shock

- knowing the symptoms of shock and how to deal with it, such as keeping the injured person warm

50

- not moving the injured person unless essential to prevent further serious harm

- noting and recording whether the injured person loses consciousness at any time

- completing any necessary records of the event.

8.2.9      Some staff may choose to develop their competence beyond the basic management requirement for professional reasons. This could include being able to deal with incidents when away from the school site, be it at a level required for teaching at locations somewhat detached from the school, or when taking groups of pupils to remote areas. Many adults delivering PESS obtain qualifications in first aid in order to enable them to take groups of pupils away from the school site with confidence. This is the individual choice of those adults. Because of the relatively isolated context of many physical-education lessons, it is highly recommended that staff have competence in resuscitation and the arrest of bleeding.

8.2.10     It is a school responsibility to ensure that the contents of **first-aid kits** are replenished as soon as possible after use in order to ensure that there is always an adequate supply of materials. Items should not be used beyond the expiry date shown on the packets. First-aid kits should be checked frequently to make sure there are sufficient quantities and that all items are still usable.

> For more information on this issue, see *Appendix 8A: First-aid Qualifications and First-aid Kits: An Explanation of the Health and Safety Executive Approved Code of Practice (HSE ACOP) on First Aid, pages 332–335.*

8.2.11     If an employee has received additional training in the treatment of **specific hazards** that require the use of special antidotes or equipment, these may be stored near the hazard area or kept in or with the first-aid kit.

8.2.12     The school is required to provide **access to first-aid provision** at all times. Thus, when groups travel off site, a travelling first-aid kit must be taken as a minimum provision for injury situations. Also, an appointed person should be available even when groups travel off site. This is easily accomplished by recognising at least one of the accompanying staff as an appointed person, providing they have the skills to fulfil the requirements of the job.

8.2.13     Good practice in school procedures for first aid when working off site may also require the staff to maintain records of who is in the party, emergency contact numbers for school leadership staff or parents and a facility to contact the emergency services, should this be required. Mobile-phone reception at the location of the activity may be poor and alternative systems of communication may need to be planned for.

8.2.14     In order to develop safe practice in schools, it is good practice to enable discussion by staff (and pupils if appropriate) of all accidents in order to inform future practice.

> For information on appropriate procedures following an injury, see *Appendix 8C: Standard Accident Procedures, pages 339–342.*

8.2.15     Employers are responsible for arranging **first-aid training** and retraining as required and through courses recognised by the Health and Safety Executive (HSE). First-aiders should be appropriately trained in techniques relevant to the circumstances in which physical-education activities will take place. Additional training should be arranged for adults involved in activities in which specific hazards are possible. For example, school staff undertaking ventures with pupils in remote areas should consider attending a relevant mountain first-aid course.

8.2.16    Specific guidance on the organisation of first-aid provision for events that are planned to occur in **public places** is contained in *Good Practice Safety Guide for Small and Sporting Events Taking Place on the Highway, Roads and Public Places* (Home Office, 2006).

8.2.17    The following extract outlines the view of the Department for Children, Schools and Families (DCSF) on children with the human immunodeficiency virus (HIV) or acquired immune deficiency syndrome (AIDS) attending school:

### Children with HIV and AIDS

*Since on all present evidence, the risk of transmitting HIV in the school setting is minimal, and since the benefits to a child with HIV or AIDS of attending school and enjoying normal social relationships far outweigh the risks of him or her acquiring harmful infections, such children should be allowed to attend school freely and be treated in the same way as other pupils.*

*It follows from this that the fact of HIV infection or AIDS should not, in the Department's view, be a factor taken into account by local education authorities, governing bodies and head teachers in discharging either their various duties concerning school admissions, transfers and attendance (in respect of an infected child or otherwise), or their powers of exclusion from school.*

**HIV and AIDS: A Guide for the Education Service
(Department for Education, 1991)**

8.2.18    School staff should consider the following points in relation to pupils with HIV or AIDS:

a.  Pupils may take part in physical education, sport and outdoor and adventurous activities, providing they do not have any other medical condition that prevents them from participating.

b.  Swimming pools and splash pools should be chlorinated or suitably treated according to standard practice. Normal precautions should be taken.

c.  Barefoot work presents no risks.

d.  Bleeding resulting from accidents should be dealt with immediately. First-aiders should wear disposable waterproof gloves and rinse wounds with water only.

8.2.19    No cases have been recorded of HIV being transmitted as a result of direct mouth-to-mouth resuscitation, although there is a theoretical risk when there are bleeding cuts or sores in the mouth. In an emergency, direct mouth-to-mouth resuscitation should not, therefore, be withheld. Rigid airways for resuscitation may only be used by first-aiders who have received appropriate specialist training.

## Recording injury situations

8.2.20    It is important that accidents are recorded on the employer's official **report form or accident book** as soon as is reasonably possible. This aids the reporting process and is also useful in the event of a liability claim.

8.2.21    An official accident report form invariably provides a brief report of an accident. It may not contain all the information that a school may be required to submit in the event of a liability claim. Schools may therefore wish to design their own accident report form, which prompts the user to provide all the details of an accident. It is advisable for this form to be completed for all accidents that result in hospital or medical treatment.

> For a sample form, see *Appendix 8B: School Accident Report Form*, pages 336–338 and the CD.

8.2.22    Schools may be required to provide relevant information several years after an accident occurred. Procedures for the storage and retrieval of such information should therefore be established.

## Reporting injury situations

8.2.23    The school should have a system for submitting an official accident report form to its employer or directly to HSE as soon as is reasonably possible in order that the employer can comply with the Reporting of Injuries, Diseases and Dangerous Occurrences Regulations (RIDDOR) 1995.

8.2.24    RIDDOR regulations apply when major injuries or death are caused by accidents. They cover workplace or work-related accidents (both on and off site) involving pupils and employees.

8.2.25    A **major injury** is defined as any resulting in death or injury requiring hospital treatment for any length of time, or injury that prevents the injured person attending work (or school) for more than three days. Notifiable injuries include fractures (other than to the bones of the hands and feet), unconsciousness resulting from electric shock or lack of oxygen, and acute illness caused by a pathogen, a substance or infected material.

8.2.26    RIDDOR requires that notifiable accidents be reported to the HSE by phone and, within seven days, in writing using the appropriate form. Some LAs may do this on behalf of the schools for which they are responsible, but, in many cases, individual schools will be responsible for fulfilling RIDDOR requirements themselves. This would be a school-leadership responsibility and not one imposed on the individual member of staff.

8.2.27    Individual members of staff are responsible for ensuring that they fulfil the school's system for the recording of accidents on the necessary forms. It is the employer's responsibility to ensure that the statutory requirements for recording and reporting notifiable accidents are fulfilled.

## 8.3    What Pupils Should Know

8.3.1    Pupils should know:

- who to report to, should anyone be injured

- not to administer first aid to someone who is injured unless an adult gives permission or, if working independently without staff close by to take responsibility, is qualified to administer first aid

- not to move anyone who is injured unless it is clearly an emergency.

## 8.4     Additional Information

Appendix 8 contains exemplar:

- first-aid kit contents *(Appendix 8A: First-aid Qualifications and First-aid Kits: an Explanation of the Health and Safety Executive Approved Code of Practice [HSE ACOP, on First Aid, pages 332–335)*

- accident report form *(Appendix 8B: School Accident Report Form, pages 336–338 and the CD)*

- accident procedures flow charts *(Appendix 8C: Standard Accident Procedures, pages 339–342)*.

### Resources

DfES (1998) *Guidance on First Aid for Schools.*

Health and Safety Executive (1997) *First Aid at Work: The Health and Safety (First Aid) Regulations – Approved Code of Practice.* London: HMSO.

Home Office (2006) *Good Practice Safety Guide for Small and Sporting Events Taking Place on the Highway, Roads and Public Places.*

# Chapter nine
## Safeguarding Children and Young People

9

This chapter provides advice and guidance relating to safeguarding children and young people. It identifies what adults working with pupils in PESS should be familiar with including the implications of directing young people to clubs and community sport.

## 9.1    Introduction

9.1.1    The demand on schools to deliver high-quality and accessible PESS for children and young people has never been higher. This demand has been matched with significant investment through the Physical Education and Sport Strategy for Young People (PESSYP) and other funded programmes to support a growth in sporting opportunities for children and young people.

9.1.2    At the same time, there is an increasing awareness of the need for all those providing these opportunities to ensure that PESS is safe and enjoyable for children and young people. Much has been invested in building the frameworks for safe and positive sport opportunities, work that has been undertaken by a range of bodies including the Association for Physical Education (afPE), Sport England, sports coach UK and national governing bodies (NGBs), coordinated and supported by the NSPCC Child Protection in Sport Unit (CPSU). This work has led to the UK being regarded as the leading nation in relation to safeguarding children and young people in sport.

9.1.3    afPE believes that:

- the welfare of children and young people is paramount

- all children and young people have the right to protection from abuse, regardless of their age, culture, disability, gender, language, racial origin, religious beliefs and sexual identity; they should be made aware of this right and also informed about where to seek help in relation to child abuse, including bullying

- all adults who work with pupils in PESS and all members of afPE should be clear about their duty of care to children and young people

- physical education and physical activity should take place in a safe, positive and encouraging environment.

### Background

9.1.4    Awareness of the risks facing children and young people in PESS has been influenced both by evidence from research and the direct experiences of sports bodies both in the UK and abroad. Research on violence towards children participating in sport, particularly from sexual abuse and harassment, has been undertaken across the UK, Europe and Australia. Interest has been generated in response to a number of highly publicised cases in the 1990s, including the reported cases of sexual abuse of athletes in Canada, Australia and the Netherlands and the conviction of a number of high-profile sports coaches in the UK.

9.1.5     The framework for much of the work undertaken by sport in addressing abuse has been provided by the UN Convention on the Rights of the Child. The Convention outlines the **rights of children and young people** and, within the international sports community, there has been a growing recognition of the responsibilities of sport in ensuring its practices do not contravene those rights. While the convention does not include direct reference to sport, there is relevance in most of the provisions of the Convention for young athletes. These include:

- the right to non-discrimination

- the right to have their views taken into account

- protection from abuse and neglect and other forms of violence

- the right to health

- the right to be protected from economic exploitation, illegal drugs and exploitation.

9.1.6     The first serious responses at national level to abuse against children in sport emerged during the 1990s. From 1997, the French authorities were particularly active in protecting child athletes from economic exploitation (including trafficking of players and illegal transfers), inappropriate intensive training regimes, doping and sexual abuse. The most developed and significant response to child protection issues in sport has taken place in the UK, primarily as a reaction to widely publicised cases of the sexual abuse of young athletes.

9.1.7     **Child-protection measures** in the UK, both for recreational and competitive sport, have focused on:

- the adoption of child-protection policies and codes of practice

- recruitment and selection processes (including criminal record checks of coaches and others involved in sport)

- awareness raising and training for coaches and other officials

- the establishment of designated person structures (child-protection officers) in sports clubs and governing bodies

- the establishment of telephone help lines

- national safeguarding standards and club accreditation systems

- research on child protection in sport issues.

There is significant overlap between the research and development outcomes in sport and developed practice in the educational context of PESS.

## 9.2    What Staff Should Know

### People

9.2.1     Physical education and physical activity should take place in a **safe, positive and encouraging environment**. There should be guidance on **expected and acceptable behaviour** towards children and young people for all staff.

## Education and training

9.2.2    In order to safeguard children and young people, and minimise the risk of abuse, all staff should have access to appropriate sources of skills and knowledge and should be able to demonstrate relevant competences. Opportunities for learning and training can be accessed through:

- basic child-protection/safeguarding awareness training
- multi-agency training
- role-specific single-agency training
- briefings from organisational management/lead designated person
- continuing professional development (CPD).

9.2.3    All **staff** with particular operational **responsibilities** for safeguarding and protecting children should:

- be able to describe what is meant by safeguarding, protecting and promoting the welfare of children and the different ways in which children and young people can be harmed
- be alert to potential indicators of abuse or neglect
- be alert to the risks that individual abusers, or potential abusers, may pose to children
- know how to communicate effectively and develop working relationships with other staff, volunteers, children and parents to safeguard, protect and promote the welfare of children
- be able to describe the roles of other practitioners and agencies in supporting and advising families and safeguarding and promoting the welfare of children
- demonstrate knowledge of organisational policies and procedures and how to apply these in practice
- understand and contribute to multi-agency processes to promote the welfare of children, assess their needs and protect them from abuse
- have knowledge of the key elements of legislation, government guidance and plans relevant to their role and responsibilities
- know the range of types of child abuse – physical abuse, emotional abuse, neglect and sexual abuse
- know what to do if they are concerned that a child may be being abused or that someone may pose a risk to a child or children generally
- understand the importance of sharing information and the dangers of not sharing information
- know what to do if they experience barriers to reporting their concerns
- know and understand the principles and values underpinning work with children, young people and parents
- be able to identify the roles of statutory agencies, including local safeguarding children boards, and other agencies to protect children and to safeguard and promote their welfare
- know how to record, store and dispose of relevant information in line with an organisation's policies and procedures, relevant to their role

- understand the importance of information sharing and know how to share information and with whom within an organisation and with other agencies, in line with reporting procedures

- know the boundaries of their own competence, role and responsibilities, and when to involve others

- appreciate the effect of witnessing upsetting situations and know how to seek advice and support

- know how to respond to a child or other person disclosing abuse or concerns about abuse

- know about the Common Assessment Framework (CAF) for children and young people and, where appropriate, how to use it.

They should be able to relate, recognise and take considered action to:

- establish rapport and respectful, trusting relationships with children, young people and those caring for them

- understand what is meant by safeguarding and the different ways in which children can be harmed (including by other children and young people and through the Internet)

- make considered judgements about how to act to safeguard and promote a child or young person's welfare, where appropriate consulting with the child, young person, or parent to inform their thinking

- give the child or young person the opportunity to participate in decisions affecting him/her, as appropriate to his/her age and ability and taking his/her wishes and feelings into account

- understand the key role of parents in safeguarding and promoting children's welfare and involve them accordingly, while recognising factors that can affect parenting and increase the risk of abuse (eg domestic abuse)

- understand that signs of abuse can be subtle and can be expressed in play and in the way children and young people approach relationships with other children and/or adults

- make considered judgements about how to act to safeguard and promote a child's welfare.

To communicate, record and report, they should:

- use appropriate verbal and written means to effectively record and report, making a distinction between observation, facts, information gained from others and opinion

- be alert to concerns about a child or young person's safety or welfare, including unexplained changes in behaviour and signs of abuse or neglect, when undertaking a PESS-based assessment on a child

- be able to recognise when a child or young person is in danger or at risk of harm, and take action to protect him/her.

Regarding their personal skills, they should:

- have self-awareness and the ability to analyse objectively

- have the confidence to represent actively the child or young person and his/her rights

- have the confidence to challenge their own and others' practice

58

- understand the different forms and extent of abuse and their impact on children's development

- develop appropriate professional relationships with children and young people.

## Child-protection coordinators

9.2.4    In accordance with DFE Circular 10/95 *Child Protection: The Role of the Education Service,* all schools must have a senior teacher with designated responsibility for child protection.

9.2.5    During off-site educational visits and school-sport activities, all adults should be aware of their responsibilities in relation to child-protection issues and should report any concerns to the teacher in charge. Where schools are working in **partnership with sports clubs**, it is recommended that safeguarding protocols are established that clarify the shared roles and responsibilities in the event of a concern arising.

## Recruitment procedures

9.2.6    All schools must have clear procedures for the recruitment of school staff and other adults who will work with children and young people. These should include:

- a clear job description/person specification

- an advertisement with clarity about the role in relation to children and young people

- application

- shortlisting

- interview

- references

- self-declaration

- Criminal Records Bureau (CRB), Disclosure Scotland or AccessNI enhanced level checks

- Independent Safeguarding Authority check

- induction

- mentoring

- review.

9.2.7    All schools need to satisfy themselves that all staff are suitable to work with children and young people, and should ensure that all the **necessary** checks are carried out and **references** obtained before any person takes up such a position. When a coach is employed or deployed, the school needs to ensure he/she holds the **appropriate qualifications and/or licence from the sport's governing body** and should seek references from the governing body.

9.2.8    *Child Protection: Preventing Unsuitable People from Working with Children and Young Persons in the Education Service* (DfES, 2002) provides details of the pre-appointment checks that should be carried out on all people who will have contact with children and young people, and explains the role of the CRB.

9.2.9    Many schools will also use **young volunteers**, often older pupils, within physical education and physical activity as part of junior sports leadership programmes. These young volunteers should never be left alone with younger pupils as they cannot assume the legal responsibility for them. Adult staff should always be present while utilising the expertise of the young volunteers, thus the young volunteers should not be affected by any need for CRB clearance. The Protection of Children Act 1999 and the Police Act 1997 specify the roles and responsibilities that are eligible for CRB checks (regulated positions), but do not refer to a minimum age that an applicant should be. Some LAs are beginning to require young leaders to have a CRB disclosure. In these instances, local regulations will apply and a CRB check needs to be made on the young leader(s).

## Context

9.2.10     All organisations that work with children share a commitment to safeguard and promote the welfare of children and young people and for many, including PESS, this is underpinned by **statutory duties**. The Children Act 2004 places a statutory duty on key people and bodies to make arrangements to safeguard and promote the welfare of children.

9.2.11     These arrangements require all agencies to have:

- senior management commitment to the importance of safeguarding and promoting children's welfare

- a clear statement of the agency's responsibilities towards children, available for all staff

- a clear line of accountability within the organisation for work on safeguarding and promoting the welfare of children

- service development that takes account of the need to safeguard and promote welfare, and is informed, where appropriate, by the views of children and families

- training on safeguarding and promoting the welfare of children for all staff working, or in contact, with children and families

- safe recruitment procedures in place

- effective inter-agency working to safeguard and promote the welfare of children

- effective information sharing.

Specific requirements for schools to safeguard and promote the welfare of children are outlined in the Education Act 2002.

9.2.12     Safeguarding and promoting the welfare of children requires effective cooperation at both local and national levels. In order to achieve this, the Children Act 2004 required each LA to establish a **local safeguarding children board** (LSCB). Their work supports the government's planned five outcomes for children outlined in Every Child Matters – Change for Children and in particular the 'staying safe' outcome.

9.2.13     Each school will have its own **child-protection policy** and procedures, developed in line with LA and LSCB requirements. These are usually whole-school policies and physical-education subject leaders will need to satisfy themselves that they are sufficient for the purposes of physical education and in line with the guidance provided in this chapter, including:

- who their child-protection coordinator is

- whether the safeguarding procedures of their school address all aspects of physical education and physical activity

- what their role and responsibility is in working with children and young people, as set out in a clear job description and clarity for each role relating to working with pupils

- how to ensure proper and secure recruitment procedures for support staff

- how to monitor and manage the work of support staff both on site and in settings beyond the school

- the safeguarding responsibilities when making links with sports and community clubs for the children and young people

- how they keep themselves updated with current issues within safeguarding.

9.2.14 Where **support staff** are deployed, they need to be made aware of the school safeguarding policy and in particular what steps they should take in the event of a concern arising.

## Photography, digital imagery, filming, Internet and mobile telephone misuse

### Parental consent

9.2.15 Parental consent should be obtained prior to filming or photographing children and young people. It is good practice to include relevant details on school admission forms to inform parents that digital imagery is used in education to support learning, and to reassure them that it will only be used in specific circumstances about which they will be advised. This information to parents should not be regarded as wholesale permission. Prior to an activity, consent needs to be obtained for taking images. For example, if digital photography is to be used in a GCSE, permission could be requested for the whole of the course rather than for each individual session.

### Photography, filming and videoing

9.2.16 The development of digital technology (eg digital cameras, camcorders and software analysis programs) has opened up an exciting and highly effective way of enhancing learning in schools. PESS and other physical activity are areas in which a great deal of visual learning takes place. Digital photographs and video clips can provide pupils with clear images of performances and specific techniques, as well as immediate visual feedback on their own movements. New software enables this process to be managed easily during physical-education sessions, school sport and off-site activities. Non-digital photography should also adhere to these guidelines where applicable.

9.2.17 However, certain **procedural and protocol issues** need to be addressed to ensure that digital images are managed effectively and securely. This is particularly important since images can now be transmitted and manipulated easily. Great care should be taken to safeguard children and young people when storing and using digital images in an educational context.

9.2.18 In-house use of digital imagery may occur within a school or group of schools as part of a defined educational project or partnership (eg between a secondary school and its feeder primary schools). The way the images are used should be controlled by the school or project manager at all times.

9.2.19 Access to the images should be controlled by authentication mechanisms (eg password protection and/or identification of specific computers).

9.2.20 Manipulation of the images needs to be restricted to appropriate formatting and display purposes (eg to enhance the content for educational use).

9.2.21    Staff should be aware of the dangers of distributing the images via email or CD-ROM. This leads to a loss of control of the images by the user group.

9.2.22    The following filming guidelines could be followed:

a.  Arrange clutter-free backgrounds to focus the attention of the learner on the specific performance issues.

b.  Care should be taken over the angles chosen for filming, in particular higher-risk sporting situations (ie swimming, gymnastics, trampolining, some athletics events).

c.  Profile shots of children and young people (side on) are generally more informative and less prone to risk of misuse.

d.  Filming pupils on poolsides should be avoided.

e.  Some specialist sports clothing (eg swimming costumes, gymnastic leotards) can create added risk and care should be taken to ensure that images cannot be misinterpreted.

f.  Names of pupils should not appear in images used on websites. If this is not possible, the images should not be used.

9.2.23    Staff should be aware that **parents are entitled to take photographs, film and video of their children** taking part in sport and other physical activities. This does not contravene the Data Protection Act. However, head teachers are within their rights to ban such activity as part of school policy.

## Publishing images

9.2.24    The publishing of images occurs when they are distributed beyond a defined group via videotape, DVD, CD-ROM or a website/Internet. Publishing images, particularly of children and young children in physical-education and sport environments, has obvious associated risks.

9.2.25    The following additional guidelines will help school staff to reduce the risks associated with the publishing of video clips:

a.  Use general-view shots to establish the theme.

b.  Shots held for a maximum of three seconds reduce risks (this makes the clip very difficult to manipulate).

c.  Children and young people shown in a video or film clip should not be identified by name and, where possible, not by school or club (ie a logo/badge on PE kit/uniform).

d.  Interviews should only show the head and shoulders of the children and young people involved. They should not be identified by name (this includes voice-overs and text-overs).

e.  Group shots should be in wide vision.

Further information can be obtained from the DfES/BECTA document *Superhighway Safety Pack – Safety for Schools* and other relevant publications/organisations.

## Guidelines for the storage of images

9.2.26      Master tapes and digital photographs should be stored in a secure environment since these are more readily manipulated if they fall into the wrong hands. Video copies, still photographs and compressed digital videos (eg Windows Media files) are less of a risk since manipulation is more difficult.

9.2.27      Libraries of tapes should be managed with care. Unnecessary storage of material should be avoided. Tapes should be stored in a locked cabinet and saved for a maximum of five years.

9.2.28      The reuse of tapes which have not been erased first can increase the risk of unwanted images being used inappropriately.

## Internet and mobile telephones

9.2.29      The use of mobile phones by staff during lessons, training sessions or at competitions, for the purposes of either making or receiving calls, is not good practice. The primary responsibility of staff is the supervision and safety of children and young people. Anything that compromises the adults' ability to maintain a safe environment and give their full attention to the supervision and coaching of children and young people should be actively discouraged.

9.2.30      There are situations where access to a mobile phone will make a positive contribution to the safety and welfare of children and young people, particularly when an emergency occurs. Therefore, there should not be a blanket ban on the use of mobile phones by adults.

9.2.31      Staff making contact with children and young people by phone, text or email should **never be undertaken without parental knowledge or consent**. Ideally, contact by coaches would be primarily on a face-to-face basis. Additional communication relating to events, training and other information should be directed to the child or young person's parents.

9.2.32      While staff should not be emailing children and young people directly as individuals, they may do so as part of a **disclosed list** (having received prior permission from parents to disclose in a group email) where they are disseminating information in relation to training or competitions. Clubs may also wish to use disclosed lists for sending club information via a designated and suitably trained adult (because of his/her position, this person should also have been subject to appropriate selection and vetting processes). Group emails should also give individuals the opportunity to have their contact details removed from the list by including a statement such as: 'If you wish to be removed from this email list, please contact the administrator'.

9.2.33      Staff should be aware of the increasing practice of **cyber-bullying**, which includes posting upsetting or defamatory remarks about an individual online and name calling or harassment using mobile phones. These may be general insults or prejudice-based bullying. Cyber-bullies use their mobile phones or emails to send sexist, homophobic or racist messages or they attack other kinds of differences, such as physical or mental disability, cultural or religious background, appearance or socio-economic circumstances. In other circumstances, bullies may physically assault other children or young people and post images of the bullying or fights online or send recordings via text messages to other people.

## Organisation

## Making links with sports clubs and other community organisations

> The Physical Education and Sport Strategy for Young People (PESSYP) safeguarding protocols for schools, endorsed by DCSF, address this issue in detail: www.teachernet.gov.uk/teachingandlearning/subjects/pe/nationalstrategy

9.2.34    It is essential that schools ensure that safeguarding is addressed in all **school-club/community sport links** to provide the best possible protection in fulfilling their duty of care towards children and young people and specifically to 'have in place arrangements for ensuring that their functions are exercised with a view to safeguarding and promoting the welfare of children' (s.175 of the Education Act 2002).

9.2.35    The **link club** should:

- have adopted the appropriate NGB safeguarding policy and set of procedures

- promote the policy and procedures to all club members and parents to show the club's commitment to a safe, friendly and supportive environment

- have guidance in place covering a range of activities and practices relevant to the sport or activity

- provide appropriately qualified, trained and CRB checked coaches to work with children and young people

- ensure appropriate training is available for coaches and others working with children and young people

- have a designated person to deal with safeguarding and welfare issues.

In addition, where a club link is established, the school should ensure that safeguarding protocols are in place that clarify the **shared roles and responsibilities** in the event of a concern arising.

9.2.36    All of the above, where relevant, apply to individual coaches and volunteers who are working with children and young people. In addition, the adults who are responsible for managing activities should be alert for any of the following **signs**:

- activities where other adults are discouraged from staying to watch

- any individual who appears to ignore organisational guidelines

- staff who appear to show favouritism or personally reward specific children or young people

- any engagement in inappropriate physical contact, such as taking part in physical activities, other than demonstrations, or physically supporting where little or no support is necessary

- poor communication from the adults and negative responses to the children and young people

- a 'win at all costs' attitude towards the sport or activity

- children and young people who drop out of an activity for no apparent reason (registers are important for curriculum, school sport and off-site activities)

- invitations offered to specific children or young people to spend time alone with the adult, such as on the pretext of individual coaching.

9.2.37    In addition, coaches who are providing high-quality delivery and have been monitored, checked and are aware of all school procedures, including evacuation and end-of-season procedures, may work at a distance from supervising staff.

> Further guidance on the direct or distant supervision of support staff on or off site is set out in *Chapter 4: Competence to Teach,* pages 31–36.

9.2.38    Many sports have adopted a **club accreditation** scheme and included within these are minimum standards for safeguarding that provide assurance for schools and others commissioning links. Clubmark is the Sport England cross-sport quality accreditation for clubs with junior sections, and NGBs accredit clubs that comply with minimum operating standards in four areas:

- the playing or participation programme
- duty of care and child protection
- sports equity and ethics
- club management.

Clubmark, or sport-specific versions (eg FA Charter Standard, Swim21, GolfMark) are an indication of quality and schools should seek to build links with clubs that have achieved or are working towards achievement of club accreditation.

## Sporting events at home and abroad: young people staying with host families – guidance for trip organisers

9.2.39    Schools will be involved in a range of sports events, tours and competitions, including overseas events. Most children will have an enjoyable sporting experience, but research has shown that they are particularly vulnerable to abuse when they are in unfamiliar surroundings, with unfamiliar people, homesick, pressured to perform and thus more dependent on other adults.

9.2.40    There may not be similar checks made in other countries to those made by CRB in the UK. Child-protection systems, policies and procedures and the culture of safeguarding young people may therefore be very different. All EU countries hold intelligence on child sex abusers, but often in different ways to the UK. Work has begun to develop a unified template, but this may take several years to reach fruition. This work will be carried out under the Council of Europe Convention that has been developed to protect children and young people against exploitation and abuse.

9.2.41    Staff need to establish what control is possible over decisions made in the foreign country prior to and during the visit, then confirm with the host school whether there is an equivalent CRB system in the host country. If there is, the host school should confirm in writing the checking process and that they have carried out checks for the host families.

9.2.42    Many LAs will already have in place **policies and procedures** to cover the welfare and duty-of-care requirements for taking youngsters away from home. This should include guidance in relation to:

- staff and other adults' roles and responsibilities
- recruitment and appropriate qualification
- contact details of relevant staff
- codes of conduct for staff and participants
- reporting procedures

- security

- health and safety

- up-to-date safeguarding information.

9.2.43    Within the sport sector, this is commonly referred to as the **event welfare plan** and many NGBs have in place comprehensive policies and procedures to cover the welfare and duty-of-care requirements for taking children away. The implementation of the welfare plan is the responsibility of the event coordinator, who will be responsible for:

- child welfare

- child protection

- health-and-safety matters

- the duty of care towards the participants and all those involved in the organisation of the sports event.

It is worthwhile for school staff to access such NGB information as additional support and guidance for their own planning of school-related sports events.

## Arrangements with the host school

9.2.44    If the foreign school or sports club has no specific child-protection policy, the host school or placing agency should be asked to ensure that they adhere to the following **safeguarding procedures** at all times when working with young people:

a.  They ensure that the UK minimum standards (ie the operating standards within the UK school) will not be compromised.

b.  Hosting arrangements should be made prior to departure.

c.  They ensure young people share placements in families with same-sex children.

d.  Where possible, two students should stay with the same host family. If this is possible, two same gender and similar age students should share a room.

e.  The UK school receives confirmation in writing from the host school of the arrangements and approves the host family.

f.  They provide to the host family a key point of contact and a clear means of communicating any concerns that might arise.

g.  They make arrangements for the host family to be informed of any special information about the placed student and what is acceptable with regard to supervision, free time and disciplinary sanctions.

## Confirming arrangements with pupils and parents

9.2.45    When requiring **written consent** from young people's parents for a trip, detailed written information should be given to them about the procedures that have been followed to ensure the safest possible arrangements for their child. They should also be made aware of the **code of conduct** that will apply during the trip and sanctions that may be imposed in the event of any breach of the code. The young people on the trip should be fully aware of the arrangements and also receive some preparation training for living abroad with host families. Parents and carers should be aware that the adults in the party may not be in a position to exercise the same degree of supervision that they would on other trips where all students are housed in a hotel or similar venue. Their child will be very much part of the host family and will be invited to take part in any activity that the family undertakes. Parents should give approval for this and set out any restrictions they feel it is important to impose.

## Preparation of young people for visits abroad

9.2.46 The status of any members of the party who may not be a British national, or who may be in the process of obtaining that status, or who are not members of a European Union member state needs to be checked, including reference to the Home Office Immigration and Nationality Directorate, concerning the right of re-entry.

9.2.47 Ensure young people have the **advice and guidance** on the following subjects:

- the language and commonly used phrases (it is recommended that at least one adult member of the group should be conversant in the language of the country)

- wearing appropriate clothing (many thin layers in cold climates, loose lightweight clothing in hot climates) and headgear for the climate, protective creams and glasses for hot climates and high altitudes

- the dangers of overexertion in hot climates and the importance of keeping fluid levels high

- the culture – body language, rules and regulations (of behaviour in host's homes, in hotels, on roads, in shops), dress codes, local customs, attitudes to gender and heritage and any celebrations at the time of visiting

- the host country's attitude to alcohol and smoking and other drugs (in addition to school rules imposed on the party)

- local food and drink – any dangers of tap water in some countries (bottled water may be preferable), raw vegetables, salads and fruit, raw shellfish, local customs of underdone meat or fish, reheated food, particularly rice and meat; host families should be advised of any special medical or dietary needs of the student placed in their home

- how to carry money and valuables discreetly

- how to use telephones abroad – a BT contact card may allow a direct call to home, and school requirements on the use of mobile telephones

- local services and, for example, have a local map or access to one

- the travelling arrangements for the party

- emergency procedures – if becoming lost or separated from the host family, main party or small group, if caught up in a local incident, if accused of an offence (it may be advisable for all young people to carry an official note in the language of the country, asking the reader to reunite the young person with the rest of the group at a prearranged meeting point, or take them to the nearest police station).

9.2.48 Ensure that all young people have an accessible **point of contact** or emergency telephone number in the host country.

9.2.49 Arrangements should enable young people to speak to a responsible adult confidentially, should they feel uncomfortable in the host-family home. A contingency fund may be advisable should an urgent need to re-accommodate a pupil arise.

## Residential events in the UK

9.2.50 Procedures should be the same as in in-school arrangements and minimum operating standards should be applied in the same way. If the centre is accredited, safeguarding policies, procedures and good-practice guidance should be in place, but it is wise never to make assumptions.

9.2.51 The vetting of host families in the UK has been seen as good practice for some time. New requirements within the Safeguarding Vulnerable Groups Act 2006 will make the vetting of host families in the UK mandatory.

9.2.52 The development of an event welfare plan will ensure that roles and responsibilities are clearly defined and that **duty-of-care responsibilities** are fully understood.

# 9.3 What Pupils Should Know

9.3.1 Pupils should:

- be aware of their right to be safe from abuse
  - in England and Wales, the law that protects them is the Children Act
  - in Scotland, the law is called the Protection of Children Act
  - in Northern Ireland, the law is called the Children Order
- be aware that the staff must look after children's and young people's rights
- manage risks by not going to unknown places alone, keeping an adult informed of their whereabouts, using mobile phones to keep contact with others and knowing what contact from adults is acceptable and what is not
- know where to go for help and advice about abuse and bullying, either from the school or club and/or know about the official helplines available
- be aware of any anti-bullying schemes within the school, sports club or community programme
- know about the advice given about electronic communication, including:
  - managing the risk of going online
  - never using real names in chat rooms – pick a special online nickname
  - never telling anyone personal things about themselves or their family online
  - never meeting people alone when the contact has only been online
  - keeping their parents informed about online and mobile contacts
  - never responding to nasty or rude messages, and never sending any
  - being careful with any email attachments or links that people send
  - agreeing rules with their parents about what can and can't be done on the Net
  - taking a look at *Hands Off!*, the NSPCC magazine for teenagers on keeping safe from abuse; it has tips on safe surfing
- not delete messages about which they could be concerned; it may be important later if some action needs to be taken
- never be alone with a person who has harmed or attempted to harm them
- know who the responsible adult/child-protection coordinator is in order to report any concerns/worries

- know that those harming them will be dealt with appropriately by adults
- be aware of what the school guidance and rules for trips abroad are.

9.3.2   There are a number of reasons why children and young people may not wish to tell anyone. They include the following:

a.  The abuser may have told the young person to keep quiet and not to talk to anybody.

b.  The abuser may have threatened the young person with what might happen to him/her or his/her place in the team if he/she tells.

c.  The abuser may have made threats about the young person's friends or family.

d.  The abuser may have said 'No one will believe you' or 'No one will do anything if you tell'.

e.  The young person may feel guilty that he/she didn't stop the abuse happening.

f.  The abuser may be someone who everyone in the school sport or activity looks up to, perhaps including the young person's parents.

g.  The young person may not want to let his/her parents down.

h.  The young person may even think the problem will go away if he/she ignores it.

## 9.4   Additional Information

### Resources

#### Government guidance

> For more information on safeguarding children, see *Appendix 2G: Safe Practice for Safeguarding Children and Young People Poster*, page 304 and the CD.
>
> For statute references, see *Appendix 1: Relevant Statute, Regulations and Guidance*, pages 287–295).

British Standards Institute (2007) *Specification for the Provision of Visits, Fieldwork, Expeditions, and Adventurous Activities, Outside the United Kingdom (BS8848)*. London: BSI. ISBN: 978-0-580505-03-4.

Department for Children, Schools and Families (DCSF) (2007) *Homophobic bullying*. Nottingham: DCSF. ISBN: 978-1-847750-29-7.
Available from:
www.teachernet.gov.uk/_doc/11911/HOMOPHOBIC%20BULLYING.pdf

Part of the DCSF guidance and resources for schools entitled: *Safe to Learn: Embedding anti-bullying work in schools*.

DCSF (2008) *Staying Safe: Action Plan*. Nottingham: DCSF. ISBN: 978-1-847751-06-5.
Available from:
www.everychildmatters.gov.uk/_files/E311A3DE50297A05E31F401F17DC67EB.pdf

DfES (2002) *Child Protection: Preventing Unsuitable People from Working with Children and Young Persons in the Education Service* (booklet).London, DfES.
Available from: www.teachernet.gov.uk/docbank/index.cfm?id=2172

DfES (2006) *Safeguarding Children and Safer Recruitment in Education.* London: Department for Education and Skills. ISBN: 978-1-844788-54-5.
Available from: http://publications.teachernet.gov.uk/eOrderingDownload/6836-DfES-Safeguarding%20Children.FinalV2.pdf

DfES (2006) *What to Do if You're Worried a Child is Being Abused.* London: Department for Education and Skills. ISBN: 978-1-844788-76-5.
Available from: http://publications.everychildmatters.gov.uk/default.aspx?PageFunction=productdetails&PageMode=publications&ProductId=DFES-04320-2006&

HM Government (2006) *Working Together to Safeguard Children: a guide to inter-agency working to safeguard and promote the welfare of children.* London: TSO. ISBN: 978-0-112711-87-2.
Available from: www.everychildmatters.gov.uk/resources-and-practice/IG00060/

### NSPCC resources

Harries, J. (2006) *Promoting Personal Safety in PSHE.* London: Paul Chapman. ISBN: 978-1-412918-23-7.

NSPCC (2003) *Learning to Protect: a child protection resource pack for teacher training.* Leicester: NSPCC.

NSPCC/EduCare (2002) *Child Protection Awareness in Education.* Leamington Spa: NSPCC.

NSPCC (2004) *Worried? Need to talk?: Teacher Support* (booklet).
Available from: www.nspcc.org.uk/Inform/publications/Downloads/WNTTteacherssupport_wdf48143.pdf

Schonveld, A. and Myko, V. (2000) *Take Care!: Self-awareness and personal safety issues in the primary curriculum.* London: NSPCC.

### Specific resources for physical education, sport and physical activity

afPE/sports coach UK (2007) *Adults Supporting Learning: School Induction Pack.* Leeds: Coachwise Business Solutions. ISBN: 978-1-905540-28-0

Boocock, S. (ed.) (2002) *Sportscheck*: *a step-by-step guide for sports organisations to safeguard children.* Leicester: NSPCC Child Protection in Sport Unit.

Child Protection in Sport Unit (2005) *Standards for Safeguarding and Protecting Children in Sport.* London: NSPCC/Sport England.
Available from: www.thecpsu.org.uk/Documents/standards.pdf

City of Edinburgh Council Education Department (2004) *The Protection of Young People in the Context of International Visits*: *Guidelines for Organisers*. Edinburgh: City of Edinburgh Council. ISBN: 978-1-902299-30-3

Earle, C. (2005) *Coaching Young Performers*. Leeds: Coachwise Business Solutions/The National Coaching Foundation ISBN: 978-1-902523-56-3.

Grange, J. and Gordon, R. (2001) *Safe Sport Away.* London: NSPCC/ASA. ISBN: 978-0-900052-35-4

Slinn, N. (2006) *Safeguarding and Protecting Children: a guide for sportspeople.* Leeds: Coachwise Business Solutions/The National Coaching Foundation. ISBN: 978-0-905540-26-6 sports coach UK (2000) *Safe and Sound* (leaflet)

Tiiva, A. and Morton, J. (2003) *Safe Sports Events: A Child-focused Resource Pack for All Sports Events Organisers.* London: NSPCC. ISBN: 978-1-842280-35-5.

## Useful websites

### Help for children and young people

www.bullying.co.uk – This site has lots of advice for children about dealing with bullying. There are also useful links to other advice sites.

www.childline.org.uk – ChildLine is the free, 24-hour helpline for children and young people in the UK. Children and young people can call on 0800-11 11 about any problem, at any time, day or night.

www.there4me.com – This is the NSPC's advice site specially for young people aged 11–16. There is on-screen advice about all sorts of things, including bullying, abuse, relationships, exams, drugs, difficulties at home. If there is a confidential private session, young people can talk one to one online in real time with an NSPCC adviser.

www.thinkuknow.co.uk – This site is all about child exploitation and online protection (CEOP) and gives advice for 5–16-year-olds, parents, teachers and trainers.

### Help and advice for adults

NSPCC
www.nspcc.org.uk
www.thecpsu.org.uk
0808-800 5000

### General websites

AccessNI
www.accessni.gov.uk

Clubmark (Sport England)
www.clubmark.org.uk

Council of Europe Convention: Strasbourg, 2007
https://wcd.coe.int/ViewDoc.jsp?id=1164093

Criminal Records Bureau
www.crb.gov.uk

Department for Education and Skills (DfES) (2004)
Every Child Matters Strategy
www.everychildmatters.gov.uk

Disclosure Scotland
www.disclosurescotland.co.uk

Every Child Matters: education, training, employment
www.everychildmatters.gov.uk/ete/

NSPCC Child Protection in Sport Unit
www.thecpsu.org.uk

Teachernet: child protection
www.teachernet.gov.uk/wholeschool/familyandcommunity/childprotection/

Worried? Need to talk? teachers' site
www.worriedneed2talk.org.uk/teachers/

For current guidance on safeguarding, legislation and resources in
Northern Ireland
www.deni.gov.uk/index/13-healthsafety/21-child-protection.htm

For current guidance on safeguarding, legislation and resources in Scotland
www.scotland.gov.uk/Topics/People/Young-People/children-families/17834

For current guidance on safeguarding, legislation and resources in Wales
http://new.wales.gov.uk/topics/childrenyoungpeople/?lang=en

Safeguarding Children: Working Together under the Children Act 2004 (2006)
Welsh Assembly Government
http://new.wales.gov.uk/topics/childrenyoungpeople/careandprotection/childprotect
ion/?lang=en

## 9.5    Case Law Examples

9.5.1    R versus Drew, Snaresbook Crown Court (2001):
*A swimming coach systematically abused young teenage boys over a long period, grooming them by claiming that his actions would help them develop physically and improve their swimming ability. The trust the swimmers had in the coach had been abused.*

9.5.2    R versus Lyte, Liverpool Crown Court (2007):
*A tennis coach was convicted of a breach of trust by grooming a 13-year-old tennis player through text messages and conversation and then being sexually active with the child.*

9.5.3    R versus Thompson, Bradford Crown Court (2008):
*A physical-education teacher groomed a 17-year-old pupil through texts and telephone calls. This led to an affair that lasted for several months. The teacher was convicted of two offences of abusing his position of trust by sexual activity with a teenage girl. He was sentenced to a nine-month prison sentence, suspended for two years, to be listed on the Sex Offenders Register for 10 years and is not allowed any unsupervised access to a child under 18. The sentence was suspended because the girl refused to give a victim impact statement as she intended to renew the relationship once she was 18.*

# Chapter ten
## Individual and Special Needs

**10**

This chapter recommends a number of teaching and learning strategies that will help to ensure that all pupils, whatever their particular needs, obtain full benefit from PESS provision.

## 10.1 Introduction

10.1.1 All pupils, irrespective of any special need, have an entitlement to a meaningful and fulfilling experience of PESS. Not only can it provide enjoyment, involvement and participation in a range of physical activities, it can also bring about significant and long-lasting gains to psychomotor and sensory development, physical health and well-being and, through the successful achievement of well-matched challenges, improve social and emotional stability.

10.1.2 In this sense, it could be argued that pupils with special needs have potentially more to gain from access to high-quality programmes of physical activity and PESS than their peers.

10.1.3 Historically, certain conditions, such as asthma, diabetes and epilepsy, were seen as debilitating illnesses, frequently inhibiting involvement in physical activity. Improved treatments and contemporary approaches to healthcare have rendered such thinking largely obsolete. With appropriate management, children and young people with special needs no longer have to experience barriers to a full and rewarding experience of, and participation in, physical activity at all levels. **Inclusion** is now high on the social agenda and is supported by significant statute and regulation.

10.1.4 Special needs can be broadly, though not exclusively, categorised as follows:

- speech and language
- sensory
- physical
- behavioural
- cognitive
- a combination of two, or more, of the above.

10.1.5 It is important to remember that all special needs tend to exist on a **continuum** from very mild to very severe. Thus, while the needs of some pupils may be very clear, for others, they may not have been previously diagnosed. Even where there is a diagnosis, it cannot be taken for granted that all pupils with a similar diagnosis or 'label' have exactly the same needs and require the same response to meet those needs. Further, some special needs may be intermittent in nature and these must to be taken into account in teaching situations. Thus, it is important that **individual needs** are recognised and responded to in an individual and specific manner. A brief overview of these categories of special needs is offered below, while more detail on some specific special needs is provided in *Appendix 4: Pupils with Special Educational Needs (SEN)*, pages 319–324 and the CD. Appropriate responses to these difficulties within the context of physical activity and teaching appear later in this chapter.

10.1.6    Those wishing to obtain more precise detail should contact their local authority (LA) specialist support team, school nurse or the many voluntary organisations that support pupils with special educational needs (SEN). A list of some of these agencies appears at the end of the chapter and in *Appendix 4: Pupils with Special Educational Needs (SEN)* (pages 319–324 and the CD).

## Speech and language difficulties

10.1.7    This covers a wide range of needs, which may include pupils who may have general receptive or expressive language difficulties, dyspraxia, dysphasia, autism or autistic spectrum disorder (ASD). Many of these children will be towards the very mild end of the continuum of difficulty and thus it is likely that their needs will not have been identified. Where needs are not taken into account, the children are likely to misunderstand or not understand what is required of them. Thus, as a consequence of this, they may not be able to carry out tasks as expected or at all and this can result in poor and disruptive behaviour as they become frustrated. They may respond poorly to criticism from adults of their poor performance. This can result in adults responding to their behaviour, rather than attending to the root cause of their difficulty, which can further exacerbate the situation.

10.1.8    Some children develop coping strategies. These can sometimes be identified, characterised by the time spent watching other pupils before starting the activity. These pupils are also noticeable for being last 'in the queue', thereby allowing themselves time to assess what is required of them.

## Sensory difficulties

10.1.9    This largely covers the areas of vision, hearing and dual impairment. Where the impairments are significant enough for them to have been diagnosed, specialist advice should be available from LA support teams. Adults should ensure that this advice is followed and used in developing risk assessments. This may include the provision of specialist equipment or support. It may involve ensuring that pupils use their spectacles or hearing aids.

> For guidance on the use of sensory aids like spectacles and hearing aids, see *14.2.3*, page 100, in *Chapter 14: Clothing and Personal Effects*.

10.1.10    Again, it is those pupils whose needs may be undiagnosed whom adults need to be aware of. For example, not all pupils with 'glue ear' have had their condition assessed. In simple terms, this is because it can affect children in different ways dependent upon their general health (ie when fully fit they may hear well; when suffering from a cold, one ear or both ears may become blocked with fluid, thus restricting the child's hearing). The intermittent nature of the condition, accompanied by its varying levels of seriousness, can sometimes make its identification difficult.

10.1.11    Some children develop coping strategies similar to those described above in paragraph 10.1.8 for children with speech and language difficulties.

## Physical disabilities

10.1.12    Where pupils have a diagnosed difficulty, help should be available from specialist support. Some other pupils may be seen to be 'clumsy' in their movements. This may be associated with a specific learning difficulty, such as dyslexia, a lack of early childhood motor experience or one of a range of other difficulties. The condition may not be formally diagnosed and, as such, no support be directly available. It is important, as with all children with SEN, to praise effort and progress. This maintains and promotes self-esteem and reduces the risk of the real difficulty being masked and behavioural difficulties arising from the frustration of failure.

10.1.13    Many schools will have a pupil or pupils who have been diagnosed with some form of physical dyspraxia. In these situations, it is likely that some support or advice will be available to those working with such pupils from a physiotherapist or occupational therapist. This can take the form of an exercise programme that can be included as part of a normal physical-education lesson. Adults working with dyspraxic children have found that including such specific exercises in warm-ups for all pupils can additionally have a positive impact on the motor development of the whole class.

## Behavioural difficulties

10.1.14    The causes of behavioural difficulties are many and often complex. As noted above, they may mask other, undiagnosed difficulties which, when left unaddressed, lead to frustration from failure, resulting in low levels of self-esteem, unwillingness to take part and disruptive behaviour. Among possible causes, difficult behaviours may arise from a particular condition such as attention deficit hyperactivity disorder (ADHD), a mental-health condition and/or poor early-childhood experiences.

10.1.15    Those working with pupils exhibiting difficult behaviours should look for signs of the possible causes of the difficulties, such as those noted earlier, and take the necessary action to respond to these. One fundamental approach is to ensure that the pupil's confidence is developed by providing a carefully graded programme using a **small-steps approach** that ensures success. Each element of success should be praised. As levels of self-esteem increase, the level of disruptive behaviour often falls.

10.1.16    In addition, it is not always possible to identify the root causes of behavioural difficulties as the outside signs of difficulty may be the same across a number of causes. Thus, a pupil's aversion to an activity may arise from a previous traumatic experience (eg an accident in water in early childhood that has left the child fearful of swimming). The school may be unaware of this. Pupils may also have experienced significant pressure to take part in activities from a young age in which they experienced a lack of success and so have become demotivated. A child may be reluctant to change for an activity due to a medical condition such as psoriasis. These are a few of many circumstances that can lead pupils to refuse or be reluctant to carry out a task. Such situations need to be handled sensitively and may require further investigation in order to promote an environment where pupils will take part and levels of disruption be reduced.

10.1.17    As with other areas, specialist advice is available from LA support teams and should be sought where necessary.

## Cognitive difficulties

10.1.18    Again, the causes of this area of difficulty can be many and varied. It is typical that children with cognitive difficulties have difficulty in grasping concepts quickly; thus, staff need to take extra care in explaining the requirements of a task. This should be done in small steps, often using **demonstration and personal support**, to ensure that all pupils understand each step before moving on to the next. Each step should be rewarded with praise and encouragement.

## Summary of general principles

10.1.19    Those working with pupils with special needs should acknowledge that whatever the origins or cause of particular needs, activities should be provided that are of equal worth, challenge and relevance to those provided for other pupils. The aim should be to maximise all pupils' participation in physical activity and sport. To this end, those providing physical activity and sport for pupils with special needs should:

- take account of the specific individual needs and the risks which may be attached to them for the pupils when taking part in a range of physical activity

- liaise with the school's special educational needs coordinator (SENCO) (or the learning support service in Scottish schools) and other specialist support (eg speech and language therapist [SALT], occupational therapist [OT], physiotherapist, school nurse) to ensure that pupils with special needs are never placed at unnecessary risk and, where appropriate, that a healthcare plan is developed

- liaise with parents to establish whether they or any other external agencies are supporting the pupil in physical activities in order to assess how their experiences of the pupil may be used to promote his/her physical activity in the school

- carefully risk assess each pupil with special needs for each planned activity. It should be remembered that, while special needs may require that significant support is in place to allow a pupil access to an activity, or an alternative activity provided, there may be other activities where the pupil is capable of taking part at his/her own level of expertise.

10.1.20    It should be recognised that support provided for pupils with special needs, such as integrating specific exercises provided by an OT or physiotherapist for a particular child into physical-education lessons, is often beneficial to most of, if not all, the pupils in the group, particularly any who may have undiagnosed conditions.

## 10.2    What Staff Should Know

### People

10.2.1    Staff working with pupils in a special-needs environment should be suitably **trained or accredited** to manage their physical needs. When working in an integrated setting, mainstream staff should be supported by additional expertise in order to effectively plan and manage a range of appropriate physical challenges for those pupils diagnosed as having additional difficulties within their right to a differentiated curriculum.

10.2.2    **Adults in charge** of a pupil with SEN should:

- know the nature of the pupil's learning difficulty, disability, or emotional or behavioural disorder

- be aware of any constraints on physical activities as a result of the disability or regime of medication

- be able to provide the emergency treatment necessary if physical activities exacerbate the disability

- have determined that they:
  - have sufficient background knowledge about the pupil
  - are confident in their approach to teaching pupils with SEN
  - have the knowledge and techniques necessary for safe teaching.

## Context

10.2.3    When planning an activity, careful attention should be paid to each pupil's needs in terms of the location, clothing, physical surroundings, equipment and general organisation of the session.

**Table 4: Checklist for planning an activity for pupils with SEN**

| Location | Clothing | Physical Surroundings | Equipment |
|---|---|---|---|
| ✓ Risk assess all locations both on and off site.<br><br>✓ Check access and egress for safety, especially where a pupil or pupils may be at risk of absconding. | ✓ Ensure that all pupils are appropriately dressed and that any special clothing (eg helmets for some pupils with epilepsy) have not been left unworn following the changing process. | ✓ Assess the acoustics of the location. Where this is an issue (eg prone to echo), ensure all pupils are able to hear instructions and support staff are well briefed to support pupils who may not hear distinctly.<br><br>✓ Assess the lighting of the location. Where there are dark areas or areas prone to bright light, ensure any pupils with a visual impairment carry out their activities in a place of optimum light for that pupil. **Note:** Different visual impairments have different optimum lighting levels.<br><br>✓ Ensure floors and flooring are suitable for activities involving those who may have motor difficulties. | ✓ Ensure that all equipment is safe for use by all pupils. Where this may not be the case for special-needs pupils, ensure access to alternative activities.<br><br>✓ Ensure that specialised equipment is available as necessary (eg sound balls for visually impaired pupils, a range of balls of different sizes and textures to support pupils with motor difficulties).<br><br>✓ **Note:** Specific guidance should be sought from specialists in the field of specific difficulty. Help can also be found on a number of websites (see *10.4 Additional Information,* page 80). |

# Organisation

**Table 5: Things to remember when giving instructions**

| When Giving Instructions |
|---|
| • Make sure all pupils' attention is gained, especially those with special needs, before the explanation of a task commences. |
| • Ensure there is little, if any, background noise as this can distract some pupils and others may find it difficult to hear all your instructions. |
| • Stand so that all pupils can see your face, with the light on your face, not behind it. This has a number of benefits, including providing a focus for pupils who are easily distracted, such as those with speech and language difficulties or those with ADHD, while making it easier for pupils who lip-read. |
| • Provide opportunities for those who lip-read to understand instructions. Remember that pupils with conditions such as glue ear may have an intermittent hearing loss that can affect either ear or both ears. Thus, to reduce any risks, the positioning of such pupils during physical activities is crucial so instructions are clear and of a volume that such pupils can hear. Clearly, for pupils who are profoundly deaf and who do not lip-read, arrangements will need to be made for alternative communication (eg signing). |
| • Work in small steps. Many pupils with special needs cannot process large chunks of information easily and these need to be broken down and supported by regular reinforcement during the activity. |
| • Speak clearly and maintain a normal rhythm without shouting. |
| • Create a climate in which pupils feel confident to ask for the instructions to be repeated as some children with special needs can feel awkward about this. |
| • Use high levels of praise for small gains in performance. This is important for all pupils, but especially those with social, emotional and behavioural difficulties (SEBD) as they tend to have low levels of self-esteem and confidence. |

**Table 6: Things to remember in sessions for pupils with SEN**

| When Preparing a Session | During a Session | At the End of a Session |
|---|---|---|
| • Plan for it to be pupil- and activity-specific. Do not assume that one risk assessment will do for all pupils with a particular special need involved in a particular activity.<br><br>• Build in the necessary control measures to allow pupils access to activities that might otherwise have been closed to pupils with special needs.<br><br>• Seek specialist support and advice, where appropriate, to ensure the efficacy of the risk assessment. Discussion should result in the development of a medical profile/healthcare plan for the pupil concerned, covering issues such as:<br><br>  ■ personal healthcare equipment (eg inhalers, syringes, incontinence pads)<br>  ■ body splints and aids<br>  ■ valves and shunts<br>  ■ administration of drugs<br>  ■ mobility aids<br>  ■ range of physical movement<br>  ■ daily living aid<br>  ■ care assistance<br>  ■ any activities identified as contraindicative by the medical profession. | • Ensure that support staff are fully briefed and clear about the activity and their role in supporting the pupils who are taking part in it.<br><br>• Ensure that the necessary equipment is readily available to those pupils who will require it (eg balls with bells inside for some pupils with a visual impairment).<br><br>• Ensure that each task is preceded by a demonstration as some pupils learn better by observing, rather than listening to instructions.<br><br>• Regularly change the activity. Some pupils, such as those with SEBD, can become easily bored or frustrated and this can lead to disruption of the whole session.<br><br>• Offer regular support, feedback and praise to pupils. Many pupils with special needs have low self-esteem and respond well to knowing that they are improving, doing well and that this is recognised by peers and significant adults.<br><br>• Encourage public acclaim by getting all pupils to recognise each other's successes. This aids the process of inclusion. | • Review pupil progress and encourage all pupils to assess their own performance and how it might be further improved.<br><br>• Ensure that, where additional support has been provided, the support worker has:<br><br>  ■ kept a record of progress<br>  ■ recorded any information to be reported to other staff, parents or other professionals<br>  ■ noted any further practice to take place before the next session<br>  ■ understood his/her role in any necessary preparation that may be needed for the next session. |

## 10.3    What Pupils Should Know

10.3.1      Pupils should know:

- to be aware of the requirements of their peers with special needs; this should ensure they act in an appropriate and safe manner, ie one that:

  ■ reduces the risk to their peers by ensuring that they are safety conscious for all involved in any activity

- encourages them to support their peers when they are frustrated or when they have achieved their goals

- to always ask for guidance when they do not fully understand the requirements of the task

- to be aware of the need to wear appropriate clothing, including protective items when involved in particular activities.

## 10.4   Additional Information

> For a risk assessment for an SEN pupil, see *Appendix 2D: Example Risk Assessment for a Pupil (SEN)*, page 301.
>
> For descriptions of a range of special needs, see *Appendix 4: Pupils with Special Educational Needs (SEN)*, pages 319–324 and the CD.

For an overview of inclusion and pupil support issues in Wales, see http://new.wales.gov.uk/topics/educationandskills/policy_strategy_and_planning/schools/339214-wag/?lang=en

National governing bodies (NGBs) of sport may provide information on disability provision in their particular sport to improve safe participation and talent development.

### Resources

Welsh Assembly Government (WAG) (2006) *Routes for Learning: Assessment Materials for Learners with profound learning difficulties and additional disabilities.* Cardiff: WAG. ISBN: 978-0-750440-57-0

### Useful websites

Autism Awareness
www.autism-awareness.org.uk

British Institute of Learning Disabilities (BILD)
www.bild.org.uk

Capability Scotland
www.capability-scotland.org.uk

DCSF
www.teachernet.gov.uk/wholeschool/sen/

National Autistic Society
www.autism.org.uk

National Deaf Children's Society (NCDS)
www.ndcs.org.uk

Royal National Institute of Blind People (RNIB)
www.rnib.org.uk

Scope
www.scope.org.uk

# Chapter eleven
## Religious and Cultural Issues

This chapter relates to the **people** aspect of risk management. It identifies a number of potential difficulties associated with faith and cultural background that could compromise full participation in PESS for some pupils. It offers a range of strategies for enabling full access to the physical-education curriculum and meaningful activity for all pupils.

## 11.1    Introduction

11.1.1    The religious and cultural diversity of modern society has brought with it a number of health-and-safety issues within the context of PESS. **Careful and sensitive management**, however, should enable all pupils to experience the full benefits of a broad and enriching programme of physical activity, whatever their faith commitment and cultural background, while allowing schools to have due regard to the relevant education, health and safety, human rights and anti-discrimination legislation.

11.1.2    Safe practice must never be compromised. Whatever solutions and strategies staff decide upon to maintain meaningful participation, this principle must be upheld in order to ensure the health and well-being of pupils in their care.

11.1.3    The most frequent health-and-safety concerns arise from:

- the wearing of certain items of clothing and/or religious artefacts

- the impact of religious/cultural festivals (eg Ramadan – Muslim month of fasting which changes from year to year)

- cultural expectations relating to prescribed areas of activity and procedures

- language issues, which may put newly arrived pupils at risk due to difficulties in understanding the requirements of the task, safety procedures, expectations relating to conduct and the simple ability to stop work immediately in the event of danger or emergency.

## 11.2    What Staff Should Know

### Clothing and religious artefacts

11.2.1    In seeking to maximise safe and meaningful participation, staff should ensure the following:

a. Any clothing worn to comply with a faith commitment is appropriate to the activity being taught. It should be comfortable and allow for freedom of movement. Clothing that is loose or free-flowing is generally not suitable for most physical activities and may compromise both the safety of the wearer (eg in gymnastics) and others in close proximity (eg in invasion games). It should be remembered that a tracksuit is considered perfectly acceptable clothing for Muslim pupils and is not seen as offending the principles enshrined in *Haya* relating to modesty and decency.

b.  Headscarves, where worn, are tight, secured in a safe manner and unlikely to catch on anything that may put the wearer at risk.

c.  Any religious artefacts are removed or made safe. Wherever removal is expressly forbidden and the article cannot be made acceptably safe by taping, padding or covering, then the activity and involvement of the wearer must be suitably modified to mitigate undue risk.

> For more information on this issue, see *Chapter 14: Clothing and Personal Effects*, pages 99–102.

## Religious and cultural festivals

11.2.2   Staff need to be aware that certain festivals (eg Ramadan, which involves **fasting** from dawn to dusk over the period of a month) require some pupils to exercise specified dietary regimes. Normal energy resources may thus become temporarily depleted and the risk of dehydration is increased. In such situations, staff expectations relating to performance (eg sustained running) may need to be reviewed and levels of challenge adjusted in order to accommodate pupil need.

11.2.3   Younger children, particularly, may be prone to a lowering of concentration levels when opting to participate in fasting. This has clear implications for the supervision and management of physical activity and care needs to be taken in maintaining a safe working environment. Thus, work on apparatus in gymnastics, for instance, may require modification and intensity levels in games activities may need to be lowered to a point where children may continue to participate safely.

11.2.4   Staff need to remain responsive to pupil needs in this area at all times, but, because of the potential for higher activity levels in the summer months, particular care needs to be taken when Ramadan or similar festivals fall at this time of year.

## Religious and cultural expectations

11.2.5   The demands made by some activities within a prescribed curriculum may initially be seen as conflicting with customs and beliefs fundamental to certain faiths. **Swimming**, for instance, presents particular issues for the Muslim community associated with unacceptable exposure of the body and mixed-gender settings. From a health-and-safety perspective, however, the ability to swim extends far beyond simply recreational or competitive activity – it embodies a potentially lifesaving skill that all children have an entitlement to access. In securing this access, school staff should apply all practical means to sustain a meaningful swimming programme that at least meets the requirements of the given curriculum, while seeking to respect any religious/cultural sensitivities involved wherever possible. Staff should try to ensure that:

- discussion with local faith leaders and parents is ongoing and policies concerning swimming provision are effectively communicated to parents and the local community

- adjustments are made in swimming attire to accommodate religious and cultural sensitivities

- changing arrangements take into account any mixed-gender issues and provide for acceptable levels of privacy

- the management of the swimming programme builds in single-sex teaching, whenever practical, wherever this preference is feasible.

## Pupils with English as an additional language

11.2.6    Pupils who do not fully understand the requirements of, or how to set about, a particular physical activity are at risk to themselves and the rest of the group. Pupils at an early stage in the acculturation process may initially have limited English language capability and consequently may struggle to interpret what is required of them in a physical-education lesson. It cannot be assumed that the complexity of the language used in physical education is any less demanding than elsewhere in the curriculum and the speed of response often required puts further pressure on the ability of pupils with English as an additional language (EAL pupils) to comprehend. The following procedures will assist in encouraging safe participation:

a.    Where learning support staff are available, they should be effectively briefed about the learning outcomes of the lesson and alerted to any safety features.

b.    Initially, time should be taken to ensure that individual EAL pupils clearly understand the command 'Stop!' and know that an immediate response to cease activity is required, should this command be necessary. Over time, other key phrases, identified through risk-assessment procedures, can be introduced into EAL pupils' vocabulary.

c.    Staff should be familiar with the names of EAL pupils in order to quickly attract and maintain their attention.

d.    The use of focused demonstration can sometimes overcome linguistic difficulty linked to an acknowledgement by the pupils that they have understood what is required.

e.    The use of a 'buddy' system, where practical, pairing an EAL pupil with another pupil known to have a responsible and mature disposition, reflects good practice.

## 11.3    What Pupils Should Know

11.3.1    Pupils should know:

- the benefits of physical activity and its contribution towards a healthy lifestyle are recognised and supported by the majority of faiths and cultures

- health-and-safety requirements have to be respected in order to protect the well-being of pupils and ensure safe participation

- never to proceed with an activity if they are unclear about its requirements and outcomes

- any apparent conflict between the needs of faith commitment and safe participation in the physical-education programme can usually be resolved by discussion, clear thinking and common sense.

## 11.4    Additional Information

### Resources

DCSF (2007) 'DCSF Guidance to Schools on School Uniform and Related Policies', http://www.teachernet.gov.uk/management/atoz/u/uniform

DCSF (2008) *The Inclusion of Gypsy, Roma and Traveller Children and Young People*. Nottingham: DCFS. ISBN: 978-1-847750-94-5.
Available from: http://publications.teachernet.gov.uk/eOrderingDownload/Inclusion%20of%20Gypsy%20Roma.pdf

Muslim Council of Britain (2007) 'Meeting the Needs of Muslim Pupils in State Schools: Information and Guidance', www.mcb.org.uk/downloads/Schoolinfoguidancev2.pdf

Whitlam, P. (2007) 'Comment on "Meeting the Needs of Muslim Pupils in State Schools: Information and Guidance for Schools", British Muslim Council, 2007', www.afpe.org.uk/public/downloads/Muslim_Council_Guidance_for_State_Schools_2007.doc

## 11.5    Case Law Examples

11.5.1    R (on the Application of X) versus Head Teachers of Y School and Another, Queens Bench Division (2007):
*A claim brought under the Human Rights Act for a pupil to be allowed to wear the niqab (veil) in school was rejected on the basis that a school could impose a school-uniform policy. The school was supported by the fact that advice was taken and was told that its existing policy conformed with the requirements of mainstream Muslim opinion.*

11.5.2    R (Begum) versus the Head Teacher and Governors of Denbigh High School, House of Lords (2006):
*The House of Lords allowed an appeal that the school had a right to set out a uniform policy and to require that the policy be followed, particularly as a recent review of the uniform policy had involved detailed discussion with the local Muslim community. Thus, a demand to be allowed to wear a jilbab (long, loose garment covering the body) was rejected as alternatives had been accepted by the local community.*

# Chapter twelve

## Equipment in Physical Education

12

This chapter concerns itself with a **contextual** aspect of risk management. It will assist staff in developing a safe working environment by suggesting procedures to enable the systematic monitoring, maintenance and upkeep of apparatus and items of equipment.

## 12.1 Introduction

12.1.1 Staff need to be confident that the equipment they plan to use is of **acceptable quality** in terms of its design, manufacture and durability. Such assurance is often obtained through reference to British and European Standards (kitemarked BS and BS EN respectively).

12.1.2 A **standard** is a document defining good practice, established by consensus and approved by a recognised body such as the British Standards Institute (BSI).

12.1.3 Standards are aspirational, rather than general practice, and are designed for voluntary use. However, local regulations, guidance and directives will frequently refer to a particular BS or BS EN standard as a means of ensuring the consistency and **fitness for purpose** of certain products and procedures. It is also worth noting that compliance with a British Standard does not in itself confer legal immunity, although it will strengthen any defence against accusations of negligence in activities involving the use of equipment.

12.1.4 Not all equipment comes with a standard. For instance, at the present time, there is no current standard for gymnastic equipment, although work is under way in the UK and Europe to compile one.

12.1.5 In such situations, staff need to seek alternative confirmation that the products they intend to purchase and use with pupils are **safe and well made** to inform their risk assessments. Suppliers should be recognised as reputable and have an established record for reliability.

12.1.6 Where appropriate, evidence should be sought of any testing or evaluation procedures that have been undertaken on particular items of equipment to determine fitness for purpose by asking the supplier for information.

12.1.7 All equipment should be subject to **systematic and regular inspection** in order to identify any signs of damage or wear and tear that may cause injury. Any items so identified must be immediately taken out of use until repaired or replaced.

## 12.2 What Staff Should Know

12.2.1 Schools and other organisations need to have **policies** in place that communicate clearly:

- how equipment is to be stored in order to maintain safe access for staff and pupils

- how and when staff should monitor the condition of equipment and the procedures for dealing with defective items

- how to use equipment correctly and not deviate from its design specification

- how pupils need to be involved in the safe handling and movement of apparatus and equipment.

12.2.2    In order to comply with good health-and-safety practice, specialist maintenance engineers will need to undertake detailed and systematic inspection of large apparatus, resulting in a written report. This is usually scheduled on an annual basis.

> For further information on the regulations, see *Appendix 1: Relevant Statute, Regulations and Guidance,* pages 287–295.

12.2.3    Criteria associated with **competent inspection and maintenance** provision would include the following:

a.  Appropriate insurance should be held by the contractor and made available for scrutiny if necessary.

b.  Human resources, tools and materials should match the agreed schedule of work.

c.  The maintenance and inspection work should seek to disrupt teaching as little as possible, but be open to observation and monitoring.

d.  An opportunity should be given to school staff to identify any equipment/ apparatus concerns prior to the inspection/maintenance work commencing.

The **inspection process** should identify:

- exactly what apparatus/equipment has been inspected (the inspection specification)

- any apparatus/equipment that is judged no longer safe through damage or deterioration

- any maintenance or repair that has been undertaken in order to restore faulty apparatus/equipment to safe usage.

The inspection process should have the following outcomes:

- a written, signed, dated report, identifying all work undertaken

- recommendations relating to any item of apparatus/equipment that merits repair, but falls outside the scope of the contract in terms of cost

- the immediate and safe disposal or decommissioning of any apparatus/equipment judged to be beyond reasonable repair.

> For a model contract, see *Appendix 5: Model Equipment Inspection/Maintenance Schedule – Gymnasia, Sports Halls and Fitness Areas,* page 325.

12.2.4    The following items of equipment merit further consideration:

- portable goalposts

- playing-area markers

- portable games posts

- gymnastic apparatus

- mats

86

- landing modules

- trampolines and trampettes.

## Portable goalposts

12.2.5   Portable goalposts are increasingly used for soccer and hockey at all levels. They provide a useful option when storage, portability and flexibility in the use of playing areas need to be considered. Such posts are made from metal, or heavy-duty plastic, and are light enough to carry. National governing bodies (NGBs) for football provide useful guidance on the handling and placing of portable goalposts.

12.2.6   Because of their relative lightness, it is essential that portable goalposts are **made secure** by the use of chain anchors or appropriate anchor weights when in use. Whether in the event of impact from the ball or unintentional collision by a player, the goalposts need to offer a stable structure. The stability of the posts should always be checked prior to use.

12.2.7   Portable goalposts should:

- be obtained from a reputable manufacturer and comply with British Standard Publicly Available Specification (PAS) 36:2000

- be assembled in accordance with the manufacturer's instructions

- be regularly checked for wear and tear and, where practical, any damage made good by a suitably qualified person

- be smooth in construction, with no sharp edges

- come equipped with a safe stabilising device that presents no hazard to players or spectators.

Any **netting** should be well fitted and not extend beyond the area covered by the base of the posts. It needs to be secured by plastic hooks or tape. Metal cup hooks should not be used.

12.2.8   Staff or pupils with responsibility for moving and positioning the posts should apply **safe lifting and carrying techniques**. Portable goalposts should be safely stored when not in use.

For a reminder of safe lifting and carrying techniques, see *12.2.15e*, page 88.

12.2.9   Clear guidance needs to be given to pupils about the **dangers arising from misuse** (eg climbing or swinging on the uprights and crossbars of both fixed and portable goalposts). Reported accidents and resulting injuries (in some cases fatal) have had their origins in such activity.

## Playing area markers

12.2.10   Clearly designated **playing areas** are essential to safe practice whether participating outdoors (eg on a field or hard play area) or indoors (eg in a school hall or sports hall).

12.2.11   Brightly coloured games discs provide the safest **alternative to goalposts** or for the reinforcement of line marking and are also relatively easy to carry to the working area. Although suitable for 'run-around' relay-type activities, cones and skittles should not be used as playing-area markers, particularly in fast-moving games activities where a fall is foreseeable. Cricket stumps or other low posts should not be used as markers or as substitute goalposts as a fall onto one could cause serious eye injury. Beanbags are not recommended as markers for indoor work and are particularly hazardous to participants on a shiny floor.

## Portable games posts

12.2.12     The hazards posed by portable games posts (eg netball posts) arise both in transit to and from the working area and when positioned on the court/playing surface.

12.2.13     It is essential that staff and, where appropriate, pupils who are given responsibility for moving and assembling such equipment are given a suitable induction into safe lifting techniques. It will be necessary for staff to supervise pupils given such responsibility and this is particularly important where heavy weights are utilised to stabilise the posts. If made of metal, regular checks should be made for rough edges and signs of rust. When in place, the bases must not intrude into the playing area.

## Gymnastic apparatus

12.2.14     Gymnastic equipment falls into two categories. In primary schools, it generally consists of **fixed and portable apparatus**, such as climbing frames, ropes, benches, movement platforms, nesting tables, boxes, planks and trestles. In secondary schools, many items associated with competitive gymnastics and more formal **vaulting and agility** activities will additionally be found.

12.2.15     Whatever the function of gymnastic apparatus, staff should ensure the following:

a. Only apparatus that has been officially provided, approved and/or Kitemarked is used and staff need to be very wary of improvising beyond its design specification.

b. All apparatus is stored in such a way as to offer safe and easy access to both staff and pupils. This may involve the use of a storeroom or location at various points around the hall or gymnasium. When stored in the latter way, it should not intrude into the working area and should have a designated space.

c. After use, apparatus is returned to its designated storage space and left in a stable position.

d. Apparatus is assembled and dismantled systematically and pupils are taught to do this, wherever possible. It needs to be checked by staff to ensure correct assembly before activity commences and pupils should be encouraged to remain alert to, and report, any unintended adjustment as work proceeds.

e. Apparatus is such that pupils are able to manage lifting, carrying and placing it in a safe manner. Pupils should have a straight back, chin tucked in, be close to the load, have feet apart with one foot in front of the other and be facing in the intended direction of travel with no twisting. Pupils should lift with knees bent using the legs as the lifting power. Everyone should have a good grip on the load before lifting and should not change their grip once carrying it. The load should not obstruct fields of view. Pupils should set the load down gently with their backs straight and knees bent.

f. Sufficient space is left between apparatus to allow safe movement around it. Dismount points and planned landing areas need to be free from obstruction and always well away from walls.

g. Apparatus is regularly inspected and repaired, where necessary, by qualified maintenance engineers, at least on an annual basis (see *12.2.2–12.2.3*, page 86). Apparatus deemed unsafe but repairable should be removed well away from the working area and clearly labelled as unsafe until made good.

Because the **annual cycle of apparatus inspection** by specialist engineers usually extends to a 12-month period, staff need to constantly **monitor the condition** of apparatus on a day-to-day and lesson-by-lesson basis. The following table identifies a number of features related to the safety of key items of gymnastic apparatus.

**Table 7: Gymnastic apparatus checklist**

|  | Check that: |
| --- | --- |
| Wooden rebound/ take-off boards | ✓ the board is stable on impact<br>✓ the surface is non-slip and free from splinters |
| Benches and planks | ✓ the construction is not warped and is free from splinters<br>✓ rubber buffers on the supporting feet are secure and the bench is stable<br>✓ the surface is clean and smooth<br>✓ fixing hooks are intact and covered with leather or plastic<br>✓ rubber pads on the top surface are in place if the bench is intended for use in an inverted position |
| Ropes and suspended apparatus | ✓ ropes are not frayed or damaged<br>✓ pull-out lines are not worn and their securing wall cleats are secure<br>✓ the runway operates smoothly<br>✓ ropes are knot-free and the leather end caps are intact<br>✓ rope ladder floor fixings are intact<br>✓ knots are not tied into the ends of the ropes |
| Hinged apparatus fixed to a wall | ✓ bracing wires are taut with no visible fraying at any point<br>✓ castors run smoothly<br>✓ floor sockets are clean and free from obstruction<br>✓ securing bolts are firmly fixed and engage properly with their floor and wall sockets<br>✓ wooden components are free from cracks or splinters<br>✓ painted components are well maintained, with no evidence of flaking |
| Single and double beams | ✓ hauling cables are free running<br>✓ trackways are well maintained, enabling smooth movement of the upright<br>✓ there are sufficient pins and wedges<br>✓ beam surfaces are clean and smooth<br>✓ beams run smoothly when lowered and raised<br>✓ floor sockets are clean |
| Vaulting apparatus and movement platforms | ✓ all wooden components are splinter-free<br>✓ all covers – vinyl, material or hide – are free from tears, clean and, in the case of hide, suitably textured<br>✓ construction is stable and solid with no weakness allowing dangerous movement on impact<br>✓ wheeling mechanisms work efficiently |

## Mats

12.2.16   It is essential that both staff and pupils understand the structure, function, capabilities and limitations of mats when used within the physical-education programme.

12.2.17   Mats are primarily designed to absorb impact. Their construction dissipates force, thereby reducing reaction to what would otherwise constitute a hard and unyielding surface.

12.2.18   Over the years, considerable improvements have been made to the design and specification of mats, enhancing safety. However, it is important pupils understand that mats, whatever their construction and size, should never be seen as fail-safe protection systems that supersede effective technique. Pupils need to be aware that a correctly performed landing contributes most to preventing injury. This technique needs to be taught and re-emphasised regularly.

12.2.19   The guidance below relating to the maintenance of mats will promote safe practice:

a. When buying new mats, care should be taken that they meet any current standard, where available, and that they fully comply with fire regulations. Assurance should be sought from manufacturers on both these requirements.

b. Mats should be covered with material that is easy to clean. In order to minimise slippage, the underside will also need to be cleaned from time to time. They should be checked regularly for any embedded objects (eg stones, pins etc).

c. Mats should be stable and lie flat to the floor. Wherever practical, mats should be stored in a horizontal position to prevent warping of closed-cell polyethylene foam and disintegration of foam padding.

d. Mats should remain free from holes and tears.

e. Mats should be light enough for pupils to handle easily, preferably in pairs if the mats are lightweight. Four pupils may need to carry mats according to their size and strength in relation to the size and weight of the mat.

f. Mats should be subject to regular inspection. Damaged mats should be immediately taken out of service until repaired by a specialist maintenance firm or replaced.

## The use of mats in gymnastics

12.2.20   Mats are used in gymnastics to:
- provide a cushioned area for aspects of floor work (eg developing rolling activities)
- identify suitable landing areas to pupils as they work around apparatus
- offer a limited measure of protection in the event of an uncontrolled or mistimed descent from apparatus.

12.2.21   General-purpose mats (approximately 25mm thick) are generally suitable for curriculum work in gymnastics. Thicker mats (eg 10cm) may be necessary for more specialised, advanced gymnastic activity in which the performer generates high levels of momentum.

12.2.22   Mats should never be indiscriminately placed around the working area. Each mat should be placed with a specific purpose in mind, associated with developing confidence, comfort in working and developing changes in direction.

12.2.23   Staff need to present pupils with appropriate gymnastic challenge following a structured and systematic progression towards identified movement outcomes. Mats should never be used to protect against the foreseeable outcomes of poorly developed skill. It is better that apparatus and task are modified to accurately reflect pupil need and capability, thereby minimising the risk of falling and poorly controlled dismounts.

12.2.24   Staff need to exercise caution when using thick weight-absorbing mattresses ('crash mats') as landing areas. Too much absorption may compromise safe dismounts onto feet. In such situations, staff are advised to 'firm up' the landing surface by overlaying the mattress with general gymnastic mats where necessary.

## Landing modules

12.2.25   Landing modules are necessary to perform high-jump technique in which the transference of weight moves from feet to some other body part (eg the Fosbury Flop and related progressions). It is strongly recommended that staff using specialised high-jump facilities have undergone appropriate training through the national governing body (NGB) – UK Athletics – or as part of a specialist PE training programme.

12.2.26   Staff should ensure that:

- multiple modules, where used, are firmly locked together and a coverall pad used to prevent slippage

- the landing area is sufficiently large and deep enough to accommodate the abilities of the pupils involved and probable variations in landing position, extending beyond both uprights

- the density of the landing module is sufficient to avoid any bottoming out.

## Trampolines and trampettes

12.2.27   Unfolding, folding and positioning trampolines are highly disciplined and systematic activities, which older pupils should be properly trained to carry out as a team. They should be taught how to erect and fold away school-model trampolines. This should always take place under the direct supervision (and often with the physical assistance) of staff. Larger trampolines (club and competition models) are heavier and may require additional adult assistance.

12.2.28   The procedures used need to be clearly understood by all involved. The guidance below will promote safe practice:

a.   Trampolines should be placed well away from any overhead obstruction (eg hanging beams, lights). There should be an overhead clearance of at least 5m from the floor to the lowest hanging object. Some trampolines may require even greater clearance.

b.   Once removed, wheel units should be placed carefully in a storage position well clear of the working area.

c.   The space under and around trampolines should be clear and free from obstructions.

d.  When unfolding a trampoline, care should be taken to ensure that:

- feet are kept well away from the wheels

- the trampoline is angled and lowered carefully, and the lower leg section held firmly, so that it does not crash to the floor

- the frame sections are opened with a firm, continuous movement, with steady force applied and maintained to prevent them from springing back

- fingers, elbows and wrists are kept clear of all hinges.

e.  Before allowing a trampoline or trampette to be used, staff should check that:

- all the leg braces have been properly fitted and the hinge units are securely housed

- all adjustments are tight

- the hooks of the springs/rubber cables are properly attached, with the hooks pointing down

- the springs/cables are all in good condition

- the safety pads are fitted and entirely cover the springs/cables

- Allen screws are tight (if present)

- the bed is clean and free from damage of any kind

- the wheeling devices are operating smoothly and the pivotal housing on the frame holds the hub of the wheeling mechanism at right angles without any movement of the hub and the housing (trampoline only)

- any weight-absorbing mattresses used are of a sufficient size and weight absorbency to meet the requirements of body impact.

f.  When folding a trampoline, care should be taken to ensure that:

- the wheels are securely housed

- the frame sections are closed using a firm, continuous movement, with steady force applied and maintained to resist the tension of the springs or cables

- fingers, elbows and wrists are kept clear of all hinges

- feet are kept well away from the wheels

- the lower frame and leg sections are positioned inside the upper frame and leg sections as the trampoline is rotated from the horizontal to the vertical.

g.  Once folded, trampolines should be locked to prevent unauthorised use. This can be done by locking together two links of one of the leg chains. Trampettes should also be *disabled* in some way when not in use or kept in secure storage.

h.  When provided, overhead support rigs should be supplied and fitted by recognised specialist manufacturers and engineers. On no account should improvised rigs be used. Training in the correct use of rigs is essential.

12.2.29   End decks are to become compulsory for competition. This is an example of where an NGB directive becomes good advice to apply within PESS situations.

For detailed guidance on the use of trampolines and trampettes, see *Part B: Trampolining Activities*, pages 187–193, in *Chapter 23: Gymnastics and Trampolining Activities*.

## 12.3    What Pupils Should Know

12.3.1    Pupils should know:

- how to manage and handle apparatus in a safe and responsible manner by:
  - assessing the object's size and shape to decide whether it is safe to proceed
  - planning enough space to reposition the load as required
  - preparing correctly and obtaining assistance if required
  - performing under supervision

- how to cooperate effectively as a team when setting out and putting away larger items of equipment

- the procedures for alerting staff to any observed dangers or defects apparent in any item of equipment

- the scope and limitations of apparatus (eg mats, landing modules) in protecting personal safety

- to use equipment for the purpose it was designed for

- never to use any equipment unless authorised to do so by a member of staff.

> For a reminder of safe lifting and carrying techniques for pupils, see *12.2.15e*, page 88.

## 12.4    Additional Information

> See also *Appendix 5: Model Equipment Inspection/Maintenance Schedule for Gymnasia, Sports Halls and Fitness Areas*, page 325.

### Useful websites

British Standards Institute
www.standardsuk.com

Continental Sports Ltd
www.continentalsports.co.uk

Sports and Fitness Equipment Association (SAFEA)
www.safea.co.uk

## 12.5    Case Law Examples

12.5.1    Beaumont versus Surrey County Council (1968):
*This ruling held the local authority responsible for the teacher not disposing of old trampette elastics adequately. A pupil picked the elastics out of a waste bin and, while playing with them, caused another pupil to lose an eye.*

12.5.2    Steed versus Cheltenham Borough Council, Gloucester County Court (2000):
*The crossbar of some rugby posts collapsed and fell onto a boy. It was judged that the posts were rusty and deteriorating and that the council did not carry out sufficiently frequent inspections of the condition of the posts.*

# Chapter thirteen
## Personal Protection

This chapter is concerned with a **contextual** aspect of risk management. It describes the scope and limitations of personal protective equipment (PPE) in selected sports and recommends how schools and organisations should proceed in enabling effective usage of PPE by pupils and other participants.

## 13.1 Introduction

13.1.1 The use of PPE is an increasing feature of participation in a wide range of physical activities and sports. PPE may be defined as 'any device to be worn or held by an individual for protection against one or more health-and-safety hazards'.

13.1.2 Protective equipment should be **fit for purpose** and regulation is extensive. Manufacturers are encouraged to ensure that their products conform to specified standards, where they exist. For example, head protectors for cricket should comply with BS 7928:1998 (a British Standard), whereas helmets for pedal cyclists, skateboarders and roller skaters should comply with BS EN 1078:1997 (a European Standard).

13.1.3 A number of national governing bodies (NGBs) of sport have introduced their own regulations, which impose the mandatory wearing of certain items of protective gear with a view to minimising injury. Such injury may arise through:

- physical contact with another player (intentional or otherwise)
- contact of some part of the body with:
  - a hard ball (usually unintentional)
  - an implement (usually unintentional)
  - a rough surface or chemically affected environment (intentional or otherwise).

13.1.4 In some sports, the legal principle of *res ipsi loquitor* – 'the thing speaks for itself' – is invoked. This applies clearly to sports such as fencing or boxing in which the wearing of protective items is inherent in the activity itself. This need, however, is not always so obvious in other activities.

13.1.5 It needs to be stressed that the wearing of PPE will not guarantee freedom from injury. It can, however, in many cases, mitigate the severity of injury by reducing a high-risk situation to one of reasonable or acceptable risk.

13.1.6 In this sense, staff should fully **inform pupils** about the purpose, function and limitations of PPE in order to counteract any false sense of security that may arise as a consequence of wearing protective gear. In all activities, the application of good technique and skill, and rigorous adherence to the rules, remain the most important features of safe participation.

## 13.2 What Staff Should Know

13.2.1 Whenever pupils become involved in competition **regulated** by an NGB, then any ruling relating to PPE must be complied with.

13.2.2 The table below summarises the requirements of a number of leading NGBs of sport relating to PPE.

**Table 8: NGB requirements relating to PPE**

| NGB | PPE Requirements |
|---|---|
| Rugby Football Union | • Mouth guards are mandatory for representative matches above school level; otherwise, they are recommended.<br>• Padded helmets are permitted. |
| Rugby Football League | • Mouth guards are recommended.<br>• Shoulder pads are permitted at all levels of participation.<br>• Padded helmets are permitted. |
| England Hockey | • Mouth guards and shin/ankle pads are recommended at all levels of participation.<br>• Specialist protection for goalkeepers is mandatory. |
| Lacrosse | • Mouth guards are mandatory at representative level.<br>• Specialist protection for goalkeepers is mandatory. |
| England and Wales Cricket Board | • Helmets (and boxes for boys) are mandatory when batting using a hard ball and also when fielding close to the bat. |
| Football Association | • Shin pads are mandatory at all levels of participation. |

13.2.3 It will often be the case that NGB rulings relating to the wearing of PPE are also directly adopted within an **educational setting**. However, a risk assessment of the activity can bring some flexibility to achieving optimum levels of participation and involvement in the taught curriculum, usually through modification of the activity in question (eg using a soft ball and plastic implements available to a number of mini versions of sports, non-contact versions of physical-contact games and practices or wearing light footwear instead of studded boots).

13.2.4 Staff should always seek to effectively **communicate** their policies relating to the wearing of PPE to parents.

### Mouth guards

13.2.5 As with any PPE item, mouth guards work by dissipating direct force relative to both time and impact, thereby offering a measure of protection to teeth and gums. In the case of mouth guards, additional benefits arise in reducing lacerations inside the mouth of the wearer while mitigating injury caused by teeth to an opponent in the event of unforeseen collision. As well as potentially minimising oral/facial injury, there is also some evidence that mouth guards can reduce incidences of concussion, but this is less certain, and only then in situations where a bespoke, personally fitted mouth guard is worn.

13.2.6 At the present time, most NGBs involved in contact sport strongly recommend that players wear mouth guards in games and in practices involving physical contact, while stopping short of making them mandatory (with the exception of the RFU in junior representative games and lacrosse at representative levels).

13.2.7 There is no doubt that a **bespoke mouth guard**, properly fitted by a dentist or dental technician, is the most effective, but cost may be prohibitive. Less effective, but relatively cheap, **'boil-and-bite'** versions are now available which need to carry a European Conformity (CE) marking. This indicates that the product has been subject to some quality assurance in assessing its fitness for purpose. There is currently no British Standard available.

13.2.8 Staff should ensure that pupils and **parents are kept well informed** about the wearing of mouth guards. A policy strongly recommending the use of mouth guards should be adopted. Should schools decide to adopt a policy of mandatory usage of mouth guards in physical-contact situations, then their duty of care obliges them to ensure that all participants always have access to one.

## Swimming goggles

For information on swimming goggles, see *26.2.55–26.2.56, page 271,* in *Chapter 26: Aquatic Activities.*

## Weather conditions

### Exposure to the sun

13.2.9 The risks associated with overexposure to the two bands of ultraviolet light from the sun are well documented and staff need to be mindful of a range of **necessary precautions** in ensuring the well-being of pupils:

a. Lengthy periods in direct sunlight, particularly around midday when the sun is at its hottest, should be avoided whenever possible.

b. Pupils should be taught how to screen themselves from the harmful effects of the sun through wearing light clothing and using suncream. Parental approval will be required to use sunscreen products, which parents should provide.

c. Sunglasses and hats can provide effective screening in selected activities where they pose no danger to the wearer or other participants in terms of the quality of the items and the nature of the activity.

For more guidance on considering weather conditions, see *18.2.28, page 129,* in *Chapter 18: Managing Sports Events, Sports Tours and Other Off-site PESS Activities.*

## 13.3    What Pupils Should Know

13.3.1    Pupils should know:

- when, and what type of, protective equipment is appropriate for a particular activity or sport

- in what ways PPE can reduce, though never eliminate, the likelihood and severity of injury

- when to replace PPE after damage or normal wear and tear

- how to judge whether an item of PPE offers genuine protection and fits appropriately

- the hygiene implications of sharing PPE and when sharing is not advisable

- how to effectively manage the potentially harmful effects of the sun.

## 13.4    Additional Information

Specific NGBs will provide regulations for the use of PPE in their sports on their websites or on request.

### Useful websites

Central Council for Physical Recreation (CCPR)
www.ccpr.org.uk

sports coach UK
www.sportscoachuk.org

UK Sport
www.uksport.gov.uk

## 13.5    Case Law Examples

13.5.1    G (a Child) versus Lancashire County Council, Burnley County Court (2000):
*A pupil received a serious mouth injury when playing hockey after being struck by a hockey stick as she attempted to make a tackle. She was not wearing a mouth guard. The judge determined that it was insufficient to simply inform pupils of the need for specific safety equipment and that staff should ensure that parents and carers are also fully apprised of the advice.*

98

# Chapter fourteen

## Clothing and Personal Effects

# 14

This chapter deals with a **contextual** aspect of risk management. It details a range of essential requirements relating to clothing, footwear and adornments that staff should seek compliance with, in order to maintain safe participation.

## 14.1 Introduction

14.1.1 Clothing and correct attire for a particular activity represent important features of safe practice that apply in equal measure to both staff and pupils.

14.1.2 **Staff** should always endeavour to change for physical education. In situations where this proves difficult or impractical, in some small primary schools, for instance, then a change of footwear and removal of jewellery, at the very least, should always be undertaken.

14.1.3 Pupils, from the earliest ages, should change into suitable physical-education clothing in order that they may participate safely and securely. Although vest and pants were, in the past, an acceptable option for the youngest children, contemporary views on safeguarding, personal development and hygiene mean this is no longer advisable practice.

14.1.4 **Clothing for PESS** should be well suited to its function. It should be light and allow good freedom of movement, without being baggy or loose, for work indoors. Clothing for outdoor lessons should again allow good freedom of movement, but will also need to offer some insulation from cold weather in the winter months. It should be remembered that pupils who are insufficiently warm and experiencing discomfort will not be appropriately focused and may lack concentration.

14.1.5 **Footwear** that is fit for purpose is essential. It should demonstrate effective grip, support and reasonable protection for outside work and games, contrasting with lightness and flimsiness for indoor activities such as gymnastics and dance.

14.1.6 **Personal effects**, such as jewellery, religious artefacts, watches, hair slides, sensory aids etc, should always be removed by pupils before participating in physical activity. Staff also need to be mindful of their own adornments. The wearing of rings, for instance, has been responsible for unnecessary injury in the past and represents a hazard to both staff and pupils involved in the lesson. Any exception to this recommendation of complete removal needs to be carefully considered and always comply with a suitable risk assessment.

14.1.7 Clear expectations should be established throughout the school, and with parents, about the management of personal effects by means of a clear and unambiguous written policy.

## 14.2 What Staff Should Know

### Jewellery and personal adornment

14.2.1　The wearing of non-essential personal effects continues to pose difficulties in many schools since such items should, ideally, always be removed in establishing a safe working environment. Staff have a duty of care to ensure that pupils are able to actively participate without unnecessarily endangering themselves or those working around them. Systems and procedures need to be in place within the changing area to check that pupils fulfil this obligation prior to participation.

14.2.2　The following procedure should be applied at the commencement of every lesson:

a. **All personal effects should be removed**. Staff should always give a verbal reminder to pupils and, where necessary, visually monitor the group and/or individuals. Particular vigilance may be required when dealing with body jewellery.

b. **If they cannot be removed, staff need to take action to try to make the situation safe**. In some situations, this may mean adjusting the activity in some way or, where a risk assessment allows, protecting the item (eg a medical bracelet) with tape, padding or a wristband. Taping over ear studs, for instance, may offer a measure of protection in some physical-activity situations where individuals are required to work within their own personal space. This would not be acceptable, however, in swimming lessons where exposure to water can easily dislodge the tape, magnifying the hazards involved, nor is it satisfactory in situations where close contact is foreseeable. Where taping is utilised, the adult supervising the group maintains the duty of care to ensure that the taping is effective in its purpose.

c. **If the situation cannot be made safe, the individual pupil(s) concerned should not actively participate**. Alternative involvement in the lesson may be possible.

> **Note:** Recent developments in the manufacture of **medical-aid wristbands** have resulted in products with an acceptably low risk factor (soft materials used, Velcro fastenings etc). Such items should be acceptable for physical participation in most activities, largely avoiding the need for removal, provided there are no hard or sharp edges that may cause injury.

14.2.3　The wearing of **sensory aids** such as spectacles or hearing aids will usually be determined by:

• the nature of the activity (ie activities involving physical contact would not be appropriate)

• a balanced judgement as to whether wearing the item constitutes greater or lesser risk to the wearer and the group in those activities where physical contact is absent.

Where the sensory aid needs to be worn for safe participation by the individual, then the staff need to apply the procedure set out above in *14.2.2* in order to determine whether participation with the sensory aid is safe for the wearer and for others in the group.

14.2.4　**Long hair** worn by both staff and pupils should always be tied back with a suitably soft item to prevent entanglement in apparatus and to prevent it obscuring vision.

14.2.5    Disclaimers from parents about the wearing of any item of jewellery by a pupil should be declined. Such indemnities have no legal status. The duty of care remains firmly with the school on such matters.

> For more information on this issue, see *Consent forms (2.2.23–2.2.24, page 17)* in *Chapter 2: Physical Education and the Law.*

## Indoor footwear

14.2.6    Suitable indoor footwear is crucial to safe participation and supervision. **Security of footing is essential**. Staff may need to respond quickly to prevent a potential injury to a pupil, making effective mobility essential. Pupils need footwear that is capable of transmitting feel for the movement and the surface they are working on in gymnastics and dance, for instance.

14.2.7    Many practitioners believe that **bare feet** offer a better alternative for these activities, providing the floor is of good quality and clean. Where any doubt exists about the suitability of the working surface, however, appropriate footwear becomes a requirement.

14.2.8    Pupils should never participate in **socks** on polished surfaces. Well-fitting socks may be acceptable on a carpet surface if traction is not affected.

14.2.9    **Training shoes**, on which the soles provide good traction, will often prove effective for a range of indoor games, but should not be worn for gymnastic activities for the reasons of 'feel' described above in *14.2.6*.

14.2.10   Staff need to avoid situations often found in games lessons when organising wet-weather indoor alternative activity in which some pupils wear training shoes and others are obliged to resort to bare feet.

## Outdoor footwear

14.2.11   Whatever the type of footwear worn to give participants stability on outdoor playing surfaces, systematic maintenance is essential. Rule 4, in The Football Association's *Laws of the Game* clearly states: 'A player must not use equipment or wear anything which is dangerous to himself or another player'. Although this reference applies to appropriate conduct in football, the principle embodied in this rule is universal. **Security of footing** is again an essential requirement, along with consideration as to whether the outdoor footwear presents any foreseeable risk to other participants.

14.2.12   Systems need to be in place whereby staff, officials and participants regularly **check the safety** of their footwear. Procedures also need to be applied whereby participants avoid, wherever possible, walking over hard surfaces to gain access to the playing area. This can result in studs and other traction devices becoming unacceptably rough and sharp, proving hazardous to opponents in competitive games and practices.

14.2.13   There is ongoing debate about the safety, or otherwise, of **bladed boots**, with some authorities deciding that they present unacceptable risk. As yet, there exists no conclusive proof, through well-documented research, that bladed boots present any greater risk than traditional studded versions, providing that adequate care and attention is given to their maintenance.

14.2.14   Where a group presents a **variety of footwear** for outdoor lessons, the adult with the group has to determine whether the lesson can proceed as planned or whether some conditions needs to be applied to enable maximum participation in safety.

## 14.3    What Pupils Should Know

14.3.1    Pupils should know that:

- clothing used for PESS should be suitable for the activity and designed with safe participation in mind

- personal items of physical-education and sports clothing should be kept clean and serviceable

- physical-education and sports footwear should be regularly checked and well maintained; this is particularly applicable to studded and bladed football boots

- jewellery should always be removed before active participation; any exception to this rule must always be sanctioned by a member of staff.

## 14.4    Case Law Examples

14.4.1    R versus the Chair and Governors of Cwnfelinfach Primary School (ex parte Roberts), High Court (2001):
*The judge determined that the school was entitled to exclude the pupil from physical activity when she wore jewellery. This was on the basis of health and safety. A claim that the exclusion breached the European Convention on Human Rights was rejected.*

# Chapter fifteen
## Buildings and Facilities

This chapter deals with a **contextual** aspect of risk management, defining how the design and usage of buildings and facilities contribute to a safe working environment. It should be read alongside *Chapter 12: Equipment in Physical Education*, pages 85–93.

## 15.1 Introduction

15.1.1 Projects such as Building Schools for the Future, the primary-school investment programme and the Private Finance Initiative have created the opportunity for extensive new-build provision for PESS. The focus has thus moved towards flexible learning spaces to meet learning outcomes. Schools will no longer have common provision. Local authority (LA) corporate estate plans will determine flexibility of provision to address the needs of PESS, community provision and provision for pathways to elite performance across networks of schools.

15.1.2 Generic aspects of health and safety in relation to facilities will remain the same as before. However, the new approach to facility provision will require a review of risk assessments specific to a particular school's use of the facilities. For example, the introduction of adaptable structures, such as portable swimming pools, or open sites that convert to squash courts, sports villages and the inclusion of more provision for personalised learning, such as climbing walls, will all impact on the way schools use facilities that become available to them, whether on site or off site.

15.1.3 Sport England and Continental Sports Limited provide excellent technical data on recommended space for buildings and court markings on their respective websites.

## 15.2 What Staff Should Know

15.2.1 Adaptable facilities require a **risk assessment** that considers the variable use of the facility, the implications of converting the facility (particularly where pupils may be involved), the particular usage the school intends and any guidelines manufacturers provide.

15.2.2 Where schools **share facilities** within a network, it is good practice to establish an understanding that the host school develops normal operating procedures and emergency action plans. These should be made available to other user groups and they in turn should accommodate these within their risk assessments for the overall experience that may include travel, shared use or other logistical issues that need to be planned for.

15.2.3 The use of facilities new to a group will need to take account of **health-and-safety issues** such as:

- access and transport implications, such as a safe embarkation/disembarkation area
- multi-use and the implications of provision for other purposes impacting on the safe work area for physical activity

- security of footing, whether on poolsides, outdoor surfaces or indoor surfaces

- storage and the management of movement in and around storage areas

- court/pitch dimensions, including location and the amount of run-off area provided

- safe access and use for those with disabilities

- sufficient space for the planned activity – freedom of movement requires more space than an activity based on restricted movement

- sources of liquid to maintain hydration where necessary.

15.2.4    The **floor area** necessary for safe practical work depends on the number of participants normally taking part, their age and the type of activity planned. The National Dance Teachers Association (NDTA) recommends a minimum of three square metres per pupil for primary-phase dance and five square metres per pupil for secondary-phase dance. Gymnastics would thus require more space than this per pupil in order to allow for safe movement and the use of apparatus.

15.2.5    Class and group sizes have tended to increase in recent years. Where this constraint applies, those leading a lesson need to consider how the activity can be presented in order to allow safe movement. For example, some types of dance require limited movement, but others are based on significant freedom to move. Without sufficient space, some variation in choreography or style may be necessary. Gymnastics sequences and apparatus arrangements may need to be planned in more compact forms. In games activities, less freedom of movement may be needed, with some form of conditioning applied to the organisation of the activity.

## General guidance for indoor spaces

15.2.6    **Floors** should be kept clean and swept regularly. Economies in floor-cleaning arrangements can make planning a safe physical-education programme difficult as dust increases the likelihood of slipping. Whenever possible, school staff should be involved in decisions about cleaning schedules. Any cleaning and/or polishing of floors should not leave a slippery finish. Loose boards, splintering, cracking and lifting edges sometimes occur with heavy use, creating an irregular surface that can affect the security of footing. Patches of condensation and residual wet mopping after school meals should be dealt with before activity begins. Sprung or semi-sprung floors are most beneficial to physical-education programmes generally in order to protect lower limbs from damage by the absorption of impact energy. Where floors are not sprung, care should be taken with high-impact landings. Where facilities are used for other purposes, such as dining, examinations and assemblies, safe use of the floor in physical-education lessons may become compromised and schools should seek to avoid this practice wherever possible.

15.2.7    **Lighting** should be uniform wherever possible. Any risk of being dazzled by sunlight coming through windows or glare reflected on water needs to be managed by the considered placement of apparatus, direction of play or movement, frequent changing of teaching position or a more permanent resolution such as tinting the glass. Artificial lighting should be made from unbreakable materials or set in protective cages. Strip lighting which produces a flickering or stroboscopic effect should be avoided, as this could impair visual focus, induce disorientation and trigger seizures.

15.2.8    **Walls** should be smooth to avoid friction injury if body contact occurs, with rounded corners where the possibility of impact is likely and facilitate safe ball-rebound activities. Background colours and the need for the safe sighting of accelerating projectiles (such as balls) need to be considered. Essential features other than physical-education apparatus should be positioned well above working height wherever possible, or recessed where this requirement cannot be met.

15.2.9      **Doors** and door frames should be flush wherever possible. Main access doors should open outwards and have some system of closure control. This is especially important on exposed or windy sites to minimise the risk of doors opening or slamming unexpectedly. Fire exits must remain clear at all times and it must be possible to open fire doors from the inside of the facility. Where possible, they should have flush mounted push pads to minimise the likelihood of injury. Glass doors can be hazardous. Where they are necessary, the glass should be smoked or coloured for visibility, unbreakable, reinforced and resistant to impact fracture. If a pane is cracked, it should be replaced as soon as possible. Door glazing should be at a height to accommodate wheelchair users. Where doors are glazed around hand-pushing height, there should be push battens across the door on both sides.

15.2.10      **Heating systems** should provide an adequate working temperature, adjustable to accommodate varying conditions and be designed so that there is no danger of any pupil being adversely affected by burns, fumes or other hazards to health. A regular inspection and maintenance programme should be established. Current building regulations indicate a minimum temperature of 15° Celsius for physical education. Where this temperature is not met, there are implications for extended warm-up, pace and whether lessons can continue with reasonable safety. There is no statutory maximum working temperature. Staff will need to be sensitive to the impact of significantly high temperature on active sessions and plan accordingly.

15.2.11      **Changing accommodation** should be of sufficient area to allow space for all pupils to change safely and keep their clothes in a tidy and clean state. Non-slip floors are essential. Pegs should not be broken, with sharp edges that may cause injury. Shower water mixer valves should be regulated by one control key, which should be positioned out of reach of pupils to reduce any risk of scalding. Broken wall tiles in shower areas can cause serious injury and should be replaced as soon as possible.

15.2.12      **Storage areas** need to be of sufficient size so as not to create hazards. Access should be as wide as possible to prevent bottlenecks. New-build facilities must have a separate fire-rated mat store.

15.2.13      **Security** of facilities is essential. All physical-education facilities should be locked when not in use to prevent unauthorised access.

## Specific guidance

### Dance studios

> Please read the general guidance provided in paragraphs *15.2.1–15.2.13*, pages 103–105, before reading this section. This will ensure a comprehensive awareness of safe-practice issues affecting physical-education facilities.

15.2.14      The NDTA recommends a fully **sprung floor**. Where a fully sprung floor is not available, a semi-sprung floor may be acceptable, with some give in it to enable pupils to jump and land safely, depending on the energy produced in the dancers' landings. The studio should have a ceiling sufficiently high so as not to restrict dancers' movements. There should be **sufficient space** for the safe use of equipment and adequate **electrical points** around the studio so that trailing wires do not present a hazard.

15.2.15  It is recommended that dance studios should provide an **even temperature** throughout, with a typical working temperature of 21–24°C and an absolute minimum of 18.3°C. The studio should be well ventilated.

15.2.16  Dance-training barres should be stable, substantial in design and set at heights appropriate for dancers of differing heights. Mirrors should be of strengthened glass.

## Fitness rooms

Please read the general guidance provided in paragraphs *15.2.1–15.2.13,* pages 103–105, as well as the guidance in *Chapter 24: Health-related Exercise,* pages 195–202, before reading this section. This will ensure a comprehensive awareness of safe-practice issues affecting physical-education facilities.

15.2.17  An **induction** process for all fitness-room users, including school staff, pupils and visitors, should be available. In addition, attention should be given to:

- sufficient space being provided between and behind items of equipment
- adequate visual supervision across the area
- firm and stable working surfaces
- accommodating free weights, weight stations and multigyms, preferably in separate areas
- access to emergency exits
- regular inspection and repair programmes by recognised specialists
- clearly posted safe weight-training procedures in the work areas
- protecting the floor area with mats in areas where free weights are used
- storing free weights on purpose-built stands
- locking collars on free weights when in use
- fixed or sufficiently weighted wedge-shaped floor bases to be used for leg squat exercises
- consistent temperature; the Sports Council recommends an air temperature of 12–18°C and adequate ventilation where heat gains are likely.

See *Chapter 24: Health-related Exercise,* pages 195–202, for further guidance on fitness issues.

## Swimming pools

Please read the general guidance provided in paragraphs *15.2.1–15.2.13,* pages 103–105, before reading this section. This will ensure a comprehensive awareness of safe-practice issues affecting physical-education facilities.

15.2.18  It is reasonable to expect owners of public swimming facilities to provide a safe working environment for users under the terms of the Occupiers' Liability Acts 1957 and 1984. However, school staff accompanying pupils, together with specialist swimming staff, should ensure that they know and implement the normal operating procedures and emergency action plan for the facility being used.

See *Occupiers' Liability Acts 1957 and 1984 in Appendix 1: Relevant Statute, Regulation and Guidance,* pages 287–295, for further information about these Acts.

15.2.19    Swimming pools are a potentially high-risk environment and should be **locked** when not in use to prevent unauthorised access.

15.2.20    Particular care should be taken on poolside surrounds where **wet surfaces** may contribute to slipping injuries.

15.2.21    **Glare** across the water surface, from natural or artificial lighting, may restrict sight to the bottom of the pool across large areas. In such circumstances, movement by supervisory staff and school staff or some other appropriate action may become necessary in order to maintain maximum visual awareness. Glare may also trigger an adverse reaction in pupils with identified special needs.

> For further information on this issue, see *Appendix 4: Pupils with Special Educational Needs (SEN)*, pages 319–324 and the CD.

15.2.22    Pools should not be used where the **water clarity** is such that the bottom of the pool cannot be seen at all depths.

15.2.23    The depth and extent of shallow or deep-water areas should be clearly marked and noted by those responsible for safety. A pool divider, usually a rope, should normally be positioned to delineate shallow from deep water whenever non-swimmers are present. It is particularly important that any sudden **changes in pool depth** are highlighted.

15.2.24    **Signs** should identify potential risks and be positioned so that pool users can see them clearly and interpret them easily. School staff should explain their significance, especially to beginners. All signs should conform to the appropriate British Standards/British Standard European Norm.

15.2.25    **Entry** from the changing rooms onto the poolside is safest where the water is shallow. Where pool design precludes this precaution, pupils should be made aware of the hazard, care should be taken when entering onto the poolside and strict behaviour standards applied.

15.2.26    The design of **steps and rails** should be such as to prevent any part of the body becoming trapped. Where this risk exists, warning signs and regular verbal reminders to pool users should be provided.

15.2.27    The Amateur Swimming Association (ASA) recommends that the temperature of the water should be about 29°C to enable young people to be comfortable and not become unduly cold during the period of time allocated to swimming. Water temperatures for disabled swimmers may be set much higher (as high as 36°C). The ambient air temperature should be slightly above that of the water, to avoid condensation, typically 1–4°C greater.

15.2.28    Those responsible for the management of pools should ensure that outlet pipes at the bottom of pools have grilles in place that are securely fastened. Holes in grilles should not be large enough for fingers to become trapped.

15.2.29    Leisure pools, many with special water features and irregular shapes, may cause potential supervisory blind spots that need to be checked regularly.

15.2.30    Pool surround, pool depth, the implications of any protruding ladders or steps and the use of electrical equipment are key considerations when determining whether the facility is suitable for **other aquatic sporting activities**, such as competitive swimming, water polo or synchronised swimming.

15.2.31    All pools need to operate swimming pool cleaning systems that meet acceptable hygiene standards.

15.2.32    **Chemical levels** should be monitored at the beginning of the day and at regular times throughout the day. At no time should chemicals be added to water directly when swimmers are present.

15.2.33    Swimming pool surrounds should be kept clear at all times. **Pool equipment** (eg floatation aids, emergency equipment, lane markers) should be stored appropriately, taking into account the need for safe access to and from the pool.

15.2.34    Adequate, well-maintained **lifesaving equipment** must be readily available in known locations and staff (and pupils as appropriate) must be trained in its use.

> See *Chapter 26: Aquatic Activities,* pages 263–279, for further guidance on the use of swimming pools.

## Sports halls

> Please read the general guidance provided in paragraphs *15.2.1–15.2.13,* pages 103–105, before reading this section. This will ensure a comprehensive awareness of safe-practice issues affecting physical-education facilities.

15.2.35    The space required for games depends on the standard of play: the higher the standard, the larger the space needed due to greater **run-off areas** and **clearance heights**.

15.2.36    **Netting** should not foul footing at any time.

15.2.37    Technical guidance is available from commercial companies, national governing bodies and national sport associations, particularly the Sport England website: www.sportengland.org/index/get_resources/resource_downloads/facilities_guidance.htm

## Playgrounds and other play areas

> Please read the general guidance provided in paragraphs *15.2.1–15.2.5,* pages 103–104, before reading this section. This will ensure a comprehensive awareness of safe practice issues affecting physical education facilities.

15.2.38    Play areas should be sited to prevent the risk of running into walls or other obstacles.

15.2.39    Play-area surfaces should be maintained in good condition, with no loose materials present in the playing area.

15.2.40    Reasonable measures should be taken to avoid allowing vehicles onto playgrounds. Where this is not possible, close and careful monitoring by school staff is essential.

15.2.41    Car-parking areas should be separate from those used for pupil play.

15.2.42    The presence of oil on playground surfaces needs to be be prevented. It makes surfaces slippery, can cause them to deteriorate prematurely and is therefore a potential hazard.

> See *Chapter 27: Play in the School Environment,* pages 281–285, for further guidance on playgrounds and other play areas.

## Playing fields and all-weather surfaces

> Please read the general guidance provided in paragraphs *15.2.1–15.2.5,* pages 103–104, before reading this section. This will ensure a comprehensive awareness of safe-practice issues affecting physical-education facilities.

15.2.43    Safety on playing fields can be adversely affected by the aftermath of **trespass**. Broken glass, cans and other rubbish generally deposited on these sites create serious risks to pupils. Deposits of dog or cat faeces infected by toxocara (roundworm) can cause toxocariasis in humans, with symptoms that include blindness, asthma, epilepsy and general aches and pains. All practical measures should be taken to keep animals off playing surfaces and to encourage owners to remove any offending deposits immediately.

15.2.44    Where playing fields are used as multi-purpose play areas, **litter** may be a problem that needs to be controlled. Gang mowers can shred plastic and metal containers into sharp shards that create significant risk.

15.2.45    Pitches should be **marked out** safely so that playing surfaces are, and remain, level (corrosive substances should not be used). Regular **maintenance** is essential. Holes (including rabbit scrapes) should be filled as soon as possible after identification. Adequate **run-off areas** at the sides and ends of pitches should be provided.

15.2.46    Pitches should be suitable in size for the **ages and abilities** of those involved. Technical guidance is available from commercial companies, NGBs and national sport associations.

> See *Facilities (22.2.3–22.2.9,* pages 166–167) in *Chapter 22: Games Activities* for further guidance on pitches.

## 15.3    What Pupils Should Know

15.3.1    Pupils should know:

- not to use any facility without permission

- how to summon staff in an emergency where supervision is remote

- what the school's safety procedures are for any facility made available to them

- how to use any of the equipment made available to them safely

- not to use a facility where footing is not secure

- what all signs mean

- where a playing surface slopes to play across the slope wherever possible

- any restrictions on footwear according to the surface being used

## 15.4 Additional Information

### Resources

afPE (2008) 'Flexible Spaces for Physical Learners',
www.afpe.org.uk/public/downloads/flexible_spaces_for_physical_learners_v1.pdf

Continental Sports (2007) 'Specifiers' Advice',
www.continentalsports.co.uk/specifiers/specifiers_advice.html

DfES (2005) *Schools for the Future: Inspirational Design for PE and Sport Spaces.*
Nottingham: DfES Publications.
Available from: www.teachernet.gov.uk/docbank/index.cfm?id=9628

DfES (2006) *Building Bulletin 98: Briefing Framework for Secondary School Projects.* Nottingham: DfES Publications.
Available from: www.teachernet.gov.uk/docbank/index.cfm?id=8104

DfES (2006) *Building Bulletin 99: Briefing Framework for Primary School Projects.*
Nottingham: DfES Publications.
Available from: http://www.teachernet.gov.uk/docbank/index.cfm?id=8117

Henshaw, D. (2007) 'A New Dance Studio',
www.ndta.org.uk/public/resources/dm028d.html

Sport England (2007) *Comparative Sizes of Sports Pitches and Courts.*
London: Sport England.
Available from: www.sportengland.org/comparative_sizes_003.pdf

Sport England (2007) *Designing for Sport on School Sites.* London: Sport England.
Available from: www.sportengland.org/designing_for_sport_on_school_sites.pdf

## 15.5 Case Law Examples

15.5.1    Bassie versus Merseyside Fire and Civil Defence Authority, Court of Appeal (2005):
*This determined that it was foreseeable that where a floor was not kept clean, it could lead to slipping injuries.*

15.5.2    Douch versus Reading Borough Council, Reading County Court (2000):
*A player stumbled and injured himself while running to retrieve a ball during a cricket match, blaming grass-covered humps in the outfield. The judge dismissed the claim on the basis that they were 'minor undulations', with only a remote likelihood of someone falling because of them. However, it was stated that playing areas need to be checked regularly in order to ensure that they are safe to use. This suggests that minor undulations can be expected on playing fields.*

15.5.3    Taylor versus Corby Borough Council, Northampton County Court (2000):
*While playing a ball game on a grassed recreation area, an adult was injured because his foot went down a 10cm hole. No regular inspection of the playing surface was carried out, with the repair of defects being reactive, rather than based on risk assessment and regular checks. It was judged that some system of regularly checking playing surfaces is necessary and that it is foreseeable that holes in playing surfaces are likely to cause serious injury.*

# Chapter sixteen
## Transporting Pupils

16

This chapter is concerned with a **contextual** aspect of risk management. It clarifies existing legislation and identifies appropriate procedures for the safe management of transporting pupils to off-site venues.

## 16.1 Introduction

16.1.1 As Building Schools for the Future creates more flexible provision for physical-education and sport facilities, and *Learning Outside the Classroom* (LOtC), sports tours, sports festivals, traditional inter-school fixtures and the increasing use of facilities across networks of schools encourage more off-site activities, so the need for planned and costed transport policies and provision evolves in PESS.

16.1.2 Where circumstances are relevant, schools should include a **policy** for transporting pupils within the school health-and-safety policy. Such a policy should set out procedures to ensure that pupils travel safely to any off-site activity.

16.1.3 Foreign **sports tours** are becoming increasingly common. Such a tour may involve school staff driving the group. This requires careful forward planning and forethought as foreign law and foreign standards will apply. Prior to the tour, it is important that adequate research is carried out, with the relevant results communicated to parents/carers and pupils.

> For guidance issues related to foreign travel, see *9.2.39–9.2.49*, pages 65–67, in *Chapter 9: Safeguarding Children and Young People*.

## 16.2 What Staff Should Know

16.2.1 Staff taking groups off site should be competent in discipline, control, organisation and dealing with any crisis that may arise. They should ensure there is an effective emergency contact system, such as via a mobile phone, or an alternative arrangement if a mobile is not available.

16.2.2 A **risk assessment** for regular activities should be carried out, as well as additional assessments for each special event involving travel.

### Minibuses

#### The minimum statutory requirements for driving minibuses

16.2.3 School minibuses are usually operated with what is called a **Section 19 permit**. Section 19 of the Transport Act 1985 allows non-profit-making organisations, such as schools, to make a charge to passengers for providing transport. Without this permit, the school would need to have a public service vehicle (PSV) operator's licence and drivers would need a passenger-carrying vehicle (PCV) entitlement on their driving licence (a full category D addition).

16.2.4 If **no charge** is made for the use of the bus at all, then no permit is required. However, any payment that gives a person a right to be carried on a vehicle (the legal term for this is 'for hire or reward') would require the operator to hold either a Section 19 permit or PSV operator's licence.

16.2.5 It is the school governors' responsibility, as the operator of the minibus, to apply for a Section 19 permit. To obtain such a permit, the minibus cannot be run with a view to making a profit. In other words, the minibus is used for **voluntary purposes** only, but a charge can be made to cover running costs and so forth, directly as a fare or indirectly as a general contribution to school.

16.2.6 **Drivers** of a minibus with a Section 19 permit must at least:

- be aged 21 or over

- have held a category B licence for at least two years

- receive no payment or consideration for driving the vehicle, other than out-of-pocket expenses.

The minibus weight must not exceed 3.5 tonnes (4.25 tonnes, including any specialised equipment for the carriage of disabled passengers) and a **trailer** must not be towed.

16.2.7 Thus, where the school offers the minibus to pupils for a charge, but on a non-profit basis under a Section 19 permit, the driver is exempt from the D1 requirement. This is because the Section 19 permit exempts the employer from holding a PSV operator's licence and exempts the driver from the D1 requirement, providing he/she receives no payment for driving the minibus.

16.2.8 Drivers who passed their car test before 1 January 1997 were automatically granted additional entitlement to drive minibuses with 9–16 passenger seats (category D1) not used for hire or reward. For as long as they hold a D1 (not for hire or reward) entitlement, these drivers may drive a 9–16-seat minibus of any weight used under a permit and may receive remuneration for this.

16.2.9 Drivers who passed their test on or after 1 January 1997 are no longer granted a D1 (not for hire or reward) entitlement. However, they may still drive a 9–16-seat minibus under a permit, provided the conditions set out above in *16.2.6* are met.

16.2.10 The argument exists as to whether school staff receive **payment** for driving a minibus as part of their contract of employment. If it is deemed that they do, then they must have a D1 addition to their basic category B licence. It is the interpretation of whether all staff are deemed to be paid to drive a minibus as part of their contract of employment that determines the conditions within which those who obtained a licence after January 1997 may or may not be allowed by their employer to actually drive a minibus without the D1 addition.

16.2.11 The Department for Children, Schools and Families (DCFS) – as the Department for Education and Skills (DfES) in 2006 – published an amendment to paragraph 134 of Chapter 6 'Planning Transport' in *Health and Safety of Pupils on Educational Visits* (HASPEV, DfES 1998, supplemented 2002). Paragraph 3 of the amending document states that:

*car drivers are exempt from the D1 PCV licensing requirement when they drive a minibus in the course of their employment and are not paid for doing so. This means that most teachers and other school staff may legally drive the school minibus on their category B car driver licence because their contract of employment does not expressly require them to drive a PCV.*

Paragraph 6 further explains:

*The exemption does not apply where a driver's employment contract expressly states that driving a PCV vehicle is part of the job. Employers of, for example, support staff hired as drivers, or of instructors at outdoor education centres, should check the contracts of these categories of staff carefully before concluding whether or not a D1 PCV licence is required. Employers of part-time teachers working extra hours and being paid additionally for driving a PCV should also check their contract(s) to establish whether a D1 PCV qualification is needed.*

As this is only guidance, rather than statute (although it sets out a very clear government position), some local authorities (LAs) and school governing bodies have determined that the D1 addition should be a requirement for all drivers of minibuses until a definitive interpretation is provided by the courts.

16.2.12   Whether a D1 addition is required or not is a temporary issue, in that the flexibility about not having a D1 licence to drive a minibus under Section 19 conditions applies only to minibuses up to 3.5 tonnes. New minibuses generally weigh more than this so, in the next 'few' years, as school minibuses are replaced, the requirement for a D1 addition will become mandatory.

16.2.13   Anyone who has obtained a driving licence abroad is not usually entitled to drive a vehicle with more than eight seats.

## Employers may make additional requirements

16.2.14   There is no national standard other than that set out in the Transport Act 1985. However, **employers** may make whatever additional conditions they wish as to who drives a minibus. Some employers choose to demand a D1 addition; others do not, but, as recommended by the Vehicle and Operator Services Agency (VOSA), they may require some additional training, such as the Minibus Driver Awareness Scheme (MiDAS), Royal Society for the Prevention of Accidents (RoSPA) or local driving course/test (hence schools having their own minibus driving tests) for what is a 'small bus'.

## Driving abroad

16.2.15   Driving a minibus under a Section 19 permit is acceptable only within the UK.

16.2.16   The governing body, as the operator of the minibus, should ensure that the requirements set out in EEC Directive 91/439 are applied when using a minibus abroad. The requirements of this Regulation include the following:

a. A specific PCV licence is required; Section 19 permits are not recognised abroad.

b. Higher medical criteria are applied; for example, insulin-dependent diabetics cannot drive a minibus.

c. The tachograph is to be completed and used. This is not a requirement in the UK.

d. Familiarity with the driving requirements and regulations in the countries to be visited is required.

e. Maximum driving hours and minimum rest requirements are imposed that are more stringent than in the UK.

f.  Vehicle documentation must be carried at all times.

g.  Passenger lists are to be carried with the vehicle.

## Management of the minibus

16.2.17    The Public Passenger Vehicles Act 1981 identifies the **operator** as the person for whom the driver drives the vehicle. If the driver is driving the bus on authorised school business then the operator is the governing body or LA, who will be responsible for the lawful use of the vehicle.

16.2.18    Best practice is where someone on the school staff has responsibility for ensuring that maintenance, confirmation of roadworthiness, scheduling, record keeping and driver management are organised effectively.

16.2.19    Only minibuses with **forward-facing seats** can be used to transport pupils. **Seat belts** must be fitted to all seats of minibuses when used for carrying children aged under 16 in a group of three or more on an organised trip. Seat belts must be worn.

16.2.20    The driver is legally responsible if a passenger under the age of 14 does not use a seat belt provided. Anyone 14 or over must wear a seat belt, but is responsible for doing so. The responsibility lies with the individual pupil and, where appropriate, the leader of the group. Staff in charge of a group on a bus may be prosecuted if they fail to ensure that seat belts are used.

> For more information on seat belts, see *Appendix 6A: The Use of Child Car Seats in Cars, Vans and Goods Vehicles – Department of Transport*, pages 326–327.

16.2.21    Adequate **wheelchair** passenger restraints must be provided to enable wheelchair users to take advantage of and travel safely on minibuses. An occupied wheelchair must itself be held securely in position using a recognised wheelchair-securing system.

16.2.22    A driver cannot drive and supervise at the same time. He/she should not be distracted except on safety grounds. Where pupil needs or behaviour warrants supervision, a second adult should be present to fulfil the supervisory duty.

16.2.23    Vehicle operators and drivers must assess the likely risk of drivers suffering from **fatigue**, especially on long journeys. If a driver is going to drive for more than four hours in any one day, then he/she must comply with British domestic rules for driver hours if operating solely within the UK and with EU rules if operating in any other EU country.

> For more information on this issue, see *Appendix 6B: Minibus Driver's Hours of Work Allowed*, pages 327–328.

16.2.24    **Trailers** should not be used unless unobstructed access is provided at all times to at least two doors, one on the nearside and one on the offside, in case of any incident that may cause the trailer load to slide forward and block the rear exit.

## Driver responsibilities

16.2.25    The driver is responsible for:

- the roadworthiness of the vehicle when the vehicle is on the road

- ensuring that the minibus is not overloaded and not carrying more passengers than allowed

- doing a risk assessment for the journey

- ensuring seat belts are worn by all passengers during journeys (see *16.2.20* page 114)

- knowing how to adjust seat belts

- ensuring all passengers have their own seat – three children sharing two seats is not allowed, neither are standing passengers

- satisfying him/herself that passenger supervision is adequate (see *16.2.22,* page 114)

- ensuring that luggage is securely stored with no obstructions on the floor between the seats or in front of any exit

- notifying the employer of any changes in his/her driving circumstances

- observing speed limits

- knowing the locations and use of the fire extinguisher and first-aid kit

- driving with the doors unlocked and good visibility through all windows.

## Cars

16.2.26  A **clean driving licence** is usually expected. Definitions of a clean licence may vary from one employer to another. Having some penalty points may be accepted as a clean licence and staff need to check with their employer.

16.2.27  The car must be **roadworthy** and have a valid MOT if relevant.

16.2.28  The driver needs to have appropriate **insurance**. For non-school support staff, this must be fully comprehensive and staff insurance should cover the use of their car for school business.

> For a model form covering these issues, see *Appendix 6C: Volunteer Driver's Declaration,* page 329 and the CD.

16.2.29  Charging is not allowed for the use of the vehicle.

16.2.30  Agreed procedures should ensure that no adult is ever alone in a car with any child other than his/her own. Appropriate **disclosure certification** should be obtained if applicable.

> For detailed guidance on this issue, see *Chapter 9: Safeguarding Children and Young People,* pages 55–72.

16.2.31  Travelling in convoy is not recommended as it can divert a driver's attention. Drivers should know the route to their destination and not rely on following others.

16.2.32  Local requirements will apply as to whether senior pupils may use their own cars to transport their peers.

16.2.33  **Parents** should give permission for their child to travel in another adult's car.

> For an example permission form, see *Appendix 6D: Parental Consent Form for a Pupil to be Transported in Another Adult's Car,* page 330 and the CD.

16.2.34 **Child restraints** (ie baby seats, child seats, booster seats and booster cushions) must be used where applicable. Schools using staff and parents' cars to transport pupils to matches and events will need to apply the requirements on the use of booster seats. It is the school's responsibility, on behalf of the parents, to ensure that booster seats are provided and used. Seat belts must be worn.

> For more information on child restraints, see *Appendix 6A: The Use of Child Car Seats in Cars, Vans and Goods Vehicles – Department of Transport,* pages 326–327.

## Taxis

16.2.35 Taxis are increasingly used to transport small groups as a more cost-effective means than hiring coaches.

16.2.36 Staff should check the employer's policy to ensure that the use of taxis is allowed.

16.2.37 Staff should also check whether or not the taxi firm is **accredited** by the employer (some LAs maintain lists of approved firms who employ Criminal Records Bureau [CRB] checked drivers). If using a firm not on an approved list, schools must make their own decisions and arrangements with the firm in relation to CRB clearance.

16.2.38 Discussion with the taxi firm to put in place a system of organisation may determine such issues as whether all taxis are to load and leave together for the journey to the venue and return to the school, and how staff supervise disembarking and check numbers.

16.2.39 The **risk assessment** should determine whether each taxi should have an adult supervisor or whether a pupil may be designated to carry a list of names and base contact details and what procedures are to be implemented in case of an accident or emergency during the journey.

16.2.40 **Seat belts**, where provided, should be worn.

16.2.41 Parents should be informed and consent obtained prior to children being transported by taxi.

## Buses and coaches

16.2.42 Where schools use buses or coaches, it is good practice to use a **reputable transport company**. Many schools and LAs maintain an approved list of companies. Coaches are now fitted with seat belts and staff should ensure that all passengers use them. However, buses are not required to have seat belts and staff should therefore seriously consider whether buses should be used to transport pupils involved in physical-education or sport activities.

16.2.43 **Supervision** levels need to be considered according to the pupils involved, the journey and any breaks in the journey. The adults should be positioned through the coach so that they can observe all pupils. Evacuation procedures need to be known by all before departure. When disembarking, it is good practice for the adults to disembark first to direct pupils to an assembly point away from the roadside or in the car-park area.

## Public transport

16.2.44 Schools should establish a **code of conduct** for pupils who use public transport for physical-education and sports events, in order to ensure that group interaction with the public is of an acceptable standard.

## 16.3    What Pupils Should Know

16.3.1    Pupils should know that:

- seat belts, where provided, must be worn

- anyone over the age of 14 has the responsibility to ensure he/she wears the seat belt provided

- they must not distract the driver other than in an emergency

- they should remain seated throughout a journey

- aisles should be kept clear of any luggage in order to allow emergency evacuation safely

- they should comply with the school's behavioural code of conduct, where one is established

- they should not be alone in a car with an adult other than their parent

- care should be taken when disembarking, particularly in public locations where traffic may be passing.


## 16.4    Additional Information

> *Appendix 6: Transporting Children* contains:
>
> - *Appendix 6A: The Use of Child Car Seats in Cars, Vans and Goods Vehicles – Department of Transport*, pages 326–327
>
> - *Appendix 6B: Minibus Drivers' Hours of Work Allowed*, pages 327–328
>
> - *Appendix 6C: Volunteer Driver's Declaration*, page 329 and the CD
>
> - *Appendix 6D: Parental Consent Form for a Pupil to be Transported in Another Adult's Vehicle*, page 330 and the CD.

### Resources

DfES (2006) 'Licensing Incidental Drivers of the School Minibus' (amending para 134 of HASPEV 1998, www.teachernet.gov.uk/docbank/index.cfm?id=9680

Vehicle and Operator Services Agency (VOSA) (2004) *Passenger Transport Provided by Voluntary Groups under the Section 19 or 22 Permit System: Guide for Operators* (PSV 385). London: VOSA.
Available from: www.vosa.gov.uk/vosacorp/repository/Passenger%20Transport%20In%20the%20Voluntary%20Sector%20July%202005%20(PSV%20385).pdf

### Useful websites

Health and safety on educational visits
www.teachernet.gov.uk/wholeschool/healthandsafety/visits/

Royal Society for the Prevention of Accidents
www.rospa.org

Vehicle and Operator Services Agency
www.vosa.gov.uk

# Chapter seventeen 17
## Crisis Management

This chapter deals with a **people** aspect of risk management. It provides essential information to assist staff in the effective management of unforeseen incidents and emergency situations within the context of PESS and in relation to a school's crisis-management plan. Factors relating to dealing with minor and major crises are set out.

## 17.1 Introduction

17.1.1    It is good practice for schools to have a **crisis-management plan** (sometimes referred to as a disaster plan) in place to enable efficient management of disasters, emergencies and critical incidents. This plan needs to be reviewed regularly.

17.1.2    Disasters and major crises happen very rarely. When they do occur, there is very little time to plan for what needs to happen. Events tend to move rapidly and the school leadership team, some governors and any staff involved will be under heavy pressure. Having agreed procedures in place will minimise the stress and enable the school to deal with the crisis more effectively.

17.1.3    The benefits of having detailed crisis-management procedures include:

- preparing governors, staff and pupils for any emergencies that may occur

- ensuring that there is a contingency plan that can be implemented swiftly in the case of an emergency caused by a disaster

- supporting staff in circumstances that are liable to strain the capacity of those managing the situation to think clearly while under great pressure.

17.1.4    With sports tours and other off-site sports events being common, it is good practice for those leading and participating to ensure that they have a clear understanding of their roles, responsibilities and essential actions should an emergency occur.

17.1.5    Crises may be considered in two groups. **Minor crises** are dealt with by the staff involved without the need to involve external agencies. **Major crises** are those of such magnitude that external agencies, such as the emergency services, automatically need to be involved. It is these that the media become aware of and they may contact the school or even the staff involved directly.

## 17.2 What Staff Should Know

17.2.1    Staff involved in any sport-related off-site activity should be familiar with the requirements of the school's crisis-management plan before the event.

17.2.2    The off-site event should be considered within the requirements of the plan so that appropriate action can be taken should a crisis occur. Consideration should be given to:

- identifying potential critical incidents
- identifying potential support agencies and personnel

- developing a contingency plan specific to the event to deal with any critical incident

- clarifying roles and responsibilities for all staff involved

- effective communication with the school

- minimising the potential for pupils involved in the incident to communicate inaccurate or misleading information to family, friends or the media.

17.2.3    In management planning of a **minor incident** (ie without the need for external support), participating staff should consider the following issues:

**Table 9: Issues for staff to consider in planning for a minor incident**

| People | Context | Organisation |
|---|---|---|
| • Attending to the injured<br>• Ensuring the safety of the rest of the group<br>• The leader and other staff's responsibilities and roles in dealing with the situation, such as:<br>  ▪ attending hospital<br>  ▪ contacting families<br>  ▪ managing the rest of the group<br>  ▪ deciding whether it is necessary to abandon the activity | • Immediate review of the risk assessment<br>• Assessing any impact on the planned session:<br>  ▪ Pre-planned contingency action may need to be implemented<br>  ▪ The event may be able to proceed or may need to be aborted or amended | • Debriefing the staff involved<br>• Any necessary reporting post-event |

17.2.4    In management planning of a **major incident** (ie needing external support in order to resolve the situation satisfactorily), the participating staff would need to consider the following issues:

**Table 10: Issues for staff to consider in planning for a major incident**

| People | Context | Organisation |
|---|---|---|
| • The leader's and other staff's responsibilities and roles in the situation<br>• Alternative leadership taking responsibility, should the designated leader become injured or incapacitated<br>• All staff involved having a full list of staff and pupils in the group in the event of separation or the need to initiate identification<br>• The role of those at school | • Ensure that any injured are placed in the care of competent personnel with first-aid expertise<br>• Accurate information needs to be collated about the incident and the staff and pupils involved<br>• Communication of the news to school would then follow, using a pre-arranged emergency contact<br>• The priority of those at the scene is to care for those at the scene | • Immediate action at the scene – identifying the injured, those not injured, preventing any escalation of the incident<br>• Procedures to contact school/the activity base/emergency services/media/ immediate families<br>• Recording essential information<br>• Establishing and tracking who is going where and under what circumstances |

120

**Table 10: Issues for staff to consider in planning for a major incident (continued)**

| People | Context | Organisation |
|---|---|---|
| | • The school's critical incident team will need to deal with families, the media and any other external agency seeking or requiring information, such as an embassy or the Foreign Office<br><br>• Evaluating the risk assessment after the event in order to establish whether improvements can be made for future events | • Effective communication channels where the incident is remote from the base, such as in the mountains or in a foreign country<br><br>• Managing the post-incident arrangements:<br><br>  ▪ Informing pupils of the true situation in a caring and supportive manner<br><br>  ▪ Assuring pupils that they will be reunited with their parents and families as soon as possible<br><br>  ▪ Post-incident care may be needed – psychological support may evolve some weeks after the incident. The emotional effects of disasters on pupils are not always immediately apparent to parents or staff. Careful monitoring of those directly and indirectly involved in an emergency is essential over time and not simply in the immediate aftermath of the event<br><br>• Effective communication is vital:<br><br>  ▪ at the scene<br><br>  ▪ with any individual or group moved to another location<br><br>  ▪ with the school. It is essential that a separate telephone link to school is established to avoid delays caused by incoming calls from families or the media<br><br>• debriefing the staff, the group and the parents after the crisis has been resolved |

## 17.3  What Pupils Should Know

17.3.1  Pupils should know:

- which member of staff they should report to in the event of any incident

- that communication with home or friends by mobile phone is not allowed, to avoid inaccurate information being communicated.


## 17.4  Additional Information

### Resources

Yule, W. and Gold, A. (1993) *Wise Before the Event: Coping with Crises in Schools.* London: Calouste Gulbenkian Foundation. ISBN: 978-0-903319-66-9

### Useful websites

Department for Children Schools and Families (DCSF) advice on emergency planning
www.teachernet.gov.uk/emergencies/


## 17.5  Case Law Examples

17.5.1  Dickinson versus Cornwall County Council, Exeter County Court, 1999:
*The police were automatically involved when a young girl was murdered during a visit to a hostel in France.*

# Chapter eighteen
## Managing Sports Events, Sports Tours and Other Off-site PESS Activities

18

This chapter identifies good practice in a key area of PESS provision relating to a wide range of off-site activity.

## 18.1 Introduction

18.1.1 Sports tours and special sports events have become popular in recent years. It is important that such events are carefully prepared, with contingency plans in place prior to any such event taking place. School staff should be aware of the employer's requirements concerning the planning and approval of such events prior to making commitments to pupils or commercial companies. Schools should apply the employer's policy relating to the safe organisation of sports fixtures and events when establishing school policy and procedures.

18.1.2 All schools should develop written **policies and procedures** for the planning, management and evaluation of sports events that take place off site, be they regular away fixtures or special sports events and tours in the UK or abroad.

18.1.3 This guidance addresses the issues to consider in the safe organisation of:

- inter-school fixtures

- sports festivals

- teams progressing to regional and national events

- swimming galas

- centralised activities where pupils travel to locations other than their own school

- tours abroad.

18.1.4 The organisation of occasional educational visits – those discrete educational experiences designed to enhance or enrich the curriculum – is addressed within the DfES guidance on *Health and Safety for Pupils on Educational Visits* (HASPEV2 – DfEE, 1998) and the supporting supplementary publications and *Health and Safety on Educational Excursions* (HASEE – Scottish Executive, 2004). It is good practice to liaise with the school educational visits coordinator in order to ensure consistent practice between educational visits and the organisation of inter-school fixtures and sports events so that procedures will be clearly understood by parents and carers.

> **Note:** In England, HASPEV will be subsumed within the *Learning Outside the Classroom* (LOtC) guidance. In Wales, HASPEV will be subsumed within the guidance document *Educational Visits*.

## 18.2    What Staff Should Know

### People

18.2.1    The **employer** has ultimate responsibility for health and safety and thus determines policy and monitors the implementation of that policy by schools. Some employers provide generic risk-assessment guidance for the safe organisation of sporting events held away from the school site. They may also set out the range and extent of insurance provision for the staff and pupils involved, provide access to advice and any professional development necessary for the safe organisation of events. They may also support any staff that may at times need to assume responsibility for pupils from other schools, but this should be clarified with the employer before being applied by individual school staff.

18.2.2    The **school governors**, where not the employer, should ensure that school policy and procedures are in place and establish systems to assure themselves of the effective implementation of agreed policy. They should decide what types of event, such as fixtures involving a long journey, merit their approval and what can be delegated to the head teacher and school staff.

18.2.3    The **head teacher** or other designated leadership representative should support the school staff involved by ensuring that:

- the governors have approved school policy

- the member of staff in charge has the leadership skills needed for successful management of the event

- management of the event meets local requirements and guidelines provided by the employer and school

- requirements for the safeguarding of pupils are met, such as disclosure certification

- any necessary approvals have been obtained (eg from parents, local authorities)

- a risk assessment has been completed

- the roles and responsibilities of all staff are clearly set out

- emergency and contingency planning is completed

- any required supervisory ratios are met

- parents have been made aware of any significant risks within the arrangements for the event and have given informed consent

- procedures for emergency contact with a school representative are in place

- parental contact information is held at the school

- transport arrangements satisfy local requirements

- access to professional development for the activities in which staff are involved is provided, where necessary.

18.2.4    Usually, there should be a minimum of one member of school staff in charge of any group going off site. This minimum requirement will need to be supplemented according to the number, age and needs of the pupils taken and the demands of the trip. Exceptionally, there may be occasions when an adult not on the school staff, but designated as support staff, leads groups going off site. Such adults will need to have been thoroughly vetted and approved by the head teacher.

18.2.5    **Those responsible for taking groups away** to inter-school fixtures and other sporting events should:

- have the confidence to ensure that the pupils' well-being is never compromised by them being placed in any dangerous situations by another adult, such as an official not applying rules consistently

- have an appropriate level of group discipline and control in order to manage the group safely

- ensure that, other than in exceptional circumstances, at least one member of school staff is present to take overall responsibility for coordination on the day of the fixture unless local requirements allow other competent adults to fulfil this role

- be satisfied about the competence of other staff, including coaches or volunteers, who are new to the school in a support role

- be aware of all pupils' individual learning needs, behaviour patterns, medical issues and their ability to undertake the activity concerned.

18.2.6    The **member of staff in charge** should ensure that:

- the head teacher is aware of all sporting events taking place on or off site and has given approval in the appropriate form, according to local requirements

- up-to-date information on the venue and the implications of its use has been obtained

- a register of participant names and emergency contact details is either taken at every off-site event or a copy is left at the school and is available, should an emergency arise

- essential medical information is known in relation to all pupils and staff involved

- a site-specific risk assessment is carried out that is based on any generic assessment provided by the employer and takes account of any specific assessment by the venue

- ongoing (sometimes referred to as dynamic) risk assessment is carried out

- local transport requirements for the use of a coach, minibus, taxis or adults' cars are met

- appropriate first-aid provision is made to deal with the immediate management of any injury arising

- parents are fully informed of arrangements

- careful regard is given to the supervisory arrangements for school fixtures, both at home and away

- staffing is sufficient to cope with any circumstances that might reasonably be foreseen, including emergencies caused by illness, injury or crisis

- there is appropriate insurance cover for any adults transporting pupils.

Where a member of staff or other appropriate adult responsible for a team is required to **officiate**, it is advantageous to have a second responsible adult present as an assistant.

18.2.7    All other **support staff** should:

- be clear about their roles and responsibilities

- have qualifications and/or experience, as appropriate

- be capable of group management before being allocated any group responsibility

- be prepared to intervene, should circumstances warrant such action, in the event that pupils are presented with unreasonable or unnecessary risks

- be aware of procedures, policies and standards, including pupil codes of conduct and standards of behaviour

- be aware of emergency procedures

- be aware of appropriate contact details (eg mobile phone numbers), including a named contact who is not at the event

- not be left in sole charge of pupils, except with the member of staff usually readily to hand or in the event of an emergency as part of the previously agreed risk assessment, unless it has been determined that the support staff have the competence and confidence to fulfil the demands of the role delegated to them

- have appropriate Criminal Records Bureau (CRB) disclosure certification, where necessary, or be otherwise vetted appropriately

- have appropriate knowledge of the pupils

- be appropriately insured.

18.2.8    **Young leaders** should be aware of their precise role and any responsibilities and receive appropriate supervision, encouragement and advice. They should not be left in sole charge of pupils, but may supervise other pupils in adult-controlled circumstances.

18.2.9    It is important that **officials** at any sporting event should have the competence (experience, expertise or qualification) to perform at the required level and know the rules and apply them consistently.

18.2.10    It is good practice for **school staff** to ensure that pupils:

- demonstrate acceptable behaviour at all times and subscribe to an agreed code of conduct as both participants and supporters

- are responsible for having personal medication to hand

- have received an appropriate preparation for the activity in which they have been invited to participate

- have skill levels, general fitness and physical maturity that are compatible with the demands of the activity

- are well informed about emergency and safety procedures

- are actively engaged in the process of risk assessment at their own level

- ensure that their parents and carers are kept fully informed about their involvement in inter-school competition, with particular attention paid to travel arrangements.

## Context

18.2.11    Policy should be subject to regular review, particularly following any major accident or incident. Systems for reviewing accidents and incidents should be established and followed.

18.2.12    It is increasingly common for school staff to carry a **register** with any necessary pupil information included, such as details of any medical conditions and treatment required in an emergency. The methodology to cover any emergency-contact situation that may occur during the event should be known by the staff involved. This should include methods for contacting parents, staff, the school or, if necessary, the local authority (LA)/governing body crisis-management team.

18.2.13 **Facilities** should be checked to ensure:

- there is sufficient space allocated for the activity

- fixtures and fittings are secure

- there are no hazards deemed to be unsafe, such as animal excreta, broken glass or a surface that may adversely affect security of footing.

> For more information on facilities, see *Chapter 15: Buildings and Facilities*, pages 103–110.

18.2.14 Equipment should be checked before use to ensure that it is compatible with any relevant BS EN/BS standards or Sports Safe UK certification, compatible with the developmental age and abilities of pupils and in a good state of repair.

> For more information on equipment, see *Chapter 12: Equipment in Physical Education*, pages 85–93.

18.2.15 **Mobile phones** are being increasingly recognised as an important item of emergency equipment when working some distance from the school buildings or when off site. They can significantly assist incident management. Careful consideration needs to be given to their usage, however, and the following procedures should be applied to obtain maximum benefit:

a. Risk assessment should determine precisely which members of staff need to carry a mobile phone.

b. The carrying of mobile phones by pupils should be strictly limited and determined by the context of the activity and school/LA policy.

c. They should be suitably protected from the elements, sufficiently charged for the duration of the activity and satisfactory reception in the work area confirmed.

d. Text messages can be more effective in some circumstances than voice messages (eg where reception may be limited).

e. In the event of an incident, all group members need to understand and comply with agreed rules of reportage and communication.

f. Pre-programming of key contacts by the group leader can help to facilitate effective distant supervision of groups working independently in remote areas, such as when on expeditions.

18.2.16 Arrangements and requirements for generic, site-specific and ongoing risk assessments should be in place at the **host school** responsible for the risk assessment on the school site. It is good practice for issues arising from risk assessments to be shared with visiting groups.

18.2.17 **Visiting staff** should always be vigilant for health-and-safety risks on sites they visit, as risk assessment is an ongoing procedure.

18.2.18 The appointed person responsible for first aid in the school should be included in discussions relating to accident procedures for away fixtures and events to ensure that decisions are compatible with general school policy. Accident procedures for away fixtures should include consideration of:

- the number of accompanying adults

- any implications relating to the modes of travel involved

- reciprocal arrangements with the host school

- the levels of competence needed by the adults involved.

18.2.19     It may be advantageous and economical for staff involved with school fixtures and sports events to consider **reciprocal arrangements**, whereby each participating school will provide for the mutual benefit of all participants.

18.2.20     When a single member of staff accompanies a number of teams to an away fixture, it would be worthwhile to discuss with the host school how certain situations will be covered. Issues may include who supervises the visiting pupils, should the visiting member of staff need to go to hospital with a child, and the arrangements necessary to hand over responsibility for visiting pupils to a third person for escort back to their own school, should the original member of staff have needed to go to hospital with a child.

18.2.21     Staff should ensure that a **travelling first-aid kit** is available at all fixtures. The appointed person responsible for first aid in the school should be responsible for the provision of a suitable travelling first-aid kit. Further provision, appropriate to the activity being undertaken, to prevent the effects of cold and shock should be readily available at fixtures and events.

18.2.22     Pupils who have suffered loss of consciousness should receive immediate hospital treatment. This should not be contingent upon the arrival of the parent.

18.2.23     Accidents occurring at fixtures and sports events should be recorded according to existing school practice. Records should be completed as soon as is reasonably possible after returning to school.

18.2.24     Considerations pertinent to any journey should be given attention prior to the trip, including:

- passenger safety and supervision

- driver competence and local conditions that may be imposed

- the type of journey

- traffic conditions

- weather conditions.

Generic safety planning issues include:

- taking a register before departure

- head counts during the journey

- collection and dispersal points

- journey time – the need for comfort stops for pupils and regulatory stops for driver(s)

- procedures in the event of an emergency

- arrangements for the dispersal of the pupils after the event.

> For more information on transport issues, see *Chapter 16: Transporting Pupils*, pages 111–117.

# Organisation

18.2.25    Sports events that involve an **overnight stay** or include a residential element fall within the remit of educational visits as defined in the HASPEV (HASEE in Scotland) guidance. Staff should check whether employers (LAs, governors, trustees) need to be informed of such events.

18.2.26    For special events, schools should undertake a **site visit** of the venue they are attending, particularly where no prior knowledge of the site can be obtained or no member of staff has visited the planned venue recently. It is usually acceptable for the venue risk assessment to be addressed by the host.

18.2.27    On occasions when refreshments and meals are provided, local hygiene requirements need to be known and met.

18.2.28    **Climatic conditions** should be considered when planning activities. Parents should be notified of the requirement for pupils to be protected from the sun, wind or excessive variations in temperatures. The administering of suncream, wearing appropriate and relevant clothing to ensure adequate protection from variable climatic effects and any requirements and arrangements for maintaining appropriate levels of fluids should be considered.

> For more information, see *Weather conditions (13.2.9,* page 97) in *Chapter 13: Personal Protection.*

18.2.29    Staff organising sports fixtures should make every attempt to arrange them with teams or players of **comparable age, standard and ability**. Wherever possible, schools should consider any national governing body (NGB) approach to selecting potential opposition. If at any stage the supervising adult identifies that there is a significant imbalance in any of these areas (eg size, age, ability, capability), the fixture should be stopped for reasons of safety and rearranged to reflect better balance and matching of pupils.

18.2.30    There may be times when **supervision** is remote, as in cross-country running or orienteering. At such times, it is important that a risk assessment of the area is carried out prior to the activity taking place, that all pupils are checked regularly and that staffing is sufficient to observe as much of the area as possible at any time.

18.2.31    It is advisable that pupils should not play more than one full sports fixture in any given day. Where it is intended or likely that pupils will participate in more than one game, care will be needed in the programming and **scheduling** of fixtures to ensure that young people are sufficiently prepared by training and levels of skill. This will ensure their safe involvement so that no one is subjected to levels of physical activity that are unreasonable in the light of their fitness and preparation. Sufficient rest periods should be provided to allow for recovery time between games so that overplay beyond a pupil's physical and mental capabilities is avoided.

18.2.32    Sports tours **abroad** should be well planned, with an awareness that health and safety and safeguarding standards differ between countries.

> For guidance on safeguarding on tours abroad, see *9.2.39–9.2.49,* pages 65–67, in *Chapter 9: Safeguarding Children and Young People.*

## 18.3 What Pupils Should Know

18.3.1      Pupils should know and follow any agreed code of conduct.

18.3.2      Pupils should know that, during off-site activities, they are expected to:

- observe normal school rules

- cooperate fully at all times with any adults involved

- fulfil any tasks or duties set prior to and during the fixture or event

- participate fully in all activities during the fixture or event

- be punctual at all times

- not leave the group without permission

- always return to any agreed meeting point at agreed times

- avoid behaviour that might inconvenience others

- respect all requirements made by school staff and accompanying adults

- abide by rules and regulations of the countries and places visited

- not purchase or consume alcohol, tobacco products, drugs or purchase any dangerous articles, such as knives.

## 18.4 Additional Information

> For information on organising events, see *Appendix 2H: Safe Practice in the Organisation of Sports Fixtures and Area Sports Events Poster,* page 305 and the CD.
>
> For guidance on accidents and first aid, see *Appendix 8: First-aid and Accident Procedures,* pages 332–342.
>
> For further guidance on issues relating to managing sports events, see *Appendix 11: Health and Safety – Managing a Sports Event – Some Issues Identified,* pages 355–357.

### Resources

City of Edinburgh Council Education Department (2004) *The Protection of Young People in the Context of International Visits: Guidelines for Organisers.* Edinburgh: City of Edinburgh Council. ISBN: 978-1-902299-30-3.

DfEE (1998) *Health and Safety of Pupils on Educational Visits* (HASPEV 2). Nottingham: DfEE Publications.
Available from:
http://publications.teachernet.gov.uk/eOrderingDownload/HSPV2.pdf

DfES (2002) *Standards for LEAs in Overseeing Educational Visits.* Nottingham: DfES Publications. Reference: DfES/0564/2002.
Available from: http://publications.teachernet.gov.uk/eOrderingDownload/DfES-0564-2002.doc

DfES (2002) *Standards for Adventure.* Nottingham: DfES Publications. Reference: DfES/0565/2002.
Available from: http://publications.teachernet.gov.uk/default.aspx?PageFunction=downloadoptions&PageMode=publications&ProductId=DfES+0565+2002&

DfES (2002) *Visits: A Handbook for Group Leaders*. Nottingham: DfES Publications. Reference:DfES/0566/2002.
Available from: www.teachernet.gov.uk/docbank/index.cfm?id=2578

Grange, J. and Gordon, R. (2001) *Safe Sport Away*. London: NSPCC/ASA. ISBN: 978-0-900052-35-4

Scottish Executive (2004) *Health and Safety on Educational Excursions*. Edinburgh: Scottish Executive. ISBN: 978-0-755943-63-5.

Tiiva, A. and Morton, J. (2003) *Safe Sports Events: A Child-focused Resource Pack for All Sports Events Organisers*. London: NSPCC. ISBN: 978-1-842280-35-5.

## 18.5    Case Law Examples

18.5.1    Woodbridge School versus Chittock (2002):
*This established the principle of a 'reasonable range of options', recognising that no single response was the correct way in which to deal with an issue, rather that some degree of flexibility according to the circumstances was a more appropriate professional response.*

# Part two
## Specific Guidance

# Chapter nineteen

## Athletic Activities

19

This chapter recommends a range of appropriate procedures and practices to ensure that athletic activity is taught safely within the context of training and competition.

> Please read the general guidance provided in Part 1 of this handbook, pages 9–131, before reading this chapter. This will help to ensure that you have a comprehensive awareness of safe-practice issues affecting athletic activities and PESS in general.

## 19.1 Introduction

19.1.1 Athletic activities are distinguished by two features, both of which have major implications for the management of risk. Firstly, athletics places significant physical demands upon individuals who are usually required to display maximal effort, whether running, jumping or throwing, irrespective of the type and nature of the competitive framework. It is thus essential that staff should maintain a good knowledge of the **health-and-fitness profiles** of their pupils. Secondly, implements are used in the throwing events that have their origins in weaponry and consequently are potentially lethal if supervised irresponsibly and without the necessary competence.

19.1.2 Although the throwing events present the greatest hazard, all athletic events require careful planning, sound organisation and appropriate supervision.

## 19.2 What Staff Should Know

### People

19.2.1 Responsibility for safety in athletics is largely determined by the location of the activity. In the school setting, staff will have an essential role to play in maintaining a safe working environment. Where athletics moves off the school site, such as to a local athletics arena, leisure-centre managers, grounds staff, and organising officials in the case of competitive activity, will share responsibility for pupils' well-being.

> For guidance on the management of off-site events, see *Chapter 18: Managing Sports Events, Sports Tours and Other Off-site PESS Activities*, pages 123–131, and *Appendix 11: Health and Safety – Managing a Sports Event – Some Issues Identified*, pages 355–357.

19.2.2 Staff concerned with the teaching and supervision of athletics should be appropriately **trained** through specialist initial teacher education (ITE) programmes, local authority (LA) professional development opportunities or have acquired athletics coaching qualifications through the national governing body (NGB), UK Athletics.

19.2.3    It is also essential that pupils learn to be safe participants and spectators. School staff need to be confident that this is the case before introducing more hazardous athletic activities, such as throwing with competition implements. Pupils should be involved in risk assessing the various athletic activities in order to develop their understanding of the potential dangers involved.

19.2.4    Pupils taking part in athletic competition should always be suitably prepared and the nature and level of competitive activity should match their physical maturity and developmental stage.

> For more information on this issue, see *19.2.9–19.2.13* under *Organisation* in this chapter.

## Context

19.2.5    The secondary-school environment presents the greatest potential for danger and the majority of recorded incidents in athletics occur in this setting. Teaching athletic activities to **mixed-ability groups** on a school playing field is potentially more hazardous than coaching specialist athletes using properly prepared facilities with full back-up resources at an athletics stadium. This needs to be reflected in rigorous risk-management procedures.

19.2.6    **Athletics facilities** need to be maintained in good condition. Running surfaces need to be level and free from hazard and finishes allocated sufficient run-off space. Jumping pits should be regularly dug, sand levels maintained, where relevant, and systematically checked for any dangerous objects. Stable, smooth and non-slip approaches are required for jumping and throwing activities.

19.2.7    Activities should be allocated sufficient **space** to avoid potential danger zones, with no possibility of any overlap. Throwing zones need to be clearly marked and procedures for entry well understood and reinforced.

19.2.8    Care needs to be taken when the **weather** is wet since many schools use grassed working areas for teaching purposes. Throwing and hurdling are particularly hazardous under these conditions and should be carefully managed, or even avoided when security of footing is compromised and the risk of injury consequently high.

## Organisation

19.2.9    Safe **techniques and procedures** must be consistently taught from the outset. This principle applies across primary and secondary phases. Soft throwing implements, for instance, while not posing an immediate danger, should be treated in the same way as authentic athletics implements and subjected to identical safety precautions.

19.2.10   The NGB of athletics – UK Athletics – issues **comprehensive guidance** on the safe organisation of athletics events. Wherever competition takes place under the remit of the NGB, any relevant directives should be considered as rules. Athletics activities that are organised by the school (curricular delivery, school athletics clubs and friendly competitions) are technically outside this remit, but staff should take note of such advice and apply it where necessary. This is particularly important when planning events and distances for pupils of different ages and stages of development.

19.2.11   With prepubescent pupils, the teaching emphasis should be on developing basic working techniques that can be applied to various forms of competitive activity.

For instance:

a. Sprint racing should be limited to 80–100m for the oldest pupils in primary schools and much less for younger pupils.

b. Hurdles should be kept low, preferably made from soft, user-friendly materials and the number of flights restricted to five.

c. Sustained running, including cross-country, can be appropriate for pupils reaching the upper stages of Key Stage 2, involving distances between 800 and 1500m, depending upon ability.

d. A variety of light throwing implements may be used with Key Stage 2/3 pupils to develop a range of throwing skills.

e. Jumping for height should be restricted to feet-to-feet jumping styles.

19.2.12    Approved practice indicates that **multi-event** athletics sessions should be restricted to four activities, only one of which should be a directly supervised throwing event.

19.2.13    The management of **spectators** and deployment of judges, recorders and timekeepers need to be carefully considered. Spectators should be allocated to specific safety zones and all officials appropriately positioned before and during activity.

> For more information on these issues, see *19.3.38,* page 142, under *Organisation,* in this chapter.

## 19.3    Further Guidance Relating to Specific Activities
### Throwing activities

> The information set out in this section should be read in conjunction with the general principles set out in the earlier part of this chapter (*19.1–19.2,* pages 135–137).

### People

19.3.1    Staff who supervise throwing events should be competent to do so. A higher level of training and expertise will be required where teaching involves the throwing of the javelin, discus, shot and hammer.

19.3.2    Pupils need to be sufficiently mature, both physically and mentally, before progressing from soft training equipment to authentic, competition-style throwing implements.

### Context

19.3.3    Throwing, in training and competition, should always be confined to a safe, clearly **demarcated area**. In restricted areas and higher-level competition, safety nets or cages conforming to UK Athletics standards should be used.

19.3.4    Approaches and release areas should be firm, level and offer a sound footing.

## Equipment

19.3.5   Discuses with worn rims, cracks or projecting rivet heads should not be used. Dimensions and weight should be appropriate to the age group. It is essential that the discus is dry at the commencement of activity to avoid unpredictable release.

19.3.6   Only purpose-made hammers in which the spindle is free to rotate and the wire is in good condition should be used for competition.

19.3.7   Metal javelins of appropriate size should only be used in secondary schools and only after pupils have been prepared in basic throwing technique.

19.3.8   Shots should present a smooth, dry surface and be of the correct weight for the age group being taught.

19.3.9   When carrying or retrieving equipment:

- the task should always be undertaken at walking pace

- implements should be carried singly, with the exception of discuses, which may be carried in a wire basket

- implements should be placed on the ground, never dropped

- javelins should always be carried vertically, preferably protected at the point and tail, and should be levered into a vertical position before removal from the ground

- staff should provide regular reminders of the need to approach javelins carefully in order to avoid possible impaling on the tail.

19.3.10   Throwing cages should conform to UK Athletics standards.

## Organisation

19.3.11   It is essential that pupils follow a suitable teaching **progression** towards the throwing of competitive implements. Control should be developed by initially teaching standing throws, with light implements where necessary, before introducing turns and approaches to add momentum.

19.3.12   The following procedures for lining up, throwing and retrieval need to be strictly complied with:

- Throwers waiting to perform should stand well behind the circle or throwing line until instructed to move forward. They should be well spaced, with eyes focused upon the thrower(s) performing. A system of auditory and visual ready and response signalling helps to heighten alertness.

- Throwers working in a group situation should throw sequentially in a predetermined order.

- Staff need to check that the line of flight is clear. A wide margin of error should be anticipated.

- Throwers always need to remain behind the circle or throwing line after throwing and only move forward for retrieval purposes when instructed to do so. Implements must be carried safely and **never** thrown back.

## Jumping activities

The information set out in this section should be read in conjunction with the general principles set out in the earlier part of this chapter (*19.1–19.2*, pages 135–137).

### People

19.3.13 Staff who supervise jumping activities should be competent to do so. A higher level of training and expertise will be required where jumping involves feet-to-body landing styles (eg Fosbury Flop, the pole vault).

19.3.14 Pupils need to demonstrate an understanding of basic feet-to-feet jumping before moving on to more advanced techniques.

### Context

19.3.15 Sandpit **landing areas** should be thoroughly prepared before and during activity to avoid a hard and impacted surface. Such areas are only suitable for horizontal jumping and low-level jumping for height involving feet-to-feet landings. For more advanced training and competitive activity, a specialist landing module is required.

19.3.16 Landing areas need to be sufficiently large to accommodate all levels of ability with no danger arising from wooden or concrete pit surrounds. The sand used in jumping areas should be sharp (ie non-caking) and deep enough to prevent jarring on landing. It should fill the pit to the level of the runway.

19.3.17 Landing areas should be systematically checked for hard or sharp objects and hazardous substances.

19.3.18 Digging or raking instruments should never be left lying near the landing area and should be stored at least 3m away from the pit. **Digging and raking** should be undertaken frequently during teaching, training and competition and should never occur while jumping is taking place. Those given responsibility for digging and raking should be given a suitable induction into how to do it effectively and safely.

19.3.19 **Runways** and approaches should offer a firm and level surface and, in the case of the horizontal jumps, should remain flush with take-off boards. Take-off boards should be clean, dry, clearly visible and always positioned to ensure that jumpers land safely in the landing area. **Multiple boards** or take-off zones are helpful in realising this requirement when working with different abilities.

### Equipment

19.3.20 Round bars are recommended for feet–to-body high-jump styles.

19.3.21 Uprights for flexi-bars, where used, should be secure so as not to collapse onto jumpers.

19.3.22 Multi-unit high-jump landing beds should:

- be large enough to accommodate all levels of ability and always extend beyond the uprights

- conform to UK Athletics standards when used for competition

- be deep and dense enough to prevent 'bottoming out' (ie the impact of the landing must be completely absorbed by the material)

- be fitted with a spike-proof coverall sheet to ensure a firm, secure and consistent landing surface

- be subject to regular inspection and systematically checked for any deterioration.

19.3.23    Fibreglass poles used for pole vaulting should:

- be systematically checked for any damage

- be discarded if cracked or spiked

- be suitably stored when not in use

- not be used in planting boxes with a vertical back plate

- be appropriately taped to prevent damage.

Fibreglass poles can be used for teaching pupils to vault without bending the pole. Only if under the supervision of sufficiently qualified staff should pupils be taught how to bend a pole.

## Organisation

19.3.24    When managing **large groups**, procedures need to be in place to ensure that landing areas and approaches remain free from obstruction and hazard.

19.3.25    Brightly coloured canes or bollards placed on the runway may be used to indicate when jumping is not allowed.

19.3.26    Where **multiple jumping** from the side of the pit is used to encourage high participation rates, groups must be sufficiently spaced out and allocated working channels to avoid any danger of collision or interference.

19.3.27    Because of the dangers associated with horizontal travel in **high jumping** – particularly when teaching beginners – take-off markers or zones should be placed towards the near upright in order to encourage jumpers to negotiate the bar at its midpoint.

## Running activities

> The information set out in this section should be read in conjunction with the general principles set out in the earlier part of this chapter (*19.1–19.2*, pages 135–137).

### People

19.3.28    Running activities are potentially less hazardous than throwing or jumping, but still require careful management. Staff need to be properly qualified and experienced, particularly relating to the suitability and appropriateness of selected running activities for different stages and age groups.

### Context

19.3.29    **Facilities** used for running activities should be level, free from hazard and relatively firm underfoot.

19.3.30    Cross-country courses should be chosen with ease of supervision as a major factor.

## Equipment

19.3.31    Hurdles used for competition should conform to UK Athletics standards and be properly positioned to allow toppling if struck. On no account should pupils be allowed to hurdle the 'wrong way', with hurdle supports on the far side of the barrier. Training hurdles should be manufactured from appropriate materials that have no sharp or protruding edges and present a relatively light, low and unthreatening barrier to the participant.

19.3.32    Finishing tapes made from easily breakable material have traditionally been used in helping to identify the precise end of a race for both officiating staff and athletes. This practice may be particularly relevant to competition involving young children. However, where experience and training allow, finishing tapes should be dispensed with.

19.3.33    Spiked shoes can cause injury to other runners. When not in use, they should be stored safely and placed with spikes facing down.

19.3.34    Firearms are not acceptable as starting devices in schools, with the exception of very small-calibre cap-firing pistols. Clapperboards or similar devices present a safer alternative. Where a starting pistol is used in higher-level competition procedures, the UK Athletics risk assessment for starting pistols should be fully complied with. Whatever starting device is used, it should be held at arm's length well away from the head.

## Organisation

19.3.35    Sufficient **space** should always be allocated for running activities, to avoid unnecessary collision. This is particularly important at the start. All races of one lap or less should ideally be run in lanes. This applies especially to relay races.

19.3.36    In **cross-country** running and competition:

a.    Courses should offer maximum visibility of runners to staff and organisers and be suitable for the age, capability and developmental stage of the runners.

b.    The slowest runner should be tracked throughout the course so as to easily identify and attend to injured or distressed runners.

c.    Starts should be sufficiently wide to safely accommodate the number of runners with a long, clear approach to the first obstacle or constricted pathway.

d.    First aid and casualty provision should be stationed at various points around the course.

e.    Runners should be counted out and back in.

19.3.37    In **indoor athletics:**

a.    The relatively confined space requires clearly designated training and competition areas well away from projections and walls.

b.    Rebound boards can be useful for sustaining fast running in a confined space, but participants should be taught how to use them safely and given sufficient practice prior to competition of any kind.

c.    Approach runs for horizontal jumping will need to be limited, usually to around four strides. Mats should be used to cushion landings. Weight-absorbing mattresses ('crash mats') should never be used for this purpose. Jumping for height, where space and facilities allow, should follow the recommendations outlined for outdoor activity.

d. Throwing implements should be appropriate for indoor use and made from plastic, foam or rubber.

e. The use of equipment should be well supervised and equipment stored safely when not in use, always well away from working areas.

f. The programme of activities should reflect the developmental stage of participants and the size of the available working space.

19.3.38    On **sports day:**

a. All judges and officials should receive an appropriate induction into safe procedures, with safety reminders provided (eg appended to recording sheets or clipboards).

b. Activity/event areas should be clearly laid out, with spectators and athletes effectively marshalled; recorders should be safely positioned; and throwing areas should be roped off at some distance from throwing sector lines.

c. Strict rules should be enforced concerning safe movement to and from events.

d. The activity programme should be suitably balanced to reflect the developmental stage and capability of the pupils involved, with the number of events taking place at any one time kept to a safe and manageable level.

e. Pupils should be well prepared for their chosen activities, which should be based on existing curricular provision and experience.

f. First-aid arrangements should be clearly communicated and understood.

g. Throwing implements should be safely stored and supervised at all times.

h. Water stations should be easily accessible and sensible precautions adopted to protect spectators and athletes from the harmful effects of the sun.

> For an example sports day risk assessment, see *Appendix 2C: Example Risk Assessment of an Event,* page 300.

## 19.4    What Pupils Should Know

19.4.1    Pupils should know:

- that safety procedures and directions require total compliance at all times because of the many potential dangers involved in athletics

- to be aware of allocated areas laid out for athletics activity and **never** intrude into a marked throwing zone

- to always remain vigilant and alert when in the vicinity of a throwing area

- never to carry more than one athletics implement at a time and always to place it in a safe location

- to always ensure that the throwing area is clear when throwing

- how to make informed judgements about the safety of landing areas and throwing implements

142

- to commence jumping only when the pit/bed is well clear of other athletes

- how to manage personal equipment (eg spiked shoes) so that it presents no danger to others

- to recognise the importance of wearing appropriate clothing and footwear and the need to remove, or make safe, any personal effects.

## 19.5 Additional Information

### Resources

Sport England (2002) *Design Guide – Athletics*. London: Sport England. Available from: www.sportengland.org/athletics.pdf

UK Athletics (2007) 'Code of Practice for the Safe Conduct of Track and Field Events – Competition', www.ukathletics.net/about-us/health--safety/code-of-practice/

UK Athletics (2007) 'Code of Practice for the Safe Conduct of Track and Field Events – Training', www.ukathletics.net/about-us/health--safety/code-of-practice/

> **Note**: This guidance refers only to competition and training that takes place on a standardised and certificated track.

## 19.6 Case Law Examples

19.6.1 Morrell versus Owen, Queen's Bench Division (1993):
*The court determined that the organisers of an indoor athletics event failed to exercise the degree of organisational care necessary when the netting in a sports hall was used for discus throwing, but someone the other side of the netting was hurt because the netting billowed out into the adjacent space and failed to absorb the momentum of the discus.*

19.6.2 Futcher versus Hertfordshire LA, Luton County Court (1997):
*A long-jump participant was awarded damages when injured by landing on compacted sand. The area had been raked, but not dug over before or during the competition.*

# Chapter twenty
## Combat Activities

**20**

This chapter deals with safety recommendations and advice on a wide range of combat activities relating to suitable practice and the use of qualified and experienced instruction.

> Please read the general guidance provided in Part 1 of this handbook, pages 9–131, before reading this chapter. This will help to ensure that you have a comprehensive awareness of safe-practice issues affecting athletic activities and PESS in general.

## 20.1    Introduction

20.1.1    Schools are increasingly offering a range of combat activities to enrich and expand both curricular and school-sport provision.

20.1.2    Combat activities involve outmanoeuvring an opponent, often utilising physical means, using a series of techniques and skills having their origins in martial combat.

20.1.3    Although many combat activities are regulated by a recognised governing body under the auspices of the national sports council, others are not, although this does not necessarily imply unsafe practice. With a view to bringing consistency of safety standards to the martial arts, the **UK Martial Arts Standards and Advisory Commission** has been established. Additionally, some local authorities (LAs) have introduced 'in-house' training programmes to accredit specified combat and self-defence instructors.

20.1.4    It is imperative that anyone teaching or coaching martial arts has appropriate insurance.

> For further information on insurance, see *Chapter 7: Insurance Issues,* pages 45–48.

20.1.5    Whatever the combat activity, **appropriate accreditation** would reflect effective technical and subject knowledge, coaching expertise and familiarity with working with young people.

20.1.6    Combat activities taught in schools include:

- boxing
- fencing
- judo
- martial arts
- self-defence
- wrestling.

## 20.2    What Staff Should Know

### People

20.2.1    **Supervising adults** should have a sound knowledge of the combat activity they intend to teach and be capable of officiating in accordance with the rules of the activity.

20.2.2    Combat activities in schools are often delivered by coaches. As the potential for injury is high, great care should be taken to appoint competent coaches who hold relevant and current coaching/instructor qualifications and who are experienced in working with young people. Where appropriate, staff should contact relevant national, regional and county agencies and associations to check coaches'/instructors' suitability to deliver combat activities in schools.

20.2.3    Coaches should have a **valid licence** for the relevant combat activity. This should provide appropriate indemnity insurance to complement the third-party liability insurance provided by schools.

20.2.4    Coaches should have comprehensive **public liability insurance** cover.

> For more information on insurance, see *Chapter 7: Insurance Issues*, pages 45–48.

20.2.5    Pupils should be adequately prepared for all activities and made aware of their personal responsibilities for their own safety and that of others.

20.2.6    Pupils should be taught to participate strictly according to the **rules** and to always respect the decisions of the officials.

20.2.7    Pupils should demonstrate respect for their peers, coaches and the work environment.

20.2.8    Pupils should understand that excessive and overzealous competitiveness, loss of temper and inappropriate language will not be tolerated. Supervising adults should always take appropriate action in the event of pupils displaying such behaviour. If necessary, the combat activity should be stopped.

20.2.9    Pupils should share in the assessment and management of the risks associated with combat activities. This is an essential part of the learning process. Due to different abilities, the risk-management process should be applied to individual pupils, to pupil groups and to the class as a whole.

### Context

20.2.10    Combat activities take place in a range of locations, including:

- gymnasia
- sports halls
- dojos
- specialist rings for boxing and wrestling
- specialist pistes for fencing.

Wherever the activity takes place, care should be taken to ensure that practice arenas used for combat activities:

- are sited away from walls and other obstructions, and are surrounded by a clear safety area

146

- are large enough to allow safe play without overcrowding
- are level, even, non-slip and clean
- are free of obstructions and the potential for tripping
- provide secure footing.

20.2.11   If **mats** are being used, it is essential they comply with the current British Standards European Norm (BS EN) requirements for the specific activity. Manufacturers' guidelines need to be followed.

> For more information on mats, see *12.2.16–12.2.19*, page 90, in *Chapter 12: Equipment in Physical Education*.

20.2.12   Arrangements should be made for the **regular inspection**, repair and maintenance of equipment.

20.2.13   Faulty equipment (eg mats, boxing gloves, fencing foils) should be clearly marked and removed from use (and access by pupils) until repaired or replaced.

20.2.14   Potentially hazardous items of equipment (eg fencing foils) should be made secure and stored in a safe place where pupils cannot access them.

20.2.15   Pupils should wear appropriate **clothing, footwear and protective equipment** for the intended activity, whether this takes place in a teaching situation or match play. This should be checked before the activity commences.

> For more information on protective equipment, see *Chapter 13: Personal Protection,* pages 95–98.
> For more information on clothing and footwear, see *Chapter 14: Clothing and Personal Effects,* pages 99–102.

20.2.16   Long hair should be tied back, nails cut short and all potentially hazardous personal effects removed prior to taking part in any combat activity.

20.2.17   The chewing of food, sweets or gum immediately before or during combat activities should never be allowed. Chewing can result in choking, which can have serious, even fatal, consequences.

## Organisation

20.2.18   It is advisable to inform parents before pupils take part in combat activities.

20.2.19   All combat activities should match the age, maturity, experience, stamina and strength of the pupils involved. Pupils should only be exposed to challenges for which they have been appropriately prepared through a progressive scheme of work.

20.2.20   The number of pupils should be appropriate for the space available. **Group sizes** may need to be reduced if the working environment demands it.

20.2.21   **Mixed-gender competition** is not permitted. Pupils should only compete against other pupils of the same gender but, in some sports, mixed-gender **practice** is acceptable.

20.2.22   An adequate warm-up should be provided prior to all combat activities.

20.2.23    Staff should not compete with pupils during combat activities. This includes 'king of the castle'-type games, in which staff take on pupils at the end of a session. It is generally advisable that staff do not demonstrate on pupils. However, on occasion, for technical guidance, it may be necessary but it is essential that great care is taken.

20.2.24    Before competitive combat begins, pupils should be taught the basic skills and **rules** involved in the intended activity. Staff should apply the rules fully and consistently.

20.2.25    The teaching of all combat activities should follow a carefully planned and graduated progression, which helps to ensure that all pupils master the necessary skills at any given level of competence before progressing to the next stage.

20.2.26    It is recommended that **weapons** are not used in a school context. These should only be introduced with experience and ideally in a structured club situation.

20.2.27    Where **strike pads** are used for practising punching and kicking, correct instruction should be given on the safe way for them to be held and the amount of impact allowed; gloves should be worn to avoid any potential soft-tissue damage.

20.2.28    In combat activities where takedowns or throws are practised, it is essential that pupils are first taught how to **land safely** (break falls) and that mats are used.

## 20.3    What Pupils Should Know

20.3.1    Pupils should know that:

- safety procedures and instructions need total compliance at all times because of the potential dangers involved in combat activities

- no personal adornments are permitted as they could cause injury to the wearer or others

- hair should be tied back to prevent injury and inconvenience to the other contestant

- the nails of the feet and hands need to be cut short

- personal hygiene needs to be of a reasonable standard, especially in activities requiring physical contact

- they need to be aware of safety procedures and have respect for each other

- they should not apply their combat skills outside the class.

## 20.4    Further Guidance Relating to Specific Activities

### Boxing

20.4.1    Boxing involves two participants of similar weight fighting each other with gloved fists in a series of 1–3-minute rounds. Technical points are scored according to the accuracy, frequency and direction of blows landed on the opponent. If there is no stoppage before an agreed number of rounds, a winner is determined through a points accumulation. If the opponent is knocked down and unable to get up before the referee counts to 10, or if the opponent is deemed too injured to continue, a knockout is the result.

20.4.2    The **British Medical Association** (BMA), as a body of medical experts, does not support the teaching or coaching of, or any participation in, boxing due to evidence indicating detrimental effects upon health. Staff may wish to

148

consider **non-contact** versions of boxing and accreditation is now available to coach this through the national governing body (NGB), the Amateur Boxing Association (ABA).

## What staff should know

20.4.3    Where schools choose to offer boxing, the general guidance for combat activities given previously in this chapter applies, as well as the following guidelines.

## People

20.4.4    Coaches need to hold approved ABA coaching qualifications. Schools have a duty to ensure that coaching is provided by responsible and **qualified coaches** in a safe environment. Only qualified and experienced coaches should be employed to teach, coach or officiate boxing in schools.

20.4.5    Schools should ensure that all parents and pupils involved are aware of, and accept, the inherent and obvious risks.

## Context

20.4.6    Amateur boxers should wear particular items of **equipment** at all times, including a mouth guard, protective hand bandages, gloves, cup protectors, force-absorbent head gear and a shirt to absorb sweat. **Women** boxers are also required to wear breast protectors. These should meet national requirements and guidance.

> For more information on protective equipment, see *Chapter 13: Personal Protection*, pages 95–98.

## Organisation

20.4.7    The Schools Amateur Boxing Association's standard scheme provides national guidance on the safe delivery of boxing activities, including non-contact versions of the sport.

## What pupils should know

20.4.8    Pupils should know that:

- the frequency of head and body blows inherent in boxing carries significant risk
- all rules relating to boxing and sparring need to be strictly applied and never compromised
- good standards of physical fitness and health are required to participate in boxing.

## Fencing

20.4.9    The three common forms of fencing are epee, foil and sabre. Safety measures need to be thoroughly addressed in order to minimise the risks involved in these potentially lethal activities. Full **personal protection** should be worn at all times, both for practice and competition. The rules of British Fencing, the NGB for the sport, must be strictly observed.

20.4.10   The general guidance for combat activities given previously in this chapter applies to fencing, as well as the following guidelines.

## People

20.4.11   Staff should hold **relevant and current NGB coaching qualifications** in order to lead this activity.

## Context

20.4.12   The fencing **environment** needs to meet British Fencing safety requirements.

20.4.13   Pistes (both competition and practice) should be well spaced out, at least 1.5m apart.

20.4.14   Practice pistes should meet British Fencing's national recommendations.

20.4.15   There should be a clear run-off at each end of a piste for the safety of participants and/or spectators.

20.4.16   Almost all serious fencing injuries are caused by broken blades. Therefore, it is essential that **only swords that are in good condition are used**; others should be condemned or taken out of use for repair.

20.4.17   Children under the age of 10 should fence with weapon blades of size 0 and children under the age of 14 should normally fence with weapon blades of size 3 or smaller, corresponding to the size they would be required to use in competitions for their age.

20.4.18   The points of swords should be covered with **purpose-made protective tips**.

20.4.19   All **swords should be checked regularly** by knowledgeable school staff/coaches.

20.4.20   Any **electrical equipment** used for scoring should be stored safely and observed carefully while in use.

20.4.21   **Adequate body protection is essential**. Pupils should only be allowed to participate in fencing activities if they are wearing the following items of protective clothing/equipment as set out in the British Fencing rules:

- a plastron

- a mask complete with bib and an effective head clip which fits correctly (substandard masks are unacceptable); all masks must be fitted with safety back straps

- a jacket long enough to cover the waistband of the trousers (the official requirement is a 10cm overlap when in the en garde position)

- gloves with a gauntlet to cover the cuff of the jacket sleeve and protect the wrist and the arm (the gauntlet should extend halfway up the forearm to ensure a safe overlap)

- breeches (optional during practice, mandatory during competitions); if wearing trousers, openings/pockets need to be zipped, sewn or taped closed

- knee-length socks (if wearing breeches) that are always covered by the bottom of the breeches so that no bare skin is showing

- shoes with a sole that grips the floor, which should be replaced if the soles are worn.

Additionally, it is compulsory for women to wear breast protectors and it is recommended that girls wear breast protectors at least from the age of 10 or from the onset of puberty, if earlier.

> For more information on protective equipment, see *Chapter 13: Personal Protection*, pages 95–98.

20.4.22    Right-handed fencers need to wear right-handed garments, which have openings on the left-hand side. The opposite applies to left-handed fencers.

20.4.23    Protective clothing needs to be marked with an appropriate label denoting a safety rating in *newtons* (N).

| **A: Those fencing with size 3 or smaller blades, electric or non-electric, all 3 weapons (both fencers) and those fencing with non-electric foil blade (both fencers)*** | | | | |
| --- | --- | --- | --- | --- |
| | **Jackets** | **Plastrons** | **Trousers/Breeches** | **Masks** |
| Either | CEN1 350N | CEN1 350N | Trousers with openings/pockets zipped/sewn/taped closed, or fencing breeches – not shorts | CEN1 (350N bib) |
| or | 350N + integrated 350N | | As above | CEN1 (350N bib) |
| or | CEN2 800N | N/A | As above | CEN1 (350N bib) |
| **B: All other fencing, all weapons** | | | | |
| | **Jackets** | **Plastrons** | **Breeches** | **Masks** |
| | CEN1 | CEN2 | CEN1 | CEN1 |
| | 350N | 800N | 350N | (350N bib) |

*'Non-electric foil blades' does not mean dummy electric foil blades fitted with a button. To qualify for this level of clothing standard, both fencers need to be using the traditional lightweight 'steam' foil blade, used universally before the invention of the electric foil.

## What pupils should know

20.4.24    Pupils should know:

- not to run in the salle

- not to point a weapon at anyone not wearing a mask

- the potential dangers of mishandling equipment

- never to use a blade that shows signs of 'softness' or is badly bent or kinked

- never to fence against anyone who is using a blade that shows signs of 'softness'

- to carry a weapon either by the pommel with the point towards the floor or by gripping the point, with the weapon hanging down vertically, when not fencing or practising

- how to put on their masks correctly and not to remove them until instructed by the coach.

## Judo

### Introduction

20.4.25    Judo involves two participants in a contest where the object is to throw the opponent largely onto his/her back with considerable force and speed. This scores 'ippon' and ends the contest.

20.4.26    Players are taught to fall in such a manner that they land safely. Great emphasis is placed on mastering the several methods of break falling since this gives players the confidence to participate fully. It is also possible to score ippon by pinning the opponent to the mat for a period of 25 seconds. In addition to the sought-after ippon, smaller scores are given for less successful throws and hold-downs broken before the 25-second limit.

20.4.27    Because of the potentially dangerous nature of the sport, strict **discipline** is essential and great importance is placed on safety, hygiene and etiquette.

### What staff should know

20.4.28    The general guidance for combat activities given previously in this chapter applies to judo, as well as the following guidelines.

### People

20.4.29    Judo should be taught by a coach with a minimum of a current Level 2 qualification and of first 'kyu' grade (British Judo Association – BJA) who has also attended a sports coach UK 'Safeguarding and Protecting Children' workshop.

20.4.30    It is essential that pupils learn to be safe participants and spectators due to the nature of this activity. Pupils should be involved in risk assessments of the various techniques in order to develop their understanding of the potential dangers involved.

20.4.31    Pupils involved in judo contests should always be suitably prepared and the nature and level of competitive activity should match their physical maturity and developmental stage.

### Context

20.4.32    A minimum ceiling height of 3.5m should be provided, with no objects hanging below this level.

20.4.33    Depending on the type of activity and intensity for practice or 'randori', there should be adequate spacing to ensure there is a safe area in which to participate. The recommended mat area per pupil is 2m$^2$.

20.4.34    Mats need to comply with BS EN 12503-3: 2001. The 'tatami' (judo area) should be firm under foot and have adequate shock-absorbing properties.

20.4.35    Mat surfaces should not be torn or tattered and mats should have a strong base to ensure they do not slide during activities.

20.4.36    The density of judo mats is such that they minimise the risk of injury from high-impact falls and throws. Gymnastic mats should not be used as a substitute, as their density is inadequate for the purposes of judo. BJA recommend 230kg per cubic metre density for club and competition.

20.4.37    The edge of the mat area should be at least 2m away from any walls, projections or open doors.

20.4.38    For competitions, it is essential to check the BJA recommendations for size of mat area in relation to the type of competition being run.

20.4.39    Canvas covers should not be used to cover or secure mats. Frames can be constructed to secure mat areas permanently but they should be covered if they present a hazard.

20.4.40    Pupils should wear suitable clothing. This should be a generous fit, as ill-fitting clothing can cause injury. Whenever possible, judogi (judo suits) should be worn. In competitions, it is mandatory to wear the correct judogi.

## Organisation

20.4.41    GCSE syllabuses provide a useful guidance tool for the organisation of judo activities.

20.4.42    **Mixed-gender practice** is permitted. Therefore, it is important pupils have respect for each other and are aware of safety implications during randori. Pupils should be matched by size, weight, age, experience, and ability. However, **mixed-gender competition** is not permitted.

20.4.43    Pupils should not practise throwing techniques while others are practising groundwork skills.

20.4.44    It is essential that pupils are taught the various ways to submit and that pupils understand how important it is to accept **submission** and stop applying any technique immediately.

20.4.45    It is advisable that **strangles and armlocks** do not form part of a school's programme of tuition.

## What pupils should know

20.4.46    Pupils should know that:

- safety procedures and instructions need total compliance at all times because of the potential dangers involved in judo

- no personal adornments that could cause injury to themselves or others are permitted

- hair should be tied back to prevent injury and inconvenience to the other contestant

- the nails of the feet and hands need to be cut short

- the personal hygiene of the contestant needs to be of a high standard

- judogi should be clean, generally dry and without unpleasant odour

- only bare feet are permitted on the tatami.

## Martial arts

20.4.47 Martial arts involve a diverse number of styles. The activities include:

- aikido
- karate
- kendo
- jiu-jitsu
- kung fu
- tae kwon do.

> **Note**: A relevant and current NGB qualification in one martial art is **not transferable** to another.

## Aikido

20.4.48 Aikido is a martial art that has been described as being as active as tumbling and as elegant and dramatic as fencing. It involves neutralising an attack by using holds and locks that are usually taught by modern/practical or classical/ceremonial methods.

### What staff should know

20.4.49 The general guidance for combat activities given previously in this chapter applies to aikido, as well as the following guidelines.

### People

20.4.50 Coaches should hold relevant and current British Aikido Board (BAB) **qualifications**, as well as taking the sports coach UK 'Coaching Children and Young People' workshop or the BAB's course on coaching children.

20.4.51 Children under 14 years of age should not practise on the same mat as adults.

20.4.52 Children under 16 years of age should not normally practise with adults.

### Context

20.4.53 The **mats** used should meet the same requirements as judo mats or other comparable health-and-safety guidelines.

> For information on judo mats, see *20.4.33–20.4.39*, pages 152–153, in this chapter.

20.4.54 Pupils should wear a **loose tunic** and, preferably, the recommended trousers.

20.4.55 The minimum ceiling height should be 3.5m, with no objects hanging below this level. If weapons are used, a greater height is needed.

### Organisation

20.4.56 Dangerous locks, holds or movements must not be taught or practised.

20.4.57 The recommended amount of mat space is 2m x 2m per person.

20.4.58 The minimum space recommendation for pairs training with weapons is 5m$^2$ per practitioner.

## What pupils should know

20.4.59    Pupils should know that:

- safety procedures and instructions need total compliance at all times because of the potential dangers involved in aikido

- no personal adornments that could cause injury to themselves or others are permitted

- hair should be tied back to prevent injury and inconvenience to the other contestant

- the nails of the feet and hands need to be cut short

- the personal hygiene of the contestant needs to be of a high standard

- gi should be clean, generally dry and without unpleasant odour

- only bare feet are permitted on the mat area.

## Karate

20.4.60    Karate is a Japanese weaponless martial art based on scientific principles that encompass physical culture, character development, self-defence and sport.

## What staff should know

20.4.61    The general guidance for combat activities given previously in this chapter applies to karate, as well as the following guidelines.

## People

20.4.62    There are many different karate organisations in the UK. It is essential that only coaches from **approved organisations** be appointed to lead karate sessions in schools. Details of approved organisations can be obtained from national sports councils.

20.4.63    Karate coaches should hold at least a first dan black-belt qualification certificated by a recognised and contactable organisation. They should also be suitably accredited to work with children and young people.

20.4.64    It is recommended that the school contacts the organisation to ensure the coach is registered with a recognised organisation.

## Context

20.4.65    Three square metres per pupil are required when practising fundamental techniques (kihon) and 4m$^2$ per pupil when practising formal exercises (kata).

20.4.66    Coaches and pupils should wear appropriate karate clothing. This should be laundered on a regular basis.

## Organisation

20.4.67    GCSE/A-level syllabuses can provide useful guidance tools for the organisation of karate activities.

20.4.68    Karate sessions that take place during curriculum time should last for no more than one hour. They usually consist of a warm-up and the three major components of karate:

- fundamental techniques (kihon)
- formal exercise (kata)
- sparring (kumite).

20.4.69    Out-of-school-hours karate sessions should last for no more than one and a half hours.

20.4.70    All kihon, kata and kumite activities should be appropriate for the ability and experience of the pupils involved.

20.4.71    The importance of developing technical competence should be emphasised.

20.4.72    There are many forms of kihon, kata and kumite. Pupils should successfully master each grade before progressing to more advanced techniques and skills.

20.4.73    **Sparring** should be introduced in a non-contact form initially, with careful progression to touch contact, which should be developed appropriately. At no time should fighting or sparring be allowed in a reckless manner.

## Kendo, kung fu and jiu jitsu

20.4.74    As the potential for harm in these activities is high, school staff are recommended to **seek guidance** from appropriate organisations (eg LA advisory support services, NGBs, activity associations) before appointing coaches to deliver these activities in their schools.

## Tae kwon do

20.4.75    The Korean martial art of tae kwon do appeals to young people as it is characterised by fast, high, spinning kicks and energetic movements, often in sequence. In addition, participants learn to apply powerful hand and joint-locking techniques. The risk of injury may be high; to minimise this to an acceptable level, great care should be taken to ensure sound discipline and respect among pupils.

## People

20.4.76    Supervising adults who deliver tae kwon do sessions should be experienced black belts with **suitable NGB coaching qualifications**. They should also have suitable accreditation to work with children and young adults.

## Context

20.4.77    If **mats** are used, they should be joined together securely so that they do not move apart.

20.4.78    Particular care should be taken to minimise risks if tae kwon do activities take place outdoors.

20.4.79    Pupils should wear appropriate **equipment** (eg headgear, knee pads) that meets recommended standards. This should be of the correct size and be washed on a regular basis.

### Organisation

20.4.80    When grouping pupils for **sparring** (especially freestyle), particular care should be taken to match pupils by gender, size, weight, age, experience and ability.

20.4.81    Pupils should be made aware of the potential for injury when performing holds and locks, and should be taught to perform them safely.

20.4.82    Pupils should strive for technical competence and a mature approach.

### Self-defence

20.4.83    Self-defence classes are becoming increasingly popular and, in schools, are mainly targeted at teenage girls in Key Stage 4. Self-defence involves control and restraint, self-protection, and elements of judo and some martial arts.

### People

20.4.84    Self-defence coaches should be experienced in working with young people in the context of formal classes and preferably hold a **relevant coaching qualification** in judo and/or one or more martial arts (eg tae kwon do, karate).

### Context

20.4.85    Facilities should be spacious enough and free from hazard to allow safe participation.

20.4.86    **Clothing** should be appropriate and not constitute a hazard to either the wearer or other participants.

### Organisation

20.4.87    Coaches should provide an in-depth syllabus of what will be taught, with clearly stated learning outcomes.

### Wrestling

20.4.88    The rules and philosophy of the internationally agreed freestyle form of wrestling (ie Olympic-style wrestling) are formulated so that two wrestlers can engage in hard physical combat without pain and/or injury. This should be the philosophy of all taking part in wrestling activities in schools (ie staff and pupils).

### People

20.4.89    Wrestling activities should always be **supervised and refereed** by competent, trained and qualified people. The coach should be British Wrestling Association (BWA) approved – Level 2 – and registered with the BWA.

20.4.90    Advice on training and qualifications for school staff wishing to deliver wrestling activities can be obtained from relevant wrestling organisations (eg the BWA).

### Context

20.4.91    The minimum ceiling height should be 3.5m, with no objects hanging below this level.

20.4.92    Any potential hazardous walls should be padded.

20.4.93    The wrestling area should measure at least 3m².

20.4.94    Wrestling mats should be Fédération Internationale des Luttes Associées (FILA) approved and firmly secured together.

20.4.95    Mats with gaps or mats that easily become parted present an immediate danger to pupils and staff alike.

20.4.96    The surface of the mats should be smooth and in good condition.

20.4.97    It is recommended that wrestling mats be disinfected before every session in order to prevent the spread of germs and disease.

20.4.98    No outside footwear should be worn on the mats.

20.4.99    Clothing should be close-fitting without being too restrictive (eg swimming costumes are ideal for training). Shorts are unsuitable and should not be worn.

20.4.100   Specifically designed **wrestling singlets** should be worn during competitions. There should be no loose parts that could trap an opponent's fingers. Tracksuits (or other similar clothing) should be worn over wrestling costumes to keep warm while waiting to compete.

20.4.101   **Footwear** for beginners should be free of metal lace tags or eyelets, and have smooth soles.

20.4.102   Protective arm and knee pads may be worn and the use of ear guards should be encouraged.

20.4.103   Suitable support protection (in line with wrestling rules) should always be worn by both male and female pupils.

## Organisation

20.4.104   A trained and experienced **mat chairperson** should be positioned at the edge of the mat during competitions. He/she should intervene immediately if any move or hold performed is likely to cause pain.

20.4.105   School staff/coaches should adopt the role of mat chairperson during practice sessions.

20.4.106   Moves that put pressure on, or twist, the **neck** are extremely hazardous.

20.4.107   Wrestlers aged under 17 are not allowed to execute any form of **full nelson**. A scissor lock with the feet crossed on the head, neck or body is forbidden. The nelson is not allowed to be used in female wrestling.

20.4.108   Pupils under the age of 11 are not allowed to use any form of nelson or bridging.

## What pupils should know

20.4.109 In all combat activity, pupils should know:

- never to lose their temper or self-control

- always to respect an opponent

- the majority of rules are designed to protect and minimise injury; consequently, rules need to be strictly complied with

- they need to be physically fit and prepared for the demands of the activity.

## 20.5 Additional Information

### Resources

Hobbs, G. and Reay, T. (1992) *The Judo Manual*. London: Hutchinson.
ISBN: 978-0091750-20-6.

Skipp, A. (1999) *Handbook of Foil Fencing*. Leeds: Coachwise Business Solutions.
ISBN: 978-1902523-27-9.

### Useful websites

Refer to NGB websites for further information on recommended safe practice in combat activities. The following may be useful:

**Aikido**

British Aikido Board
www.bab.org.uk

**Boxing**

Amateur Boxing Association of England
www.abae.co.uk

British Medical Association
www.bma.org.uk/ap.nsf/Content/boxing

Irish Amateur Boxing Association
www.iaba.ie

Scottish boxing
www.scottishboxing.co.uk

Welsh Amateur Boxing Association
www.welshboxing.co.uk

**Fencing**

British Fencing
www.britishfencing.com

England Fencing
www.englandfencing.org.uk

Welsh Fencing
www.welshfencing.org

**Judo**

British Judo Association
www.britishjudo.org.uk

**Karate**

British Karate Association
www.thebka.co.uk

English Karate Federation
www.englishkaratefederation.com

# Chapter twenty-one

## Dance Activities, Movement and Creative Development

21

This chapter recommends a range of practices and procedures designed to promote safe delivery of dance-related activity.

> Please read the general guidance provided in Part 1 of this handbook, pages 9–131, before reading this chapter. This will help to ensure that you have a comprehensive awareness of safe-practice issues affecting dance-related activities and PESS in general.

## 21.1    Introduction

21.1.1    Dance is a distinct area of experience that offers unique learning opportunities within the school curriculum and is part of physical education and arts education. It contributes to pupils' physical, aesthetic, artistic, creative, cultural and social development, playing an important role in promoting physical fitness, well-being and maintaining a healthy lifestyle.

21.1.2    There are many forms of dance, which involve a range of styles, movements and techniques. From the Foundation Stage through to the final stages of formal education, children and young adults should be provided with opportunities to acquire and develop technical skills in order to achieve high-quality performance and approaches to working creatively that are safely executed. These will range from simple actions to very complex movements, all of which should be introduced progressively.

21.1.3    Although it might be assumed that dance activities are relatively hazard-free in comparison to other areas of the physical education curriculum, comprehensive and informed risk management remains essential.

## 21.2    What Staff Should Know

### People

21.2.1    **Staff** should be appropriately qualified or experienced, and should be knowledgeable about the structure and function of the human body, understanding its potential, as well as limitations, and how to prevent injury. All staff involved in the activity should be aware of emergency procedures and how to implement them.

> For general information on injury and emergency procedures, see *Chapter 8: Accident Procedures and First-aid Management,* pages 49–54.

21.2.2     **Pupils** should share in the assessment and management of the risks associated with dance activities. This is an essential part of the learning process. They should be given opportunities to think about safe practice in relation to themselves and others, as well as the environment they are working in.

## Context

21.2.3     Dance activities are frequently taught in **facilities** which are not designed for that purpose, such as school halls or gymnasia. In these circumstances, great care should be taken to ensure that any modifications or adaptations meet satisfactory safety standards.

      a. Facilities should be maintained in good order and remain hazard-free, with risks reduced to an acceptable level.

      b. Floors should be non-slip, preferably sprung and checked regularly, with doorways and fire exits kept clear at all times.

      c. Heating and lighting should be suited to the dance activity.

      d. Dance equipment and props should be maintained in good order. All risks associated with their use should be properly assessed and managed.

      e. Pupils should preferably work in bare feet if it is safe to do so. Any footwear should be appropriate for the activity and in good repair, with appropriate support to prevent injury during high-impact activities.

      f. Clothing needs to be safe and comfortable while allowing staff to quickly spot any incorrect body alignment.

      g. All personal effects should be removed or made safe.

> For further information on these issues, see *Dance studios (15.2.14–15.2.16, pages 105–106)* in *Chapter 15: Buildings and Facilities*.

## Organisation

21.2.4     There should be sufficient time for an adequate **warm-up** before strenuous exercise. Staff should ensure that pupils are properly prepared for the physical demands of the dance activity. **Cooling down** at the end of a session should include gentle stretching of muscle groups used during the activities undertaken. This will help to relax the muscles and prevent tension or involuntary contraction, which may otherwise occur after vigorous activity has taken place.

21.2.5     Some dance forms, including health-related activity, may involve exercise of moderate to vigorous intensity. Correct **technique** should be emphasised in order to maximise the associated benefits and minimise any risks.

21.2.6     Class and **group sizes** should be organised in relation to the space available and the levels and techniques being taught. Age and ability should be taken into consideration when planning suitable activity.

21.2.7     Safety procedures need to be well understood by staff and pupils.

21.2.8    To avoid unnecessary damage and injury, care needs to be taken to ensure that, during dance exercises or activities:

- the neck is not cramped when rotating the head or taking the head backwards

- there is no bumping or banging when landing or taking the weight onto different body parts

- there is good alignment of the head, spine, hips, knees and feet and no overarching of the back

- knees are positioned over toes when bending and ankles do not turn outwards when on the toes.

> For further information on safe exercise principles, see *Chapter 24: Health-related Exercise*, pages 195–202.

21.2.9    Staff should observe pupils carefully to check that they do not overstress themselves through poor technique and that they have good control of the body when working creatively.

21.2.10   When working in pairs or small groups on exercises involving **lifting or supporting**, extra care should be taken to ensure that pupils have worked through progressive practices and are sufficiently strong, spatially aware and mature enough to meet the requirements of the movement.

21.2.11   Good practice frequently shows that partnerships between schools and external agencies such as **professional dance companies** enhance pupils' learning and experience. Staff need to be satisfied that any adults involved are suitable and that there is an effective system of monitoring and support in place.

> For further information on monitoring adults working with children, see *Chapter 9: Safeguarding Children and Young People*, pages 55–72.

## 21.3    What Pupils Should Know

21.3.1    Pupils should know that they:

- should share in the assessment and management of the risks involved in dance activity

- need to maintain high levels of concentration and take responsibility for others when taking weight, lifting, supporting and working with partners and in groups

- need to prepare for vigorous activity and be physically able to meet the demands of the intended style, technique and finished dance.

## 21.4    Additional Information

### Useful websites

Dance UK
www.danceuk.org

National Dance Teachers Association
www.ndta.org.uk

## 21.5    Case Law Examples

21.5.1    Hill versus Durham County Council, Court of Appeal (2000):
*A teacher participated in a dance session during a professional development course and ruptured a tendon during the warm-up. The claimant argued that the warm-up should have been gentler to accommodate varying abilities. The claim was dismissed on the basis that warm-up activities can never rule out possible injury.*

164

# Chapter twenty-two

## Games Activities

22

This chapter identifies a number of essential safety principles associated with the different types of game – invasion, net/wall, striking/fielding – that contribute to safe teaching and learning.

> Please read the general guidance provided in Part 1 of this handbook, pages 9–131, before reading this chapter. This will help to ensure that you have a comprehensive awareness of safe-practice issues affecting games activities and PESS in general.

## 22.1 Introduction

22.1.1 One of the most significant features of games activities, in terms of assessing and managing risk, is that they challenge participants to work in situations that are constantly changing, where the body may be still or moving. Participants are required to demonstrate a range of technical skills with features such as:

- physical contact

- accuracy

- maximal effort

- application of force

- timing.

The degree of challenge faced will vary significantly, depending upon the demands of each particular game and the level at which it is played.

22.1.2 The use of a range of equipment in games activities, including projectiles, some of which are very hard, and a range of implements, such as bats and rackets, further complicates the situation. Careful planning, organisation, supervision and the direct involvement of the pupils in risk assessment and management will assist in significantly reducing risk.

22.1.3 National governing bodies of sport (NGBs) play a central role in developing games activities. They are responsible for establishing the rules, regulations and conventions of their respective activities, as well as providing guidance that supports staff in ensuring safe practice. Staff should be familiar with the guidance provided by the specific NGB for each games activity.

## 22.2 What Staff Should Know

### People

22.2.1 All **staff** involved in the delivery or supervision of games activities should have a current **working knowledge** and understanding of the activity being taught through initial teacher education (ITE), appropriate and relevant continuing professional development (CPD) courses, and the advice given by NGBs. There is a concern in games activities that some NGB teaching/coaching awards do not require renewal once successfully obtained. With this in mind, it is vital that staff maintain an up-to-date knowledge of the areas in which they work and remain engaged in the process of CPD, fundamental to good, and therefore, safe practice.

22.2.2 **Pupils** play a crucial role in safe practice in this area. Staff must ensure that pupils learn about the inherent risks in the different types of games activities and are fully involved in the processes of risk assessment and risk management. The range of abilities and needs that present themselves when staff are working with any group of pupils requires careful consideration.

## Context

### Facilities

22.2.3 **Playing surfaces** need to be suitable for the activity and the needs of all pupils (including those with reduced mobility, or wheelchair users), in addition to being in sound condition. They should be routinely and regularly checked by those responsible for site and facilities maintenance to ensure that security of footing is not compromised by damage, such as holes, cracks or splinters, or debris, such as loose grit, dust or rubbish, all of which increase the risk of accident. This routine check should also be followed up by the member of staff who goes to work with the pupils in each particular area. The pupils should be effectively involved in this process, although it would be inappropriate for them to be directly physically involved in resolving any significant problem, removing any hazard or dealing with any hazardous substance. Staff must report problems to whoever has the relevant responsibility within the organisation and check that they have been resolved before using the area again. When not in use, all facilities should be locked or made secure, wherever reasonably practicable.

22.2.4 It is important that any facilities under the direct jurisdiction of the school are checked very carefully by staff and pupils to ensure that they are safe, and that appropriate routine maintenance is evident at all times. Staff are responsible for the health and well-being of their pupils wherever they are expected to work with them.

22.2.5 **Weather conditions** require careful consideration. The physical demands of games activities are such that the body is often moving quickly so it is essential that the weather conditions do not impede safety. On a damp or frosty morning, the risk of slipping on a grass or court surface is increased and needs to be carefully assessed.

> For more information, see *Weather conditions (13.2.9, page 97)* in *Chapter 13: Personal Protection*.

22.2.6 The position and brightness of the sun in relation to pupils and the types of activities they have been asked to undertake can impact upon performance. Similarly, in the indoor environment, the effectiveness of artificial lighting needs to be taken into account. It would be hazardous to ask pupils to undertake any activity where their safety was compromised due to inadequate lighting.

22.2.7 The **playing surface** should be kept free of all equipment not in use during the activity and pupils should be taught and encouraged to apply this principle consistently.

22.2.8 There should be a suitable distance between the playing area and the perimeter of the working space in which it is located, particularly if there are other pupils working in adjacent areas, and proximity to hazardous fixtures and fittings should be avoided. There needs to be a sufficiently clear space to **run off** the pitch or court without danger of collision with objects or people (typically a minimum of 2m but reference should be made to Sport England's publication *Comparative Sizes of Sports Pitches and Courts*). It is important to ensure that the distance between the playing surface and features such as boundary fences, roads, and windows are sufficient to avoid accident or injury, and that directions of play account for this. All pitch/court/area markings need to be clearly visible.

22.2.9 **Remote facilities** require additional consideration. Staff who are working away from the main building, on fields, courts or other play areas, should be equipped with radios or alternative reliable communication devices in order to make immediate contact with colleagues if necessary. Some emergencies necessitate immediate support, frequently including access to first aid.

> For general information on facilities, see *Chapter 15: Buildings and Facilities*, pages 103–110.

## Equipment

22.2.10 Games activities require the use of a range of equipment, some of which may be inherently hazardous.

22.2.11 The state of **repair, maintenance and replacement** is a key consideration for staff who need to ensure that all equipment is fit for purpose and functional. Any equipment that is broken or damaged should be effectively removed from service, either permanently or until it has been satisfactorily repaired. Pupils should be encouraged to report any defective or damaged equipment to a member of staff.

22.2.12 Equipment should be stored in a safe manner in suitable containers and locked in designated storage areas when not in use. Larger items of **unfixed equipment**, such as netball posts or portable football goals, that cannot be stored inside the building need to be secured at all times.

22.2.13 **Outdoor posts** need to be correctly located, fixed to the ground and have protective padding applied, where relevant, taking note of NGB guidelines.

22.2.14 In order to ensure that pupils are able to work as safely as possible, as well as with appropriate challenge, the suitability of equipment should reflect pupil need and ability. Considerations such as the size, weight or shape of implements and projectiles should be carefully assessed when planning activities to make sure they are compatible with the developmental stage of the pupils.

22.2.15 When making use of **markers or posts** within activities, they need to be fit for purpose. The height and size of cones should not compromise safety. Marker discs or throw-down lines may provide a safer option.

22.2.16 **Adapting equipment** for use may occasionally be appropriate, such as the use of cones to create mini goals, but this requires careful risk assessment. Some adaptations may be required when modifying the activity for a particular playing surface or space, possibly involving the use of lighter-weight balls for hockey on a hard court space.

> For general information on equipment, see *Chapter 12: Equipment in Physical Education*, pages 85–93.

# Clothing

22.2.17  All **personal adornments** should be removed. Clothing should be suitable for the activity and for the environmental conditions within which the activity is taking place. If pupils are required to work in high or low temperatures or a range of weather conditions if outside, and to undertake a range of activities demanding different levels of exertion then the clothing worn should allow for sufficient warmth without being bulky or obstructive. Clothing should also reduce the risk of injury, where possible and practical. This may require long-sleeved tops and tracksuit bottoms when playing on hard or synthetic surfaces.

22.2.18  Crucially, a number of games activities, on the advice of NGBs, require specific **personal protective equipment** (PPE) to be worn. Such safety equipment should be fit for purpose and in good repair. For the most part, the activities requiring very specific safety wear are those where there is a likelihood of contact with other players, hard projectiles are used and there is unpredictability in terms of speed and force. Examples are detailed later in this chapter.

> For further information on PPE, see *Chapter 13: Personal Protection*, pages 95–98.

22.2.19  **Footwear** should be appropriate for both the activity being undertaken and the condition and nature of the playing surface. If trainers are required, then they should be tied and have gripping soles. Where fields or grassed areas are wet or slippery, but still considered safe for working, boots with no sharp studs are advisable. On AstroTurf pitches, either trainers with good grip or Astro boots should be worn, according to NGB advice. All footwear should be correctly tied in the manner of its design to ensure appropriate support for the ankles. As fashion evolves, there are often items of casual or leisure footwear on the market that have the appearance of trainers. It is important that staff check to ensure that footwear has the required specification and provides the necessary support for safe participation.

22.2.20  Eating or chewing should never be allowed. Some games require particular attention to be paid to personal matters; for example, in passing games, fingernails should be short to prevent injury to oneself and others in the course of the activity.

22.2.21  Many schools make clothing and footwear available for pupils to use in the event of their own clothing not being available for activities. It is essential that such clothing and footwear allows pupils to participate safely and incorporates good hygienic practice.

22.2.22  It is recognised good practice to work closely with parents in order to raise awareness about what is required to ensure safe participation. This, in conjunction with making pupils aware of what to look for in both their own attire and that of their peers, will further support staff in their role.

> For general guidance on clothing, see *Chapter 14: Clothing and Personal Effects*, pages 99–102.

## Travel

22.2.23 Many games activities take place on fields or playing surfaces that require staff and pupils to travel to reach them, be it on or off the school site. It is essential that appropriate guidelines on transport and travel, including emergency contact procedures are followed. As with any emergency procedures, departmental, school and local authority (LA) policies must be adhered to.

> For more information on these issues, see *Chapter 16: Transporting Pupils*, pages 111–117, and *Chapter 18: Managing Sports Events, Sports Tours and Other Off-site PESS Activities*, pages 123–131.

## Organisation

### Preparation

22.2.24 Effective planning, knowledge of facilities and equipment, and risk assessment underpinned by good subject knowledge (both game-specific and general) will allow staff to create a safe learning environment. In planning, staff need to ensure that there is safe configuration of practices and playing areas in relation to the direction of play, proximity of other groups, the number of players involved in both practices and games and, where there is any likelihood of contact, that account is taken of the size, gender and ability of pupils.

22.2.25 Pupils' needs, age, prior experience, confidence, ability and any special educational needs (SEN) should form the basis of decisions made about:

- learning activities and planned and expected progression within them
- the equipment and space used
- the organisation of the learning environment
- the level of designated pupil responsibility and independence
- teaching style.

> For further guidance on pupils with SEN, see *Chapter 10: Individual and Special Needs*, pages 73–80.

22.2.26 Gender issues should also be considered in any activity where contact may occur.

## Class organisation

22.2.27 The procedures and routines that staff and pupils engage in as part of class organisation represent an important foundation for safe practice. The more fully involved at their own level pupils are in understanding safe practice and working safely, with clear and consistent guidance, the safer the environment will be.

22.2.28 In striking and fielding games, for instance, there should be agreed minimum **fielding distances**, which are marked where possible and practical. It is also good practice to designate waiting or watching areas for the various roles that pupils might undertake, such as batting, coaching, observing, or substitute player.

22.2.29 When setting up the learning environment and packing away, pupils need to be taught how to safely **carry equipment** and be provided with appropriate instruction. Guided demonstrations by the staff or other pupils can be effective in developing understanding. Pupils need to be clear about:

- efficient and safe lifting techniques

- how to carry different sizes and types of equipment

- how many people are required

- whether special care needs to be taken with particular items, such as large portable equipment requiring a designated team, rather than an individual.

> For general information on handling equipment safely, see *Chapter 12: Equipment in Physical Education*, pages 85–93.

22.2.30 **Communication** is a key skill in games activities, but also in safe practice. Pupils need to learn the importance of eye contact and ensuring that all other players are ready before activity begins, for example, ensuring the batter is ready before the ball is bowled or pitched.

## Teaching style

22.2.31 Pupils need to learn how to participate independently, where appropriate, and opportunities need to be provided to develop their confidence through a range of teaching styles. The nature of the activity and its safety demands will determine the most suitable approach.

22.2.32 A feature of good practice in any area of learning is the clarity of instruction. **Instructions** should be clear and consistent and make use of appropriate vocabulary. A clear expectation should be established that rules are followed by all, both the rules of the specific activity and those that staff have put in place as part of their routine practice. Staff need to consistently ensure this is maintained and be willing to take steps to reinforce it whenever necessary.

22.2.33 In planning the use of appropriate teaching styles, staff should take into account any specific SEN. Particular examples include pupils who face any challenges with their hearing or sight, in order to ensure that all pupils can be safely and appropriately included in the learning activities within games. Where necessary, specialist guidance can be sought from LA support teams or national organisations such as the Royal National Institute of Blind People (RNIB).

> For further guidance on working with pupils with SEN, see *Chapter 10: Individual and Special Needs*, pages 73–80.

22.2.34 Staff should limit their active involvement in games activities to that of demonstration and, where appropriate, keeping the game moving; they should not involve themselves on a competitive basis with pupils.

## Progression

22.2.35 As with all areas of physical activity, planning for progression is essential. Progression in games activities can benefit from the opportunities that recognised mini games offer (eg pop lacrosse, short tennis, High 5 Netball) and information on these can be obtained from the relevant NGB. **Conditioned practices and games** should also be used to allow activities to be matched to the age, prior experience, needs and ability of pupils. Particular care needs to be taken when working with activities that require contact, as well-structured development work is essential to reduce the risks to pupils. Careful consideration is also needed with regard to when and how to introduce competition. Its nature and organisation should take into account the requirements for learning, along with the pupils' ability and confidence. At all times, pupils should be encouraged to play in the 'appropriate spirit' of the game, with rules and conventions consistently modelled and reinforced by staff.

22.2.36 Whatever approach staff take to planning for progression, it is crucial to build up skills gradually and this can be assisted through effective **differentiation**. Various features may be altered within the learning situation to differentiate for all learners. These features include:

- space

- distance

- the size, weight and shape of equipment

- direction

- level

- speed

- force

- grouping (pairs, small groups etc)

- combining skills

- the role of the opposition (passive, semi-passive, competitive).

When grouping pupils, it is essential to consider matching them in terms of capability, size, strength and confidence.

## Emergency action

22.2.37 Any emergency action should follow department, school and LA (or relevant organising body) policy. The procedures should be clearly documented and all staff made fully aware of their practical application.

> For further information on these issues, see *Chapter 8: Accident Procedures and First-aid Management,* pages 49–54, *Chapter 17: Crisis Management,* pages 119–122, and *Appendix 8: First-aid and Accident Procedures,* pages 332–342.

## 22.3 Further Guidance Relating to Specific Activities

22.3.1 This section outlines further key safety features within the three types of games activity.

### Invasion games

> The information set out in this section should be read in conjunction with the general principles set out in the earlier part of this chapter (*22.1–22.2,* pages 165–171).

22.3.2 'Invasion games' is a collective term applied to team games in which the objective is to attack and defend parts of the playing area with the aim of scoring more goals or points than the opposition. They include fast-moving activity, frequently involve physical contact and, in some games, hard implements. Consequently, the most common causes of accidents include:

- unintended collision with other players

- being struck by a hard implement or ball

- poor application of technique, such as when tackling.

### Association football/soccer

22.3.3 Halls with hazardous projections, unprotected windows, low-level mirrors or fixed equipment that encroaches onto the playing area should not be used for indoor football.

22.3.4 Care needs to be taken in maintaining **studded and bladed boots** to an appropriate safety standard.

22.3.5 **Shin pads** offer protection to the lower leg and should be worn for competitive matches and whenever there is a risk of injury.

22.3.6 **Goalposts** – fixed and portable - should not be improvised; they should comply with recognised safety standards and be made secure at all times.

> For further guidance, see *Portable goalposts (12.2.5–12.2.9, page 87)* in *Chapter 12: Equipment in Physical Education*.

### Basketball

22.3.7 The court surface should be clean, firm, dry and non-slip.

22.3.8 The court perimeter should be free from hazard with a safe zone of at least 1m around the edge. Protruding obstacles should be removed or made safe behind and in line with the backboards. Where this is impracticable, careful officiating and management of the situation is essential.

22.3.9 Backboards should have an overhang of 1.25m on match courts and 0.75m on practice courts.

22.3.10 Basketballs should be inflated correctly and be free from splits and tears.

22.3.11 Players should keep fingernails well trimmed.

### Gaelic games

22.3.12 In all hurling games and practice sessions, it is mandatory for all players up to and including under-21 grade to wear a helmet with a facial guard.

22.3.13 Gaelic Games Authority (GAA) policy with regard to the use of hurling helmets is that they should comply with IS 355 (ie the official hurling helmet specification that was set out by the National Standards Authority of Ireland [NSAI] in 2006).

### Handball

22.3.14 A safe, non-slip playing area should be maintained, particularly in attacking areas where perspiration from players making contact with the ground may constitute a hazard.

### Hockey

22.3.15 Playing surfaces – whether grass or synthetic – need to be true and flat.

22.3.16 Hockey sticks should be maintained in good condition and never used when damaged.

22.3.17 The type of ball used should take into account the nature of the playing surface and the capability of the players. For example, a softer ball is appropriate for hard playground surfaces.

22.3.18    Shin pads and mouth guards are highly recommended for match play and competitive practices and mandatory at junior representative level.

22.3.19    Goalkeepers need to be suitably equipped and protected with:

- pads and kickers

- gauntlet gloves

- body protectors

- a full helmet

- a throat guard.

They should also try to remain on their feet whenever possible.

22.3.20    Players should seek to develop and exercise good stick and ball control at all times.

22.3.21    Controlled pushing should be well established before the introduction of hitting.

### Lacrosse

22.3.22    Players should protect their hands and wrists with suitably padded gloves/gauntlets.

22.3.23    Head protection is recommended for men's lacrosse, but is not acceptable for women's lacrosse. Mouth guards are recommended in both versions of the game.

22.3.24    Goalkeepers should be suitably protected with protective equipment for both the head and body.

### Netball

22.3.25    There should be at least 2m of space between adjacent courts.

22.3.26    Posts need to be stable, with suitably weighted bases, where used, which should not project onto the court area.

22.3.27    During competitive matches, gloves may only be worn at the discretion of the umpire.

22.3.28    Players should keep fingernails short and well trimmed.

### Rugby football

22.3.29    A suitable playing surface is essential and should be soft enough to safely accommodate falls during tackles.

22.3.30    Goalpost uprights should be protected by padding.

22.3.31    Corner flags should be flexible and sufficiently high so as not to constitute a hazard to falling players.

22.3.32    Mouth guards are strongly recommended for all players at all levels and mandatory at junior representative level. The wearing of other forms of personal protection (eg shin pads, shoulder pads, padded helmets) should be encouraged following appropriate risk assessment.

22.3.33    Contact versions of the game should only be introduced and managed by suitably experienced staff and coaches following recognised teaching progressions, guidelines and NGB (Rugby Football Union [RFU] and Rugby Football League [RFL]) regulations.

22.3.34    Mixed-gender competition is generally suitable for children of primary age, but is not appropriate for secondary-age pupils.

## Net/wall and racket games

The information set out in this section should be read in conjunction with the general principles set out in the earlier part of this chapter (*22.1–22.2*, pages 165–171).

22.3.35    Net/wall and racket games are comparatively safe compared to other types of game but injuries do occur, predominantly involving eye damage. The most common causes of accidents include:

- being struck by a racket or fast-moving missile
- tripping or slipping
- collision with obstacles, equipment or another player
- crossing a court when in use.

### Badminton

22.3.36    There should be sufficient space on court to accommodate group practice and to avoid pupils playing over post bases.

22.3.37    Background lighting should permit clear visibility of the shuttle in flight.

22.3.38    Rackets with broken strings should not be used.

22.3.39    Nets should be in good condition and free from holes and tears.

22.3.40    Portable posts should be stored and positioned safely.

### Squash and racquetball

22.3.41    Squash is played in a confined area. A maximum of six pupils per court is recommended for coaching and practice sessions.

22.3.42    Safe procedures should be established for entering and leaving the court.

22.3.43    Players should only move on to doubles play when a high standard of singles play has been achieved.

22.3.44    Protective eye shields are advisable to protect from eye injury.

22.3.45    Short-lever rackets are recommended for beginners.

### Tennis

22.3.46    Broken wire surround fencing is particularly hazardous and pupils should maintain a safe distance until it is repaired.

22.3.47    When posts are removed, caps should be used to cover the holes, particularly on multi-use areas.

22.3.48    Lighter, shorter rackets and sponge balls, or other types of soft ball, are recommended where space is limited.

22.3.49    When pupils are practising serving, smashing or lobbing, safe procedures should be adopted. During service practice, there should be a maximum of six pupils behind the baseline. For smashing practice, feeders should be safely positioned, never directly in front of the player practising the smash. Waiting players should remain alert, off the court.

22.3.50    A court may be used safely by two groups for rallying purposes, although care needs to be taken by players moving backwards.

22.3.51    Players should be encouraged not to look round at a serving player, jump over a net or attempt to play strokes outside their designated playing area.

22.3.52    Courts should be arranged in the same direction of play in order to avoid the possibility of being hit by a ball from another game.

### Volleyball

22.3.53    All lights above the court should be guarded.

22.3.54    Weighted posts should be made secure by retaining wires to adjacent walls above head height; bases should not protrude onto the court.

22.3.55    Free-standing or weighted posts are not acceptable for competitive matches.

22.3.56    Players practising smashes or serves should be well spaced out and direct the ball to empty spaces on the court.

22.3.57    Balls should be rolled back during match play and carried back when both sides of the court are used for practice.

## Striking and fielding games

> The information set out in this section should be read in conjunction with the general principles set out in the earlier part of this chapter (22.1–22.2, pages 165–171).

22.3.58    Striking and fielding games involve throwing, running, bowling, catching and striking using an implement. Potential risk is increased when using a hard ball. The most common causes of accidents are:

- being unintentionally struck with a fast-moving hard ball
- being unintentionally struck with a bat or stick
- collision with another player or an item of equipment.

### Cricket

22.3.59    The wicket – grass or synthetic – should be reasonably true and well maintained.

22.3.60    Batters, wicketkeepers and fielders close to the bat should wear appropriate protective equipment, including helmets.

22.3.61    Rules administered by the cricket NGBs relating to close-in fielding by junior players should be strictly enforced.

22.3.62    Bowlers should bowl in a controlled order and always ensure that the batsman is fully ready.

22.3.63    Waiting batsmen should observe from a safe position.

22.3.64    Practice netting should be free of holes and tears, positioned so that players in adjacent areas are not at risk and preferably include roof netting.

22.3.65    Care needs to be taken when retrieving balls from the netting and should only happen when bowling has been halted.

### Rounders, softball and baseball

22.3.66    Running areas should be flat and free from hazard.

22.3.67    Rounders posts should be securely based, of appropriate height and have rounded tops.

22.3.68    Catching mitts/gloves should be worn as appropriate for baseball and softball.

22.3.69    The ball should not be pitched until all players are fully ready.

22.3.70    Rounders bats should be carried when running between bases and never thrown down.

22.3.71    Backstops should consider the use of head and body protection and always position themselves so as to avoid backswing.

## Target games

> The information set out in this section should be read in conjunction with the general principles set out in the earlier part of this chapter (*22.1–22.2*, pages 165–171).

22.3.72    Target games involve striking or projecting a missile, often at great speed, towards a designated area. Consequently, most accidents are caused by:

- other players, spectators or passers-by inadvertently wandering into the line of shot

- waiting players standing too close to the hitter and being struck by an implement.

### Archery

22.3.73    Archery in schools should always be organised and supervised by suitably qualified and experienced personnel. Advice on training, accreditation and safe procedure can be obtained from the NGB for archery, the Grand National Archery Society (GNAS).

### Golf

22.3.74    Golf activities should take place on a golf course or driving range.

22.3.75    When a net is being used for practice:

- a well-maintained special net with fine mesh that is at least 2.5m high and hangs clear of any supports should be used

- only light (airflow) balls should be used when pupils are practising on both sides of the net

- suitable protective mats should be used when indoors.

22.3.76  When practising in group situations, care needs to be taken to ensure that all players have sufficient space and can hit the ball in a safe direction.

22.3.77  Individual players should always ensure they have sufficient personal space around them to swing safely.

22.3.78  Balls should only be retrieved on a given signal after all players have completed their shots.

22.3.79  Careful supervision is essential to ensure that pupils' actions and behaviour do not create a hazard for other pupils.

## Other Game-type Activities

The information set out in this section should be read in conjunction with the general principles set out in the earlier part of this chapter (22.1–22.2, pages 165–171).

22.3.80  These activities – usually competitive in nature – are normally found in primary school and are frequently used as warm-up activities to develop speed, agility and spatial awareness. Accidents are commonly caused by:

- pupils inadvertently colliding with each other or an obstacle of some kind

- slipping or falling.

### Relay racing and tag games

22.3.81  Playing surfaces should be sound and dry.

22.3.82  Clear boundary markings are necessary for tag-type activity.

22.3.83  In relays, walls are unsuitable for turning points; lines and marker discs provide a safe alternative.

22.3.84  Highly challenging skills (eg running backwards at high speed) should only be practised with advanced performers.

## 22.4  What Pupils Should Know

22.4.1  Pupils should know:

- the importance of their role in risk assessment and management in relation to others, clothing, equipment and working/playing surfaces; they should understand the significant impact they can have by being aware, and making both staff and other pupils aware, of any safety concern they might encounter

- never to lose their temper and self-control in competitive situations

- the importance of adhering to rules and conventions relevant to each activity, in order to reduce levels of risk to themselves and others

- the vital role played by officials in maintaining a safe playing environment

- how PPE can help to minimise the risk of, but never completely protect them from, potential injury

- that games activities require significant levels of cooperation and communication with both teammates and opponents
- that effective non-verbal communication plays a vital role in ensuring everyone's safety; having agreed additional signals (eg for pupils who are hearing impaired) and making effective use of eye contact (eg before bowling or fielding a ball) can significantly reduce risk.

## 22.5    Additional Information

### Resources

Sport England (2007) *Comparative Sizes of Sports Pitches and Courts*. London: Sport England.
Available from: www.sportengland.org/comparative_sizes_003.pdf

### Useful websites

### Governing bodies of sport

### Invasion games

### Basketball

Basketball Scotland
www.basketball-scotland.com

Basketball Wales
www.basketballwales.com

England Basketball
www.englandbasketball.com

### Football

The Football Association
www.TheFA.com

The Football Association of Wales
www.faw.org.uk

The Irish Football Association
www.irishfa.com

The Scottish Football Association
www.scottishfa.co.uk

### Gaelic games

Gaelic Games Association
www.gaa.ie

### Handball

England Handball
www.englandhandball.com

Scottish Handball
www.scottishhandball.com

## Hockey

England Hockey
www.englandhockey.co.uk

Scottish Hockey
www.scottish-hockey.org.uk

Ulster Hockey
www.ulsterhockey.com

The Welsh Hockey Union
www.welsh-hockey.co.uk

## Lacrosse

English Lacrosse
www.englishlacrosse.co.uk

Lacrosse Scotland
www.scottish-lacrosse.org.uk

The Welsh Lacrosse Association
www.lacrossewales.com

## Netball

England Netball
www.england-netball.co.uk

Netball Scotland
www.netballscotland.com

The Welsh Netball Association
www.welshnetball.co.uk

## Rugby league

The Rugby Football League
www.rfl.uk.com

## Rugby union

The Rugby Football Union (England)
www.rfu.com

Scottish Rugby Union
www.sru.org.uk

Ulster Rugby Union
www.ulsterrugby.com

Welsh Rugby Union
www.wru.co.uk

# Net/wall and racket games

## Badminton

Badminton England
www.badmintonengland.co.uk

Badminton Ireland
www.badmintonireland.com

BADMINTONscotland
www.badmintonscotland.org.uk

Welsh Badminton
www.welshbadminton.net

## Squash

England Squash
www.englandsquash.com

Irish Squash
www.irishsquash.com

Scottish Squash
www.scottishsquash.org

Squash Wales
www.squashwales.co.uk

## Tennis

The Lawn Tennis Association (England)
www.lta.org.uk

Tennis Ireland
www.tennisireland.ie

Tennis Scotland
www.tennisscotland.org

## Volleyball

Northern Ireland Volleyball
www.nivb.com

The Scottish Volleyball Association
www.scottishvolleyball.org

Volleyball England
www.volleyballengland.org

# Striking and fielding games

## Baseball

BaseballSoftball UK
www.baseballsoftballuk.com

### Cricket

Cricket Scotland
www.cricketeurope4.net/SCOTLAND/home.shtml

Cricket Ireland
www.irishcricket.org

The England and Wales Cricket Board
www.ecb.co.uk

The Welsh Cricket Association
www.welshcricket.org

### Rounders

The National Rounders Association
www.nra-rounders.co.uk

## Target games

### Archery

The Grand National Archery Society
www.gnas.org

### Golf

The English Golf Union
www.englishgolfunion.org

The Golfing Union of Ireland
www.gui.ie

The Golf Union of Wales
www.golfunionwales.org

The Scottish Golf Union
wwwscottishgolfunion.org

## 22.6　Case Law Examples

22.6.1　Affutu-Nartay versus Clark and Another, Queen's Bench Division (1994):
*A 15-year-old pupil was tackled by a member of staff during a game of rugby and became temporarily paraplegic. The school was found to be in breach of its duty of care. The teacher was deemed to be negligent for taking a full participative role in the game.*

22.6.2　Bell versus Staffordshire County Council, Stoke-on-Trent County Court (2003):
*An eight-year-old girl suffered a nasty eye injury when struck by a tennis ball hit fiercely by a pupil playing on an adjacent court where the group had altered the direction of play on their court. The council was found liable for inadequate supervision and control, ie:*

- *The boys playing tennis ought to have been playing in the same direction as the girls.*

- *The games were too close in proximity.*

- *The boys' rackets were powerful enough to make such an accident foreseeable.*

22.6.3　Peacey versus Havering LA, Central London County Court (2000):
*A lunchtime supervisor lost an eye when hit by a badminton racket as she walked across the court, believing the game had finished. She was struck by a player (pupil) moving backwards. The claim for compensation was dismissed and the lunchtime supervisor judged not to have kept a proper lookout.*

22.6.4　Smolden versus Whitworth, Court of Appeal (1996):
*A referee allowed rugby scrums to regularly collapse without insisting on RFU rules being applied. A player in the front row of the scrum broke his neck when a scrum again collapsed. The referee was judged to be negligent for not applying the rules strictly and consistently.*

22.6.5　Condon versus Basi, Court of Appeal (1985):
*During a football match, a player made a late tackle on an opponent, breaking the opponent's leg. The case established that a player has a duty of care to an opponent not to recklessly cause injury outside the laws and spirit of the game.*

# Chapter twenty-three
## Gymnastic and Trampolining Activities

23

Although common safety principles apply across both activities, this chapter is divided into two sections, covering gymnastics in Part A and trampolining in Part B. It makes recommendations relating to key practice and equipment issues to assist safe delivery of gymnastic activity in schools.

> Please read the general guidance provided in Part 1 of this handbook, pages 9–131, before reading this chapter. This will help to ensure that you have a comprehensive awareness of safe-practice issues affecting gymnastics and trampolining activities and PESS in general.

## Part A:  Gymnastic Activities

### 23.1    Introduction

23.1.1    Gymnastic activity involves subjecting the body to a wide experience of movement challenges, which might include at various times managing the body in flight, climbing, hanging, descending, swinging, inverting and balancing, often at some distance from the ground, and rolling on sloping and narrow surfaces. The aim of gymnastic activity is to develop and refine a broad range of movement skills using the floor and large gymnastic apparatus.

23.1.2    It is recognised that work on apparatus provides a potentially more hazardous environment, with the majority of recorded incidents typically involving falls or misjudged descents from gymnastic equipment. However, work at a low level – on the floor or when using benches and mats – requires equally rigorous risk management.

23.1.3    Gymnastic activity in schools is characterised by two contrasting teaching and leaning styles that generate different considerations in terms of health and safety. Most primary schools deliver a curricular gymnastic-activity programme of study through a task-centred or **problem-solving approach**, building in some direct teaching where progress and safety issues require a specific focus. The ability of staff to set realistic and appropriate movement challenges based on the existing abilities of their pupils is key to safety in this approach. In secondary schools, partly reflecting the specialist physical-education training of the staff involved, there is often more recourse to direct instruction of recognised **formal gymnastic skills** associated with vaulting and agility, and trampolining, although not to the exclusion of task-centred content. A sound knowledge of technical progression relating to specified skills is essential to safe practice here.

23.1.4 Whatever the teaching approach, or combination of approaches, used, staff involved in the teaching of gymnastics should be appropriately trained since technique and effective body management are fundamental to safe performance. Training in task-centred gymnastics is usually located within the context of initial teacher education (ITE), supplemented, where necessary, through local authority (LA) professional development programmes and sometimes by the support of visiting specialist physical-education teachers. This is also the case with secondary physical-education specialists who may additionally benefit from acquiring national governing body (NGB) – British Gymnastics (BG) – coaching awards.

23.1.5 When staff wish to offer formal gymnastics – primary- or secondary-school-based – through an out-of-hours club, or when seeking to involve and prepare pupils for competitive involvement, an appropriate BG coaching award is strongly advised.

> **Note:** A BG Teacher Award does not accredit a member of school staff to coach within an external gymnastics club context.

## 23.2  What Staff Should Know

### People

23.2.1 Staff and coaches teaching gymnastics should be appropriately trained and qualified to do so. Any identified lack of confidence or competence should be addressed through a suitable programme of professional development.

23.2.2 Staff should only work at a level in gymnastics at which they feel comfortable about their **own expertise** and are able to effectively plan, deliver and evaluate the gymnastics programme.

23.2.3 Wherever practicable, pupils should be involved in the management of risk in gymnastics and provision needs to be made for this to become part of the learning process. They should clearly understand the range and nature of movement activity that different gymnastics equipment is designed to facilitate and to apply this knowledge effectively.

23.2.4 Pupils should understand the importance of **body preparation**. Becoming stronger and more flexible will not only enhance performance but will also reduce the likelihood of injury.

### Context

23.2.5 The **working surface** should be clean, free from obstruction or hazard, and non-slip. It should be subjected to a systematic and regular maintenance programme. This is particularly important where the facility is multi-purpose and used for additional activities outside the physical education-programme.

> For general information on facilities, see *Chapter 15: Buildings and Facilities*, pages 103–110.

23.2.6 There should be **sufficient space** and equipment to match the needs of the group. In order to ensure safe practice, strategies may need to be employed to accommodate large groups working in limited space through alternating periods of observation with practical involvement.

23.2.7 Gymnastics **apparatus** should conform to appropriate standards (eg BSI, BS EN). It needs to be stored safely and be readily accessible. Prior to the commencement of activity, staff should ensure it is safe to use and, over the longer term, is subject to an annual specialist inspection.

> For more information on this issue, see *Gymnastic apparatus (12.2.14–12.2.15, pages 88–89)* in *Chapter 12: Equipment in Physical Education.*

23.2.8 On no account must defective equipment be used. It needs to be clearly labelled as such and, wherever possible, securely stored. Equipment that is judged to be irreparable should be safely and immediately disposed of.

23.2.9 Care needs to be taken when using **mats** in gymnastics, particularly with regard to their placement. There is a concern that when an informed decision is made to use mats as a precautionary measure (eg pupils are working at a height, using climbing frames or ropes), it may encourage some pupils to work beyond their capabilities. It is essential that all pupils fully understand the purpose as well as the protective limitations of mats used in this way and never develop a false sense of security through their presence. In this sense, particular care needs to be taken with pupils who consistently display poor discipline, are known to be hyperactive or suffer from attention deficit hyperactivity disorder (ADHD). In such cases, the activity of pupils at greater risk may have to be modified or limited in the interests of their own safety and that of their peers.

> For more information on mats and their use in gymnastics, see *Mats (12.2.16–12.2.24, pages 90–91)* in *Chapter 12: Equipment in Physical Education.*

23.2.10 **Clothing** for gymnastics should allow free, unrestricted movement without being loose. Very loose clothing may snag on equipment and cause injury. Footwear needs to be light and flexible (eg gymnastic slippers or plimsolls), enabling pupils to 'feel' the movement. Taking part in bare feet can enhance aesthetic awareness, providing working surfaces are acceptably clean and free from hazard.

23.2.11 Training shoes with thick, inflexible soles are not suitable for work in gymnastics and pupils should never participate in **socks** on polished surfaces. Well-fitting socks may be acceptable on a carpeted surface if traction is not affected.

23.2.12 Long hair should be tied back and all personal effects removed before activity commences.

> For more information on these issues, see *Chapter 14: Clothing and Personal Effects,* pages 99–102.

## Organisation

23.2.13 Comprehensive and progressive schemes of work should inform and encourage a consistency of approach, and give direction to the work in gymnastics. Such schemes should be subject to periodic review and updated in the light of emerging practice, ongoing risk assessments and accident reports.

23.2.14 **Curricular gymnastic sessions** should typically involve four phases:

a. a warm-up undertaken as a whole-class activity

b. development and/or consolidation of particular skills or movement tasks using the floor or mats

c.  application of the skills, focused on an apparatus setting or progressed through partner/group work

d.  individual cool-down.

23.2.15    **Differentiated practice**, taking into account the varying abilities and progress of individual pupils, provides the basis for safe and successful learning. Skills already learned will need to be revisited on a regular basis and frequent **consolidation** should be a feature of planning. Care needs to be taken with pupils who have experienced a prolonged absence and whenever units of gymnastic activity are punctuated by long periods of time. A record of attendance, work covered and pupil achievement will help to ensure suitable progression and appropriate challenge.

23.2.16    **Training schedules** designed to support pupils involved in competitive gymnastics need to ensure their well-being. Care needs to be taken that the frequency, intensity and duration of the training sessions reflect the physical and mental maturity of those involved. Injuries to young gymnasts frequently have their origins in fatigue and lack of concentration. Whenever pupils display any sign of physiological or psychological tiredness, staff should be prepared to stop, or modify, the activity.

23.2.17    It is considered good practice for pupils from the earliest ages to be involved as much as possible in the movement and assembling of **apparatus**. It is essential that pupils are given clear instruction about safe lifting techniques and how to cooperate effectively with others in the process of setting out apparatus.

> For more information on this issue, see *Gymnastic apparatus (12.2.14–12.2.15, pages 88–89)* in *Chapter 12: Equipment in Physical Education.*

23.2.18    On no account should any gymnastics session ever be left unsupervised. In the event of an emergency, all gymnastic activity needs to cease immediately until the member of staff/coach is able to resume acceptable levels of supervision.

23.2.19    Effective communication between the class teacher and any support staff is essential and time should be allocated for joint planning activity. Each should understand their respective roles in ensuring a well-structured and disciplined working environment.

23.2.20    In the case of more **complex skills** (eg rotational vaulting activities), physical support may be necessary to carry out movements safely, usually to prevent under- or over-rotation. Pupils need to be clearly informed about the manner and purpose of such support, which should always follow accepted and common practice. Staff will need to have been appropriately trained in support technique and be equipped with a good understanding of the body mechanics involved.

23.2.21    In the event of an accident during a gymnastics session, all activity should cease immediately and emergency procedures be enacted. It is essential that a clear record of the incident is completed as soon as possible after the event in order to inform future practice.

> For more information on this issue, see *Chapter 8: Accident Procedures and First-aid Management,* pages 49–54.

## 23.3    What Pupils Should Know

23.3.1    Pupils should know:

- that concentration levels need to be kept high during gymnastic activity, with clear focus and attention maintained throughout the session

- they need to remain vigilant when working on apparatus and to alert staff immediately to any concerns relating to the safety and stability of apparatus

- the importance of working effectively and responsibly as a team when assembling, setting out and putting away apparatus, or when producing joint movement sequences with others

- how to lift and move pieces of apparatus safely, using accepted techniques

- they should work within their personal limits and capabilities, always seeking advice and support from staff in areas of uncertainty

- that body preparation, practice and consolidation are essential in gymnastics to acquire reliable technique, confidence and freedom from injury

- never to work or practise in an unsupervised setting in gymnastics

- that personal attire for gymnastics has to meet health-and-safety requirements for safe participation

- that good technique is the key to safe practice and the protective capacity of mats, mattresses and pads is limited

- that different pieces of apparatus, including mats, have specific and different functions in developing skilled activity and performance needs to comply with these expectations.

## Part B:  Trampolining Activities

## 23.4    Introduction

23.4.1    Trampolining can offer a challenging and developmental gymnastic experience to pupils of all abilities, including those with special educational needs (SEN). Trampolines and trampettes, however, have proved to be unforgiving pieces of equipment in the absence of adequate control of body movement by performers at all levels. Great care needs to be taken to ensure the well–being of all pupils who participate in this popular and exciting activity. Because of the highly technical nature of trampolining and the potential risks associated with rebound jumping, trampolining and trampettes are not considered suitable for use in primary schools.

## 23.5    What Staff Should Know

### People

23.5.1    School staff/coaches involved in teaching or coaching trampolining should be **appropriately trained**. They should be knowledgeable about the basic skills and techniques of jumping, and understand the biomechanics of the moves they teach. Even the basic skill of feet-to-feet jumping involves a number of fundamental requirements that should be understood, taught and learned so that full control of the body can be maintained.

23.5.2    School staff/coaches who wish to teach or coach trampolining at a more advanced level (eg forwards and backwards rotational movement in a horizontal plane) or to enter pupils in competitions should attend courses organised or approved by **BG** and be appropriately qualified, with at least a Level 2 coaching award or BG Trampoline Teacher's Award.

23.5.3    Pupils should share in the assessment and management of the risks associated with trampolining activities. This is an essential part of the learning process. Due to differentiation in abilities, the risk-management process should be applied to individual pupils, pupil groups and the class as a whole.

## Context

### Facility

23.5.4    Trampolining equipment should be sited well away from walls, fire exits and overhead obstructions. In sports halls, it should generally be separated by drawn netting from any other activities taking place.

23.5.5    The ceiling should be at least 5m high for curriculum and recreational purposes and at least 8m for competition.

> For general information on facilities management, see *Chapter 15: Buildings and Facilities,* pages 103–110.

### Equipment

23.5.6    The procedure for positioning, assembling and folding trampolines should be systematic and deliberate. It should always be undertaken by at least two trained staff or, where pupils are mature and strong enough to assist, under the close supervision of qualified staff ready to give immediate hands-on assistance whenever necessary. It requires closely coordinated teamwork in which the roles of individual pupils are clearly understood and implemented. Injuries may occur during this exercise, mainly when the end of the trampoline frame has been opened or folded, but has not been held with sufficient force to counter the tension caused by the springs.

23.5.7    During use, the roller stands should be placed in a secure manner well away from the working area.

23.5.8    Two trampolines may be positioned end to end, with a large weight-absorbing mattress covering the frames and frame pads at the adjoining ends. Non-slip mats of a suitable thickness and consistency should be placed around the frame and should not impede the movement of spotters or performers accessing or dismounting from the trampoline bed. It is accepted practice for weight-absorbing mattresses to be placed on the ends of trampolines, providing they are suitably supported by 'end decks'.

> For more information on mats, see *Mats (12.2.16–12.2.19,* page 90) in *Chapter 12: Equipment in Physical Education.*

23.5.9    The metal frame and springs or cables of trampolines should be covered by fixed **coverall pads** which should be regularly checked for wear and tear.

23.5.10 **Spotters** as an additional line of defence may be positioned one or two at each side, plus one at each end, unless end weight-absorbing mattresses are provided, in which case spotters will only be needed at the sides. It is essential that anybody required to spot is suitably mature, strong enough and effectively trained to do so.

> For further guidance on spotting, see *Appendix 7: Summary of British Gymnastics' Advice on the Use of Spotting,* page 331.

23.5.11 An **overhead support rig** may be used to teach pupils movements involving rotations or twists on the trampoline. The supporter (usually an adult) should be competent in using the rig, and capable of holding the weight and controlling the descent of a pupil. Care should be taken to ensure that the centre of the trampoline is vertically aligned with the centre of the rig. The BG 'Use of a Trampoline Rig' course is recommended for staff using rigs.

23.5.12 Damaged trampolines and trampettes should **never** be used until they have been repaired or replaced.

> For general guidance on trampolining equipment, see *Trampolines and trampettes (12.2.27–12.2.29,* pages 91–92) in *Chapter 12: Equipment in Physical Education.*

## Clothing and personal effects

23.5.13 Clothing for trampolining is similar to that worn for gymnastics, except that non-slip socks or trampolining slippers are necessary to prevent pupils slipping and to prevent their toes entering gaps in the webbing when they make contact with the trampoline bed. Cotton and wool socks are suitable but nylon socks on a webbed nylon bed are unlikely to provide adequate traction. A long-sleeved top is advisable to prevent friction burns to the forearms when performing front drops.

23.5.14 Before trampolining sessions start, long hair should be tied back and nails trimmed. All personal effects (eg jewellery, watches) should be removed or the situation made safe if they cannot be removed. Injuries, some serious, have occurred in the past when these requirements have not been met.

> For general guidance on these issues, see *Chapter 14: Clothing and Personal Effects,* pages 99–102.

## Organisation

23.5.15 As for gymnastics, written schemes of work are necessary to ensure that skills are taught in a logical sequence, using appropriate progressions.

23.5.16 A record of attendance could be kept, together with a record of the skills and tasks covered, and the levels of performance attained. This will enable effective progression and inform other staff of pupils' capabilities.

23.5.17 Gradual, step-by-step **progression** over time should be provided, with the emphasis on basic skills, correct techniques and quality of movement. Pupils should be dissuaded from making over-rapid progress and taking unnecessary risks. Basic skills should be learned and consolidated in isolation before being combined into sequences.

23.5.18 Some pupils may wish to progress beyond basic jumping to more exciting moves involving rotation (eg back drops, front drops and somersaults). Not all pupils will be capable of doing so; those that are should first demonstrate that their basic straight jumps are well consolidated. Trampolining accidents frequently occur when pupils try to progress too quickly before they have mastered basic skills. It is important to resist pressure from pupils to move on to the next stage before they are ready to do so.

23.5.19    During **competitions or displays**, pupils should only perform movements that they have successfully practised and consolidated during training. It is not acceptable for pupils to be put at risk by changing their sequences in a bid for higher marks during a competition.

## Accidents

23.5.20    Trampolining accidents should be very rare if the activity is taught well and pupils learn sound techniques that enable them to exercise good control. However, accidents do occasionally happen, usually as a result of:

- unfolding or folding the trampoline (resulting in arms or fingers becoming trapped)
- landing awkwardly on the trampoline bed and placing a hand down ahead of the body (resulting in a broken arm).

23.5.21    Falling from trampolines does not happen very often and is unlikely if competent spotters and weight-absorbing mattresses are in place. Very **serious injuries** have resulted from landing inverted during an attempted rotating movement so that the head strikes the bed and the neck is either hyperflexed or hyperextended on impact (causing a potential neck fracture and/or spinal damage).

23.5.22    The procedure in the event of an accident is the same as for gymnastics. In the case of a suspected **spinal injury**, the injured pupil should be kept as still as possible on the trampoline bed until expert medical help arrives, since any movement may exacerbate the damage caused.

> For general guidance on these issues, see *Chapter 8: Accident Procedures and First-aid Management,* pages 49–54.

## Procedures

23.5.23    Subject to employers' requirements, staff with suitable trampolining qualifications should always be present when trampolining activities take place in schools, whether during curriculum time or as a school-sport activity. On no account should pupils ever be left unsupervised. If the qualified person is called away from the session for any urgent reason, all trampolining activities need to stop immediately, the trampoline(s) should be folded to prevent unauthorised jumping and an alternative supervised activity provided.

23.5.24    With suitable qualifications and experience, it is possible to supervise several trampolines at once. When this is the case, it is important to observe all the activities taking place so that intervention and advice may be provided when necessary. At such times, pupils should only practise and consolidate skills that they can already perform correctly and confidently unless they are working under the direct supervision of a member of staff.

23.5.25    Beginners with little or no previous experience, or pupils who are learning new skills, should always be directly supervised.

23.5.26    Appropriate **warm-up** exercises, similar to those for gymnastics, should be carried out at the start of trampolining sessions. Initial jumping should also contribute to body warm-up.

23.5.27    Only one pupil at a time should normally be allowed on the trampoline. Work should only begin when everyone is appropriately positioned and ready. The pupil should rebound in a position as near to the centre of the bed as possible, at a height at which he/she is able to maintain complete control.

23.5.28    If **loss of control** is experienced, the pupil performing should flex at the knee and hip joints during the very next contact of the feet with the bed. This will effectively deaden the jumping. Following discussion on how and why control was lost, and what measures should be taken to address the problem, the pupil should return to the centre of the bed and recommence work.

23.5.29    Beginners should work for periods of around 30 seconds. This time can be gradually extended (up to one minute), but pupils should stop jumping immediately if they begin to tire or lose concentration.

23.5.30    It is accepted practice to provide support for pupils who need it when learning movements on the trampoline. Staff should be suitably trained and skilled in accepted **support methods** (eg using overhead support rigs or throw-in mattresses).

23.5.31    Pupils should understand, and be constantly reminded of, the disciplined approach required when trampolining. Pupils need to remain vigilant at all times, regardless of whether they are jumping on the trampoline or spotting for others.

23.5.32    Trampolining skills are very specific and should be taught correctly from the very start. Basic straight jumping may appear simple and straightforward, but this can be deceptive. There is little room for trial and error in teaching and learning trampolining skills. Pupils should be taught how to jump correctly and what to do by way of immediate remedial action if they begin to move away from the centre of the bed. This will nearly always mean stopping, returning to the middle and recommencing jumping.

23.5.33    Pupils should appreciate the importance of using the correct techniques in order to **maintain control** when jumping, and understand that loss of control can result in injury. Total concentration is necessary when jumping and spotting for others, since incidents tend to happen very suddenly and require a swift response.

23.5.34    Pupils acting as **spotters** may sometimes be tempted to give vocal encouragement to the pupil jumping. This can be distracting for the jumper, affecting their concentration and causing loss of control, and should not be permitted. Discussions should only take place between phases of jumping.

23.5.35    **Tag-on-type games**, in which pupils in turn add a movement to the sequence or routine of the previous pupil, are not recommended. They may encourage pupils to jump beyond their abilities.

23.5.36    Pupils should be constantly monitored for signs of **fatigue**. Those displaying any symptoms (eg deterioration in the quality of performance and/or loss of concentration or persistent travel) must stop immediately and rest.

## Trampettes

23.5.37    Because of the specialist nature of the activity and the potential risks associated with rebound jumping, trampolines and trampettes are not recommended for use in primary schools.

23.5.38  Particular care needs to be taken when using trampettes in secondary schools. Basic trampette skills are the same as those for trampolining, except that forward travel occurs and landing takes place on a thick weight-absorbing mattress (or mattresses). Following the guidance below will promote safe practice:

a.  Appropriate footwear should be worn when using trampettes with webbed beds.

b.  Basic jumping skills using a double-foot take-off should be well developed before progressing to the trampette.

c.  Beginners should approach a trampette in an unhurried and controlled manner, using just a few paces.

d.  When a trampette is used as part of one activity within a gymnastics session, close attention should be paid to the performance of basic trampette skills. Observation and control of the class as a whole should be maintained.

e.  Each trampette skill should be thoroughly practised, learned and consolidated before progressing to the next.

f.  Support should be provided that is appropriate to the skill being practised. It should provide a physical check for pupils as they land, preventing them from pitching forwards or falling backwards. Responsible, mature pupils may be trained to provide support.

g.  Rotational skills in the horizontal and vertical plane during flight from a trampette are potentially dangerous and should never be attempted by beginners. The same applies to forward rolls after landing.

h.  Special care needs to be taken when teaching somersault actions, which should only be undertaken by pupils who are judged to have the potential ability to complete them successfully and who have mastered basic skills. Direct supervision is required.

i.  Somersault actions are most safely taught on a trampoline using an overhead support rig. When transferred to a trampette, competent support to counter possible under-rotation or over-rotation should always be provided until the movements have been thoroughly consolidated.

j.  The use of standard single trampettes is recommended. The use of double trampettes (where two or more jumps precede the final action of flight and landing) is only suitable for advanced performers.

k.  It is recommended that trampettes are not used during vaulting activities, as pupils who are not specifically trained in their use find it difficult to cope with the added height and rotation produced by the trampette.

## 23.6    What Pupils Should Know

23.6.1  Pupils should know:

- **never** to attempt to unfold or fold a trampoline on their own or without supervision

- that appropriate footwear – trampoline shoes or non-nylon socks – should be worn if there is a danger of their toes going through the bed

- **never** to trampoline alone; trampolining should always be supervised

- that they should always concentrate fully when performing or spotting

- the importance of taking care when leaving the bed and dismounting slowly, always stepping directly from the bed onto the frame

- that they need to beware of fatigue; it is recommended that intermediate jumpers bounce for no longer than a minute and less than this for beginners.

## 23.7 Additional Information

> For further guidance on spotting, see *Appendix 7: Summary of British Gymnastics' Advice on the Use of Spotting*, page 331.
>
> For an exemplar risk assessment, see *Appendix 2E: Example Risk Assessment of Primary Gymnastics*, page 302.

### Useful websites

British Gymnastics
www.british-gymnastics.org

## 23.8 Case Law Examples

23.8.1    Heffer versus Wiltshire County Council, Devizes County Court (1996):
*A pupil was injured in a gymnastic lesson while attempting a straddle vault over a buck. The class had progressed from leapfrog with support to the buck, where support was withdrawn if not requested by pupils. The pupil was hesitant and managed initially to successfully clear the buck using a one-foot take-off. In finding for the claimant, the court judged that the pupil was supported throughout the leapfrog activity so support should not have been withdrawn on the buck; it should not have been left to the pupil to 'opt in' for support (peer-group pressure may have prevented opting in), reduction in support was judged to be premature and total rather than gradual and it was deemed that progression to the buck constituted a new activity requiring a continuation of support.*

23.8.2    Villella versus North Bedfordshire Borough Council, Queen's Bench (1983):
*A young girl trampolining in bare feet caught her toe in the webbing and fractured her femur. The claim for damages was upheld.*

23.8.3    Kenyon versus Lancashire County Council, Oldham County Court (2001):
*A pupil was injured performing a back drop on a trampoline. She claimed incorrect tuition and succeeded in the claim. Care needs to be taken when teaching technical skills.*

# Chapter twenty-four
## Health-related Exercise

# 24

This chapter defines the nature of health-related exercise and identifies a range of considerations and procedures to assist effective and safe planning and delivery of this key area of the curriculum.

> Please read the general guidance provided in Part 1 of this handbook, pages 9–131, before reading this chapter. This will help to ensure that you have a comprehensive awareness of safe-practice issues affecting health-related exercise and PESS in general.

## 24.1    Introduction

24.1.1    Health-related exercise is physical activity associated with health enhancement and disease prevention. Health-related exercise in schools involves the teaching of knowledge and understanding, motor and behavioural skills, and the development of positive attitudes and confidence associated with lifelong participation in physical activity.

24.1.2    This section contains general guidance that applies to all forms of health-related exercise, including specific 'health-and-fitness' activities, such as aerobics, step, skipping, circuit training, weight training and fitness testing. Health-and-fitness activities are growing in popularity in schools and are important in terms of their links with the recreational habits of young adults.

24.1.3    Children and young people should be encouraged and helped to maintain or improve their own health and engage in regular physical activity. In particular, they should be assisted in meeting the current physical-activity recommendations for children and young people, which involve participating:

- in physical activity of at least **moderate intensity** (this is equivalent to brisk walking) for **an hour a day** (ie 60 minutes accumulated during the day)

- at least twice a week in activities that help to enhance and maintain muscular strength and flexibility and bone health.

## 24.2    What Staff Should Know

### People

24.2.1    Staff contributing to the delivery of health-and-fitness aspects of the curriculum (such as aerobics, circuits, multigym sessions and weight training) should have newly qualified teacher (NQT)/qualified teacher status (QTS) and/or a relevant fitness qualification and/or professional development from a recognised trainer (eg YMCA Fitness Industry Training). Supervising adults utilising fitness facilities with pupils should ensure they are familiar with the safe use of the equipment and are appropriately inducted in the use of any new, unfamiliar equipment.

## Context

24.2.2     The venue for health-and-fitness activities (eg fitness room, gymnasium, dance studio) should be **hazard-free** and **conducive to safe participation and effective learning**. There should be sufficient space for pupils to exercise safely. A matted floor area or mats should be used for strength and endurance exercises and stretches performed in sitting or lying positions.

> For general guidance on facilities, see *Chapter 15: Buildings and Facilities, pages 103–110.*

24.2.3     Specialist facilities (eg fitness room) should be secure and have systems in place to guard against inappropriate access and usage. Pupils should **never work unsupervised** in fitness facilities. Fitness equipment (eg dumb-bells, bars, pins, collars) should be stored safely and securely when not in use. Pupils should be taught how to safely store fitness equipment.

24.2.4     Some activities, such as aerobics and circuits, are often delivered to large groups or whole classes. The selection of actions/exercises in the session and the instructions should take into consideration the space available and the numbers involved to ensure that all pupils can **move safely and effectively** without colliding with each other or with equipment.

24.2.5     Fitness equipment (eg multigym equipment, free weights) needs to be maintained in good condition. It should be **checked regularly** and repaired or replaced, as appropriate. Maintenance should be carried out by suitably qualified contractors.

24.2.6     Equipment used should be **compatible with the age, size, strength, ability and experience of the participating groups and individuals**. For example, there should be a range of different weights from which pupils can select, and it should be possible to adjust multigym equipment to suit individuals of different shapes and sizes. Older secondary pupils should be taught how to make these adjustments and how to use the equipment safely.

> For general guidance on equipment, see *Chapter 12: Equipment in Physical Education, pages 85–93.*

24.2.7     Clothing should be appropriate. It should allow **free, unrestricted movement** but should not be so loose that it inhibits or hinders movement or could catch on any equipment being used. **Supportive footwear** should be worn when performing high-impact and vigorous cardiovascular activities (eg skipping, star jumps, step ups) and when using fixed or free weights.

> For general guidance on clothing, see *Chapter 14: Clothing and Personal Effects, pages 99–102.*

24.2.8     The chewing of food, sweets or gum during health-related exercise sessions should never be allowed. Chewing can result in choking, which can have serious, even fatal, consequences.

## Organisation

24.2.9     Staff contributing to the delivery of the curriculum should be clear about the progressive learning to be developed within health-and-fitness activities, and know how to involve pupils in their own learning (eg through student-centred teaching approaches) and how to assess and record their achievement and attainment.

24.2.10 Staff should review medical records to **identify pupils at risk** from vigorous or strenuous activity (eg low fit, low active, obese, asthmatic) and be able to offer individuals modified or alternative activities. Pupils who are unwell or recovering from a recent illness should avoid exercise until they have fully recovered and feel well.

24.2.11 Staff should be informed about the appropriateness of specific exercises and avoid those considered to be controversial or contraindicated (eg straight-legged sit-ups, standing toe touches, deep knee bends) which expose major joints to unnecessary risk. Instead, they should **offer safe alternatives** to achieve the desired outcomes.

24.2.12 Staff should know how to adapt tasks/exercises to ensure they are **appropriate to the developmental stage of the pupils** and involve every child. For example, they should be able to offer different versions of an exercise at varying intensities (eg knee lifts with and without jumps, box and full-length push-ups). This will provide pupils with opportunities to select tasks compatible with their own health, activity and fitness status, and to use this as a personal baseline for improvement over time.

24.2.13 Staff should ensure their instructions and teaching points can be heard over the volume of any music they are using.

24.2.14 Careful thought should be given to the frequency, intensity and duration of exercise, particularly when working with prepubescent pupils. Factors associated with physiological immaturity and growth spurts place limits on training overload. **Physical demands should gradually progress over time and reflect individual proficiency**. Staff should emphasise the importance of developing efficient technique and should be aware of the potential dangers resulting from poor technique, progressing too quickly, and irregular participation.

24.2.15 The teaching of health-and-fitness activities should follow a **carefully planned and graduated progression**. For example, pupils should learn a variety of muscular strength and endurance exercises that use their own body weight (eg curl ups) or use light resistance equipment (eg low-weight dumb-bells) prior to performing similar, but more complex exercises using fixed equipment (eg multigym equipment).

24.2.16 Pupils should be deemed competent at performing exercises in their own time (eg continuous curl ups) prior to being asked to perform them at speed (eg performing as many curl ups as possible in one minute). Careful monitoring is required of participants performing exercises at speed, as control and technique could be lost, risking injury. In terms of safety and effectiveness, **quality is more important than quantity.**

24.2.17 Education relating to diet and nutrition, and achieving and maintaining a healthy body weight should be **delivered sensitively** and should take account of body-image problems experienced by some pupils. Pupils should be encouraged to be 'in shape', rather than a particular size or shape. A healthy, balanced diet and an active lifestyle should be promoted, in line with current recommendations from the relevant country's department of health.

24.2.18 Within the curriculum, the focus of health-and-fitness activities should be on learning and inclusion. Over time, every pupil should develop identifiable knowledge, understanding and skills associated with a particular activity. Within curriculum time, it is not appropriate for pupils to engage in drill-like workouts without any identified learning taking place.

## 24.3 Further Guidance Relating to Specific Activities

### Preparation for and recovery from physical activity

24.3.1 Physical-education lessons should include **safe preparation for and recovery from physical activity**. This involves performing activities of gradually increasing intensity as part of a warm-up and gradually decreasing intensity within a cool-down. Exercises designed to enhance mobility and flexibility should form part of the warm-up and cool-down. Effective preparation and recovery include activities that are specifically related to the demands of, and skills inherent in, the main activity and involve appropriate selection of mobility exercises, cardiovascular activities and stretches that relate to the joints, energy systems and muscles associated with the activity.

24.3.2 Pupils should demonstrate a good understanding of procedures associated with safe participation, such as knowing the importance of warming up in terms of effective physical and psychological preparation for activity. They should know that an effective **warm-up** commences with low-intensity, low-impact activities related to the main activity followed by gradually more energetic activities and static stretches of the major muscle groups associated with the activity. The stretches should not be performed until the muscles involved feel warm and they should be held still for 6–10 seconds.

24.3.3 Pupils should also know that an effective **cool-down** comprises activities that gradually decrease in intensity, finishing with low-intensity, low-impact activities followed by static stretches of the major muscle groups worked in the activity. The stretches should be held still and for longer than in the warm-up (up to 30 seconds).

24.3.4 Dynamic flexibility involves repeatedly lengthening muscles (as opposed to holding them still in a lengthened position, as in static stretching). There is some debate about the relative benefits of different types of flexibility. However, the research is equivocal and does not provide sufficiently robust evidence to warrant changing current good practice, which recommends static stretching with pupils in curriculum time. All pupils should be taught to **stretch statically with good technique**. Dynamic flexibility often requires participants to have good body awareness, coordination, balance and control and is therefore only considered suitable for use with young people with these attributes.

24.3.5 Pupils should share in the assessment and management of the risks associated with health-related exercise. For example, they should be involved in designing, conducting and evaluating their own and others' preparation for and recovery from activity. To do this effectively, pupils need to be taught the required knowledge base over time and given regular opportunities to plan and perform parts of warm-ups and cool-downs (eg performing mobility exercises for the joints used in the activity and suggesting the muscles which need to be stretched for the particular activity).

### Resistance exercise (including weight-bearing activities, body-weight exercises, weight training and weightlifting)

24.3.6 Resistance exercise, in the form of weight- or load-bearing activities, is recommended for pupils of all ages. Resistance exercise should be part of a balanced physical-education programme.

24.3.7 Primary-school children should be involved in a wide range of weight-bearing activities for both the upper body (eg climbing, throwing, pushing, pulling) and the lower body (eg running, jumping, hopping, skipping).

24.3.8 Older primary-school children (aged 9–11 years) can additionally be involved in **developmentally appropriate** low-level exercises involving their own body weight, such as curl ups (eg with legs bent and hands reaching towards feet) for the abdominal (tummy) muscles and push-ups (eg against a wall or in a box position) for muscles in the arms and chest.

24.3.9 The use of specific fitness equipment with primary-school children is neither essential nor desirable; they can instead be involved in a broad and balanced range of physical activities to develop their physical competence and self-confidence and to promote positive attitudes towards physical activity.

24.3.10 Secondary-school children can safely use low-to-medium-resistance external weights (eg light dumb-bells, elastics and tubing). The use of medium-to-high-resistance external weights (eg as is possible with fixed equipment, such as multigym equipment, dumb-bells and barbells) is advisable only with older secondary-age children (age 14–18 years). The focus should initially be on endurance work in which the number of repetitions performed is gradually increased.

24.3.11 Lifting heavy loads or near-maximal weights is appropriate only for young people aged 16–18 years who have reached the final stage of maturation. A **systematic record should be maintained** for pupils involved in progressive resistance-exercise programmes to ensure that the rate of progression is appropriate.

24.3.12 Resistance exercise in the form of weight training and weightlifting should always be supervised. **Pupils should never be allowed to weight train or weightlift on their own.** All pupils should receive instruction in how to use weights with correct technique. Light, easily manageable weights should be used prior to gradually progressing over time to heavier weights.

24.3.13 Weightlifting is fundamentally a test of strength, usually within a competitive setting, whereas weight training is concerned with the development of muscular strength and endurance associated with health-and-fitness goals. Weightlifting includes Olympic lifts, strength tests and other competitive work with barbells and dumb-bells.

24.3.14 Weightlifting can be hazardous for post-pubescent pupils as the risk of joint and spine injuries is high. Overloading should be avoided and competitive lifting should be delayed until skeletal growth is complete. During weightlifting competitions, post-pubescent pupils should not lift weights that are heavier than their body weight. Their performance should preferably be judged on the style of lift, rather than the amount of weight lifted. A safe weightlifting environment requires a focus on trained, alert spotters.

24.3.15 As the risk of injury is high, **weightlifting should only be taught by adults with a specific qualification in the activity**. A minimum requirement for teaching weightlifting in schools is a British Weightlifting Association (BWLA) teaching or coaching award.

## Fitness Testing

24.3.16 If conducting fitness testing, it is advisable to perform a thorough and relevant warm-up before fitness tests and a cool-down afterwards. For example, prior to performing a 'sit and reach' flexibility test, participants should ensure their body is warm, especially their hamstring and lower-back muscles. A shorter, gentler warm-up may be appropriate for tests that begin slowly and increase in intensity gradually.

24.3.17    Some fitness tests, such as the Multistage Fitness Test (also known as the 'bleep test') and the Abdominal Curl Conditioning Test are maximal, in the sense that they require participants to exercise to exhaustion. These tests were initially designed for use with elite adult populations and are very challenging. Consequently, they are problematic to use with groups of children for the following reasons:

a.  They can impose inappropriate physiological demands on developing and immature bodily systems.

b.  Self-imposed and peer pressure can encourage participants to exercise beyond safe limits and to suffer disorientation, lack of control of their actions and severe fatigue.

c.  **Screening** of participants is required prior to such tests to ensure that only those with good health take part.

d.  **Close and continuous monitoring** of participants is essential to ensure they can cope with the demands of the test.

In addition, fitness testing can be offputting for some children (often the least healthy, fit and active) and children's fitness-test scores from field tests are, at best, only an indicator of their fitness and do not closely reflect their activity levels. Given these limitations, it is recommended that any fitness testing included within the curriculum:

- is part of an educational programme of study (in which pupils learn about the components of fitness and their links with health and activity)
- is a positive experience for all pupils
- is personalised (with individual scores from which to improve)
- promotes involvement in physical activity.

In order to achieve the latter, schools should also monitor pupils' activity levels, as well as, or even instead of, their fitness.

24.3.18    Time/distance runs (eg running as far as possible in six minutes or running as fast as possible over one mile) and timed muscular strength and endurance tests (eg performing as many push-ups as possible in one minute) are also maximal tests but they differ significantly from the Multistage Fitness Test and Abdominal Curl Conditioning Test in that they permit pupils to pace themselves during the time or distance allowed. Pupils should be advised to pace themselves in order for the experience to be more comfortable and manageable.

24.3.19    Timed tests and sub-maximal tests (eg step-up tests) are recommended for use within the curriculum, as they make more appropriate demands on children's developing systems and provide an indicator of fitness within a context that helps pupils to learn about fitness components and their association with everyday and sporting activities. This learning can also be achieved through the context of challenging skill-related activities, rather than through formal fitness testing.

24.3.20    Pupils of the same chronological age can be up to four years apart in terms of their maturational stage and, consequently, it is **not considered good practice to create and/or use age-related norm tables to compare pupils' fitness test scores**. The use of criterion-referenced 'health-and-fitness standards' alongside the monitoring of physical-activity levels is considered more appropriate, in terms of personalising learning and encouraging pupils to meet the physical-activity recommendation of 'one hour a day' for young people.

## 24.4     What Pupils Should Know

24.4.1      Pupils should know:

- that they should adopt a preferred level of working and not be influenced by peer pressure

- that they should never exercise unsupervised in a fitness facility

- not to chew food, sweets or gum when exercising

- the importance of choosing activities that suit them: if the exercise feels too easy, a more demanding version should be chosen; if it feels too difficult, an easier version should be chosen

- that if an exercise hurts, they should slow down and/or stop

- low-impact exercises place less strain on joints than medium-to-high-impact exercises

- the importance of the application of good technique

- the importance of easing into (ie warming up) and out of (ie cooling down) activity, which helps the body and mind to effectively prepare for and recover from the demands of the activity

- that the benefits of exercise will only be achieved through regular and systematic activity

- not to exercise if they are unwell or recovering from an illness.

## 24.5     Additional Information

### Useful websites

Central YMCA Qualifications
www.cyq.org.uk

**Central YMCA Qualifications (CYQ)** offers a range of health-and-fitness qualifications that are part of the National Qualifications Framework (NQF) and approved by the Qualifications and Curriculum Authority (QCA) and Sector Skills Council (SkillsActive).

CYQ Level 2 qualifications are equivalent to NVQ Level 2 and provide entry onto the national Register of Exercise Professionals (REPs). CYQ Level 2 qualifications offer routes into teaching different disciplines, such as studio cycling, step and circuits.

More information is available from: www.cyq.org.uk/level-2

Individuals who are qualified fitness, health, aerobics or gym instructors and personal trainers should hold CYQ Level 2 Awards in:

- Circuit Training

- Step Exercise to Music

- Studio Resistance Exercise

- Group Indoor Cycling

- Instructing Exercise for Children

and CYQ Level 2 Certificate in: Fitness Instructing.

Oxford, Cambridge and RSA Examinations
www.ocr.org.uk

**Oxford, Cambridge and RSA Examinations (OCR)** is a leading UK awarding body, committed to providing qualifications that engage learners of all ages at school, college, in work or through part-time learning programmes to achieve their full potential. OCR also offers health-and-fitness qualifications.

More information is available from: www.ocr.org.uk/qualifications/vocationally-relatedcertificate/fitness_instructing_level_2_certificate/index.html

Individuals who are qualified fitness, health, aerobics or gym instructors and personal trainers should hold OCR Fitness Instructing Level 2 (gym-based exercise, water-based exercise and exercise to music).

Register of Exercise Professionals
www.exerciseregister.org

The **Register of Exercise Professionals (REPs)** has been set up to help safeguard and promote the health and interests of people who are using the services of exercise and fitness instructors, teachers and trainers. The Register uses a process of self-regulation that recognises industry-based qualifications and practical competence, and requires exercise professionals to work within a code of ethical practice. Members of the Register are given a card and registration certificate to prove their qualification and membership. Also known as the Exercise Register, it operates in the UK and across the world to recognise the personal achievement and competences of qualified exercise professionals.

The Register is a charity, owned by SkillsActive, the Sector Skills Council for Active Leisure and Learning.

REPs provides a list of approved training providers that are also approved centres for an awarding body (eg Central YMCA Qualifications [CYQ], Oxford Cambridge and RSA Examinations [OCR]).

## 24.6    Case Law Examples

24.6.1    A (a Minor) versus Leeds City Council, Leeds County Court (1999):
*This case emphasised the need for clear and careful organisation of free-moving activities where the possibility of collisions needed to be anticipated.*

# Chapter twenty-five

## Outdoor Education and Adventurous Activities

**25**

This chapter provides information about safety recommendations and procedures across a broad range of land- and water-based outdoor/adventurous activities. Where relevant, it directs the reader towards the national governing body (NGB) for a specific activity. The NGB can provide specific information on the levels of qualification necessary for effective and responsible leadership in adventurous activities. A matrix summarising relevant NGB qualifications current at the time of printing (April 2008) for different levels of activity is set out in each appropriate activity-specific section.

> **Note:** Further essential guidance for off-site visit organisation and leadership is set out in *Health and Safety of Pupils on Educational Visits* (HASPEV – DfES, 1998). In England, HASPEV will be subsumed within the *Learning Outside the Classroom* (LotC) guidance. In Wales, HASPEV will be subsumed within the guidance document *Educational Visits*.

> Please read the general guidance provided in Part 1 of this handbook, pages 9–131, before reading this chapter. This will help to ensure that you have a comprehensive awareness of safe-practice issues affecting outdoor education, adventurous activities and PESS in general.

## 25.1   Introduction

25.1.1   The inclusion of adventurous activities in the curriculum recognises the value of these activities in contributing to pupils' educational development. A progressive programme of activities, emphasising the benefits of environmental education and adventure, offering real-life experiences and encouraging pupils to take responsibility for their own actions in appropriately challenging situations lies at the heart of this approach to education.

25.1.2   Competent leadership and appropriate safety-management systems (which anticipate the many variables inherent in working with people in the natural environment) are essential in delivering safe, high-quality adventurous activities. The spirit of adventure needs to be balanced against a concern for the well-being and safety of those participating in these activities.

25.1.3　**The general principles set out below apply to all adventurous activities and should be read and applied to each of the areas described later in the chapter.** Further common principles applicable to land-based activities and to water-based activities are given at the start of the relevant sections and these should also be applied. In addition, activity-specific guidance is given within each section of this chapter. The overall guidance thus builds through common principles to activity-specific guidance. Staff should familiarise themselves with this information and apply it to their unique set of circumstances.

## 25.2　What Staff Should Know

### People

25.2.1　**Competent leadership is central to safe practice in the outdoors.** Being competent implies the leader can demonstrate the ability to operate to current standards of recognised good practice, with an appropriate knowledge and understanding of the employer's guidance, establishment procedures, the group, the staff, the activity and the venue. This is often (but not always) reinforced by some form of structured and approved training and, in some cases, qualification.

25.2.2　Technical competence to lead an activity can be demonstrated by holding one of the following:

- a relevant and current NGB award for the activity/terrain (see the activity-specific sections of this chapter) plus logged evidence of recent and relevant experience

- an assessment of competence by an appropriate technical adviser which confirms the leader has the required experience, leadership and technical skills for the specified activity. Appropriate qualifications for technical advisers are given in the NGB matrix within the activity-specific sections of this chapter.

25.2.3　In situations involving basic activity using the school and its immediate local environment (eg problem solving, orienteering using the school grounds or walking in local lowland countryside), a degree of self-regulation is acceptable through application of the general principles outlined in this chapter and appropriate risk assessment.

25.2.4　Where an adventurous activity is to be led by a member of the school staff, he/she should first check that he/she meets the requirements of the employing body (school or local authority [LA]). Staff leading adventure activities should additionally be monitored from time to time by their employer to ensure they operate within the limitations of their competence and in line with current good practice, and to identify any further training needs.

25.2.5　Where the activity is to be led by an external provider, organisers should check that the provider employs suitably competent staff. Depending upon the type of activity, an external provider may be required to hold a licence issued by the Adventure Activities Licensing Service (AALS). Further information may be obtained from the AALS website: www.aals.org.uk

> **Note:** The AALS is not applicable in Northern Ireland.

25.2.6　School staff should have knowledge of the pupils involved, including any special, medical, behavioural or other needs and should effectively communicate this information to the leader if using an external provider.

25.2.7　The AALS recommends the formulation and use of working documents outlining 'Definitions of Competent Persons', which describe the required skills to lead activities in particular environments. This information is normally set out by the employing organisation (LA or school governing body).

25.2.8　Good judgement is most likely to be made when the adult with a group has:

- the relevant qualifications and skills

- experience or knowledge of the intended location, taking into account weather conditions/forecasts and other variables

- clear educational objectives in mind

- a good knowledge of the pupils for whom he/she will be responsible

- taken reasonable steps to ascertain the fitness and experience of pupils and matched them with the proposed activity

- an appreciation of his/her common-law duty of care

- proven qualities of leadership and responsibility that are evident from other aspects of his/her work

- a flexible approach to altering the plan appropriately if conditions dictate

- the necessary mental and physical fitness to undertake the proposed activity

- established safe adult:pupil ratios, taking into account all relevant variables.

25.2.9　It is important that management systems are applied to monitor staff to enable them to operate within the limitations of their experience, qualifications and expertise (in line with current best practice).

25.2.10　**Adult:pupil ratios** should be determined through informed risk assessment and be compatible with employer requirements. Appropriate ratios may be determined for particular circumstances according to specific needs in relation to the pupils' abilities and behaviours, the staff expertise and confidence, the demands of the activities and the designated area and variable conditions such as weather. Some NGBs provide recommended ratios. In the absence of employer requirements, reference to such NGB guidelines is strongly advised.

> For more information on the factors relating to securing appropriate ratios, see *Chapter 3: Risk Management*, pages 23–30, and *Appendix 2: Risk Assessment Models and Guidance*, pages 296–309 and the CD.

25.2.11　It is common, but not a requirement, that a minimum of two responsible adults accompany groups participating in adventurous activities, one of whom may be a member of school staff. Where this is not feasible, a thorough risk assessment should be carried out to ensure the activity can proceed safely.

25.2.12　If both male and female pupils are involved, it is advisable, but not a requirement of all employers, to have at least one responsible adult of each gender, one of whom should be a member of school staff. This is particularly true for overnight stays. Where this is not possible, parents should be informed prior to giving their consent for their child to take part in the activity.

25.2.13　Where leaders operate alone, the group should be trained to take appropriate action in the event of leader incapacitation. An assistant leader, who is able to keep the group together and raise the alarm, should be present in environments where the group would be placed at high risk if the leader was removed.

25.2.14  Systems should be in place to carry out **thorough employment and vetting checks** to ensure all adults, including instructors and volunteers, who will have close access to pupils during activities or residential courses are suitable to work with children. Schools should also ensure all such adults are fully aware of, and able to fulfil, their duties.

> For more information on this issue, see *Chapter 9: Safeguarding Children and Young People*, pages 55–72.

25.2.15  School staff should clarify their roles, expectations and duty-of-care responsibilities when working with external providers.

## Context

### Activities away from the main base

25.2.16  The activity leader should have recent knowledge of the venue to be used. When the intention is to visit a new location, a **pre-course visit** to the proposed venue by those leading the activity should be undertaken, wherever possible. Guidance from technical experts may be useful in certain circumstances.

25.2.17  Travelling times to and from the venue need to be taken into account when planning off-site activities. The legal requirements for minibus driving and group transport must be observed at all times.

> For more information on these issues, see *Chapter 16: Transporting Pupils*, pages 111–117.

25.2.18  Appropriate **information should be left at the base** with a responsible person, to allow him/her to act as emergency contact if required. This should include relevant information such as activity locations, expected times of arrival and return, equipment carried, names and numbers of participants and staff, together with agreed procedures to be followed in the event of an incident or emergency.

25.2.19  Schools should have an **emergency policy** for out-of-school activities. There should be a planned means of communication between the group and base and/or emergency services and group leaders are advised to carry mobile phones.

25.2.20  It is good practice to test the emergency procedures from time to time. A simple and realistic flow chart of emergency procedures detailing lines of communication, with contact telephone numbers, and responsibilities should be agreed at the planning stage.

25.2.21  High levels of vigilance and concentration are required by the staff to ensure safe practice and **staff ratios should reflect the needs of the group**.

25.2.22  Rigorous risk assessments should take account of **individual pupil needs**, such as epilepsy or diabetes.

### Activities at outdoor and residential centres

25.2.23  Many schools use outdoor and residential centres to provide pupils with experience of the outdoors and specialist staff can do much to further schools' educational aims. Centres may be run by LAs or commercial/private agencies.

25.2.24  School staff should satisfy themselves that centres are appropriate for their group and the planned educational aims before booking. Centres offering activities that are subject to licensing under the **Adventure Activities Licensing Regulations 2004** must demonstrate to the licensing authority that they meet acceptable standards of safe practice in those activities; accredited centres are then issued with a unique licence number. Centres that hold a current AALS licence are listed on the AALS website: www.aals.org.uk

25.2.25    Prior to booking with an outdoor centre or adventure activity provider, staff should carry out checks, undertaking, wherever possible, a visit to the proposed centre in advance to:

- establish the educational credentials and reputation of the centre

- establish whether the centre requires an AALS licence and, if so, to find out what it is licensed to provide

- ensure the centre's fire and emergency procedures are satisfactory

- check facilities and services offered

- discuss their group's needs and agree the activity programme with an appropriate representative of the centre staff

- determine whether or not the school will have sole use

- clarify insurance arrangements

- establish who is responsible at particular times of the day (eg for evening activities).

25.2.26    School staff should resolve any unsatisfactory issues with the centre manager before booking and advice should be sought from the LA or technical experts if necessary.

25.2.27    LA/employing authority requirements for staff:pupil ratios for the journey to and from the centre must be observed.

25.2.28    Where a **specialist instructor** is involved in the delivery of an activity, he/she is responsible for the technical aspects but the accompanying member of staff has overall duty of care for the pupils involved. These duty-of-care responsibilities should be explicit and preferably agreed in writing prior to booking the activity.

25.2.29    Wherever possible, it is strongly advised that the number of school staff present during residential courses is sufficient to enable one member of staff to accompany each activity group under instruction.

25.2.30    In the event of school staff becoming concerned that pupils may be at **unnecessary or unreasonable risk** during an activity, the instructor(s) involved should be approached during a safe interval and appropriate measures taken to ensure the continued safety and well-being of all pupils. Depending upon the nature of the concern, school staff may wish to inform the centre manager.

25.2.31    School staff should have repeated opportunities to hold **regular meetings** during residential courses to evaluate progress and resolve issues that may arise, particularly those relating to safety. A morning joint meeting for school and centre staff is the typical forum for daily planning and information sharing.

## Organisation

25.2.32    The educational aims of the proposed trip should be established at the outset and should inform the planned activity programme.

25.2.33    Schools should follow requirements set out by their employing body relating to the organisation and leadership of off-site activities. Home-country departments with responsibility for education may also provide guidance.

25.2.34 The AALS scheme of accreditation (www.aals.org.uk) gives assurance that good safety-management practice is being followed by the provider. Anyone who provides, in return for payment, adventure activities within the scope of the scheme to young people aged under 18 must have a licence and abide by its conditions. Though the scheme does not cover activities offered by voluntary associations to their members, schools to their pupils or provision for young people accompanied by their parents, its guidance on safety in the outdoors is clearly appropriate to schools' provision.

25.2.35 When external agents or **tour operators** are used, schools should follow their employer's requirements for engaging their services. Systems should be in place to ensure they are reputable, meet relevant statutory requirements, including financial bonding arrangements, and are able to fully satisfy the school's duty-of-care expectations. When dealing with commercial agencies, some knowledge of the Package Travel, Package Holidays and Package Tours Regulations 1992 will enhance safe planning.

## Risk assessment

25.2.36 A suitable risk assessment must be carried out for the venue/activity/group. Legally, it is the responsibility of the employer. In practice, this responsibility is normally delegated to the visit/activity leader, who should ensure the risk assessment meets employer requirements.

25.2.37 For activities led by an external provider, the provider assumes responsibility for risk assessing its services and provision. School staff should note that they retain responsibility for risk assessing those elements of the visit/activity falling directly under their supervision. This allocation of duty needs to be understood and agreed by both parties.

## Long-term planning for adventure activities

25.2.38 Staff should ensure employer (school or LA) requirements with regard to adventure activities are met and sufficient time should be allowed for necessary **planning and coordination** and, where appropriate, visit approval.

25.2.39 Staff competence, availability (eg enforced staff-substitution arrangements) and staff ratios should be clarified at an early stage in the planning process (see www.aals.org.uk). Appropriate staffing allocations should form an integral part of the risk-management process.

25.2.40 It may be useful to compile a written checklist and agree timescales covering important aspects of the itinerary. Depending on the duration and nature of the activity, this might include:

- a preliminary visit to the intended location

- educational visit coordinator (EVC) clearance and submission of any necessary paperwork (eg risk assessment), as required by the employer

- a detailed plan for the proposed trip, with timescales

- written information to parents, including outline plan, consent forms, educational aims and a proposed programme of activities

- expectations and codes of behaviour

- times of meetings and information evenings

- finance details and pupil costs

- travel arrangements, including the management of breaks in the journey

- accommodation details with arrangements for mixed-gender groups
- information concerning personal insurance and the limit of the school's liability
- appropriate equipment lists
- Criminal Records Bureau (CRB) checks and designation of approved-adult status
- responsibilities and supervision arrangements for the duration of the trip
- meal arrangements
- individual needs, such as diet, educational and medical information
- an accurate register of participants and appropriate adult:pupil ratios
- contingency arrangements for use when adverse circumstances prevent the planned programme from taking place
- anticipation of staff changes and their effects on continuity
- agreed and workable emergency procedures
- the appointment of a named school contact.

25.2.41 School staff should submit plans to the leadership team, as required by their employer and, where appropriate, school governing body for approval, accepting advice from senior, more qualified and experienced staff and agreeing on safer options or alternatives if necessary. A named representative of the leadership team should act as the **point of contact** and communication in the event of an emergency.

25.2.42 Schools should consider the benefits of a **code of conduct** that governs pupils' behaviour. Agreed with pupils and parents prior to the activity, such a code can help to assure consistency and fairness by encouraging pupils to realise they have a vital part to play in the success of the venture.

25.2.43 Activities should provide an appropriate level of challenge for participants. As a principle, a progressive approach to skill acquisition will eventually encourage pupils to safely take part in more challenging activities, thereby developing enhanced self-esteem and independence.

## Medium-term planning for adventure activities

25.2.44 A schedule for the **supervision** of pupils should be devised and agreed with all staff concerned before the activity takes place. Contingency arrangements should also be made for the care of pupils in the event of an accident, illness or inability to participate in the proposed programme. Staffing levels should always be adequate in numbers and competence to assure acceptable margins of safety.

25.2.45 **Equipment requirements** should be established: it should be in good condition, fit for purpose and correctly sized to fit the pupils involved. If pupils are to use their own clothing and equipment, this should be checked to ensure it is appropriate.

> For more general guidance on equipment, see *Chapter 12: Equipment in Physical Education,* pages 85–93.

25.2.46 Using all available disclosed information, the staff should make reasonable efforts to ensure pupils are emotionally and physically fit for the proposed activity; a specialist instructor, having expert knowledge, if involved, is the key decision maker relating to the technical aspects of the activity and school staff retain pastoral-care responsibilities for their pupils. Close cooperation between the two is essential to maximise both sets of expertise.

25.2.47　The school staff or centre staff should obtain a **weather forecast** and the leader should be able to interpolate general information to the proposed mountain, cave, gorge, coastal or marine venue, and take account of this corrected forecast in planning activities.

25.2.48　Workable incident/accident-reporting procedures should be in place as an essential part of the risk-management process.

## Short-term planning for adventure activities

25.2.49　Flexibility on the day is important, taking into account variables such as weather, the presence of other groups and the disposition of the group in question. Such decisions highlight the importance of leader competence.

25.2.50　**Plans** for the event should include consideration of:

- the educational aims of the event
- staff ratios and appropriate supervision arrangements for the group
- the capabilities, individual needs and physical state of pupils and adult staff
- the development of weather systems as the day progresses
- site-specific issues relating to the proposed venue
- transport logistics and travelling times.

25.2.51　**The adult in charge** should:

- follow accepted current good practice in the conduct of the activity
- ensure the group is adequately clothed and equipped
- ensure the group is adequately briefed on the plan for the day
- take into account the medical background of pupils and staff and ensure prescribed medication, such as asthma inhalers, is accessible
- ensure accessories such as watches and jewellery are removed if they pose a danger or are liable to be damaged; long hair should be tied back and spectacles secured if necessary
- check any equipment used is fit for purpose
- monitor and take account of changes in the physical and mental state of pupils during activities
- carry out the plan, unless unforeseen circumstances dictate otherwise, so the group can be located in the event of an emergency
- ensure emergency equipment is adequate and readily accessible
- consider the experience and abilities of other members of staff, clearly define roles and responsibilities and delegate only appropriate levels of supervision
- consider communications systems and emergency procedures in the event of an accident.

25.2.52　Activities should provide an appropriate level of challenge for the individuals involved. Allowances need to be made for the least able pupils and activities should be modified as necessary to encourage their safe participation.

25.2.53　**Discipline** must be maintained at all times and school staff must be prepared to intervene if pupils take potentially unsafe action.

25.2.54    It is accepted practice, and an integral part of high-quality provision, for pupi[ participating in activities such as the Duke of Edinburgh's Award scheme to undertake carefully planned expeditions under **remote supervision**, providing th have been properly trained to do so. Before taking part in more independent activities, pupils should first demonstrate sufficient skill, experience and maturity under supervision. Adequate safeguards should be put in place by relevantly qualified and experienced staff before proceeding with these activities.

25.2.55    In anticipating the possibility of **changed circumstances**, the staff should ensure adult:pupil ratios are always sufficient to ensure safety by having workable and realistic contingency plans.

25.2.56    Staff should not unduly pressure group members; individual apprehensions and levels of ability should always determine progress.

## 25.3    What Pupils Should Know

25.3.1    Pupils should:

- know that commitment and willingness to take responsibility are essential to successful participation
- be made aware of their personal responsibilities for safety and be introduced to the concept of residual real risk
- should behave in accordance with the safety instructions given by the staff and, as part of the educative process, should be made aware of the variables informing the risk-management strategy and approach to the activity
- never participate in adventurous activities that are:
  - unplanned
  - unsupervised
  - not approved by the school staff leader.
- know who the responsible adult is.

## 25.4    Additional Information

### Resources

#### Essential

DCELLS (2006) *Educational Visits: All Wales Guidance for Learning Outside the Classroom*. Cardiff: DCELLS.

DfEE (1998) *Health and Safety of Pupils on Educational Visits* (HASPEV 2). Nottingham: DfEE Publications.
Available from:
http://publications.teachernet.gov.uk/eOrderingDownload/HSPV2.pdf

HASPEV is currently being updated in England and Wales.

## General

AALS (2004) 'The Adventure Activities Licensing Regulations 2004', www.aals.org.uk/documents/AALR2004StatutoryInstruments.doc

Bailie, M. (2006) 'Risk Assessments, Safety Statements and all that...Economy of Effort!', www.aals.org.uk/guidance_details.php/pArticleHeadingID=166

British Standards Institute (2007) *Specification for the Provision of Visits, Fieldwork, Expeditions, and Adventurous Activities, Outside the United Kingdom* (BS8848). London: BSI. ISBN: 978-0-580505-03-4.

HSE (2007) *Guidance to the Licensing Authority on The Adventure Activities Licensing Regulations 2004.* Sudbury: HSE Books. ISBN: 978-0-717662-43-2.

Macnae, A. (2001) 'Risk, freedom and the law', www.thebmc.co.uk/feature.aspx?id=1544

Tomlinson, A., Ravenscroft, N., Wheaton B. and Gilchrist, P. (2005) 'Lifestyle sports and national sport policy: an agenda for research', www.sportengland.org/lifestyle_sports_and_national_sports_policy.pdf

# Part A: Land-based Activities

## 25.5    Introduction

> It is essential that reference is made also to the **general principles** set out at the beginning of this chapter (*25.1–25.3*, pages 203–211) as they will apply to all the specific activities included in this section.

## 25.6    Further Guidance Relating to Specific Activities

### Walking and mountaineering

> It is essential that readers understand the **general principles** set out at the beginning of this chapter (*25.1–25.3*, pages 203–211) as they apply to all the specific activities included in this section.

### Introduction

25.6.1    Walking can take place in a variety of locations, from local walks in urban areas to high-level mountain and fell walking in remote areas. Though there are hazards associated with low-level walking, particularly on or near beaches, rivers, cliffs and quarries, the guidance provided in this section mainly relates to high-level walking, since risks are likely to be more significant in these areas.

25.6.2    Detailed information relating to the safe and effective planning and management of walking and mountaineering activities may be obtained from Mountain Leader Training United Kingdom (MLTUK) through www.mltuk.org

### What staff should know

#### People

25.6.3 Walking and mountaineering activities should be carried out by competent, appropriately qualified and relevantly experienced staff.

25.6.4 The relevant qualifications for leaders and technical advisers for walking and mountaineering are set out below (correct at time of publication – April 2008):

| Activity | Leader Qualifications | Technical Adviser Qualifications |
|---|---|---|
| **Walking** | | |
| Mountainous terrain in the UK: winter | Winter Mountain Leader (Winter ML) | Mountain Instructor Certificate (MIC) |
| Mountainous terrain in the UK: non-winter | Summer Mountain Leader (Summer ML) or International Mountain Leader (IML) | Mountain Instructor Award (MIA) with Winter ML |
| Hilly or moorland terrain in the UK: non-winter | Walking Group Leader (WGL) | Winter ML |
| Lowland country in the UK: non-winter; overnight | Sports Leader UK Award in Basic Expedition Leadership (BEL) | Summer ML |
| Lowland country in the UK: non-winter; day | Sports Leader UK Level 2 Award in Day Walk Leadership (DWL) | WGL or Summer MLStaff |

Staff should ensure anyone leading groups in mountain activities holds the relevant qualification or endorsement.

#### Context

25.6.5 **Competent staff** with the appropriate accreditation, knowledge and experience should carefully choose appropriate venues and plan routes, taking into account all variables.

25.6.6 Mountainous areas can modify the **weather** significantly, causing, for example, increases in wind speed and rainfall intensity and reductions in temperature. Wind chill and topographical funnelling effects should also be anticipated by the staff in choosing appropriate venues.

25.6.7 Venues should offer levels of educational, environmental and/or adventurous challenge appropriate to the abilities, confidence and experience of the group.

25.6.8 If the route to be taken involves planned scrambling or gorge walking, the use of helmets may be required. Gorges may also require the use of wetsuits and buoyancy aids.

> For more information on this issue, see *Combined water/rock activities* (*25.6.41–25.6.56*, pages 219–221) in this chapter.

**Organisation**

25.6.9    Adult:pupil ratios should be decided based on an informed risk assessment, taking account of relevant factors within the three key dimensions of people, context and organisation.

> For general guidance on this issue, see *Chapter 3: Risk Management,* pages 23–30.

25.6.10   Each **group member** should carry or wear suitable clothing and equipment to ensure their comfort. This will typically include:

- waterproof and windproof clothing
- food and drink
- appropriate spare clothing
- appropriate footwear.

25.6.11   In addition, the **group** should carry equipment to allow them to deal with emergencies. This will typically include:

- first-aid kit
- group shelter and/or survival bags
- map and compass
- torch
- whistle
- emergency procedures aide-memoire
- mobile phone.

25.6.12   Groups who are to be **remotely supervised** need to be clearly briefed, informed of potential hazards and left in no doubt as to action to take in the event of emergencies. They should carry suitable emergency equipment to deal with foreseeable incidents and to contact the leader if required. The group leader should be satisfied that the pupils have acquired the necessary skills and have the necessary confidence, physical ability and judgement to be left without direct supervision. The withdrawal of direct supervision should be a gradual four-stage process, evolving through:

- accompanying the group
- shadowing the group
- checking regularly at agreed locations
- checking occasionally at agreed locations.

## Climbing and abseiling

### Introduction

> It is essential that readers understand the **general principles** set out at the beginning of this chapter (*25.1–25.3,* pages 203–211) as they apply to all the specific activities included in this section.

25.6.13   Climbing and abseiling require degrees of balance, agility, strength, endurance and mental control that are dependent on the standard of routes selected at the chosen venue. The activities also require that individuals take responsibility for their own and others' safety in what can be potentially hazardous environments.

25.6.14 Detailed information relating to the safe and effective planning and management of climbing and abseiling activities may be obtained from MLTUK through www.mltuk.org

### What staff should know

#### People

25.6.15 Climbing and abseiling activities should be carried out by competent, appropriately qualified and relevantly experienced staff.

25.6.16 Though NGB rock-climbing awards accredit individuals to operate at any appropriate crag (as defined in their terms of reference), it is advisable for leaders of rock-climbing and abseiling activities to have prior knowledge and experience of the proposed venue.

25.6.17 The relevant qualifications for leaders and technical advisers for climbing and abseiling are set out below:

| Activity | Leader Qualifications | Technical Adviser Qualifications |
|---|---|---|
| **Climbing and Abseiling** | | |
| Winter climbing | Mountain Instructor Certificate (MIC) or British Mountain Guide (BMG) or Aspirant Guide | MIC or BMG |
| Multi-pitch rock climbing and teaching of leading on any crag | Mountain Instructor Award (MIA) | MIC or BMG |
| Single-pitch climbing and abseiling | Single Pitch Award (SPA) | MIA |
| Climbing wall | Climbing Wall Award (CWA) | MIA |
| Teaching leading on a climbing wall | SPA or CWA with additional Teaching Leading module award | MIA |

Staff should ensure anyone leading groups in climbing or abseiling holds the relevant qualification or endorsement.

#### Context

25.6.18 Ropes, karabiners and all other technical gear should conform to Conformite European (CE) standards and be **fit for purpose**.

25.6.19 The development of artificial climbing and bouldering walls has had a significant influence on the development of climbing. Though generally designed with safety in mind, these seemingly controlled environments can wrongly give the impression of being less serious. **Belaying** correctly using appropriate methods in line with current best practice remains essential.

25.6.20　Managers of commercial indoor walls will have their own **risk-management systems** and procedures and these should be fully understood and observed by the staff with responsibility for the session. Account should be taken of the commercial risk assessment within the school's own risk assessment for the event.

25.6.21　**Matting** under bouldering walls is designed to provide a more comfortable landing for climbers falling or jumping. It should not be assumed that matting makes the climbing any safer. Staff should encourage pupils to understand and manage the hazards involved when climbing above such matting.

### Organisation

25.6.22　Adult:pupil ratios should be decided based on an informed risk assessment, taking account of relevant factors within the three key dimensions of people, context and organisation.

> For general guidance on this issue, see *Chapter 3: Risk Management,* pages 23–30.

25.6.23　**MLTUK** provides comprehensive guidelines and terms of reference but particular consideration should be given to the following:

a. The venue and chosen route(s) should be suitable for the group, taking into account the capabilities of the group's least able climbers.

b. Clear safety rules should be established before climbing or abseiling begins. Careful consideration should be given to the control and supervision of all members of the group – climbers and non-climbers – especially at the top of the crag, when on descent routes, after finishing activities or when approaching an abseil.

c. Recognised and fully understood systems of communication should be established before the session begins.

d. The type of footwear permitted should be considered carefully. The weather, type of rock and nature of the approach and descent are all relevant.

e. Where appropriate, the group should be made aware of the climb's descent route and its associated hazards; levels of supervision should be appropriate. If students are acting independently on descent routes, this should be carefully managed.

f. Helmets and harnesses should be correctly fitted and procedures should be in place to ensure they are worn correctly at all times. This includes time spent waiting at the bottom of the crag, unless the group are out of range of any rockfall or dropped equipment.

g. The use of screw-gate or similar locking karabiners should be demonstrated and practised and the vital importance of the gate being locked when climbing should be emphasised.

h. Group members need to be correctly attached to the rope before starting to climb.

i. Climbing or bouldering should not take place unless the group leader is present and gives his/her consent.

216

j.  Lead climbing should not take place without the express consent and supervision of the qualified adult.

k.  Abseiling should always be supervised by a qualified adult and a suitable safety back-up system should always be used.

## Camping and expeditions

### Introduction

It is essential that readers understand the **general principles** set out at the beginning of this chapter (*25.1–25.3*, pages 203–211) as they apply to all the specific activities included in this section.

25.6.24    There are various forms of camping, ranging from standing camps, with some permanent on-site facilities, to lightweight camping and backpacking expeditions, which demand greater levels of skill and knowledge. It is essential that potential hazards relating to sites and associated activities are identified at the planning stage.

### What staff should know

#### People

25.6.25    Site-specific **risk assessments** must be carried out for each venue by appropriately competent, qualified and relevantly experienced staff.

25.6.26    For camping in hill and mountainous country, staff should be appropriately trained and qualified for the terrain, in accordance with MLTUK guidelines.

25.6.27    If the party is to camp **near water**, group leaders should be familiar with the issues relating to water safety.

#### Context

25.6.28    All sites should be thoroughly **risk assessed** by an appropriately qualified and experienced person and appropriate control measures put in place. Sites close to mines and quarries, busy main roads and steep ground should be avoided wherever possible.

25.6.29    Staff should plan **progressive** schedules in which pupils gradually develop appropriate levels of skill. The first camp should be held under controlled conditions and located near permanent shelter.

25.6.30    Wild camping requires a high degree of leadership and pupil skill. Staff and students should work within parameters that find the correct balance between adventure, personal development and enjoyment.

#### Organisation

25.6.31    Adult:pupil ratios should be decided based on an informed risk assessment, taking account of relevant factors within the three key dimensions of people, context and organisation.

For general guidance on this issue, see *Chapter 3: Risk Management*, pages 23–30.

25.6.32    It is good practice to introduce young people to camping through a **progressive series of activities** in which pupils gradually develop appropriate levels of skill. For example, a first camp for young pupils could be held in a relatively sheltered location close to vehicle access. The end of the progression might be wild camping in a more remote location, but this requires a high degree of leader competence (dictated by the terrain and activity required to access the camp area), pupil maturity and environmental sensitivity.

25.6.33    Group leaders should ensure pupils receive **adequate training** in key aspects of camp craft, including effective pitching of tents for anticipated weather, the importance of hygiene, the safe packing and carrying of loads and a minimum-impact approach to the environment.

25.6.34    **Contingency plans** for alternative routes, venues or activities, in the event of bad weather, should be agreed at the planning stage.

25.6.35    Careful thought needs to be given to the type(s) of **stoves** used, fuel storage, refuelling and the training and supervision required for safe use.

25.6.36    Stoves should be refuelled carefully after the stove has cooled, in a ventilated area and when other nearby sources of ignition have been extinguished.

25.6.37    Menu planning should reflect the need for healthy nutrition, cooking convenience and hygiene, fuel efficiency and palatability. Pupils should be taught how to safely prepare and store food and clean utensils with environmental and hygiene considerations in mind.

25.6.38    Wherever possible, sufficient space should be left between tents to allow free movement and prevent the spread of fire.

25.6.39    **Wild camping** in remote upland areas away from roads and habitation demands high levels of skill and expertise. Food and human waste pollution have the potential to adversely affect the environment and particular attention should be paid to hygiene arrangements. These are important not only for comfort and health but also for the long-term sustainability of the site. Pupils should be clearly briefed on this issue.

25.6.40    All rubbish should be taken away and disposed of thoughtfully.

### Additional information

#### Resources

Long, S. (2003) *Hill Walking: The Official Handbook of the Mountain Leader and Walking Group Leader Schemes.* Conwy: MLTUK. ISBN: 978-0-954151-10-2

MLTUK (2005) *Mountain Leader Training's National Guidelines for Climbing and Walking Leaders, 2nd Edition.* MLTUK: Conwy: MLTUK. ISBN: 978-0-95441511-2.

Mountain Leader Training England (MLTE) *Remote Supervision Guidance Notes.* Available from: www.mlte.org/content.php?nID=56&pID=23

#### Contact details

Mountain Leader Training UK
Siabod Cottage, Capel Curig
Conwy LL24 0ES
Tel: 01690-720 272
www.mltuk.org

**Mountain Leader Training UK** (MLTUK) provides comprehensive training and assessment in the extensive range of skills and qualifications required to lead groups safely in the British hills. The *National Guidelines for Climbing and Walking Leaders* produced by MLTUK provide detailed advice for those having responsibility for mountain-related activities.

British Association of Mountain Guides
Siabod Cottage, Capel Curig
Conwy LL24 0ET
www.bmg.org.uk

The **British Association of Mountain Guides** (BMG) administers the highest internationally recognised qualification for instruction and guiding in rock and ice climbing, mountaineering, off-piste skiing and ski touring – the International Federation of Mountain Guides Association (IFMGA) carnet.

## Combined water/rock activities

### Introduction

It is essential that readers understand the **general principles** set out at the beginning of this chapter (*25.1–25.3*, pages 203–211) as they apply to all the specific activities included in this section.

25.6.41    Combined water/rock activities are adventure activities where those hazards associated with the rock environment may, at times, combine with those of the water environment. These include:

- gorge walking

- sea-level traversing

- coasteering

- canyoning

- adventure swimming

- river running.

25.6.42    MLTUK and MLTE have worked closely with the AALS, British Canoe Union (BCU), DCSF and HSE to produce guidance notes, which make essential reading. For more details, see www.mltuk.org

Further good advice is contained in the DCSF/Central Council for Physical Recreation (CCPR) resource *Group Safety at Water Margins* (2003).

### What staff should know

#### People

25.6.43    Combined water/rock activities should be carried out by a competent leader. Specific competence requirements will depend on the nature of the activity/location but will normally involve a combination of mountain/rock climbing with water-safety competence. Staff planning to undertake a combined water/rock activity should check with a suitable technical adviser prior to commencement. A suitable technical adviser will usually be MIA qualified with water-safety qualifications and a sound knowledge of the venue. Local outdoor education centres may be able to offer useful advice on venues.

**Context**

25.6.44    There are many hazards associated with combined water/rock activities: water causing a risk of drowning, cold-water immersion causing hypothermia, flowing water causing possible entrapment on downstream obstacles and fast-moving water potentially sweeping individuals away completely. Tripping, slipping and stumbling on wet or loose rock may cause bruising, sprains and fractures. There is also a possibility of concussive injury from falls or loose rock. Consideration should also be given to the possibility of new hazards developing over time as a result of water erosion in these dynamic and changeable environments.

25.6.45    Staff should obtain a **weather forecast** and apply this general information to the proposed venue by taking into account site-specific information and local topographic factors. These corrected forecasts should also take into account the lasting effects of recent weather patterns. Fluctuations in water levels will be rapid in certain circumstances.

25.6.46    When working in coastal, marine or estuarine environments, a thorough knowledge of weather conditions and their effects on tide times, sea states and escape routes should be used to plan safe activities.

**Organisation**

25.6.47    Adult:pupil ratios should be decided based on an informed risk assessment, taking account of relevant factors within the three key dimensions of people, context and organisation.

> For general guidance on this issue, see *Chapter 3: Risk Management,* pages 23–30.

25.6.48    All group members should be equipped with **suitable, well-fitting clothing** and equipment for warmth and mobility, depending on the venue. The type of footwear permitted should be considered carefully.

25.6.49    Staff should determine the need for helmets on the basis of a risk assessment of the activity and venue.

25.6.50    For activities involving jumps into deep water, buoyancy aids or similar floatation devices should be used and wetsuits should be considered, as they can offer the dual benefit of warmth and protection from bumps and scrapes.

25.6.51    Appropriate **safety equipment** should be available according to the conditions and location (eg spare clothes, emergency shelter, throw line and first-aid kit).

25.6.52    On arrival at the venue, the actual conditions should be assessed. Wind direction and rain intensity are crucial factors in affecting local conditions and valley-to-valley characteristics can differ significantly in certain weather conditions. Water erosion may degrade gorges so rapidly that predications based on previous experience may not be reliable. Staff must always make safety the top priority and should not succumb to pressure to do otherwise.

25.6.53    **Escape routes** should be noted before the activity commences.

25.6.54    Cold-water immersion results in the rapid onset of **hypothermia** many times faster than in air at the same temperature and the full implications of getting wet should be considered, not only for the individual but also for the success of the day as a whole.

25.6.55    Staff should use sound judgement when it comes to using ropes or in-situ protection left by others.

25.6.56    Staff should safeguard the fragile and ecological nature of these environments by appropriate group-management strategies.

### Resources

MLTUK (2005) *National Guidelines for Climbing and Walking Leaders 2005: Appendix VIIa: 'Combined Water and Rock Activities – Safety Check List'*. MLTUK: Conwy

MLTUK (2005) *National Guidelines for Climbing and Walking Leaders 2005: Appendix VIIb: 'Group Safety at Water Margins'*. MLTUK: Conwy

## Underground activities: caving and mine exploration

### Introduction

> It is essential that readers understand the **general principles** set out at the beginning of this chapter (*25.1–25.3*, pages 203–211) as they apply to all the specific activities included in this section.

25.6.57    Underground systems, other than show caves and tourist mines, present many of the challenges and adventure opportunities associated with mountains and water and these, associated with darkness and confined spaces, make the underground experience uniquely challenging and exciting. Well-organised underground activities can provide numerous educational opportunities for personal and group development.

25.6.58    Detailed information about underground activities and appropriate leadership awards can be obtained from the **British Caving Association** (BCA), the NGB that administers training and assessment courses in this activity for teachers and leaders in Britain.

### What staff should know

#### People

25.6.59    Underground activities should be carried out by competent, appropriately qualified and relevantly experienced staff.

25.6.60    The relevant qualifications for leaders and technical advisers for underground activities are set out below:

| Activity | Leader Qualifications | Technical Adviser Qualifications |
|---|---|---|
| **Caving** | | |
| Cave/mine systems with pitches >18m | Cave Instructor Certificate (CIC) | CIC |
| Systems with several unavoidable pitches <18m | Local Cave and Mine Leader Award (LCMLA) Level 2 | CIC |
| Systems with one unavoidable pitch <18m | LCMLA Level 2 | CIC |
| Systems with avoidable pitches <18m | LCMLA Level 2 | CIC |
| Systems with no pitches | LCMLA Level 1 | CIC |

Staff should ensure anyone leading groups in caving holds the relevant qualification or endorsement.

### Context

25.6.61 The LCMLA is a venue-specific award and appropriately qualified staff will have first-hand knowledge and experience of the caves to be used. Pupils should never be taken into caves that are unfamiliar to the leader.

25.6.62 The activity leader should obtain a **weather forecast** and interpolate this general information to the proposed cave or mine by taking into account site-specific information and local topographic factors. These corrected forecasts should also take into account the lasting effects of recent weather patterns. Fluctuations in water levels will be rapid in certain circumstances.

25.6.63 **Wind-chill** effects outside the cave or mine, as well as water temperatures inside, should be taken into account. Cold-water immersion may result in the rapid onset of hypothermia.

### Organisation

25.6.64 Adult:pupil ratios should be decided based on an informed risk assessment, taking account of relevant factors within the three key dimensions of people, context and organisation.

> For general guidance on this issue, see *Chapter 3: Risk Management,* pages 23–30.

25.6.65 On the journey to, and on arrival at, the cave, the actual conditions should be assessed. Wind direction and rain intensity are crucial factors affecting local conditions within caves or mines.

25.6.66 In caves or mines with active streamways or liable to flooding,, the adult in charge should assess **indicators of potential flooding** (eg the level of nearby streams) and, if unsure, make a quick reconnaissance of the cave or mine itself. In such caves or mines, it is advisable to have identifiable water-level indicators within the system to allow the leader to identify if conditions are changing while the group is underground.

25.6.67 The group should be clearly briefed about any specific hazards within the cave or mine at an appropriate time. Leaders should maintain effective supervision of the group at all times.

25.6.68 In-situ ropes or protection left by other people should be treated with caution.

25.6.69 All **group members** should be equipped with suitable clothing and equipment for warmth and mobility. Depending on the characteristics of the cave or mine, this might include:

- appropriately warm clothing – preferably fleece-wear
- waterproof and windproof clothing or protective overgarment
- a helmet with hands-free lighting
- wellington boots or other appropriate footwear.

5.6.70    In addition, the **group** should carry equipment to deal with foreseeable emergencies. This might include:

- group shelter or survival bags
- spare lighting
- first-aid kit
- whistle
- emergency procedures aide-memoire
- mobile phone.

25.6.71   Particular attention should be paid to pupils on their first underground trip. Pupils need to understand that being in confined spaces may be part of this activity. To forestall factors likely to hinder pupils' safe involvement and progress, staff should be adequately perceptive in detecting poor reactions at an early stage. Pupils should be monitored and reassured appropriately.

### Additional information

#### Contact details

The British Caving Association
The Old Methodist Chapel
Great Hucklow, Buxton
Derbyshire SK17 8RG
www.british-caving.org.uk

## Orienteering

### Introduction

It is essential that readers understand the **general principles** set out at the beginning of this chapter (*25.1–25.3*, pages 203–211) as they apply to all the specific activities included in this section.

25.6.72   The challenge, excitement and achievement of orienteering is in finding the fastest route between a series of controls on an orienteering course, using physical and mental abilities in combination.

25.6.73   The **British Orienteering Federation** (BOF) is the NGB that administers the various training and assessment schemes in orienteering for coaches, teachers and leaders in Britain.

### What staff should know

#### People

25.6.74   Orienteering activities should be carried out by competent, appropriately qualified and relevantly experienced staff.

25.6.75   The relevant qualifications for leaders and technical advisers for orienteering are set out overleaf:

| Activity | Leader Qualifications | Technical Adviser Qualifications |
|---|---|---|
| **Orienteering** | | |
| Complex or high-level terrain | BOF Level 4 Coach or Mountain Leader (ML) with orienteering experience | BOF Level 4 Coach Tutor or Mountain Instructor Award (MIA) with orienteering experience |
| Forest or open-country sites | BOF Level 3 Coach or Walking Group Leader (WGL) with orienteering experience | BOF Level 4 Coach or ML with orienteering experience |
| Larger parks or small woods | BOF Level 2 Coach or Day Walk Leader with orienteering experience | BOF Level 3 Coach WGL with orienteering experience |
| Local parks | BOF Level 1 Coach or local approval by a technical adviser | BOF Level 2 Coach or WGL with orienteering experience |

Staff should ensure anyone leading groups in orienteering away from the school site holds the relevant qualification or endorsement.

25.6.76  Competent adults who have some experience of orienteering are perfectly able to deliver a basic introduction in the school grounds, local parks or small areas of woodland with clear boundaries and observable paths.

**Context**

25.6.77  Prior **permission** should be sought from the landowner; the existence of orienteering maps does not necessarily indicate a right of access.

25.6.78  Wherever possible, the orienteering course should not require pupils to cross busy roads or negotiate major geographical hazards (eg crags or areas very close to deep water).

**Organisation**

25.6.79  Adult:pupil ratios should be decided based on an informed risk assessment, taking account of relevant factors within the three key dimensions of people, context and organisation.

> For general guidance on this issue, see *Chapter 3: Risk Management,* pages 23–30.

25.6.80  Appropriate route setting is an essential part of the risk-management process.

25.6.81  Appropriate **clothing** should be worn to suit the prevailing conditions and the type of orienteering course. Complete coverage of the arms and legs is strongly advised for events in thick vegetation and woodland.

25.6.82  **Footwear** should be suitable for the course terrain and prevailing weather conditions.

25.6.83    All pupils should carry a whistle or other means of calling for help if orienteering in areas where they will be out of sight of the leaders. A **call-back signal** and prearranged cut-off time should be agreed. Escape instructions may be issued to enable pupils to retreat safely to a prearranged point.

25.6.84    Pupils should be briefed with clear and unambiguous ground rules. All foreseeable hazards that they may come across should be identified and brought to the attention of pupils.

25.6.85    Inexperienced pupils should compete in pairs or small groups and remain together.

> **Note:** Orienteering skill development in pairs is less effective than solo orienteering.

25.6.86    If groups are to be left **unaccompanied**, consideration should be given to:

- educational aims
- the potential hazards associated with proposed routes
- the potential threat from other people
- emergency procedures in the event of injury or getting lost
- a realistic cut-off time
- the boundaries of the course.

25.6.87    Only experienced and relevantly trained pupils should take part in **night-time orienteering**, except on the most straightforward sites (eg school grounds).

25.6.88    Procedures for locating pupils who get lost should be handled by the leader. First-aid kits should be available.

### Additional information

#### Resources

McNeill, C., Cory-Wright, J. and Renfrew, T. *Teaching Orienteering (2nd Edition)*. Champaign, IL: Human Kinetics. ISBN: 978-0-880118-04-0.

#### Contact details

British Orienteering Federation
8a Stancliffe House, Whitworth Road
Darley Dale
Matlock DE4 2HJ
www.britishorienteering.org.uk

## Cycle touring and mountain biking

### Introduction

> It is essential that readers understand the **general principles** set out at the beginning of this chapter (*25.1–25.3*, pages 203–211) as they apply to all the specific activities included in this section.

25.6.89    There are many forms of cycling, ranging from recreational activities in the rural environment to competitive events in mountainous terrain, from cycling as a way of getting to school or work to competing at the highest levels in the velodrome. In all its guises, cycling, as an aerobic activity, provides the type of exercise that is particularly effective at promoting good health. There are, of course, many other benefits of cycling, not least its potential to encourage young people to explore the wider world in a local context.

25.6.90 Further information about awards for cycling and mountain biking may be obtained from the British Cycling Federation, the NGB of cycle sport in Great Britain.

## What staff should know

### People

25.6.91 Biking activities should be led by competent, appropriately qualified and relevantly experienced staff.

25.6.92 The relevant qualifications for leaders and technical advisers for mountain biking are set out below:

| Activity | Leader Qualifications | Technical Adviser Qualifications |
|---|---|---|
| **Mountain biking** | | |
| Routes with high levels of technical difficulty | Scottish Mountain Bike Leader Award (SMBLA) or combination of alternative mountain-biking leader qualification and Mountain Leader (ML) or Walking Group Leader (WGL) | SMBLA Tutor Assessor or Mountain Instructor Award who is also an alternative mountain-biking award tutor/assessor |
| Routes with low to medium levels of technical difficulty | SMBLA Trail Cycle Leader Award or alternative mountain-biking leader award (eg BSCA) | SMBLA or alternative mountain bike leader award tutor/assessor |

Staff should ensure anyone leading groups in mountain-biking activities holds the relevant qualification or endorsement.

### Context

25.6.93 There is the potential for serious accidents in all forms of cycling and great care should be exercised when planning and organising activities. In deciding on appropriate rides for young people, risk assessments should take into account the levels of technical difficulty, objective dangers, overall distance (including height gain and loss), escape routes and whether a leader with a mountain-biking qualification will be required (and available) to ensure acceptable margins of safety.

25.6.94 **Weather** variables will have effects on the riding surface, as well as on the physical capabilities of the group. Wind strength and direction, wind chill and the possibility of frozen ground at higher altitudes will have significant effects on progress and safety margins.

25.6.95 **Bikes** should:

- be roadworthy, with all parts in good condition

- have tyres that are appropriately inflated for the nature of the riding

- have wheels that are locked in place and not buckled, with hubs running smoothly

- have correctly adjusted brakes that are capable of stopping the cyclist effectively

226

- be correctly sized with securely adjusted handlebars, brake levers and saddle
- have correctly adjusted and smooth-running gears
- be fitted with suitable lights (if appropriate)
- have safe stowage and pannier systems (if appropriate).

25.6.96  Cyclists should **wear** clothing, and carry equipment, suitable for the activity, venue and conditions. This will normally include:

- gloves
- helmets
- appropriate footwear; trainers are normally acceptable but it should be remembered that riders can be susceptible to cold feet when wet
- long sleeves and full-length, close-fitting trousers
- waterproof/windproof top (in warm weather, it is usual to carry this in a rucksack; otherwise, riders may suffer from overheating).

**Organisation**

25.6.97  Adult:pupil ratios should be decided based on an informed risk assessment, taking account of relevant factors within the three key dimensions of people, context and organisation.

> For general guidance on this issue, see *Chapter 3: Risk Management,* pages 23–30.

25.6.98  Cycling frequently involves transporting bikes and pupils by minibuses and trailers; the legal requirements must be observed.

> For general guidance on this issue, see *Chapter 16: Transporting* Pupils, pages 111–117.

25.6.99  The competence of the group should be assessed before taking to the road or trail and this assessment should take place in controlled conditions in a safe area.

25.6.100  Cyclists should be briefed on key safety measures relevant to the planned route. These will normally include:

- bike controls
- body positions when ascending and descending
- braking
- skid control
- riding as part of a group at different speeds
- specific venue hazards, including weather variables.

Pupils need to maintain safe braking distances between their bike and the one in front.

25.6.101  **Venues** should be chosen that take account of the fitness, ability and experience of the group.

25.6.102  Consideration needs to be given to the position of the staff in the group when riding; this 'position of most usefulness' may involve the leader dismounting to check individuals at certain points.

25.6.103    Pupils should be forewarned of **hazards** such as very steep descents, difficult bends, unusually rough terrain or other unusual riding surfaces, and other track users. Such situations should be managed according to the ability of the group, whether on or off-road. Safe progressions with appropriate levels of challenge and development should characterise the session.

25.6.104    Each **group** should carry equipment to deal with foreseeable emergencies. Depending on the route and other variables, this will normally include:

- first-aid kit
- group shelter
- puncture repair/maintenance kit
- map and compass
- emergency procedures aide-memoire
- mobile phone.

### Additional information

### Contact details

British Cycling Federation
British Cycling
National Cycling Centre, Stuart Street
Manchester M11 4DQ
Tel: 0870-871 2000
Email: info@britishcycling.org.uk
www.britishcycling.org.uk

Off Road Training Consultancy
PO Box 1506
Sheffield S6 2JZ
www.otc.org.uk/

Off Road Training Consultancy (OTC) provides the National Mountain Bike Leader Award (NMBLA).

Scottish Cyclists Union
The Velodrome, Meadow Bank Stadium
London Road
Edinburgh EH7 6AD
www.scuonline.org

Scottish Cyclists Union offers training and assessment courses for the Scottish Mountain Bike Leaders Award Scheme (SMBLA).

## Horse riding and pony trekking

### Introduction

It is essential that readers understand the general principles set out at the beginning of this chapter (*25.1–25.3*, pages 203–211) as they apply to all the specific activities included in this section.

25.6.105    Horse riding and pony trekking are popular activities with many young people. Schools should use only approved riding schools, trained horses and qualified staff when offering equestrian activities.

228

25.6.106    The Trekking and Riding Society of Scotland, Association of Irish Riding Establishments, Welsh Trekking and Riding Association and the British Horse Society (BHS) have worked together to develop qualifications for those working in equestrian tourism.

25.6.107    The Equine Tourism Qualifications are administered by the BHS.

25.6.108    The Trek Leader Certificate is administered by the **Association of British Riding Schools** (ABRS).

### What staff should know

### People

25.6.109    Riding activities should be led by competent, appropriately qualified and relevantly experienced staff.

### Context

25.6.110    Only BHS or ABRS approved centres should be used.

25.6.111    School staff should discuss the needs of their pupils with the riding school to ensure the standards of rides chosen are appropriate for the needs of the group.

### Organisation

25.6.112    Staff **ratios** should reflect the demands of the terrain, the needs of the group and the risk-assessment requirements of the riding centre. Clear, comprehensive and concise guidance from the centre's staff should be given to all responsible adults if they are to lead particular horses.

25.6.113    Horses and riders should be relevantly equipped in line with BHS standards and guidelines.

### Additional information

### Contact details

Association of British Riding Schools (ABRS)
Queen's Chambers, 38–40 Queen Street
Penzance, Cornwall TR18 4BH
www.abrs-info.org/index.htm

British Horse Society
Stoneleigh Deer Park, Kenilworth
Warwickshire CV8 2XZ
www.bhs.org.uk/content/default.asp

## Skating

### Introduction

It is essential that readers understand the **general principles** set out at the beginning of this chapter (*25.1–25.3*, pages 203–211) as they apply to all the specific activities included in this section.

25.6.114 The advice in this section applies to ice, roller and in-line skating.

25.6.115 The National Ice Skating Association (NISA), Federation of Artistic Roller Skating (FARS) and British Roller Skating provide detailed information on relevant qualifications and the safe and effective planning and management of skating activities.

### What staff should know

#### People

25.6.116 Skating activities should be carried out by competent, appropriately qualified and relevantly experienced staff.

25.6.117 Pupils should be taught how to skate safely. To assist with this process, many leaders introduce the acronym **SLAP**, which means skaters should be:

- **S**mart
  - always wear protective gear
  - master the basics, including stopping and turning
  - skate at a speed that is safe and appropriate for the level of competence
- **L**egal
  - observe the venue's protocol for overtaking
- **A**lert
  - skate in control at all times
  - watch out for hazards
  - be vigilant for changes to the skating surface
- **P**olite
  - announce an intention to pass
  - always yield to novices and pedestrians
  - accept the need to skate thoughtfully and with care.

25.6.118 Leaders should have previous experience of skating at rinks and of leading groups in similar environments.

#### Context

25.6.119 The **skating surface** should be free from obstructions, regularly checked and maintained and inspected before use. Skating should only take place on an even surface.

25.6.120 Though in-line skating is increasing in popularity, guidance should be sought from the relevant LA or employing organisation for its policies on skating in public areas and/or on highways.

25.6.121    Site-specific risk assessments must be carried out by appropriately qualified or experienced staff.

25.6.122    A pre-visit inspection of the **location** by the leader is highly recommended prior to its use by the school.

25.6.123    For recreational skating, the terms and conditions of the particular commercial venue must be observed and duty-of-care arrangements should be explicit.

25.6.124    For taught sessions, skating should be supervised by school staff and a competent instructor should always be present.

### Organisation

25.6.125    Staffing **ratios** should be in line with LA or school guidelines for educational visits or based on an informed risk assessment taking account of relevant factors within the three key dimensions of people, context and organisation.

> For general guidance on this issue, see *Chapter 3: Risk Management,* pages 23–30.

25.6.126    It is sensible, in pre-visit information to parents, to explain the nature of the risks inherent in visits to skating rinks.

25.6.127    Pupils should wear suitable **clothing** that provides adequate protection. Beginners should wear gloves. Helmets may be required in certain circumstances. Elbow and knee protection is advisable. Ice/roller boots should provide firm ankle support.

25.6.128    The group should observe any local requirements for direction of skating. This is usually an anticlockwise direction, skating on the right and passing on the left.

25.6.129    Where possible, it is advisable for beginners and advanced skaters to skate in separate groups.

### Additional information

### Contact details

British Roller Skating
www.british-roller-skating.org.uk

Federation of Artistic Roller Skating
10 The Broadway, Thatcham
Berks RG19 3JA
Tel: 01635-877 322
www.fars.co.uk/

National Ice Skating Association
Lower Parliament Street
Nottingham NG1 1LA
Tel: 0115-988 8060
www.iceskating.org.uk

## Problem-solving Activities

### Introduction

It is essential that readers understand the **general principles** set out at the beginning of this chapter (*25.1–25.3*, pages 203–211) as they apply to all the specific activities included in this section.

25.6.130    Problem-solving and team-building activities can develop trust, communication and leadership skills using simple equipment in safe, controlled environments. Activities that are easy to set up, using resources that are obtainable locally, can address the central challenges of education by:

- helping individuals find solutions by discovering the right balance of creativity and subjectivity on the one hand, and logic and objectivity on the other

- encouraging individuals, through adopting the techniques of critical thinking, to realise they can make a difference to the outcomes of their own lives

- fostering and developing teamwork.

### What staff should know

#### People

25.6.131    Problem-solving activities should be led by competent, appropriately qualified and relevantly experienced staff.

25.6.132    Pupils often think creatively when problem solving and experienced staff's active approach to risk management is crucial. Sensible precautions can reduce risk without stifling initiative, enterprise and excitement.

25.6.133    There is a danger with these activities, which can appear contrived and innocuous on occasions, that pupils may not fully appreciate the real risks involved. All participants should act in a safe manner and take responsibility for their own and others' well-being.

#### Context

25.6.134    Problem solving embraces a wide range of activities, some of which have significant hazards. Special consideration should be given to the height from which pupils could fall. Some common activities involve working in awkward positions some distance from the ground and there may be a need for protective equipment, such as helmets, for some activities. In these cases, it is vital staff have the specialist knowledge and competence to lead the activity safely. The required levels of skill and expertise for particular activities should be stipulated in the risk assessment.

#### Organisation

25.6.135    Pupils should be adequately **briefed** on the potential hazards of the activity, and the parameters within which they may act independently should be carefully defined.

25.6.136    Pupils should be adequately clothed and equipped to afford acceptable levels of protection.

25.6.137    The hazards and consequences of overtly competitive activities should be considered.

25.6.138    If the activity involves **independent** work, staff should be positioned at specified locations if hazards, such as busy roads, entrances and exits and deep water, are to be managed.

25.6.139    Activities that involve pupils physically supporting each other should be carefully managed, with time given for familiarisation and practice.

25.6.140    Consideration should be given in the risk-assessment process to the appropriateness of all equipment to be used in problem-solving activities. This is particularly important when using equipment that has not been designed specifically for the task. Due consideration should also be given to the nature and size of the equipment relative to the capabilities of the group and individuals concerned.

## Skiing and snowboarding

### Introduction

> It is essential that readers understand the **general principles** set out at the beginning of this chapter (*25.1–25.3*, pages 203–211) as they apply to all the specific activities included in this section.

25.6.141    Skiing and snowboarding can encourage pupils to develop a wide range of physical skills and qualities, including general fitness, coordination, balance and strength. Foreign residential visits, as cultural experiences, also offer wide-ranging opportunities for personal and social development in challenging new environments.

25.6.142    High-energy activities in winter pose particular physiological challenges and care should be taken to plan, organise and deliver skiing and snowboarding in accordance with an activity-specific risk assessment. Particular care needs to be taken in choosing appropriate venues that are suitable for the prevailing weather and snow conditions.

25.6.143    Detailed information on relevant awards and guidelines on the organisation of snow-sport activities may be obtained from Snowsport England, Snowsport Scotland, Snowsport Wales and the Northern Ireland Ski Council.

25.6.144    The British Association of Snowsport Instructors (BASI) delivers UK coach-education programmes. BASI qualifications are recognised by the International Ski Instructors Association as the benchmark awards for skiers working abroad. For more information, go to www.basi.org.uk

### What staff should know

#### People

25.6.145    Skiing and snowboarding activities should be led by competent, appropriately qualified and relevantly experienced staff.

25.6.146    The relevant qualifications for leaders and technical advisers for snow sport are set out overleaf:

| Activity | Leader Qualifications | Technical Adviser Qualifications |
|---|---|---|
| **On-piste skiing and snowboarding** | | |
| Skiing and snowboarding – instruction | BASI II or local ski school approved | BASI trainer or head of local ski school |
| Skiing and snowboard leading | Alpine Ski Course Leader, Ski Party Leader Award (Snowsport Scotland) | Alpine Ski Course Leader/coach/tutor/assessor, Snowsport Scotland coach/tutor |
| Ski trip organisation only | Snowsport Course Organiser (SCO) | Snowsport appointed SCO coach/tutor |
| Artificial slopes instruction | Club Instructor or Artificial Slope Instructor (ASI) | Snowsport Club Instructor, Tutor or Assessor ASI Tutor/Assessor |

Staff should ensure anyone leading groups in skiing holds the relevant qualification or endorsement.

### Context

25.6.147 Skiing in Britain in mountainous terrain should be planned in the same way as other mountain activities. Particular attention should be paid to the qualifications, knowledge and experience of teaching staff. The BMG Carnet and Snowsport Scotland's Mountain Ski Leader (MSL) are relevant qualifications for operating in this context.

25.6.148 The wearing of **ski helmets** for children up to 14 years old is now compulsory under Italian law and, though helmets are not yet mandatory for skiing in other countries, their use should be considered. LAs are currently formulating their own guidance on this issue.

> For general guidance on this issue, see *Chapter 13: Personal Protection*, pages 95–98.

25.6.149 **Mobile phones** and/or closed-circuit radios make communication on the slopes considerably more manageable and their use is recommended.

25.6.150 Boots, skis and bindings should only be selected and adjusted by qualified technicians.

25.6.151 Ski brakes should be checked to ensure they function properly in the event of skis being released.

25.6.152 **Clothing** should be appropriate to provide protection from snow, wind and cold. The combined cooling effects of wind chill with the burning effects from reflected radiation should not be underestimated, particularly when skiing at altitude. Depending on location, items may include:

- ski suit or ski jacket
- ski trousers or salopettes
- gloves or mittens

234

- goggles and sunglasses
- hat
- suncream and lip salve.

### Artificial slopes

25.6.153   On artificial slopes, full body cover should be worn to protect the arms, legs and hands from friction burns in the event of falls.

### Snow sport abroad

25.6.154   The following points should be considered when **planning** ski or snowboarding trips abroad:

a.   Staff:pupil ratios for every aspect of the proposed itinerary (travel, pastoral-care requirements, evening activities, instruction) should be sufficient to ensure acceptable margins of safety.

b.   Comprehensive travel arrangements to and from the resort need to be planned well in advance and a full risk assessment made (ABTA/ATOL cover is essential).

c.   Pupils must have adequate insurance cover (including medical, rescue and repatriation).

d.   European Health Insurance Cards (EHIC) for each pupil must be regarded as essential documentation for trips within Europe.

e.   Accommodation should be appropriate, safe, secure and risk assessed.

f.   The resort should have slopes with adequate lift systems, appropriate for the skill level of the group.

g.   For package tours, the hired equipment should be modern and well serviced.

h.   A qualified ski technician should be available for the duration of the trip.

i.   Adequate and secure drying and storage facilities should be available.

j.   Ski instructors should be qualified and operate under the insurance arrangements of a recognised ski school.

k.   Staff should have adequate information regarding resorts they have not visited before; a pre-trip inspection is strongly recommended.

25.6.155   **Adult:pupil ratios** for skiing should be based on an informed risk assessment, taking account of relevant factors within the three key dimensions of people, context and organisation.

> For general guidance on this issue, see *Chapter 3: Risk Management*, pages 23–30.

### Organisation

25.6.156   It is important to know the pupils' whereabouts at all times.

25.6.157    Schools should ensure adequate arrangements for **supervision** are in place at all times. If pupils are allowed on the slopes at times when not receiving professional instruction, they should be supervised by school staff who are competent to lead and who have adequate experience and knowledge of the area.

25.6.158    Groups should be graded as beginners, intermediate or advanced according to the demands of the skiing.

25.6.159    School staff should watch for reckless **behaviour** and manage it appropriately. If ski codes are persistently infringed, pupils should be sanctioned to prevent further repetition.

25.6.160    Pupils should not be allowed to ski **alone or outside** marked ski areas and trails.

25.6.161    Group leaders should have access to **emergency equipment**, as appropriate. On piste, this will normally be the responsibility of the instructor and ski patrol.

25.6.162    Safe skiing practice should be taught to pupils (eg the International Ski Federation **Safe Skiing Code** or Snowsport Skiway Code). The main points include the following:

   a.  Pupils should ski in control and adapt their speed and manner of skiing to their ability, the weather, the terrain, the quality of snow and the frequency of other skiers.

   b.  Pupils should choose routes in such a way that, when overtaking, they do not endanger others.

   c.  When entering a marked piste, or starting again after stopping, pupils should look up and down the piste to ensure they will not endanger others.

   d.  Wherever possible, pupils should avoid stopping on the piste in narrow areas or when visibility is restricted; any rests must be taken well to the sides.

   e.  If climbing or descending on foot, pupils should keep to the sides of the piste.

   f.  Pupils should respect all signals and markings.

   g.  If an accident occurs, every skier is duty-bound to assist.

25.6.163    Pupils may need instruction in a number of areas and these should be discussed by school staff prior to the first day on the slopes, for example:

   • use of the various types of lift

   • use of piste maps

   • what to do if skiers become separated from the group.

### Additional information

### Contact details

British Association of Snowsport Instructors (BASI)
Glenmore
Aviemore
PH22 1QU
Tel: 01479-861 717
www.basi.org.uk

236

Northern Ireland Ski Council
43 Bally Maconnell Road, Bangor
Co Down, Northern Ireland
Tel: 01247-450 275

Snowsport England
Area Library Building, Queensway Mall
The Cornbow, Halesowen
West Midlands B63 4AJ
Tel: 0121-501 2314
www.snowsportengland.org.uk

Snowsport Scotland
Hillend, Biggar Road
Midlothian EH10 7EF
Tel: 0131-445 4151
www.snowsportscotland.org

Snowsport Wales
Cardiff Ski and Snowboard Centre
Fairwater Park, Fairwater
Cardiff CF15 3JR
Tel: 029-2056 1904
www.snowsportwales.net

# Part B:  Water Activities

## 25.7  Introduction

25.7.1  A vast range of opportunities and challenges are available involving activity in, on and around water. It is essential that all participants fully recognise the potentially hazardous nature of the water environment and consistently apply appropriate safety procedures.

> It is essential that readers understand the **general principles** set out at the beginning of this chapter (*25.1–25.3*, pages 203–211) as they apply to all the specific activities included in this section.

## 25.8  What Staff Should Know

### People

25.8.1  Water activities should be led by competent, appropriately qualified and relevantly experienced staff.

### Context

25.8.2  The **weather** can be notoriously changeable and accurate weather forecasts, corrected for the locality, are essential. The collective effects of wind strength and direction and air and water temperatures, as environmental variables, need to be taken into account during the planning of water activities.

25.8.3    **Cold-water immersion** causes rapid and sudden cooling unless adequate protective clothing is worn. Added to this are the cooling effects of the wind which, once they have been rescued, chills wet pupils still further. The effects of cold-water immersion and wind chill on pupils' physical and mental states should be monitored rigorously.

25.8.4    The effects of cold-water immersion need to be fully appreciated by the staff responsible for planning water activities, even at warm times of the year, and careful consideration given to what type of insulating and windproof clothing to use. The risks associated with open-water swimming, particularly without the use of wetsuits, should be obvious.

25.8.5    Appropriate **clothing and footwear** should be worn, including wetsuits and helmets, if appropriate. Footwear type will be dependent on a number of factors. The main aim is to protect the feet while not impeding the ability to swim. Wellingtons, for instance, may be appropriate for sailing, canoeing and those water activities where the advice is to stay with the boat or craft as the main source of buoyancy.

25.8.6    For water activities, all participants should wear **CE-approved buoyancy aids or life jackets**; the CE marking testifies that the buoyancy aid has been successfully tested and all fabrics and materials used in its manufacture comply with European standards. 50-newton ISO 12402-5:2006 buoyancy aids are suitable for canoeing, kayaking, windsurfing, dinghy sailing and waterskiing.

25.8.7    Particular care should be taken on **inland waterways, canals and lakes**. Group leaders should:

- check for potentially hazardous debris, which may lie on or under the water

- recognise the health risks associated with contaminated water (Weil's disease)

- take action to minimise the risk from infection if this risk exists; such actions might include:

  - ensuring abrasions are covered with plasters
  - advising pupils to avoid swallowing water
  - ensuring pupils take a shower at the end of the activity.

25.8.8    For activities on larger areas of inland water and the **sea**, consideration should be given to:

- the potential seriousness of these environments and the essential requirement for high levels of competence, suitable qualifications, experience and leadership ability in those who are responsible

- the extent to which weather conditions, tide state and sea state can change very rapidly

- the dangers associated with offshore winds

- local environmental anomalies

- the need to inform the coastguard of activities on the open sea

- the requirement for additional safety equipment (eg flares, charts, VHF radios).

25.8.9    Weil's disease (leptospirosis) is a dangerous condition that, in extreme cases can result in serious illness or death. Leptospirosis, also known as caver's flu or sewerman's flu, is a bacterial infection resulting from exposure to the **Leptospira interrogans** bacterium, which is carried in rodents' urine. The means of infection is via open cuts, scratches and abrasions. In the event of flu-like symptoms appearing after exposure to contaminated water, pupils should see a doctor.

238

25.8.10    Algal scum can cause illness, skin rashes, eye irritation, vomiting, fever and diarrhoea if swallowed. Although not always harmful, it is a sensible precaution to avoid contact with the scum and water close to it.

25.8.11    Staff should consider whether one or more powered **rescue boats** is required to ensure safety and/or assist with the educational aims of the session. If used, safety boats need to be:

- seaworthy and adequately buoyant, with hulls that are properly inflated

- driven by approved people who are suitably qualified and experienced for the level of operation involved

- equipped with suitable emergency equipment (eg first-aid kit, fire extinguisher, survival bag, towlines and 'kill cords')

- adequately fuelled.

25.8.12    The sea, coastal areas and large stretches of open water should be recognised as hazardous environments to work in and great care should be exercised in selecting appropriately competent staff as group leaders in these contexts.

25.8.13    As many water-based activities involve immersion, care should be taken at the planning stage to anticipate the combined effects of wind strength, direction and air and water temperatures on pupils' well-being and enjoyment.

25.8.14    The site-specific risks relating to the activity area should be assessed and managed appropriately.

25.8.15    Adults should remember that stretches of open water with which they have become familiar over many years may appear very intimidating to young eyes and can change unexpectedly in unusual weather or tidal conditions.

## Organisation

25.8.16    Staff should ascertain the level of **water confidence** of each member of the group and consider what level of ability is required to be able to take part in the activity.

25.8.17    Staff should put measures in place to safeguard pupils when afloat and ashore. They should be briefed on the safe movement and handling of boats and be made aware of any areas that are out of bounds. On the water, pupils should stay within the limits of a clearly defined safe activity area.

25.8.18    Activity groups should operate in a manner that is considerate to other water users and makes minimum impact on the natural environment. Leaders should always work within the International Regulations for the Prevention of Collisions at Sea (IRPCS) and pay due regard to local by-laws.

## 25.9    What Pupils Should Know

25.9.1    Pupils should:

- be aware of their personal responsibilities for safety and be introduced to the concept of residual real risk

- behave in accordance with the safety instructions given by staff and, as part of the educative process, be made aware of the variables informing the risk-management strategy and approach to the activity

- never participate in adventurous activities that are:
  - unplanned
  - unsupervised
  - not approved by the school staff leader
- know who the responsible adult is
- be made aware of site-specific hazards (eg crumbling banks, quicksands, height and speed of tides, tidal bores and slippery weed-covered rocks)
- understand the factors relating to water safety, particularly those relating to hypothermia.

## 25.10 Further Guidance Relating to Specific Activities

### Angling

#### Introduction

> It is essential that readers understand the **general principles** set out at the beginning of this chapter (*25.1–25.3*, pages 203–211) as they apply to all the specific activities included in this section.

25.10.1    Angling is popular with many young people. It can provide opportunities to develop an awareness of environmental issues, address conservation matters and promote respect for other water users.

#### What staff should know

#### People

25.10.2    Angling activities should be carried out by competent, appropriately qualified and relevantly experienced staff.

25.10.3    Group leaders should be proficient anglers who have practical experience of the waters in which angling will take place.

25.10.4    Group leaders are strongly recommended to ensure at least one member of the angling party is trained in lifesaving and first aid.

#### Context

25.10.5    Angling can take place in many environments:

- fast-flowing rivers
- meandering streams
- ponds, lakes and reservoirs
- from the seashore
- on the open sea.

In every case, a risk assessment should be made of the venue and its hazards.

25.10.6    An accurate weather forecast and knowledge of local water conditions (eg susceptibility of the venue to flooding, tide times and the effects of wind on tide and sea states) should inform the risk assessment.

240

25.10.7    When fishing from a **boat**:

- it should be fit for purpose and appropriately licensed

- it should not be overloaded and there should be sufficient space

- there should be a method to retrieve anyone who falls in

- that is hired, the boat should conform to the requirements laid down by the Maritime and Coastguard Agency (MCA) and other relevant agencies

- staff members should be vigilant at all times.

### Organisation

25.10.8    Adult:pupil ratios should be decided based on an informed risk assessment, taking account of relevant factors within the three key dimensions of people, context and organisation.

> For general guidance on this issue, see *Chapter 3: Risk Management*, pages 23–30.

25.10.9    Pupils need to be adequately equipped for the prevailing weather conditions.

25.10.10   Appropriate footwear (usually wellingtons) should be worn.

### What pupils should know

25.10.11   Pupils should know:

- the basic principles associated with water safety (*25.7.1–25.9.1*, pages 237–240)

- not to fish within 30m of overhead power lines; electricity can spark across the gap

- not to fish near locks or weirs, where there is a danger of falling in.

### Additional information

#### Useful websites

Environment Agency fishing information
www.environment-agency.gov.uk/subjects/fish/246986/1749840/?lang=_e

## Canoeing and kayaking

### Introduction

> It is essential that readers understand the **general principles** set out at the beginning of this chapter (*25.1–25.3*, pages 203–211) as they apply to all the specific activities included in this section.

25.10.12   Canoeing and kayaking take place in a wide variety of contexts and environments; from open boating in the Lake District to offshore sea kayaking on the coasts of Scotland, and from flat-water marathon racing on the Thames to play boating in Wales. They epitomise, in every way, the notion of sport as a route to adventure.

25.10.13   Further detailed guidance and information on awards may be obtained from the British Canoe Union (BCU – the lead body for canoeing and kayaking in the UK), the Scottish Canoe Association, the Welsh Canoeing Association and the Canoe Association of Northern Ireland.

## What staff should know

### People

25.10.14   Canoeing and kayaking activities should be led by competent, appropriately qualified and relevantly experienced staff.

25.10.15   The relevant qualifications for leaders and technical advisers for canoeing and kayaking are set out below:

| Activity | Leader Qualifications | Technical Adviser Qualifications |
|---|---|---|
| **Canoeing and kayaking Inland water** | | |
| Very sheltered water | BCU UKCC Level 1* plus site specific training** + Valid First Aid + CRB (or Home Nation Equivalent) + over 18yrs | As a general rule, technical advisers should hold qualifications at least one level above the leaders being accredited and demonstrate more extensive experience. |
| Sheltered inland water | BCU UKCC Level 1* plus site specific training** + Valid First Aid + CRB (or Home Nation Equivalent) + over 18yrs OR BCU UKCC Level 2 | |
| Moderate; white water – grade 2–3 and equivalent weirs. Open water no more than 500m from shore and winds below force 4 | BCU UKCC Level 3 | |
| Advanced; white water grade 3–4 and above. Open water more than 500m from shore and/or winds above force 4 | BCU UKCC Level 3 + 5* Leader Award (White Water) | |
| Moderate; white water descents up to grade 2, and equivalent weirs. Open water no more than 500m from shore and winds below force 4 | BCU UKCC Level 3 | |
| Advanced; white water grade 3 and above, very large lakes/lochs | BCU UKCC Level 3 + 5* Leader Award (Canoe) | |
| Moderate; white water descents up to grade 2, and equivalent weirs. Open water no more than 500m from shore and winds below force 4 | BCU UKCC Level 3 (Touring) | |
| Advanced; white water descents up to grade 3. Open water more than 500m from shore and/or winds above | force 4 BCU UKCC Level 3 + 5* Leader Award (Touring) | |

*safe practice* in physical education and school sport

**Continued:**

| | Sea | |
|---|---|---|
| Sheltered tidal water | BCU UKCC Level 2 | As a general rule, technical advisers should hold qualifications at least one level above the leaders being accredited and demonstrate more extensive experience. |
| Moderate tidal water | BCU UKCC Level 3 | |
| Advanced sea | BCU UKCC Level 3 + 5* Leader Award (Sea) | |
| | **Surf** | |
| Moderate surf | BCU UKCC Level 3 (Surf) | As a general rule, technical advisers should hold qualifications at least one level above the leaders being accredited and demonstrate more extensive experience. |
| Advanced surf (>1m) | BCU UKCC Level 3 + 5* Leader Award (Surf) | |

**Note**: At the time of writing, this matrix is under further review by BCU. See the BCU website.

Staff should ensure anyone leading canoeing and kayaking activities has the relevant NGB qualifications or necessary alternative endorsement.

### Context

25.10.16    The NGB awards, administered by the home-nation boards, are divided into two areas: coaching and personal skills/leadership. They are specific to a variety of craft and a wide range of environments. Specialist knowledge (for kayaks and canoes) is available in the following areas:

- racing

- slalom

- wild-water racing

- surfing

- open canoeing

- polo

- freestyle

- sea kayaking

- white-water kayaking

- flat water.

25.10.17    Pupils should be adequately equipped for the prevailing conditions. Appropriate footwear should be worn at all times to afford the necessary level of protection. To avoid problems with footrests in kayaks, shoelaces should be neat with small loops.

25.10.18    If **spraydecks** are to be worn, the quick-release strap should be securely fastened to the spraydeck material. When attached to the kayak, the safety strap needs to be visible.

25.10.19  **Helmets** should be worn on river trips (although open canoeing on gentle rivers may not require this), for surfing, polo and when kayaking on shallow lakes where there is a possibility of concussive injury. Some raft games will require helmets and, for polo, a protective face mask should be attached.

> For general guidance on this issue, see *Chapter 13: Personal Protection*, pages 95–98.

25.10.20  Paddle sports cover a wide range of craft in a very wide range of environments and organisation on the water will vary according to:

- the staff's appraisal of their own personal ability, accreditation, experience, knowledge and motivations

- the availability, experience and qualifications of accompanying staff

- the number, age, ability and previous experience of the group

- the weather forecast and, in particular, the wind strength and direction

- the air and water temperatures

- the available clothing and equipment, its condition and suitability

- site-specific factors, including the proximity of escape routes

- the need for a workable and appropriate group-management strategy while on the water.

25.10.21  For activities on moving inland waters, risk assessment will include consideration of the following:

a.  Travelling times and transport logistics should be appropriate.

b.  The trailer must be securely and correctly loaded. Lights and other safety features must comply with legal requirements. This is the responsibility of the driver.

c.  The leader should have prior knowledge of the river (eg access agreements, weirs, fallen trees, difficulty of rapids and escape routes).

d.  If travelling on moving water, the boats should be appropriately equipped for this.

e.  Levels of water will affect the levels of difficulty (in large catchment areas, river levels may remain high for a number of days after heavy rain, particularly if lake-fed).

f.  Additional safety equipment will normally be required. Depending on the type of canoeing or kayaking, this may include helmets, spraydecks, split paddles, repair kit, throw lines, group shelter and first-aid kit.

25.10.22  For activities on larger areas of inland water and the sea, risk assessment will include consideration of:

- the potential seriousness of these environments and the essential requirement for high levels of competence, appropriate qualifications, experience and leadership ability in those who are responsible

- the extent to which weather conditions, tide state and sea state can change very rapidly

- the dangers associated with offshore winds

- local environmental anomalies

244

- the need to inform the coastguard for some activities on the sea
- the requirement for additional safety equipment; depending on the activity and venue, this may include flares, charts and VHF radios.

### Organisation

25.10.23 Adult:pupil ratios should be decided based on an informed risk assessment, taking account of relevant factors within the three key dimensions of people, context and organisation.

> For general guidance on this issue, see *Chapter 3: Risk Management,* pages 23–30.

25.10.24 Pupils should be well briefed in capsize procedure and aware of rescue options available according to the type and nature of the canoeing/kayaking activity.

25.10.25 A **signalling and communications** system should be agreed with all members of the party for trips on moving water.

25.10.26 Group leadership and risk management on the water will be a dynamic process where the leader will place him/herself in a position of most usefulness, taking into account all context-specific factors. The ability to think clearly and manage risk appropriately when above the rapids, on reaching the headland or in the surf is critically important.

25.10.27 By appointing an experienced paddler to bring up the rear, the leader can reduce the chance of individuals becoming separated from the group. The parameters for the delegation of any leadership responsibility need to be concisely and clearly defined.

25.10.28 Safe lifting and handling techniques should be observed when portaging boats.

### What pupils should know

25.10.29 Pupils should know:

- the basic principles associated with water safety (*25.7.1–25.9.1,* pages 237–240)
- the requirement for the group to stay together at all times
- the requirement for an effective system of communication on the water
- the propensity of canoes to drift in the wind
- the need for appropriate clothing and well-maintained equipment
- what action to take in the event of a capsize.

### Additional information

### Resources

British Canoe Union (2006) *British Canoe Union Coaching Handbook.* Caernarfon: Pesda Press. ISBN: 978-0-954706-16-6.

Ferrero, F. (2006) *White Water Safety and Rescue.* Caernarfon: Pesda Press. ISBN: 978-0-954706-15-9.

### Contact details

British Canoe Union
British Canoe Union HQ
18 Market Place, Bingham
Nottingham NG13 8AP
Tel: 0845-370 9500
www.bcu.org.uk

Canoe Association of Northern Ireland
Unit 2 Rivers Edge, 13–15 Ravenhill Road
Belfast BT6 8DN
Tel: 0870-240 5065
www.cani.org.uk

Scottish Canoe Association
Caledonia House, South Gyle
Edinburgh EH12 9DQ
Tel: 0131-317 7314
www.canoescotland.com

Welsh Canoeing Association
Canolfan Tryweryn
Frongoch, Bala
Gwynedd LL23 7NU
Tel: 01678-521 199
www.welsh-canoeing.org.uk

## Rafting

### Introduction

> It is essential that readers understand the **general principles** set out at the beginning of this chapter (*25.1–25.3*, pages 203–211) as they apply to all the specific activities included in this section.

25.10.30   White-water rafting involves paddling purpose-made inflatable rafts on white-water rivers.

25.10.31   Improvised rafting using barrels and planks as building materials is an outdoor activity that is often used for team building and management-development programmes.

### What staff should know

#### People

25.10.32   Rafting activities should be led by competent, appropriately qualified and relevantly experienced staff.

25.10.33   For **improvised rafts**, group leaders should be experienced in construction techniques. Rafts may distort when placed on the water and care will be needed, during design and construction, to anticipate the effect of this.

25.10.34    An appropriately staffed **safety boat** may be required for rafting activities that take place on stretches of open water where individuals may have difficulty reaching the shore in the event of capsize.

25.10.35    The **British Canoe Union Raft Guide scheme** is the nationally recognised award scheme for guiding commercial rafts.

### Context

25.10.36    The vast majority of those wishing to white-water raft will choose a commercial organisation employing qualified raft guides. These companies need to have adequate risk-assessment and risk-management strategies in place that are in line with current best practice.

25.10.37    For improvised rafts, all pupils should be made aware of the hazards involved in lifting and handling the construction materials, which should be fit for purpose. Clear construction and safety guidelines should form part of the initial briefing.

25.10.38    At the construction stage, helmets may be useful.

> For general guidance on this issue, see *Chapter 13: Personal Protection*, pages 95–98.

25.10.39    Pupils should be adequately **dressed for immersion** and helmets and buoyancy aids should be worn, even in shallow water. The risk of entrapment must be anticipated and managed appropriately.

### Organisation

25.10.40    Adult:pupil ratios should be decided based on an informed risk assessment, taking account of relevant factors within the three key dimensions of people, context and organisation.

> For general guidance on this issue, see *Chapter 3: Risk Management*, pages 23–30.

25.10.41    Clear **communications** will be necessary to ensure safe lifting and handling techniques are used.

25.10.42    A **capsize or break-up** of the improvised raft should be considered a real possibility and an appropriate action plan established to rescue anyone in the water.

25.10.43    If safety boats are to be used, appropriate procedures should be followed in the event of capsize or break-up. Safety boat 'kill cords' should be used, and the instructor should carry a knife.

### What pupils should know

25.10.44    Pupils should:

- know the basic principles associated with water safety (*25.7.1–25.9.1*, pages 237–240)

- be made aware of the requirement for the group to stay together at all times; they will initially be unaware of the propensity of rafts to drift in the wind.

# Dinghy sailing

### Introduction

It is essential that readers understand the **general principles** set out at the beginning of this chapter (*25.1–25.3*, pages 203–211) as they apply to all the specific activities included in this section.

25.10.45 Sailing is a long-established adventure activity that has become a core component of outdoor education. It offers opportunities for developing physical skills, self-confidence and self-esteem and is used frequently for team building, leadership and management-development programmes.

25.10.46 The **Royal Yachting Association** (RYA) and **National School Sailing Association** (NSSA) provide detailed guidance and information on relevant awards.

### What staff should know

### People

25.10.47 Sailing activities should be carried out by competent, appropriately qualified and relevantly experienced staff.

25.10.48 The relevant qualifications for leaders and technical advisers for sailing are set out below:

| Activity | Leader Qualifications | Technical Adviser Qualifications |
|---|---|---|
| **Sailing** | | |
| Sea/tidal waters; coastal journeys | RYA Advanced Instructor Coastal | Senior Instructor Coastal and Advanced Instructor Award |
| Confined sea/tidal waters | Instructor Coastal | Senior Instructor Coastal |
| Inland waters | Instructor Inland | Senior Instructor Inland |

Staff should ensure anyone leading groups in sailing holds the relevant NGB awards or has the necessary alternative endorsement.

### Context

25.10.49 Prior knowledge and experience of the **sailing area** should be sought at the planning stage and venues should be selected that are appropriate to pupils' level of skill, knowledge and experience.

25.10.50 The combined effects of wind strength, direction and air and water temperatures will have significant effects on pupils' well-being and enjoyment and staff should structure the session accordingly.

25.10.51 The site-specific risks relating to the sailing area, such as offshore winds, lee shores and shallows, should be assessed and managed appropriately.

25.10.52    Though helmets are not usually used in sailing, they may be of use in certain circumstances for groups of beginners.

> For general guidance on this issue, see *Chapter 13: Personal Protection*, pages 95–98.

25.10.53    If training shoes are worn, the laces should be fastened securely. Wellingtons, appropriate in many circumstances, may impede pupils' ability to swim but staying with the boat as the main source of buoyancy will reduce the impact of this.

25.10.54    Wetsuits and footwear that facilitates swimming is recommended in circumstances where capsizes are likely.

### Organisation

25.10.55    Adult:pupil ratios should be decided based on an informed risk assessment, taking account of relevant factors within the three key dimensions of people, context and organisation.

> For general guidance on this issue, see *Chapter 3: Risk Management*, pages 23–30.

25.10.56    Boats should be checked to ensure they are seaworthy, adequately buoyant and **fit for purpose**.

25.10.57    The number of pupils allocated per dinghy should be in line with the recommendations of the manufacturer and RYA, and good practice.

25.10.58    Pupils should be instructed on what to do in the event of **capsize**.

25.10.59    The effects of cold-water **immersion and wind chill** on pupils' physical and mental states must be monitored at all times and the consequences of capsizes considered. The need to reef should be considered in good time.

25.10.60    **Safety cover** needs to be available, in line with RYA recommendations. Rescue craft, where used, should be staffed by competent and appropriately qualified adults. Safety-boat 'kill cords' should be used and staff should carry a knife.

### What pupils should know

25.10.61    Pupils should:

- know the basic principles associated with water safety (*25.7.1–25.9.1*, pages 237–240)

- be instructed in the appropriate course of action in the event of capsize

- stay within the defined sailing area and be made aware of the recall signal.

### Additional information

#### Resources

NSSA (1998) *Sailing Across the Curriculum: A practical handbook for teachers, centre leaders, club leaders and all interested adults*. Windermere: The National Schools' Sailing Association. ISBN: 978-0-953213-30-6.

RYA Training (2005) *Dinghy Coaching Handbook & Logbook*. Southampton: RYA. ISBN: 978-0-901501-96-7.

**Contact details**

National School Sailing Association
Green Moss
Oakthwaite Road, Windermere
Cumbria LA23 2BB
www.nssa.org.uk

Royal Yachting Association
RYA House, Ensign Way
Hamble, Southampton
Hampshire SO31 4YA
Tel: 023-8060 4100
www.rya.co.uk

Royal Yachting Association Northern Ireland
House of Sport, Upper Malone Road
Belfast BT9 5LA
Tel: 02890-383 812
Email: admin@ryani.org.uk

Royal Yachting Association Scotland
Redheughs Rigg
South Gyle
Edinburgh EH12 9DQ
Tel: 0131-317 7388
Email: admin@ryascotland.org.uk

Welsh Yachting Association
8 Llys-y-Mor
Plas Menai
Caernarfon
Gwynedd LL55 1UE
Tel: 01248-670 738
Email: admin@welshsailing.org

## Windsurfing

It is essential that readers understand the **general principles** set out at the beginning of this chapter (*25.1–25.3*, pages 203–211) as they apply to all the specific activities included in this section.

### What staff should know

#### People

25.10.62   Windsurfing activities should be carried out by competent, appropriately qualified and relevantly experienced staff.

25.10.63   The relevant qualifications for leaders and technical advisers for windsurfing are set out on the next page:

| Activity | Leader Qualifications | Technical Adviser Qualifications |
|---|---|---|
| **Windsurfing** | | |
| Sea/tidal waters | RYA Start or Intermediate Instructor Coastal | RYA Windsurfing Senior Instructor Coastal |
| Inland Waters | RYA Start Windsurfing Instructor Inland | RYA Windsurfing Senior Instructor Inland |

Staff should ensure anyone leading groups windsurfing holds the relevant NGB award or necessary alternative endorsement.

### Context

25.10.64 **Dry-land simulators** form an essential part of the recognised teaching scheme. They should be used carefully to ensure safe practice; they should be low and stable, and boards should be securely fastened to meet RYA standards.

25.10.65 The use of tethered boards should be considered when working with beginners in the early stages of learning on water.

25.10.66 The wearing of wetsuits is recommended in all weather conditions to afford an element of protection from bumps and scrapes.

25.10.67 Soft-soled **shoes** that grip the board should be worn and laces should be fastened securely.

25.10.68 Though helmets are not usually worn when windsurfing, they may be of use in certain circumstances for groups of beginners.

> For general guidance on this issue, see *Chapter 13: Personal Protection,* pages 95–98.

25.10.69 **Wetsuits** provide some buoyancy, as do most waist harnesses. If buoyancy aids are worn with harnesses, they can obstruct hooking to and unhooking from the mast. It is for this reason that proficient windsurfers tend not to wear buoyancy aids. In all cases where pupils are not using harnesses, they should wear buoyancy aids (buoyancy aids also provide thermal insulation and protection). Approval should be sought from appropriately qualified staff if pupils are to use harnesses without buoyancy aids.

### Organisation

25.10.70 Adult:pupil ratios should be decided based on an informed risk assessment, taking account of relevant factors within the three key dimensions of people, context and organisation.

> For general guidance on this issue, see *Chapter 3: Risk Management,* pages 23–30.

25.10.71 Boards should be checked to ensure they are seaworthy, adequately buoyant and fit for purpose.

25.10.72 Pupils should be made aware of the dangers of jumping off the board in shallow water.

25.10.73 Strong winds can take windsurfers a long way very quickly, even when drifting. Safety cover should be available, in line with RYA recommendations, with rescue craft, where used, staffed by competent and appropriately qualified adults. Safety boat 'kill cords' should be used and staff should carry a knife.

### What pupils should know

25.10.74 Pupils should know:

- the basic principles associated with water safety (*25.7.1–25.9.1*, pages 237–240)

- the hazards associated with shallow water.

### Additional information

#### Resources

RYA (2006) 'RYA National Windsurfing Scheme Start Windsurfing Teaching System', www.rya.org.uk/NR/rdonlyres/EAB7F751-60FF-4F1F-A983-93B78970F2FC/0/W4a.pdf

RYA (2006) 'Buoyancy afloat – windsurfing supplement', www.rya.org.uk/NR/rdonlyres/A0CBE7F6-0FED-487F-B04B-C63DBA5EFB04/0/Buoyancyafloatwindsurfingsupplement.pdf

## Surfing

### Introduction

> It is essential that readers understand the **general principles** set out at the beginning of this chapter (*25.1–25.3*, pages 203–211) as they apply to all the specific activities included in this section.

25.10.75 Surfing provides cardiovascular exercise by using upper-body muscles to paddle through the surf and leg muscles to guide the board once up and riding. It develops balance, strength and coordination while demanding high levels of personal commitment to learning about, and staying safe in, surf.

25.10.76 The **British Surfing Association (BSA)** is the NGB for surfing in the UK. The **Royal Life Saving Society UK (RLSS)** and the **Surf Life Saving Association of Great Britain (SLSA)** also offer specialist training in lifesaving and first aid.

### What staff should know

#### People

25.10.77 Surfing activities should be led by competent, appropriately qualified and relevantly experienced staff.

25.10.78 In any surf where pupils will be out of their depth, they should be able swimmers who are capable of swimming strongly. Weaker swimmers may need to wear a buoyancy aid and only surf in small waves close to shore.

25.10.79 **Qualified lifeguards** should be present at all times for organised school-led activities.

### Context

25.10.80    The site-specific **risks** relating to the surf beach should be assessed and managed appropriately and sea conditions need to be appropriate for the pupils' levels of ability and experience.

25.10.81    Pupils should surf in recognised surfing areas, where these are defined (usually the area between black and white chequered flags).

### Organisation

25.10.82    Adult: pupil ratios should be decided based on an informed risk assessment, taking account of relevant factors within the three key dimensions of people, context and organisation.

> For general guidance on this issue, see *Chapter 3: Risk Management*, pages 23–30.

25.10.83    The instructor needs to gauge the levels of **swimming ability** of pupils who arrive on the day.

25.10.84    Pupils should wear wetsuits, preferably those providing arm and leg cover, that protect against excessive convective heat loss in water and air.

25.10.85    Surfers should be clearly **briefed** about site-specific hazards, such as no-go zones, the location of rips, undertows, longshore drift, rocks and groynes, dumping waves and other surfers, before entering the surf.

25.10.86    Surfers should be clearly briefed on, and keep to, any planned outgoing and incoming lane system.

25.10.87    Surfers should wear a surf leash to:

- prevent loss of the board
- assure the continued presence of a vital source of buoyancy
- increase visibility from the beach
- prevent other surfers from being hit by the board.

25.10.88    A good group-management system is to pair surfers up with a shore-based **buddy** who is responsible for observation at all times. High levels of concentration are required to 'buddy' effectively and leaders should not rely on pupil buddy systems alone.

25.10.89    Leaders should ensure surfers do not overtire themselves if this could lead to difficulties in getting safely to shore.

### What pupils should know

25.10.90    Pupils should:

- know the basic principles associated with water safety (*25.7.1–25.9.1*, pages 237–240)
- understand the surfers' code of conduct:
  - when paddling out, avoid surfers who are riding waves by paddling into the broken (white) water
  - if someone else is already up and riding on the wave, another surfer must not take off (known as 'dropping in')

- if two surfers are paddling to catch a wave, the surfer closest to the peak (breaking part of the wave) has priority
- stay within the defined surfing area and stay with the board
- be aware of the agreed visual or audible recall signal.

### Additional information

#### Resources

Bradford, J. (2001) 'Surfing Info Sheet', www.aals.org.uk/guidance_details.php/pArticleHeadingID=33

BSA 'BSA Code of Conduct', www.britsurf.co.uk/html/code_of_conduct.asp

Marine and Coastguard Agency Beach Safety Information www.mcga.gov.uk/c4mca/mcga-home/education.htm

#### Contact details

British Surfing Association
International Surfing Centre
Fistral Beach, Newquay
Cornwall TR7 1HY
Tel: 01637-876 474
www.britsurf.co.uk

Royal Life Saving Society UK
River House
High Street, Broom
Warwickshire B50 4HN
Tel: 01789-773 994
www.lifesavers.org.uk

Surf Life Saving Association of Great Britain
1st Floor, 19 Southernhay West
Exeter EX1 1PJ
Tel: 01392 218007
www.surflifesaving.org.uk

## Sub-aqua activities

### Introduction

> It is essential that readers understand the **general principles** set out at the beginning of this chapter (*25.1–25.3*, pages 203–211) as they apply to all the specific activities included in this section.

25.10.91   Underwater exploration often begins with snorkelling but the proficient use of scuba equipment significantly enhances the levels of enjoyment, challenge and opportunities for sub-aqua activities farther afield.

25.10.92   Further information may be obtained from the **British Sub-Aqua Club (BSAC)** and the **Professional Association of Diving Instructors (PADI)**.

### What staff should know

#### People

25.10.93    Sub-aqua activities should be led by competent, appropriately qualified and relevantly experienced staff.

25.10.94    Diving instructors and skippers of boats used by divers should be competent and appropriately qualified.

25.10.95    Due to the specialist nature of sub-aqua activities, only recognised and fully **accredited teaching centres** should be used to deliver diving programmes.

25.10.96    Snorkellers should be competent swimmers. The ability to swim at least 50m is an accepted indicator of swimming competence.

#### Context

25.10.97    The site-specific **risks** relating to the diving area should be assessed and managed appropriately, taking into account relevant variables, including:

- water temperature
- depth of water
- currents
- pollution
- underwater obstructions
- condition of the lake or seabed
- other water users
- proximity to safe egress.

25.10.98    Swimming/snorkelling/diving areas need to be clearly defined.

25.10.99    All **equipment** should be fit for purpose and conform to CE standards.

#### Organisation

25.10.100    The following points should be considered in planning open-water dives:

a. An appropriately staffed and equipped support boat should be available.

b. Appropriate diving suits should be available for the prevailing conditions. If dry suits are to be used in open water because of conditions, then pool training for all participants should be given to familiarise them with usage.

c. The group leader should be satisfied that pupils are sufficiently physically fit and have received appropriate instructions to complete the dive safely.

d. Pupils suffering from fatigue, colds or other infections should not be permitted to dive.

e. Divers should work in pairs, using agreed 'buddy' system procedures.

f. All divers should know and observe the BSAC Divers' Code of Conduct.

## What pupils should know

25.10.101  Pupils should:

- know the basic principles associated with water safety (*25.7.1–25.9.1*, pages 237–240)

- understand the many issues covered in the BSAC Divers' Code of Conduct (BSAC) under the headings:

  - On the beach, river bank or lakeside

  - In and on the water

  - On conservation

  - On wrecks

- know to stay within the defined diving area and stick to the protocols of the 'buddy' system throughout.

## Additional information

### Resources

BSAC (2004) 'Risk Assessment Guidelines for Swimming Pools', www.bsac.org/uploads/documents/Resources/Risk_Assessment/rapool2.pdf

BSAC (2006) 'Divers Code', www.bsac.org/page/129/divers-code.htm

Ellerby, D. (2002) *The Diving Manual*. Richmond, Surrey: Circle Publishing/BSAC. ISBN: 978-0-953891-92-4.

HSE (2007) 'Diving at Work Regulations 1997: List of approved qualifications dated 18 May 2007', www.hse.gov.uk/diving/qualifications/index.htm

### Contact details

British Sub-Aqua Club
Telford's Quay, South Pier Road
Ellesmere Port, South Wirral
Cheshire CH65 4FL
Tel: 0151-350 6200
www.bsac.org

Professional Association of Diving Instructors
Unit 7, St Philips, Central Albert Road
St Philips, Bristol BS2 OPD
Tel: 0117-300 7234
www.padi.com/padi/default.aspx

## Rowing

### Introduction

It is essential that readers understand the **general principles** set out at the beginning of this chapter (*25.1–25.3, pages 203–211*) as they apply to all the specific activities included in this section.

25.10.102    Rowing, as a leisure sport, provides high-quality aerobic exercise that benefits the heart and lungs and strengthens all the major muscle groups in a smooth, impact-free, rhythmic motion. Competitive rowing, in which anaerobic and strength conditioning form an integral part of the training regime, has a long tradition as an Olympic sport in Britain. Whether for leisure or competition, rowing offers diverse opportunities for training and enjoyment, both on and off the water. Perhaps more importantly, with increasing obesity rates in children now posing major challenges for the future of the nation's health provision, it should be noted that rowing burns calories faster than cycling at the same perceived level of exertion.

25.10.103    Additional guidance and information may be obtained from the **Amateur Rowing Association** (ARA).

### What staff should know

#### People

25.10.104    Rowing activities should be led by competent, appropriately qualified and relevantly experienced staff.

25.10.105    In line with ARA recommendations, every school/organisation should appoint a named competent **safety adviser** whose role is to implement and offer advice on the ARA Water Safety Code.

25.10.106    The main purpose of the **coxswain** is safety. He/she must be fully aware of his/her responsibilities to his/her crew and other water users, in line with ARA recommendations.

#### Context

25.10.107    A **competent member of staff** should ensure the weather and water conditions are appropriate for rowing.

25.10.108    Site-specific **risk assessments** for the stretch of water should be carried out, noting hazards such as weirs, sluices, locks and the effects of tides and currents. A plan of the local rowing area with egress points, public telephones and marked hazards is very useful.

25.10.109    All rowers should be able to swim, in accordance with the ARA safety guidelines. Rowers should:

- be able to swim at least 50m in light clothing, 25m to be performed on the back when swimming with the boat as the life raft

- be able to swim to pick up an object from the bottom of the pool

- practise using throw bags in rescue scenarios

- rehearse the capsize/immersion drill, accepting it as a crucial element of training

- gain experience of the available self-rescue options that complement the golden rule of 'staying with the boat'.

25.10.110 Rowing as a sport has developed without the use of buoyancy aids because they can impede rowing movement and lead to overheating during strenuous activity, but the ARA strongly advises their use for beginners who have not completed the swim test or capsize/immersion drill. In any event, members of school staff should follow the guidance of their employing authority and the use of rowers' life jackets (approved by the ARA) is recommended.

25.10.111 Coxswains, umpires, coaches and launch personnel should wear life jackets or buoyancy aids when afloat. The manual gas inflation life jacket is recommended, where inflation occurs when the rower pulls a cord, which releases carbon dioxide from a cylinder in the jacket.

25.10.112 Before being allowed on the water, pupils should be fully briefed on:

- local navigation rules and site-specific hazards

- the effects of currents, weirs, sluices, tides and winds

- the rights and customs of other water users

- the course of action in the event of swamping or capsize.

25.10.113 Rowers should be appropriately equipped and clothed for the prevailing weather conditions. They should be physically fit enough to safely undertake the proposed activity.

25.10.114 **Boats** need to be seaworthy, with adequate buoyancy. Particular attention should be paid to any heel restraints, fitted shoes and quick-release mechanisms; these should be in good working order.

25.10.115 Boats should be launched with their bows facing in accordance with the agreed rowing circulation pattern.

25.10.116 Coxswains need to be able to see beyond the bow of their boat.

### Organisation

25.10.117 Adult:pupil ratios should be decided based on an informed risk assessment, taking account of relevant factors within the three key dimensions of people, context and organisation.

> For general guidance on this issue, see *Chapter 3: Risk Management,* pages 23–30.

25.10.118 Throw ropes should be available and carried by trainers/coaches if coaching from tow paths.

25.10.119 All coaching launches and safety boats should be equipped and staffed appropriately and in line with ARA recommendations.

### What pupils should know

25.10.120 Pupils should:

- know the basic principles associated with water safety (*25.7.1–25.9.1,* pages 237–240)

- stay with the boat as a source of buoyancy in the event of a capsize.

## Additional information

### Resources

Amateur Rowing Association 'Water Safety Code',
www.ara-rowing.org/Asp/uploadedFiles/File/Safety_code.pdf

ARA (2008) 'Safety Aids',
www.ara-rowing.org/render.aspx?siteID=1&navIDs=1,249,258

Concept 2 'Rowing – An Effective Calorie-burning Exercise',
www.concept2.com/us/training/goals/weightcontrol/wt_effective.asp

### Contact details

Amateur Rowing Association
The Priory, 6 Lower Mall
Hammersmith, London W6 9DJ
Tel: 020-8237 6700
www.ara-rowing.org

## Swimming in open water

It is essential that readers understand the **general principles** set out at the beginning of this chapter (*25.1–25.3*, pages 203–211) as they apply to all the specific activities included in this section.

### What staff should know

#### People

25.10.121   Swimming activities in open water should be carried out by competent, appropriately qualified and relevantly experienced staff.

25.10.122   Swimming in open water needs to be closely supervised by **competent staff**, able to affect rescue and resuscitation procedures.

25.10.123   Additional information may be obtained from the Amateur Swimming Association (ASA), the Swimming Teachers' Association (STA) and the Marine and Coastguard Agency's Beach Safety Information.

#### Context

25.10.124   It is unlikely the water will be clear. Precautions should be taken to check for underwater obstructions, the depth of the water, the extent of weed, composition of the bottom and the likelihood of hazardous rubbish before allowing anyone to enter the water. While the extent of pollution is difficult to establish, a professional judgement may need to be made on the quality of water and its suitability for recreational or competitive swimming.

25.10.125   The existence and possible effects of any current, tidal flow, wave height or wind-chill factor need to be established before allowing anyone to enter the water.

25.10.126   Easy entry and exit points are essential.

25.10.127   Venues should be selected where water traffic will not impinge on safety.

25.10.128   Parents should be informed when it is planned to offer open-water swimming to pupils and their consent obtained.

### Organisation

25.10.129    A thorough **risk assessment** of the event or occasion needs to be made prior to allowing open-water swimming to take place. Consultation with agencies having local knowledge of the venue needs to be part of the risk assessment wherever possible. A local weather forecast is an important part of the risk assessment.

25.10.130    Groups should be **briefed** thoroughly and made aware that the temperature of open water is often less than what they would be familiar with in a swimming pool and that they should proceed with caution when first entering the water, particularly after spending time in the hot sun.

25.10.131    **Boundaries** for swimming in open water should be set, clearly visible and over a manageably contained area. Swimmers should not venture outside the boundaries. Regular head counts should be carried out. Weaker swimmers should keep to areas where it is easier to stand and they should be monitored frequently.

25.10.132    Groups should be briefed on the requirements for the open-water situation prior to entering the water.

25.10.133    Supervising staff should be positioned around the boundaries to monitor swimmers in relation to cold, fatigue, discomfort or fear and to prevent any excursions outside the boundaries. Regular head counts should be standard practice.

25.10.134    Staff should also monitor the effects of sun, wind, tide, sea state, current or weather forecast on the group. A review of whether to continue the event or occasion should be made according to the particular circumstances.

25.10.135    Staff must be able to rescue any swimmer in difficulty. Depending on the nature of the event, this may involve the need for **lifeguards** with an open-water endorsement, safety boats, rescue equipment, provision of facilities to treat hypothermia, the presence of emergency services and changing accommodation.

25.10.136    **Adequate clothing** needs to be available for swimmers to change into when they leave the water.

25.10.137    Appropriate footwear is advisable when swimming in open water in order to avoid the likelihood of foot injuries.

### What pupils should know

25.10.138    Pupils should know:

- the basic principles associated with water safety (*25.7.1–25.9.1*, pages 237–240)

- that swimming in open water is very different to swimming in a heated pool and they should not enter open water other than in a supervised activity or an emergency

- that currents, tides, underwater obstructions, water depth and weeds may create hazards additional to those encountered in swimming pools

- that sudden or unexpected immersion in cold water can have a sudden and dramatic effect on the body that may impair an individual's ability to swim any distance to safety

- the appropriate safety procedures

- to stay in the defined swimming area.

### Additional information

**Contact details**

Amateur Swimming Association
Harold Fern House
Derby Square, Loughborough
Leicestershire LE11 5AL
Tel: 01509-618 700
www.britishswimming.org

Swimming Teachers' Association
Anchor House
Birch Street, Walsall
West Midlands WS2 8HZ
Tel: 01922-645 097
www.sta.co.uk

**Useful websites**

Marine and Coastguard Agency Safety Information
www.mcga.gov.uk/c4mca/mcga-safety_information.htm

# Part C: Emerging Activities

# 25.11 Introduction

25.11.1  As participants seek additional and varied challenges relating to the outdoor and adventurous environment, a number of activities are beginning to emerge that are potentially high risk. Examples of such activity might include parkour (free running/urban gymnastics), kite surfing, free diving and land boarding.

25.11.2  Because emerging activities are **not regulated** by an NGB or national association, principles relating to safe practice are inevitably in their infancy and lack an effective communication network. Some emerging activities groups would not welcome intervention and oversight in the sense of compromising and limiting independence, creativity and individual choice in seeking out extreme and potentially dangerous pastimes.

25.11.3  This poses particular difficulties for staff charged with a duty of care in safeguarding the health and well-being of pupils.

25.11.4  It is advisable for staff to refrain from actively promoting involvement by pupils in activities that lack a regulatory structure and identified code of practice, whether within the curriculum or as part of school sport provision.

25.11.5  At the time of writing, discussions are ongoing between British Gymnastics and representatives from parkour/free running with a view to establishing an accreditation and training process.

## 25.12    Case Law Examples

25.12.1    Dickinson versus Cornwall County Council, Exeter County Court (1999):
*This case emphasised the importance of security of premises being a key aspect of forward planning and ongoing risk assessment, in order to ensure the safety of groups when using residential venues.*

25.12.2    R versus Kite, Court of Appeal (1996):
*The Lyme Bay canoeing tragedy occurred, in part, because of the inexperience and lack of relevant qualifications of the staff provided by the adventure company to lead the activity. The managing director was held responsible for failing to maintain proper safety standards and provide sufficiently experienced staff. This incompetent leadership was deemed to be a substantial cause for the deaths of the students involved.*

25.12.3    Ramsay versus Kings School and the Ministry of Defence, Lincoln County Court (1999): *The Army Youth Team managed an adventure camp for schools. A pupil broke his arm during a mountain-biking activity that was judged to be inadequately risk assessed and not modified to accommodate pupils. Only one member of the army staff was present and the bikes had not been matched to pupil size, nor the route adapted to suit the inexperience of the group. The army staff had little experience of working with young people.*

25.12.4    Woodroffe-Hedley versus Cuthbertson, High Court (1997):
*An experienced mountain guide was judged to have caused the death of an adult client while climbing an ice wall on an Alpine peak by not following regular and approved practice, in that he failed to fix the usual number of ice screws into an anchor point in order to save time. The belay point gave way, causing the death of the client.*

# Chapter twenty-six
## Aquatic Activities

26

This chapter identifies a comprehensive range of responsibilities, practices and procedures that staff need to implement in ensuring safe practice within the potentially high-risk environment of the swimming pool.

> Please read the general guidance provided in Part 1 of this handbook, pages 9–131, before reading this chapter. This will help to ensure that you have a comprehensive awareness of safe-practice issues affecting aquatic activities and PESS in general.

## 26.1 Introduction

26.1.1 Swimming and its related activities are health-promoting and provide great satisfaction to all practitioners. Learning to swim and being confident in water provides the essential foundation for many water-based recreational choices.

26.1.2 Due to the evident hazard of drowning, the teaching and learning of swimming and related water skills require the utmost care on the part of all concerned. The aim must be to teach the basic skills to as many young people as possible.

26.1.3 The Health and Safety at Work Act 1974 places responsibilities on pool owners, managers (including head teachers and school staff) and users to establish and apply sound procedures to reasonably ensure that swimming-related activities are carried out safely.

26.1.4 The Health and Safety Executive (HSE) has clearly identified that the risk to the safety of swimmers may be limited when undertaking programmed activities, compared to swimming in an unprogrammed public session, in 'free' swimming when allowed as a contrasting activity at the end of a structured session or in 'fun' activity sessions. Swimming lessons are programmed activities with structure, supervision and continuous monitoring from the poolside. Unprogrammed sessions, such as leisure and play sessions, may require higher levels of supervision and lifeguard expertise because of the less controlled nature of the session.

26.1.5 This chapter sets out the fundamental considerations when planning, delivering and evaluating a range of aquatic programmes in swimming pools and open water. It addresses good practice in terms of qualifications, responsibilities, ratios, supervision and both day-to-day and emergency procedures.

# Part A:  Swimming, Water Safety and Related Sports

## 26.2    What Staff Should Know

### People

### Responsibility for safety

26.2.1    Good practice operates where nominated staff are delegated responsibility for **managing and monitoring the school swimming programme**, particularly in the areas of staff confidence and competence for the roles delegated, pupil progress, the application of policies and standards, informing other school staff of procedures and standards and ensuring that risk assessments are carried out.

26.2.2    The duty of care for pupils involved in swimming remains at all times with school staff. **Specialist swimming teachers** may be employed by local authorities (LAs) to assist with swimming lessons. Where their role is to lead the lesson, it is essential the school staff remain on poolside to provide an assisting role. The specialist swimming staff may also provide essential **lifesaving cover**. In these situations, it is important that another responsible adult is available to supervise the pupils in any situation where the specialist swimming teacher has to enter the water to affect a rescue.

26.2.3    It is necessary for school staff and specialist swimming teachers to enjoy a good working relationship, with good **communication**, to ensure a safe environment with clear shared aims. It should be clearly understood that the school staff have the responsibility for monitoring the progress of the pupils regardless of who directs the session.

26.2.4    The teaching and lifesaving awards of the Amateur Swimming Association (ASA), the Swimming Teachers' Association (STA) and the Royal Life Saving Society (RLSS) are desirable qualifications for swimming teachers, but it should be remembered that these may not indicate up-to-date competence in lifesaving and the teaching of swimming skills unless retaken from time to time. LAs and school governing bodies should ensure that specialist swimming teachers, physical-education specialists and other school staff, where appropriate, are afforded the opportunity to update their skills in these areas regularly through local or awarding-body professional development modules.

26.2.5    School staff should regularly practise their previously learned lifesaving skills and, where appropriate, lifeguarding skills. They should also check that all lifesaving equipment is adequate, appropriately placed for ready access and in good condition.

26.2.6    It is not advisable to deploy staff to poolside responsibilities if they **lack confidence** in the role, cannot swim or are reticent about being on the poolside. School staff should have the opportunity to express such a lack of confidence or ability before being deployed in a poolside role.

26.2.7    School staff responsible for the delivery of swimming pool programmed aquatic activities, including swimming lessons, should be aware of the recommendations by the HSE with regard to school staff, coaches and lifeguards holding an appropriate current lifesaving award or lifeguard qualification (see Health and Safety Executive Guidance HSG 179).

26.2.8 Where school staff are responsible for the safety of a programmed session, such as a swimming lesson, it is essential that they have, as a minimum, a **current swimming pool lifesaving award**, such as the Rescue Award for Swimming Teachers and Coaches (NRASTC)/National Rescue Standard for the Pool Safety Award for Teachers (NaRS SAT).

26.2.9 Those directly responsible for the supervision of a swimming pool during unprogrammed sessions are recommended to provide a current nationally recognised **pool lifeguard** qualification, such as the RLSS National Pool Lifeguard qualification or National Rescue Standard Pool Lifeguard (NaRS PL) qualification. These awards are recognised by the ASA, the RLSS, Institute of Swimming Teachers and Coaches and the STA.

26.2.10 Systems need to be in place to ensure that lifeguards are diligent and effectively organised.

26.2.11 School staff should be aware of the standard pool operating procedures for the venue they use.

26.2.12 The supervision of activities such as canoeing or scuba-diving in pools requires specialist knowledge in both teaching and lifesaving, as identified in the appropriate risk assessment and with any necessary adjustments made to the operating procedures.

26.2.13 All staff working on the poolside need to be **appropriately dressed** so that they can fulfil the requirements of their role without restriction.

26.2.14 Where an adult has responsibility for teaching more than two pupils, the recommended **teaching position** is from the side of the pool, as this provides the best position to oversee the whole group and respond quickly to any teaching or emergency situation. Additional adults may be in the water to assist individual pupils or small groups.

## Pupil:school staff ratios

26.2.15 As specific circumstances and the building design of swimming pools vary greatly, definitive sets of **ratios** are not always appropriate. For example, shallow-depth learner pools are much easier to supervise than large public pools where the presence of public swimmers can present problems. The starting point for any such policy should be the completion of a thorough **risk assessment** based on considerations of staff and pupils, the context and organisation. However, where local requirements (eg LA requirements) are specified, these must be followed.

26.2.16 In any pool, the pupil:school staff ratio should be such that it safely meets the varying risks imposed by the pool environment and from the public who may be in the pool at the same time. Whatever the conditions, there must always be a supervisory presence able to meet any rescue and resuscitation needs that may arise among the pupils.

26.2.17 Determining the safe ratio of pupils to swimming staff is an obligation on all owners/operators/occupiers of swimming pools. This is in accordance with the general duties and responsibilities placed upon them by the Health and Safety at Work Act 1974 and by the Management of Health and Safety in the Workplace Regulations 1999.

26.2.18    The ratio determined safe may be set out in the normal operating procedures and should be based on a risk assessment that includes:

- pupil:
  - numbers
  - behaviour
  - confidence
  - abilities
  - understanding
- staff:
  - qualifications
  - expertise
  - confidence
  - discipline and control
- pool:
  - design
  - space
  - depth and slope
  - equipment
  - operating procedures
  - emergency provision
- organisation:
  - joint or sole use
  - programmed or unprogrammed activity
  - what the activity involves
  - group management.

26.2.19    Some national governing bodies (NGBs) and other awarding bodies for swimming activities recommend maximum staff:pupil ratios. These should be considered within the risk assessment as useful guidance, but they do not take into account the variable circumstances each teacher may encounter. Decisions on ratios may vary according to the specific circumstances.

26.2.20    Where ratios are larger than allowed by local requirements, or larger than deemed to be safe, organisational arrangements need to be put in place to accommodate this, such as having only half a group in the water at any time. Such organisational arrangements should apply throughout the lesson, including any less-structured time at the end, with adequate supervision of the non-swimming group at all times.

## Pupil conduct/behaviour

26.2.21    The conduct of pupils when they attend for swimming tuition is of obvious importance. The accepted procedures and underlying reasons should be fully explained to all participants.

26.2.22    All jewellery should be removed or made safe and the chewing of sweets or gum during a lesson should never be allowed.

26.2.23    Pupils should not be permitted to run on the pool surrounds.

26.2.24    Emergency procedures to clear the pool should be practised at regular intervals and should be effected by means of a specified signal, both audible and visual. The signal needs to be understood by school staff and pupils alike. Standard whistle signals are applied in many facilities in the form of:

- one short blast for the attention of all pool users

- two short blasts for the attention of a lifeguard or other pool staff

- three short blasts to indicate a lifeguard taking action

- one long blast for the pool to be cleared.

26.2.25    Pupils should be encouraged to look for and report unseemly or unacceptable behaviour, especially when safety is compromised.

26.2.26    Pupils should be encouraged to carry out the usual hygiene procedures before entering the water.

26.2.27    Pupils should be aware that it is their responsibility to report any illness or skin complaint to school staff.

## Pupils with particular needs

26.2.28    Infants and young primary children are best taught in shallow-water beginner pools, with the availability of appropriate aids to floatation.

26.2.29    Care should be taken when teaching very young non-swimmers who are unable to touch the bottom of a pool. The children should wear appropriate floatation aids, to ensure confidence.

26.2.30    Additional adult support in the water may be considered according to the age, ability and confidence of the pupils. In circumstances where manual support (physical contact) is provided, care needs to be taken to avoid embarrassment to the pupil or adult, ensure that the use of manual support is provided in an appropriate form that cannot be misunderstood and is provided with the knowledge and approval of the pupil, and parents, where they are in attendance with very young children.

## Pupils with special educational needs (SEN)

26.2.31    Where swimming involves young people with SEN, the class size should be reduced, or staffing increased, to take account of the age, ability, confidence and experience of the pupils. Additional suitably qualified or experienced adult support in the water may be considered according to the age, ability and confidence of the pupils.

26.2.32    Individual needs should be communicated to any adult not familiar with an individual pupil in order to ensure the individual needs are met and situations can be addressed without disruption to the session.

## Pupils with medical conditions

26.2.33    Pupils with serious medical problems need clearance provided through the written permission of parents before they can be allowed to participate in school swimming programmes. Additional advice may also be necessary from relevant organisations with regard to specific risk factors relating to aquatic activity.

For more information on this issue, see *Chapter 10: Individual and Special Needs*, pages 73–80 and *Appendix 4: Pupils with Special Educational Needs (SEN)*, pages 319–324 and the CD.

26.2.34    The needs of pupils with epilepsy may vary according to whether a medication regime applies. They should, in all cases and at all times, be observed from the poolside and should work alongside a responsible person in the water when out of their depth. Shimmering water or flickering light may trigger an attack. A 'buddy' system of a co-pupil or helper in the water provides an unobtrusive system of paired supervision that avoids embarrassment.

## Context

## Procedures

26.2.35    **Pool safety operating procedures** (PSOPs) should be written, specific to the pool and consist of normal operating procedures (NOPs) and an emergency action plan (EAP). They should contain the supervisory and safety requirements for all sessions in the pool and should be followed by whoever is responsible for any group using the pool, be it in curriculum time or otherwise. The procedures may vary according to the particular circumstances of the pool and the users.

26.2.36    NOPs are simply the day-to-day organisational systems based on risk assessment. All who assume responsibility for the supervision and safety of any groups using the pool should be made aware of the procedures. Periodic review is important in order to maintain up-to-date, consistently applied levels of practice.

For more information on risk assessment, see *Chapter 3: Risk Management*, pages 23–30.

26.2.37    **NOPs** would typically include information relating to:

- pool design and depth
- potential areas of risk
- arrangements for lessons
- responsibility for safety
- staffing levels and qualifications
- supervision and pupil conduct
- arrangements for pupils with particular needs (eg very young children, those with SEN or medical conditions)
- pool safety and equipment
- clothing and equipment
- maximum numbers
- first-aid provision
- water quality.

## Supervision

26.2.38    Whenever there are pupils in the water, a suitably qualified adult should be present at the poolside who is able to effect a rescue from the water and carry out cardiopulmonary resuscitation (CPR).

26.2.39    A minimum of two people on the poolside is common and good practice to cover eventualities in the teaching and safety aspects of swimming. Where only one adult is present, the risk assessment needs to indicate clearly why this ratio is acceptable and should highlight alternative emergency arrangements.

26.2.40    All **adults accompanying pupils** to swimming sessions should:

- be given a clear role

- understand the limits of the role

- be confident on the poolside

- communicate with the other adults on safety issues

- have the necessary discipline and control standards

- regularly carry out head counts during, as well as at the beginning and end of, sessions

- know, understand and be able to apply the pool NOPs and EAP

- be suitably dressed for the role they are to play in the lesson.

26.2.41    Routines, deep and shallow water and relevant notices should be brought to the attention of pupils before and when they first visit the pool and re-emphasised on subsequent visits. Notices must be clear to users who may have problems with reading. Standard emergency procedures should be practised at regular intervals, for instance each term, with the children.

26.2.42    Pupils should be taught to report any mishap to the staff. It is helpful if they are paired to check on the well-being of their partners at any time.

26.2.43    Pupils should be **registered or counted** both before and after the lesson. A **head count** at times during the lesson would also be appropriate.

26.2.44    Where possible, separate school **changing areas** should be made available. Where this is not possible, changing times different to the public should be attempted. Whatever the circumstances, changing rooms should be adequately supervised. Ideally, a male and female member of staff should accompany each class in order to supervise fully the changing areas. Staffing pressures may mean that a known adult volunteer of the opposite gender is used. He/she would need disclosure and Independent Safeguarding Authority (ISA) (barring and vetting) clearance due to the situation of supervising children while undressing. Where this level of staffing is not available, it may be possible to enlist the cooperation of pool staff to supervise the other changing room. This arrangement, through the pool management, needs to be assured and consistent. If only one suitable adult is available, he/she would need to establish procedures to deal with any emergency in the other changing room. If these arrangements are not to the school's satisfaction, it may be necessary to combine classes and take single-gender groups, where appropriate staffing allows this. Adults supervising pupils need to be familiar with and adhere to the relevant safeguarding issues.

> For more information on safeguarding, see *Chapter 9: Safeguarding Children and Young People,* pages 55–72.

26.2.45    Pupils in school pools should always have relevant qualified poolside adult supervision.

26.2.46    When carrying out a risk assessment and preparing **written procedures**, those doing so should consult with swimming teachers, coaches, school staff and all who take groups to the swimming facility. This will ensure that the fullest consultation is effected.

## Emergency action plan

26.2.47 Risk assessments should be used to identify foreseeable hazards and risks. Those using a particular pool should be familiar with the recommended action to be taken as set out in a written emergency action plan.

> For general guidance on risk assessments, see *Chapter 3: Risk Management*, pages 23–30.

26.2.48 EAPs should establish who assumes leadership in managing emergencies and the action to be taken in relation to such issues as:

- serious injury to a bather
- dealing with casualties in the water
- sudden overcrowding in a public pool
- sudden lack of water clarity
- disorderly behaviour
- emergency evacuation due to:
  - fire alarm
  - bomb threats
  - power failure
  - structural failure
  - toxic-gas emission.

26.2.49 School staff should be aware of any **notices** referring to the action to be taken in an emergency evacuation and ensure that the pupils have a basic understanding of what to do, should such a situation occur.

26.2.50 Adequate lifesaving and buoyancy aids, and first-aid equipment, including a blanket, should be immediately to hand.

26.2.51 Consideration needs to be given to the fact that, during an **emergency evacuation**, swimmers will have bare feet, little clothing and may be outside for an extended period of time. Pool operators should make provisions for these factors in their emergency plans, such as the provision of space blankets and possibly Rubberoid surfaces near the emergency exits.

26.2.52 There should be known access to a **telephone** giving direct contact from the pool to the emergency services. The system for providing this access should be guaranteed during all hours when the pool is in use.

26.2.53 Pool lifeguard staff should be trained in the use of **spinal boards/special recovery stretchers**, which more easily meet the need of recovering patients, especially where such patients may have suffered head and neck injury. School staff and those on poolside duty should know how to assemble and use such equipment, where it is available and where their role may include responsibility for water rescues.

## Equipment

26.2.54 **Swimwear** should be suitable for the purpose. For reasons of safety, swimwear should be sufficiently tight fitting to allow freedom of body and limb movement without causing unsafe water resistance. Cultural or religious sensitivity needs to be demonstrated, but staff should ensure the correct balance between safety,

270

cultural requirements and the need to be able to see the limb movements of pupils to ensure appropriate learning and safe practice. In the first instance, the staff and the pupil should make themselves aware of the effects of swimming while wearing additional clothing. Liaison with community leaders can do much to minimise any problems that may arise.

> For more guidance on this issue, see *Chapter 11: Religious and Cultural Issues*, pages 81–84.

26.2.55 **Goggles** or masks should only be allowed exceptionally in school swimming lessons, when chemicals in the water may adversely affect eyes. When used, these items should be made of unbreakable plastic or rubber materials. Pupils should be taught to remove them by slipping them off the head and not by stretching the retaining band, as wet plastic is slippery and may cause severe eye injury. Where goggles are not properly fitted, they may mist up and adversely affect visibility. Pupils learning to swim or improving their ability often do not swim in straight lines, become close together and clash heads or hit each other with arms while swimming, causing possibly more severe eye injuries if goggles are worn. Dependency on goggles for underwater swimming is not a factor in being judged to be safe in water, neither are goggles designed for such activity as the eye pressure cannot be relieved.

26.2.56 Long, regular training sessions are where goggles become an important item of equipment. Goggles usually are not necessary within short curriculum swimming lessons (typically 20–25 minutes of water time) or for single, short races in school galas unless a pupil has particularly sensitive eyes. In these rare instances where the use of goggles may be allowed, the adult responsible for the group should have the prerogative to require the pupil to remove them for reasons of safety if the pupil constantly adjusts or removes and replaces the goggles.

26.2.57 Where loose hair is long enough to impair vision, a swim cap is advised or, as a minimum, long hair should be tied back at all times.

26.2.58 **Safety equipment**, such as poles, throwing ropes or throw bags, first-aid provision and emergency alarms, needs to be sufficient in quantity, regularly checked and positioned so as to be readily available when needed without creating additional hazards to pool users.

26.2.59 Any **electrical equipment** on the poolside needs to be designed for that specific purpose, of low voltage or battery operated, located so as not to create additional hazard, have current circuit breakers attached and be checked regularly. No one in the water should handle any electrical equipment.

26.2.60 Leisure or **play equipment** is often large and may adversely affect supervision, requiring observation from both sides of any large inflatables. Careful thought should be given to the wisdom of introducing such equipment into the water where additional lifeguarding provision is not available.

26.2.61 Equipment for sports such as water polo should be checked for stability, fixing and smooth surfaces.

26.2.62 A variety of teaching and **buoyancy aids** should be available. Equipment should:

- conform to any CE or BSI standard, where available

- be checked before the session to ensure they are safe to use

- be close at hand for easy access and use during the lesson

- placed tidily on the poolside to minimise tripping or other safety hazards

- be used appropriately to avoid over-reliance

- be appropriate and safe for the needs of the pupils

- be correctly fitted or held according to the design and purpose of the aid.

> For more information on swimming facilities, see *Swimming pools* (*15.2.18–15.2.34*, pages 106–108) in *Chapter 15: Buildings and Facilities*.

## Organisation

26.2.63   Arrangements for the **safe supervision** of lessons will need to take account of whether the group has sole or shared use of the pool. Shared use with the general public would have further implications for the supervision and designated responsibility for safety, which would need to be satisfactorily addressed.

26.2.64   Schools will often use pools on premises other than their own and, by law, the responsible manager must ensure that the facilities are safe and present no risk to health for visiting groups. This applies equally when schools use swimming pools belonging to other schools. It is regarded in law as a place of work under the responsibility of the host school. However, staff with the duty of care for the lesson should always ensure that they make whatever checks they can each visit before allowing pupils to use the facility.

> For more information on this issue, see *Chapter 2: Physical Education and the Law*, pages 13–21.

26.2.65   School staff and/or specialist swimming staff should be able to see all the pupils throughout the lesson. The bottom of the pool should be **clearly visible** and any problems of **glare** or light reflected from the water surface should be satisfactorily overcome.

26.2.66   Teaching should be from the poolside. Except in emergencies, school staff or instructors should not enter the water if this leaves no other supervising adult on the poolside.

26.2.67   The **teaching position** should allow observation of maximum numbers and maximum space.

26.2.68   Fatigue, stress, fear, coldness and activity levels should be monitored by staff regularly.

26.2.69   Staff should **walk around the pool** at the end of the lesson to ensure the pool is clear.

26.2.70   It is wise to allow a reasonable time from ending a meal before pupils are allowed to enter the water. This will enable the process of digestion to be sufficiently advanced to minimise the hazardous possibility of vomiting during a swimming session, which could be life threatening if air tubes become blocked. Where pupils swim in the session that follows the midday lunch break, it is advisable for them to eat lightly and as early as possible during this break period to enable the necessary time from eating to swimming to elapse.

## 26.3   What Pupils Should Know

26.3.1   Pupils should know:

- never to enter the water unless told to do so by a responsible adult

- chewing can be dangerous and should not occur in swimming lessons

- basic hygiene practices, such as using the toilet, using a handkerchief and taking a shower before swimming are for their benefit in maintaining clean water

- they should be aware of any safety signs around the pool, understand what they mean and always follow the instructions

- where any changes in water depth occur

- understand and follow the signals an adult may use in an emergency

- the importance of remaining within designated work areas

- they should report to an adult if they feel unwell during a lesson

- never to swim immediately after a large meal.

## Part B: Diving

## 26.4 What Staff Should Know

26.4.1 In addition to relevant information given above, the following issues specific to diving need to be considered.

### People

26.4.2 Diving, by its very nature, can be dangerous and there have been a number of serious diving accidents recorded in recent years. To avoid such occurrences, safety measures need to be followed.

26.4.3 Diving sessions should be **supervised** by adults who are thoroughly familiar with modern practice and competent in the teaching of diving.

26.4.4 Pupil **numbers** should be low enough to allow the school staff to watch all the divers.

### Context

26.4.5 Appropriate **warning signs and notices** should be clearly displayed and regularly drawn to the attention of pool users. Pool signs should indicate clearly those areas that are appropriate for diving.

26.4.6 The pool freeboard (the distance from the poolside to water surface) should be less than 0.3m.

26.4.7 A sufficient area of **forward clearance** (the horizontal distance at which the minimum depth of water is maintained) is needed, typically in excess of 7.5m.

26.4.8 The **depth of a dive** is affected by:

- the height from which the dive is made – higher will be deeper

- the angle of entry – a steeper entry leads to a deeper dive

- flight distance – a short flight leads to a deeper dive

- the strength and drive from the diver's legs.

## Organisation

26.4.9    Prior to any dives being taught, pupils should have developed watermanship, confidence and competence in water practices, followed by feet-first and head-first entries from the poolside.

26.4.10   Pupils should be thoroughly familiar with the water space and environment in which they learn to dive. Diving should never take place in unknown waters.

26.4.11   To ensure that the risk of collisions during simultaneous dives is avoided, there should be:

• sufficient pool space

• sufficient forward clearance (ie the distance forward over which the minimum depth of water is maintained)

• no underwater obstructions

• clearly understood exit routes from the entry area on resurfacing from a dive.

26.4.12   **Good class organisation** and discipline is paramount during diving activities. Staff and pupils should be fully aware of the safety implications involved to ensure safe practice. These include the following:

a. Divers with long hair should wear caps.

b. Goggles should not be worn.

c. Toes should be curled over the pool edge.

d. Dives should be performed from a stationary position.

e. Arms should be extended beyond the head with the hands clasped for a safe entry.

26.4.13   Where diving provision is made in a main pool, rather than a specific diving pit, the area designated for diving should be **clearly defined** and other swimmers discouraged or prohibited from entering that area. Where swimmers are permitted into that area, divers and their supervisors need to take responsibility for ensuring that the diving area is clear before performing a dive.

26.4.14   When diving forms part of lessons, the **water depth** should ideally be at least full standing height plus arms and fingers fully extended. However, this advice must be considered as exemplary as very few existing swimming pools can provide water of sufficient depth to meet this requirement for adults or tall children. Where this is not practicable, the deepest water available, with a **minimum depth of 1.8m**, should be used, with the exercise of additional caution.

26.4.15   Prolonged **underwater swimming** after a dive should be discouraged.

26.4.16   Generally, entry into water less than 1.5m in depth may be best effected from a sitting position on the side of the pool. Care should be taken with feet-first entry jumping, which may cause damage to the ankles, arches of the feet or lower spine from striking the pool bottom with force in shallow water. The activity needs to be taught bearing in mind the importance of bending the knees and the variables of:

• water depth

• freeboard height

• size and weight of the participant.

## 274

## Plunge dive

26.4.17    All pupils should be taught to perform, and understand when to use, a plunge dive from the poolside. It is important that any pupil taking part in a competitive swimming race commencing with a plunge-dive racing entry should be checked for his/her competence to do so safely, especially when the entry is from a starting block.

26.4.18    A competitive shallow-entry dive should be taught into water no less than 1.8m in depth. When pupils have achieved the standard of the ASA Competitive Start Award and can execute a competitive shallow dive consistently, they may execute such a dive in water of no less than 0.9m in depth.

26.4.19    Pupils should always exercise great care when diving into swimming pools. Staff should ensure dives are executed into the deeper end of the swimming pool as a matter of routine safety.

26.4.20    Diving blocks should always be fitted at the deepest end of the swimming pool. Diving from starting blocks into shallow water, and a depth of not less than 0.9m, should only be allowed when pupils have achieved the standard of the ASA Competitive Start Award and can execute a shallow dive consistently.

26.4.21    Raised starting blocks for racing dives should only be used by capable swimmers who have received instruction on the techniques required and with the approval of school staff. It is not recommended that raised blocks are used for school swimming instruction.

26.4.22    Vertical poolside dives and diving from a board should not form part of mainstream school swimming unless only delivered in a specialist environment by a qualified diving teacher.

26.4.23    Where vertical plain header dives are taught, the water should be a minimum of 3m in depth and pupils should understand clearly the technique of manoeuvring underwater by extending the hands at the wrists immediately after entry to level and raise the body to the surface.

## Board diving

26.4.24    Only one person should be allowed on any part of the board at any one time.

26.4.25    The water should be checked by both the diver and the supervisor to ensure that it is clear of swimmers or any obstruction before a dive.

26.4.26    Board divers should demonstrate their competence at low level before progressing to greater heights.

26.4.27    Diving boards should be checked before use to ensure they are not slippery and that the surface is not damaged in any way that would affect the security of footing and movement.

26.4.28    For dives from a height of 3m or more, the surface of the water should be disturbed, such as by the provision of a specialist facility or a hosepipe with a spray nozzle played across the surface, to avoid mistiming of entry leading to subsequent injury.

## 26.5    What Pupils Should Know

26.5.1    Pupils should know that:

- it is dangerous to dive into water without checking there is sufficient depth and that they are competent to dive in a controlled manner

- they should check that the designated diving area is clear before commencing a dive.

## Part C:  Lifesaving

## 26.6    What Staff Should Know

26.6.1    In addition to relevant information given above, the following issues specific to lifesaving need to be considered.

### Organisation

26.6.2    When teaching lifesaving, only reaching with a pole or similar item and throwing rescues should be taught to children below eight years of age. Contact rescues should not be taught to children under 13 years of age.

26.6.3    Advice on teaching packs and awards for lifesaving at the appropriate key stages in primary and secondary education is available from the RLSS, STA and ASA.

## 26.7    What Pupils Should Know

26.7.1    Pupils should know:

- that valuable contributions to lifesaving can be made without entering the water through contacting the emergency services or effecting land-based rescues

- the rescue sequence of selecting reach rescues, throw rescues or wading rescues before swimming rescues are utilised

- the importance of taking a stick or similar implement into a water rescue to monitor water depth and possibly use to effect a non-contact rescue.

## Part D:  Personal Survival Skills

## 26.8    What Staff Should Know

26.8.1    In addition to relevant information given above, the following issues specific to personal survival skills need to be considered.

### Context

26.8.2    Swimming is a life skill and it is important that personal survival skills are taught. Pupils should understand the **dangers of cold water**, their ability to assess a survival situation and the application of the principles of personal survival.

26.8.3    As well as personal survival techniques, pupils should be taught the effects of cold water in order for them to be able to apply the skills effectively.

26.8.4    **Swimming in clothes** differs considerably from styles and techniques used in normal swimming lessons. Pupils should be taught how to conserve energy and body heat through the use of gentle swimming movements and holding particular body positions. The wearing of everyday clothing helps simulate real situations.

## 26.9    What Pupils Should Know

26.9.1    Pupils should know:

- how to conserve energy in water

- how to conserve body heat in water

- the effects of cold water

- not to attempt to swim long distances in cold water, but to conserve energy and use whatever floatation aids are available.

## Part E:   Swimming in Open Water

> For information on this topic, see *Swimming in open water*
> (*25.10.121–25.10.138*, pages 259–260) in *Chapter 25: Outdoor Education and Adventurous Activities*.

## Part F:   Hydrotherapy Pools

## 26.10    What Staff Should Know

26.10.1    In addition to relevant information already given, the following issues specific to hydrotherapy pools need to be considered.

26.10.2    Hydrotherapy pools in special schools provide the opportunity for pupils to exercise in warm water. This is of particular benefit to pupils with complex physical difficulties.

26.10.3    Hydrotherapy-pool activity programmes usually involve team teaching by the class teacher, learning support/care assistants and a physiotherapist. Whether a specialist swimming teacher is present is an issue to be determined by the particular circumstances. As hydrotherapy pools tend to be shallow in depth and small in size, it is not usual to require a lifeguard to be present. However, the staff involved need to be confident and have the competence to complete any water-based rescue that may become necessary.

26.10.4    The adult:pupil ratio should not be determined in accordance with any swimming-specific written guidelines that may exist. A safe ratio can only be determined by carefully examining individual pupils' medical profiles and healthcare plans in conjunction with relevant medical staff.

26.10.5    Safe practice in hydrotherapy pools should be as rigorous as in swimming pools. In addition, a **pool watcher** should be present on the poolside, whose sole duty is to observe all pool activities and draw attention to any problems developing in the water.

26.10.6    As the pool will be used by pupils with complex physical difficulties, particular attention should be given to the development of risk-management schemes for:

- lifting and carrying pupils

- transporting pupils between the changing rooms and the pool

- dressing/undressing areas and support staff

- emergency equipment and procedures.

26.10.7    Due to the temperature, it is recommended that regular maintenance of the plant, filtration system and sterilisation system, and a comprehensive programme of water testing are carried out to ensure the safe use of hydrotherapy pools.

## 26.11    Additional Information

> For further guidance, see *Appendix 2J: Safe Practice for Swimming Poster*, page 307 and the CD.

### Resources

ASA, STC, RLSS UK, ISLM (2002) 'Safe Supervision for Teaching and Coaching of Swimming', www.sportcentric.com/vmgmt/vfilemgmt/page/filedownload/1,8202, 5157-51138-121152-0-file,00.pdf

ASA, NSPCC (2004) 'Wave Power: Child Welfare in Swimming: Procedures and Guidelines', www.sportcentric.com/vmgmt/vfilemgmt/page/filedownload/1,8202,5026-49221-84094-0-file,00.pdf

British Standards Institute (2004) *Management of Public Swimming Pools: General Management. Code of Practice (BSI PAS 65:2004)*. London: BSI. ISBN: 978-0-580441-65-2.

British Standards Institute (2005) *Specification for the Management and Operation of Swimming Pools (BSI PAS 81:2005)*. London: BSI. ISBN: 978-0-580465-77-2.

Institute of Sport and Recreation Management (ISRM) (2001) *Diving and Jumping in Swimming Pools and Open Water Areas*. Loughborough: ISRM. ISBN: 978-1-900738-60-0.

Sport England and HSE (2003) *Managing Health and Safety in Swimming Pools*. Sudbury: HSE Books. ISBN: 978-0-717626-86-1.

### Useful websites

Amateur Swimming Association
www.britishswimming.org

Institute of Sport and Recreation Management
www.isrm.co.uk

Marine and Coastguard Agency: Beach Safety Information
www.mcga.gov.uk/c4mca/mcga-home/education.htm

Royal Life Saving Society UK
www.lifesavers.org.uk

Scottish Swimming
www.scottishswimming.com

Swimming Teachers' Association
www.sta.co.uk

## 26.12    Case Law Examples

26.12.1    Burke versus Cardiff City Council, Court of Appeal (1986):
*A weak swimmer nearly drowned in the deep end of a large pool. An inadequate level of lifeguard provision and attention was held to be responsible.*

26.12.2    Jones versus Cheshire County Council, Manchester County Court (1997):
*A teacher took a larger group to the pool than the LA ratios allowed, but used a paired system so that only half the group were in the water at any time other than 'free' time at the end of the lesson when all were in the water. A child was injured during the free time, doing an activity the group had not been taught. The teacher was held responsible for going beyond the LA ratios and not limiting the end of lesson activity to pre-learned skills instead of free time.*

# Chapter twenty-seven 27
## Play in the School Environment

This chapter details a range of recommendations associated with facilities and personnel which will contribute towards safe play provision.

> Please read the general guidance provided in Part 1 of this handbook, pages 9–131, before reading this chapter. This will help to ensure that you have a comprehensive awareness of safe-practice issues affecting play in the school environment and PESS in general.

## 27.1 Introduction

27.1.1 Opportunities for physical play abound in the school environment and may take a number of forms, depending upon the age and developmental stage of pupils.

27.1.2 Structured physical play within the taught curriculum typically involves the youngest children using a range of mobile and static equipment, has predetermined learning outcomes and assumes direct supervision and intervention, where necessary, by suitably qualified staff.

27.1.3 Playground activity occurring at break and lunchtime, preschool or at the end of the school day is much more varied and involves pupils of all ages. Activity may be **pupil-regulated**, with minimum levels of adult supervision, or **directly controlled** and supervised by a member of staff. It may consist of highly creative activity or be based upon traditional sports and games.

27.1.4 Schools should have in place a clearly communicated **policy** relating to all aspects and dimensions of play for which they have responsibility. The information below will assist in compiling such a policy with a view to ensuring consistency and safe practice across the full extent of provision.

## 27.2 What Staff Should Know

### People

27.2.1 All adults who have responsibility for supervising play activity should be suitably qualified, trained and competent to do so. The level and type of **supervision** to be undertaken should be clearly understood and not exceeded. It is recommended that, where activity consistently involves competitive play (eg invasion games), a basic national governing body (NGB) award should be considered as useful professional development.

27.2.2 All supervisory adults should be fully aware of **emergency procedures** and how to rapidly access first aid in the event of injury or accident.

> For more information on this issue, see *Chapter 8: Accident Procedures and First-aid Management*, pages 49–54.

27.2.3    Pupils need to comply with **behavioural expectations** and the school code of conduct, where established. They should adhere to safety principles learnt within the taught curriculum, which may extend to the wearing of correct attire and footwear for some activities. **Zoned playing areas** should be respected and activities restricted to their particular designation.

27.2.4    Any pupil given **leadership responsibility** for play activity (eg junior sports leaders, play monitors) must work under the direct supervision of a member of staff.

## Context

## Outside facilities

27.2.5    Staff need to ensure that **playing surfaces** are acceptably safe and free from hazard. The types of hazard that may be encountered include the following:

**Table 11: Potential hazards relating to play areas**

| Play-area Surface | Surrounding Plants/Shrubs etc |
|---|---|
| • Uneven or cracked<br>• Loose grit<br>• Slippery in wet weather<br>• Vegetation growing on or through<br>• Litter<br>• Patches of silt from poor drainage | • Possibility of pupils overrunning into plants/shrubs etc<br>• Type of plants/shrubs etc (eg shrubs with large thorns)<br>• Possibility of poisonous berries adjacent to play area |
| **Play-area Drainage** | **Access to Play Area** |
| • Standing water after rain<br>• Drain grids below or above surface level<br>• Drain grids with oversized spaces<br>• Drain grids broken or missing | • Possibility of unauthorised pupil access<br>• Possibility of vehicular access<br>• Vehicular deposits on play area if used as a car park outside school hours<br>• Use as public right of way<br>• Secure to prevent access by unauthorised adults |
| **Play Area Built on Sloping Ground** | **Fixed Climbing Equipment** |
| • Steep steps<br>• Lack of secure handrail<br>• Condition of steps<br>• Presence of rubbish or vegetation on steps<br>• Possibility of pupils overrunning play area<br>• Possibility of stones etc rolling onto play area | • Lack of inspection and repair schedule<br>• Peeling paint and rust<br>• Inappropriate or lack of safety surfaces<br>• Proximity to other hazards (eg windows, projections)<br>• Excessive fall height |
| **Buildings Around Play Area** | |
| • Exposed external corners adjacent to play areas<br>• Projections below head height (adult) | • Outward-opening windows<br>• Outward-opening doors<br>• Non-toughened glass |

For general guidance on facilities, see *Chapter 15: Buildings and Facilities*, pages 103–110.

*safe practice* in physical education and school sport

## Climbing equipment, including traversing walls

27.2.6 All equipment should meet appropriate **British Standards European Norm** (BS EN) requirements, where available. In the absence of a formal standard, purchasers should ensure the product has been subjected to appropriate safety testing and is installed by a specialist contractor. **Installations** should always be inspected and approved by a qualified specialist before usage commences and written confirmation be obtained; they should then be inspected on a regular basis.

27.2.7 **Surfaces** should be level, non-slip and even. Research has shown that recommended impact-absorbing surfaces reduce injuries. It is essential to bear this in mind when selecting play-area surfaces.

27.2.8 Staff should be competent in setting out any equipment where required to do so. An appropriate **safety surface** should be provided beneath and around all climbing equipment, whether indoors or outdoors. All-purpose gymnastic mats may be used to provide a temporary safety surface where the climbing equipment is located indoors. This should extend at least 1.75m beyond the outermost points of the base of the frame. Impact-absorbing surfaces are not required beneath frames that are less than 600mm high. However, it is good practice to provide one, as this helps to cover all eventualities and displays an attention to detail in risk assessments.

> For information on mats, see *Mats (12.2.16–12.2.24, pages 90–91)* in *Chapter 12: Equipment in Physical Education.*

27.2.9 All **climbing equipment** should be appropriate for the age and developmental needs of the pupils who will use it. Particular attention needs to be paid to any dangers posed through entrapment. **Signs** displaying instructions and guidance can assist safe supervision.

27.2.10 Pupils using climbing equipment should wear **suitable footwear** that provides good grip and traction, with any laces securely tied.

27.2.11 No adult should be placed in sole charge of a lunchtime play area and climbing equipment at the same time.

27.2.12 The **maximum number** of pupils who can safely use the whole climbing area of equipment at any one time should be determined by experienced staff and clearly communicated to all supervisors. Pupils need to understand these limits.

27.2.13 Young pupils, who may be timid and less skilful (eg nursery-age pupils), should not use climbing equipment at the same time as older pupils. Suggested rota systems to enable this should be included in school play policies.

27.2.14 Outdoor climbing frames should not be used in inclement weather.

## Soft-play and mobile items

27.2.15 **Wheeled equipment** (eg trikes) should be confined to designated areas and checked at regular intervals for stability.

27.2.16 **Soft-play shapes** should offer firm and predictable support. Depending upon the frequency of usage, such items do succumb to normal wear and tear and a programme of replacement needs to be in place.

27.2.17 Arrangements should be made for the surfaces of soft-play items to be periodically cleaned and sterilised. Any damage should be made good by a qualified person and the item safely stored until such repairs have been completed. Where repair is not feasible, the damaged item must be quickly and safely disposed of.

> For general guidance on equipment, see *Chapter 12: Equipment in Physical Education,* pages 85–93.

## Organisation

27.2.18 Supervisors need to ensure that **sufficient space** is allocated for selected activities, particularly those that involve rapid movement and sudden changes in direction (eg competitive ball games). Designated or **zoned areas** should be provided for such activity. Similarly, the use of **balls and bats** can prove hazardous in restricted space and careful planning and oversight are required to ensure that children and pupils are not exposed to unnecessary risk. **Quiet areas** of the playground should be respected and not intruded upon.

27.2.19 Wherever practical, pupils should be grouped for play activities according to age and developmental stage. Staggering break times for different age groups can assist in achieving a play environment in which everyone feels comfortable and secure.

27.2.20 Both staff and pupils need to be aware of **emergency procedures**. In the event of an accident, rapid access to first aid has to be ensured. Systems need to be in place that safeguard all pupils while the accident is being managed.

> For more guidance on these issues, see *Chapter 8: Accident Procedures and First-aid Management,* pages 49–54.

27.2.21 **Written risk assessments** of play provision need to be in place and effectively communicated to all staff responsible for supervision and to pupils, at an appropriate level of understanding. These need to be reviewed at regular intervals, taking into account any injuries and recorded incidents or 'near misses'.

# 27.3 What Pupils Should Know

27.3.1 Pupils should know that:

- safety principles taught and enacted during the formal curriculum are equally applicable to play activity

- vigilance is required in the playing area; any observed hazard should be avoided and reported immediately to a member of staff

- they need to use any equipment provided responsibly and always ensure that it poses no danger to anybody else

- they should use the designated playing zones only for the purpose for which they are intended.

## 27.4    Additional Information

### Resources

afPE/sports coach UK (2007) *Adults Supporting Learning: School Induction Pack.* Leeds: Coachwise Business Solutions. ISBN: 978-1-905540-28-0.

British Standards Institute (2006) *Playground Equipment and Surfacing. Part 10. Fully Enclosed Play Equipment* (EN 1176-10). London: BSI. (Draft)

NPFA (1997) *Impact Absorbing Surfaces for Children's Playgrounds.* London: NPFA. ISBN: 978-0-9460 85-35-X
Available from: www.fieldsintrust.org/downloads/surfaces.pdf


## 27.5    Case Law Examples

27.5.1    Morgan versus Blunden and Another, Reilly versus Blunden and Another, Court of Appeal (1986):
*Two six-year-old children were injured in an adventure playground managed by an unincorporated group. The playground was closed with no supervision, but not secure. The boys were injured playing on an abandoned car that had been pushed into the playground. Although the claim was dismissed on the grounds of foreseeability, the judge stated that had the boys been injured on playground equipment then the defendants would have had considerable difficulty in defending a claim for damages.*

27.5.2    Burton versus Canto Play Group, Queen's Bench Division (1989):
*Adult staffing of a playgroup was supplemented by a 14-year-old helper who was left alone to supervise a climbing frame. She had been given no training, nor did she have the experience to anticipate the action of a young child who had not been on the apparatus before. The child jumped and injured herself.*

### Relevant to *Chapter 2: Physical Education and the Law*

*Statutes* are Acts of Parliament and take legal precedence over any other form of law. These set out the principles the law addresses and often provide for *Regulations*.

Regulations and *Statutory Instruments* have statutory status and provide a more detailed framework, setting out how the law is to be applied. In this handbook, the term 'must' has been used where Statute and Regulation apply to the particular situation.

*Guidance* and *codes of practice* do not have statutory status. They are advisory, providing fuller detail on how to put the legal requirements into practice. The term 'should' – or similar – has been used here to indicate that the issue is advisory, but something that should be carefully considered within an ongoing or written risk assessment. The range of formal guidance is extensive and only a small, but relevant, sample is provided here.

Where schools are required by legislation to have regard for guidance, schools must comply and follow the guidance unless the circumstances of a particular case are exceptional and justify departing from it. Schools should also take account of relevant non-statutory guidance and, as a general rule, should follow such guidance. For example, staff should follow the safe-practice guidelines issued by their employer, unless they consider they have a good reason for not doing so on the facts of a particular case.

## Statute (Acts of Parliament)

### Health and Safety at Work etc Act 1974 (HSWA)

Under the terms of the Health and Safety at Work Act 1974 (HSWA), employers are required to do all that is reasonably practicable to ensure the health and safety of employees (eg school staff) and non-employees (eg pupils, parents and other visitors to the school premises) who are affected by their actions. This requirement extends to people who are not employers, but who have control of premises, such as management responsibilities, whatever the extent. Such people are required to do all that is reasonably practicable to provide a safe environment and safe systems of work, including safe access to, and exit from, their premises.

The employer varies according to the type of school:

a. In community schools, the local authority (LA) is the employer.

b. In voluntary-aided or foundation schools, the governing body is the employer.

c. In independent schools (including city technology colleges and city academies), the proprietor or governing body is usually the employer.

Under the terms of Section 2(3) of the HSWA, employers are required to prepare (and revise, when necessary) a written statement containing a general policy relating to the health and safety at work of employees, and guidelines on its implementation. Employers must inform their employees about the statement and any revision of it.

The policy applies to all organised activities both on and off the school site.

The Health and Safety Executive (HSE) and LA health and safety inspectors have powers to ensure that schools comply with the requirements of the HSWA. Failure to comply may result in prosecution.

## Occupiers' Liability Acts 1957 and 1984

The Occupiers' Liability Acts 1957 and 1984 impose a duty of care on those who manage premises to ensure that visitors (eg pupils and parents) are reasonably safe on the premises for the purposes for which they are invited or allowed to be there. School leadership teams are therefore responsible for ensuring that school premises are safe to use.

A higher duty of care is imposed on an occupier if children are involved. Objects that may, in legal terms, be classed as *allurements* should be safeguarded. It is essential to do so with equipment associated with physical education (eg javelins, trampolines). A warning notice does not necessarily absolve an occupier from liability, unless it enables visitors to be reasonably safe. It is only one of many factors that will be considered when deciding whether or not an occupier has exercised the duty of care required.

## Children Act 1989 and 2004 (England), Children (Scotland) Act 1995, Children's (Northern Ireland) Order 1995

Under the terms of the Children Act 1989, everyone who has substantial access to children is required to provide evidence of their suitability to work with children. This evidence should be vetted by the authority concerned. In the context of education, this applies when recruiting school staff and other adults who contribute to the PESS programmes.

Many LAs and independent agencies now provide codes of conduct on purposeful physical contact with children. Those working with pupils in situations where physical contact is sometimes deemed to be necessary (eg when teaching certain gymnastic skills) should ensure they are aware of, and follow, such guidance. Physical contact should only occur when it is necessary to ensure the safety of a pupil and when the pupil is aware that it will take place. Contact should be such that it cannot be misconstrued.

The Children Act 2004 established local safeguarding boards from 1 March 2005 and departments for children's services from 1 April 2005.

Section 175 of the Education Act 2002 imposed duties on governing bodies and LAs to ensure they carry out their functions concerning safeguarding and promoting the welfare of pupils. This does not imply direct liability on any individual teacher if there is a failure to put the arrangements into place. Section 38 of the Education and Inspections Act 2006 also places duties on governors relating to the 2004 Act, in that it established a duty to ensure the well-being of pupils.

> See *Chapter 9: Safeguarding Children and Young People*, pages 55–72, for further information about child-protection issues relating to physical education.

**Protection of Children Act 1999, Protection of Children (Scotland) Act 2003, Protection of Children and Vulnerable Adults (Northern Ireland) Order 2003**

The Protection of Children Act 1999 (POCA) has four principal objectives:

a. To make statutory the Department of Health Consultancy Service Index list – the *Protection of Children Act (POCA) List* – which contains the names of people considered unsuitable to work with children.

b. To amend Section 218 of the Education Reform Act 1988 to enable what was the Department for Education and Skills (DfES), now the Department for Children, Schools and Families (DCSF), to identify people placed on *List 99* because they are considered unsuitable to work with children.

c. To amend Part V of the Police Act 1997 to enable the Criminal Records Bureau (CRB) to disclose information about people who are included on the *POCA List* or *List 99*, along with their criminal records, thereby creating a *one-stop shop* system of checking people seeking to work with children.

d. To require regulated childcare organisations to check the names of anyone they propose to employ in posts involving regular/substantial access to children against both the *POCA List* and *List 99*.

Sports organisations are not covered by the mandatory aspects of POCA 1999, as they are not childcare organisations. However, they are encouraged to refer names to be considered for inclusion on the *POCA List*.

See *Chapter 9: Safeguarding Children and Young People*, pages 55–72, for further information about child-protection issues relating to physical education.

**Special Educational Needs (SEN), Disability Act 2001 and Disability Discrimination Act 2005, Special Needs and Disability (Northern Ireland) Order 2005**

The *SEN and Disability Act 2001*, together with the *Disability Discrimination Act 2005* (which amended the *Disability Discrimination Act 1995*) set LAs and school governing bodies a duty not to treat disabled pupils less favourably, without justification, than their non-disabled peers (the 'less favourable treatment duty') and to make reasonable adjustments to ensure that disabled pupils are not put at a substantial disadvantage compared to non-disabled pupils (the 'reasonable adjustments duty'). The reasonable adjustments duty requires schools to think ahead, anticipate the barriers that disabled pupils may face and remove or minimise them before a disabled pupil is placed at a substantial disadvantage. This planning should include consideration of health-and-safety issues in physical education, such as accessibility plans to take account of SEN and disabilities.

**Safeguarding Vulnerable Groups Act 2006, Safeguarding Vulnerable Groups (Northern Ireland) Order 2007, Child Protection: Pre-employment Checks of Persons to Work in Schools – New Arrangements (circular 2008/03, Northern Ireland)**

This Act established a new vetting and barring scheme for people who work with children and vulnerable adults by introducing the Independent Safeguarding Authority (ISA). This agency has the responsibility for maintaining an up-to-date online list of anyone barred from working with children or vulnerable adults through a centralised vetting process that everyone working with children and vulnerable adults will need to go through.

Two barred lists are being created – one for children and one for vulnerable adults – that will prevent those barred from engaging in 'regulated' activity (ie a range of specified activities involving close contact with children or vulnerable adults). Teaching is one such activity.

Everyone registered with the ISA will be monitored and their data kept up to date. If someone's circumstances change in relation to the vetting and barring system, anyone checking the list online will be able to see this. Also, anyone who has made an enquiry about such individuals will be notified of the change in circumstances.

From 2008, it will become a criminal offence not to register or to work in a school without being registered or for anyone to appoint someone without checking the barred list prior to the person commencing work.

Disclosure certification through the CRB will continue, as the barring system identifies only those actually barred, not those with some form of information held in relation to the disclosure process. In effect, the Act establishes whether it is legal to appoint someone to a position. The disclosure system establishes whether it is safe to appoint someone.

## Corporate Manslaughter and Corporate Homicide Act 2007

This law is meant to make it easier to prosecute medium- and large-sized organisations for serious mismanagement in health and safety that results in death (corporate manslaughter in England and Wales, corporate homicide in Scotland) through a collective criminal responsibility for deaths. Any poor management judged to be grossly criminally negligent will be deemed to be manslaughter. The target for possible prosecution is intended to be the leadership group. The Act does not require proof of any individual being guilty of an offence, but targets the organisation as being criminally deficient. There are no new obligations, safety measures or management processes built into the Act. Instead, the sanctions available have increased.

The new Act is designed to make it easier to prosecute a school leadership without identifying an individual directing mind. Any governing body of a school, as a corporate body, is liable under the new Act – as it also appears under health-and-safety law – but is most unlikely to face prosecution where it has complied with relevant health-and-safety statutory requirements.

Schools are advised to review existing health-and-safety policies and procedures to ensure they are of sufficient detail for the safe and detailed planning, management and evaluation of school organised events.

### The Law Reform (Contributory Negligence) Act 1945

This established that liability – or responsibility for the injury – may be apportioned by the court where it is judged that the claimant's action contributed to the outcome.

# Regulations

### The Activity Centres (Young Persons' Safety) Act 1995 and Adventure Activities Licensing Regulations 2004

> **Note**: The Activity Licensing Regulations 2004 are not applicable in Northern Ireland.

Under the terms of the Activity Centres (Young Persons' Safety) Act 1995 and Adventure Activities Licensing Regulations 2004, commercial providers of climbing, water sports, trekking and caving activities, in remote or isolated areas, for young people under the age of 18, are required to apply for a licence to offer such activities. All applicants must undergo an inspection and will only be awarded a licence if their safety-management systems are deemed to be adequate.

From October 1997, it became a legal requirement that only licensed activity providers could offer outdoor and adventurous activities on a commercial basis. Some activity centres are exempt from licensing requirements (eg school-operated centres, non-profit-making centres).

The Adventure Activities Licensing Authority (AALA) has ceased to be an independent body and its powers have been transferred to the HSE, with TQS Limited now trading as the Adventurous Activities Licensing Service (AALS). The same rigorous licensing regulations have been maintained.

School staff planning to take pupils to an activity centre should ascertain whether the planned programme falls within the remit of the AALS and, if so, whether the centre is licensed. Holding a licence demonstrates that the centre's safety management has been inspected and that it meets AALS requirements. However, a licence does not cover aspects of provision such as accommodation.

If the work of the centre falls outside the remit of AALS, school staff should be satisfied that the quality of the staffing, equipment and accommodation at the centre is adequate, and should advise the school governors accordingly.

### Regulatory Reform (Fire Safety) Order 2005

Under the Regulatory Reform (Fire Safety) Order 2005 (FSO), all the pre-existing fire-safety regulations and requirements for safety certificates were rescinded. Schools in the UK are subject to the revised FSO.

Persons responsible for premises (ie the LA, governors, trustees or proprietor according to the status of the school) are now solely responsible for ensuring the safety of the premises and the occupants, but the task will normally be delegated to the head teacher. All schools are expected to have in place a comprehensive fire-safety system based on relevant risk assessments. Fire risk assessment no longer involves an annual visit and certification by the fire brigade. The brigade's new role is to carry out spot checks to see if buildings comply with the new requirements.

Schools should ensure that their current fire-safety arrangements and, in particular, fire equipment, fire notices and fire drills are in place and up to date in order to manage and minimise the risk from fire, as failure to comply may lead to prosecution.

Schools should have in place policies and procedures that aim to keep the risk of fire to a minimum. The head teacher and governors must ensure that fire-safety policies are known and implemented.

In the event of a fire, the availability of completed attendance registers and a plan of the school buildings would be helpful to the fire and rescue services.

### Management of Health and Safety at Work Regulations 1999 and 2002

Under the terms of the Management of Health and Safety at Work Regulations, employers are required to carry out risk assessments by:

- formally identifying the hazards present in any undertaking

- estimating the extent of the risks involved, taking into account any precautions that are already in place

- introducing measures for planning, organising, controlling, monitoring and reviewing their management of health and safety.

Risk assessments are central to any health-and-safety system. Assessments must be made of the risks to which employees, pupils and others who visit the school premises are exposed so that appropriate action can be taken to protect their health and safety.

All risk assessments must be suitable and sufficient, and show reasonable forethought.

> See *Chapter 3: Risk Management,* pages 23–30, for further information.

### Reporting of Injuries, Diseases and Dangerous Occurrences Regulations 1995

The Reporting of Injuries, Diseases and Dangerous Occurrences Regulations 1995 (RIDDOR) apply to accidents or occurrences that take place during both curricular and school-sport activities, both on and off the school premises (eg outdoor activity centres, sports centres).

The employer should be informed of any such accident or occurrence, as it is likely to manage the reporting procedure to the HSE, if required.

School staff should familiarise themselves with the requirements of the Regulations so that they are aware of which accidents have to be reported. Failure to comply may result in prosecution.

> See *Chapter 8: Accident Procedures and First-aid Management,* pages 49–54, for further information about RIDDOR.

### Provision and Use of Work Equipment Regulations 1998

Under the terms of the Provision and Use of Work Equipment Regulations 1998, employers are required to ensure that work equipment is maintained in good working order. To achieve this, they should arrange for equipment to be inspected at regular intervals, particularly where a risk assessment has identified a significant risk arising from the installation or use of the equipment.

The extent of the inspection will depend on the type of equipment, its history, how it is used, how often it is used and the potential risks arising from its use or failure.

School staff are advised to ensure that specialist physical-education equipment (eg gymnastic equipment) is inspected on an annual (or more frequent) basis. LAs often make arrangements for an annual inspection of gymnastic apparatus in the schools for which they are responsible. The schools are subsequently responsible for implementing any recommendations made in the inspection reports.

> For more information, see *Chapter 12: Equipment in Physical Education*, pages 85–93.
>
> For a model contract, see *Appendix 5: Model Equipment Inspection/ Maintenance Schedule – Gymnasia, Sports Halls and Fitness Areas*, page 325.

### The Education (School Premises) Regulations 1999

These are often referred to as the 'building regulations' and are updated every few years. The Regulations set out what must be provided in schools of particular types and sizes. Schedule 2 sets out the area and quality standard for playing fields. There is no longer any specific requirement for indoor spaces.

### Education (Specified Work and Registration) Regulations 2003

The Education (Specified Work and Registration) Regulations 2003 impact on how adults, who are not qualified teachers, work within the school setting. The conditions are set out under which school staff other than qualified teachers may undertake the following *specified teaching activities* in schools:

- planning and preparing lessons and courses for pupils

- delivering lessons to pupils, including delivery via distance learning or computer-aided techniques

- assessing the development, progress and attainment of pupils

- reporting on the development, progress and attainment of pupils.

The Regulations ensure that all such specified teaching activities are supervised by a teacher. The degree of supervision is up to the professional judgement of head teachers. For example, it is not assumed that a teacher will always be physically present when a member of staff without qualified teacher status is carrying out specified teaching activities.

### School Staffing (England) (Amendment) Regulations 2006

It is now mandatory to obtain enhanced CRB disclosures for all new appointments to the schools workforce and those who have been out of the workforce for more than three months. All volunteers who work regularly with children must also obtain an enhanced disclosure certificate. This change is part of an ongoing process by the government to tighten current vetting and barring procedures to ensure that the system is as robust as possible.

The regulations apply to all maintained schools and include LA-appointed staff. The school workforce includes anyone employed by the school, including those employed to deliver extended services. Independent schools are also required to undertake CRB checks under the Education (Independent School Standards) Regulations 2003.

### The Health and Safety (Safety Signs and Signals) Regulations 1996

The Regulations place duties on schools to safeguard staff and pupils. The principle duty is to ensure that safety signs are in place where required. All signs should be of a pattern to comply with the regulations, ie to BS 5378 (or in the case of fire-safety signs with BS 5499).

The Regulations require schools to ensure that safety signs are provided and maintained where risk assessments have identified that other risk-control measures are insufficient or inappropriate in themselves. In other words, if typical risk-control measures do not work fully, then put a warning sign in place. They are not intended simply as a substitute for other control measures but as a reminder that risk remains or that particular action needs to be taken to remain safe.

A safety sign may take various forms, such as an illuminated sign or acoustic signal, a verbal communication or hand signal or a signboard – something that provides information or instructions by a combination of shape, colour and a symbol or pictogram that is rendered visible by lighting of sufficient intensity. In practice, many signboards may be accompanied by supplementary text (eg 'Fire exit') alongside the symbol of a moving person.

Signs can be of the following types:

- *prohibition sign* – a sign prohibiting behaviour likely to increase or cause danger (eg 'No running')

- *warning sign* – a sign giving warning of a hazard or danger (eg 'Danger: wet floor')

- *mandatory sign* – a sign prescribing specific behaviour (eg 'Eye protection must be worn')

- *fire emergency escape or first-aid sign* – a sign giving information on emergency exits, first-aid or rescue facilities (eg 'Emergency exit/escape route').

## Guidance and Codes of Practice

### Approved Code of Practice for First Aid 1997

The First Aid Regulations 1981 place a duty on schools to ensure there is adequate first-aid provision for employees who become ill or are injured at work. First aid is defined as immediate attention to prevent minor injuries becoming major ones. It excludes giving tablets or medicines to treat illness. The Approved Code of Practice (ACOP) sets out the detail to meet the requirements of the Regulations.

Where there are 50 or more employees, a suitable, trained first-aider must be appointed. In schools with fewer employees, an appointed person needs to be identified to take charge of any situation relating to an ill or injured employee. Further arrangements should be based on an appropriate risk assessment. The school must inform the staff of the arrangements made for first aid.

There is no specific legislation to provide first-aid cover for those on the premises who are not at work (eg pupils), but a note in the ACOP states that employers who regularly have such persons on the premises 'may wish to make some provision for them'. This is now seen to be standard practice in schools because of the duty of care schools have for pupils.

It is advisable that records are kept of any aid given.

Provision must be made for those working away from the main site. Groups going off site should be equipped with the minimum of a travelling first-aid kit.

Schools should have at least one first-aid box and probably more, according to the particular circumstances. All staff should know where the first-aid boxes are kept. They should contain a 'sufficient quantity' of first-aid material. There is no longer a mandatory list of items for a first-aid kit. A suggested minimum is given, with possible items added according to the location and type of injury likely to be encountered. See also *Guidance on First Aid for Schools* (DfEE, 1998).

## Schools for the Future: Inspirational Design for Physical Education and Sport Spaces (2005)

The DfES (now DCSF) has produced design guidance with actual school examples to show how well-designed physical-education and sport facilities can contribute to exciting teaching and learning. The guidance is intended to support the Building Schools for the Future initiative.

## Building Bulletins 98 and 99: Briefing Framework for Secondary/Primary School Projects (2006)

**Note**: The Schools for the Future guidance is not yet applicable in Northern Ireland.

These documents aim to help school staff and governors with LAs and other agencies to develop a brief for new-build and refurbishment projects. As non-statutory guidelines, these documents provide a basis for which the government will fund school buildings. Decisions on the use and provision of space rest with the agency determining the building or refurbishing of a facility.

## Comparative Sizes of Sports Pitches and Courts (2007)

Sport England has updated the excellent technical guidance relating to the design and provision of sports-related pitches and courts. The tables set out the recommended or required sizes of pitches and courts, including ceiling heights and run-off areas, for the different standards of competition. It includes recommendations for schools' age-related pitch sizes, where appropriate.

## Health and Safety of Pupils on Educational Visits (1998) plus Supplementary Papers (2002) and Group Safety at Water Margins (DfES with CCPR, 2003)

The DfES (now DCSF) produced detailed guidance on the organisation and management of off-site experiences. The initial publication was supplemented later by five additional sets of guidance:

- *Health and Safety: Responsibilities and Powers*

- *A Handbook for Group Leaders*

- *Standards for Adventure*

- *Standards for LEAs in Overseeing Educational Visits*

- *Group Safety at Water Margins.*

**Note:** Further essential guidance for off-site visit organisation and leadership is set out in *Health and Safety of Pupils on Educational Visits* (HASPEV – DfES, 1998). In England, HASPEV will be subsumed within the *Learning Outside the Classroom* (LotC) guidance. In Wales, HASPEV will be subsumed within the guidance document *Educational Visits*.

## Appendix 2A: A Generic Risk-assessment Prompt Sheet for Physical Education

| People | Context | Organisation | Controlling Risks |
|---|---|---|---|
| **1. Pupils/performers** <br> ■ Group sizes <br> ■ Teacher:pupil ratio <br> ■ Additional supervision required <br> ■ Control/discipline/behaviour <br> ■ Individual and group abilities <br> ■ Needs match demands of activity <br> ■ Clothing appropriate for activity <br> ■ Jewellery <br> ■ Safety equipment/personal protection <br> ■ Medical conditions known <br> ■ Policy on physical contact/ substantial access applied <br> ■ Disability Discrimination Act requirements re access and involvement in PE for those with cognitive, visual, hearing or motor impairment <br> ■ Pupils/performers know routines and procedures <br> ■ Other aspects <br> **2. Staff** <br> ■ Qualifications/ experience/confidence | **1. Facility** <br> ■ Changing rooms safe <br> ■ Work area hazard-free – no obstructions <br> ■ Clean, non-slip floor/water clarity <br> ■ Sufficient space for group size/activity <br> ■ Any shared-use issues <br> ■ Access issues for those with disabilities <br> ■ Operating procedures known/applied <br> ■ Fire regulations applied <br> ■ Safety signs in place <br> ■ Secured when not in use <br> ■ Other aspects <br> **2. Procedures/routines** <br> ■ Orderly movement to work area <br> ■ Access to facility <br> ■ First-aid equipment/ procedures/responsibilities <br> ■ Notices <br> ■ Other aspects <br> **3. Equipment** <br> ■ Used for purpose designed <br> ■ Suitable for the activity | **1. Class organisation** <br> ■ Numbers known/register check <br> ■ Regular scanning/head counts <br> ■ Group organisation/ management procedures <br> ■ Warm-up/preparation/safe exercise <br> ■ Demonstrations accurate <br> ■ Involvement of pupils with visual, hearing, motor or cognitive impairment <br> ■ Other aspects <br> **2. Teaching style** <br> ■ Planned sessions <br> ■ Appropriate teaching style used <br> ■ Rules consistently applied <br> ■ Regular and approved practice used <br> ■ Support techniques known and applied <br> ■ Intervention appropriate <br> ■ Tasks differentiated <br> ■ Other aspects | **1. Ensuring the people work safely** <br> ■ Provide protective equipment/clothing <br> ■ Provide necessary CPD <br> ■ Devise appropriate procedures <br> ■ Set appropriate discipline and control standards <br> ■ Develop observation skills <br> **2. Ensuring the context is safe** <br> ■ Inspect facility periodically <br> ■ Place warning notices/protective devices where risks exist <br> ■ Buy high-quality equipment <br> ■ Inspect equipment <br> ■ Repair/service equipment <br> ■ Modify equipment <br> ■ Teach how to use equipment/facility <br> ■ Amend how equipment is used <br> **3. Ensuring the organisation is safe** <br> ■ Teach progressive practices thoroughly <br> ■ Explain any inherent risks <br> ■ Emphasise playing within the rules |

- CPD needed
- Supervision at all times
- Knowledge of individuals and group
- Observation and analysis skills adequate
- Control and discipline adequate
- Clothing/personal effects appropriate for teaching PESS
- Teaching position in relation to performers
- Assistants know limits of role/responsibility
- Effective communication between teacher and support staff
- Insurance cover where needed
- Disclosure certificates seen
- Parents informed and involved as necessary
- Other aspects

- Handling/carrying/siting issues
- Accessibility/storage
- Safety/rescue equipment present
- Annual/periodic inspection check
- Checked before use by performers
- No improvisation
- Routines for collection/retrieval/changing
- Other aspects

**4. Transport**
- Roadworthiness
- Safe embarkation
- Seat belts used
- Driver requirements/responsibilities
- Passenger lists
- Other aspects

**3. Preparation**
- Written scheme of work sets out safety issues to be followed
- Equipment – size/type/quality/suitability
- Carrying/moving/placing equipment
- Storage
- Safety policy applied
- Other aspects

**4. Progression**
- Progressive practices known/applied
- Appropriate activities
- Other aspects

**5. Emergency action**
- Emergency/accident procedures/contingency plans known and applied
- Other aspects

- Change the way the activity is carried out
- Group by ability or some other factor
- Stop the activity
- Avoid the area
- Use a safer alternative

**Appendix 2B: Risk Assessment in Physical Education – Facility**

School: *Holly Bush*

Work area: *Hall*

| Aspects to Consider (List only actual hazards) | Satisfactory? (tick ✓) Yes | Satisfactory? (tick ✓) No | Who is Affected? Pupils (P) Staff (S) Visitors (V) | Is Further Action Necessary? Risk Control (Comment) What? | By When? | Completed? |
|---|---|---|---|---|---|---|
| **1. People** | | | | | | |
| **1.1 Pupils** | | | | | | |
| **1.2 Staff** | | | | | | |
| • NQT with no gymnastic experience required to teach gymnastics | ✓ | | P | • Support through shared teaching, INSET and lesson observations | Ongoing | |
| **2. Context** | | | | | | |
| **2.1 Facility** | | | | | | |
| • OHP stand not always pushed into corner of hall | | ✓ | P | • Notice to be placed on wall<br>• Notice via staff meeting<br>• Emphasise in handbook – procedures | 1/4 | 25/3<br><br>Disk updated |
| • 1 fire extinguisher missing | | ✓ | S/V/P | • Site manager informed – replacement ordered 23/3 | 15/4 | ✓ checked 15/4 |
| **2.2 Procedures** | ✓ | | | | | |
| **2.3 Equipment** | | | | | | |
| • Condemned mats not removed from storeroom – still available for use | | ✓ | P/V | • Condemned mats removed and disposed of immediately – firm doing annual inspection asked to remove in future | 23/3 | ✓ checked 23/3 + letter 15/4 |
| **2.4 Transport** | N/A | | | | | |

| Aspects to Consider (List only actual hazards) | Satisfactory? (tick ✓) | | Who is Affected? Pupils (P) Staff (S) Visitors (V) | Is Further Action Necessary? Risk Control (Comment) | | Completed? |
|---|---|---|---|---|---|---|
| | Yes | No | | What? | By When? | |
| **3. Organisation** | | | | | | |
| **3.1 Class organisation** • Warm-ups frequently insufficient and not monitored by teachers | | ✓ | P | • Staff INSET on safe exercise and activity-specific warm-up • Guidelines in handbook to be further developed | 21/7 | ✓ checked 8/5 |
| **3.2 Teaching style** | ✓ | | | | | |
| **3.3 Preparation** | ✓ | | | | | |
| **3.4 Progression** | ✓ | | | | | |
| **3.5 Emergency action** | ✓ | | | | | |

Signed:  Head teacher  .........*JB*.................   Date of assessment: .........*23 March 2008*.................

       Subject leader  .........*MM*.................

       Review 1 .................... (date and initial)
       Review 2 .................... (date and initial)
       Review 3 .................... (date and initial)

## Appendix 2C: Example Risk Assessment of an Event Using a Different Format
School Sports Day (school site)

| Hazard | Risk Rating | Who is at Risk? | Control Measures |
|---|---|---|---|
| **People** | | | |
| Lack of expertise of some staff | Low | Competitors and spectators | Whole-staff briefing and induction prior to event; deployment of less-confident staff to track events |
| Pupils known to exhibit challenging behaviour | Low/med | Competitors and spectators | Maximise participation rates for all pupils as competitors and assistant judges; appropriate supervision levels; pupil code of conduct clearly communicated and understood |
| Spectator and athlete compliance | Low | Competitors and spectators | Newsletter to pupils' homes prior to event clearly explaining organisation, procedures and expectations; effective microphone/speaker communication system used on the day; sufficient number of staff undertaking marshalling duties |
| **Context** | | | |
| Surface irregularities and dangerous substances on school field | Low | Competitors | Check working areas prior to event and remedy any deficiencies |
| Faulty, worn equipment | Low | Competitors and spectators | Ensure all equipment is in good condition before transporting to competitive area |
| Facility quality | Low | Competitors | Jumping pits well dug and raked; approaches prepared; approach markers provided for athletes |
| Harmful effects of the sun | Low | Competitors and spectators | Sunscreen application advised and water stations easily accessible |
| Inclement weather | Low | Competitors and spectators | Alternative, fallback dates identified; decision to postpone made as early as possible; routines and procedures for orderly dispersal clearly established and communicated in case of abandonment. |
| **Organisation** | | | |
| Transport of throwing implements to designated throwing areas | Low | Pupils | Pupils and staff inducted into safe carrying procedures and placement |
| Supervision of throwing implements | Low | Competitors and spectators | Throwing implements never left unattended by members of staff responsible; returned safely to storage when used |
| Injury to competitors | Low | Competitors | First-aid provision and emergency action plan clearly communicated to pupils and staff |

300

# Appendix 2D: Example Risk Assessment for a Pupil (SEN)

**Activity**: Swimming     **Pupil**: TS

| Hazard | Risk Rating | Who is at Risk? | Control Measures |
|---|---|---|---|
| **People** | | | |
| TS – autistic; reacts to changes in sunlight, glare; can become distressed, may try to run away; loses focus and fails to respond to staff support | High | TS Staff Other pupils | Whole-staff briefing regarding TS, his response to light changes and safety measures to be put in place |
| Staff – possible lack of expertise in dealing with TS when he is distressed | Med | TS Staff Other pupils | Ensure one-to-one specialist support in circumstances where light change may be an issue |
| Other pupils – may follow TS if he tries to run away or copy other behaviours | Low | TS Staff Other pupils | All staff taking part in activity fully briefed on their role, should there be an incident with TS |
| **Context** | | | |
| School pool – north facing with high windows with shades to reduce action of light | Low | TS Staff Other pupils | Risk assess for any possible ingress of sharp light likely to cause TS difficulties; make good any possible causes of ingress of sharp light; check before each session |
| Local pool – all glass, regular changes in intensity of light on water | High | TS Staff Other pupils General public | Risk is so high that TS should not attend local pool until he has developed the skills to respond to light changes |
| **Organisation** | | | |
| Use only school pool until TS has developed skills to cope with light changes experienced at local pool | Low | TS Staff Other pupils | Ensure TS is restricted to school pool only for swimming activity |
| Ensure one-to-one support for TS in school pool | Low | TS Staff Other pupils | Ensure all other staff present are trained in how to support TS, should an incident occur |

## Appendix 2E: Example Risk Assessment of Primary Gymnastics

| Hazard | Risk Rating | Who is at Risk? | Control Measures |
|---|---|---|---|
| **People** | | | |
| Pupils with SEN | Low | All pupils | Teaching staff to be aware of any constraints/limitations on SEN pupil activity and movement; ensure presence of support staff, where necessary, and brief appropriately about their role and input during the lesson |
| Graduate teacher | Low | All pupils | Subject leader/mentor to monitor all aspects of teaching and exercise direct presence where appropriate (eg apparatus work) |
| Absence of current first-aid qualification of some teaching staff | Low | All pupils | Ensure all staff are familiar with emergency accident procedures identified in physical-education handbook |
| **Context** | | | |
| School hall | Low | All pupils Staff | Ensure working area is free from hazard (eg piano, OHP, chairs); alert children to the need to remain within designated working area; ensure floor is clean and free from any spillage |
| Faulty equipment | Low | All pupils | Always check for damage/wear and tear prior to work commencing; ensure equipment has been properly assembled |
| Inappropriate clothing, personal adornment and footwear | Low | All pupils Staff | Staff and pupils to be in correct attire with all jewellery removed or made safe |
| **Organisation** | | | |
| Compliance with scheme of work and pupil progress records | Low | All pupils | Subject leader to ensure planning of all teaching staff complete and up to date and any concerns about individual pupil progress clearly identified |
| Movement from classroom to hall | Low | All pupils | All children to be given clear understanding of procedures for entering hall and when to commence work |

302

# Appendix 2F: Safe Practice in Physical Education Poster

**Pupils** engaged in physical education should be:
- given opportunities to think about safe practice in relation to themselves and peers
- guided to develop their knowledge and understanding relating to responsible participation and progress
- sufficiently skilled and confident in the tasks set
- appropriately supervised when undertaking a leadership role.

**Preparation** requires:
- comprehensive schemes of work in place, differentiated to meet the needs of all pupils
- a safety policy and guidelines
- up-to-date risk assessment.

**Teaching style and class organisation** should ensure that:
- pupil capability is matched to task
- the methodology is appropriate to safety demands inherent within the activity
- pupils are always appropriately prepared and confident through progressive practices.

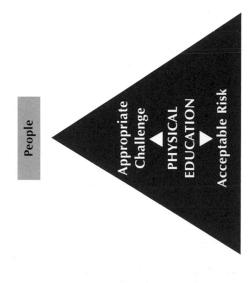

People

Organisation

Appropriate Challenge ◀ PHYSICAL EDUCATION ▶ Acceptable Risk

Context

**School staff** delivering physical education need to:
- understand their obligations relating to their duty of care
- be suitably experienced and competent to teach the physical activity being offered
- use regular and approved practice
- be aware of any child/pupil at risk
- ensure acceptable pupil behaviour at all times
- clarify the role of and monitor the work of other support staff.

**Physical-education facilities** should provide:
- hazard-free playing surfaces
- sufficient space allocated to the activities and be subject to:
  – a regular and systematic maintenance programme
  – appropriate usage.

**Procedures** should involve:
- safety rules and regulations clearly understood by both pupils and staff
- attendance and assessment records consistently maintained
- all accidents and 'near misses' comprehensively logged and reported to the appropriate body where required
- communication with parents about school policies and practice.

**Physical-education equipment** should be:
- inspected annually
- regularly maintained
- regularly monitored for wear and tear
- checked before use
- used appropriately and stored safely
- disposed of when condemned.

association for
**Physical Education**

The Scottish
Government

Department of
**Education**
www.deni.gov.uk
AN ROINN
**Oideachais**
MANNYSTRIE O
Lear

department for
**children, schools and families**

Available at: www.afpe.org.uk or hard copies of this poster are available from: DCSF Publications at www.teachernet.gov.uk/pesafety or telephone 0845-602 2260

# Appendix 2G: Safe Practice for Safeguarding Children and Young People Poster

**Children and Young People (CYP)** should:
- be aware of their right to be safe from abuse
- know where to go for help and advice about abuse and bullying.

**Environment:**
- Physical activity should be carried out in a safe, positive and encouraging atmosphere.

**Procedures:**
- Practice should be exemplary and unlikely to cause concern to other adults or harm to CYP.
- There should be published codes of conduct, good practice and ethics.
- There should be guidance on expected and acceptable behaviour towards CYP.
- Disciplinary measures and sanctions should be non-violent and not involve humiliating CYP.
- There should be appropriate education and training to raise awareness of issues about safeguarding CYP.
- There should be a published process for dealing with behaviour that is unacceptable.
- There should be a process of support for adults and CYP who are suspected of inappropriate behaviour towards CYP.
- There should be clear procedures for the recruitment of staff.

**Staff** should:
- promote a culture that ensures that CYP are listened to and respected as individuals
- be clear on how to respond appropriately to concerns about CYP
- be clear on how to respond appropriately to allegations of abuse by other adults and abuse by CYP on CYP
- respond to suspicions and allegations of abuse swiftly using agreed procedures.

**Policies:**
- Schools should have a mandatory CYP safeguarding policy, which is promoted within the school, informs suitable recruitment and is reviewed every three years.
- Policies should be clearly written and understood by all adults.
- There should be a designated child protection coordinator (CPC) in the school and a designated CPC for off-site activity.
- There should be a process for recording incidents and dealing with concerns.

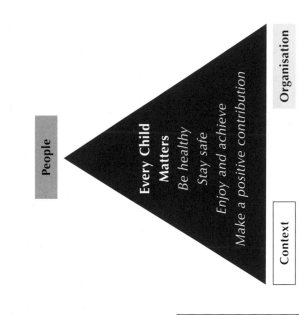

People

**Every Child Matters**
*Be healthy*
*Stay safe*
*Enjoy and achieve*
*Make a positive contribution*

Context

Organisation

**Staff Guidance and Training** is needed on:
- procedures to safeguard CYP
- awareness raising about abuse in order to overcome barriers to CYP reporting their concerns
- helping adults recognise the signs and indicators that might give rise to concern
- how to respond to concerns about abuse of CYP
- how to respond to CYP making an allegation of abuse
- ways in which adults can raise concerns about unacceptable behaviour by other adults
- specific issues such as ratios, photography, imagery on the Internet, supporting performers, physical contact, one-to-one coaching, journeys in cars, conduct on school trips etc.

304

# Appendix 2H: Safe Practice in the Organisation of Sports Fixtures and Area Sports Events Poster

**People**

**Curriculum enrichment and extension**

◄ *Inter-school Competition* ►

**Acceptable Risk**

**Organisation**

**Context**

**School staff** need to:
- be competent in managing inter-school events, whether located on or off site
- keep senior management reliably informed of their planning and organisation
- establish clear procedures with home and visiting staff for managing an emergency situation, including first aid.

**Employers** need to:
- communicate their policy and monitor its implementation
- provide risk-assessment guidance
- offer appropriate advice and professional development necessary to ensure safe practice.

**Senior management** need to:
- ensure governors receive appropriate information about this aspect of school life
- confirm a suitable risk assessment has been completed, including all travel, supervision and emergency arrangements.

**Support staff** need to:
- comply with any school or LA policy requirements relating to the safe conduct of inter-school competition
- clearly understand the extent of their supervisory role in relation to that of the teachers.

**Pupils** need to:
- demonstrate acceptable behaviour at all times
- exercise appropriate responsibility for their own well-being and that of others
- ensure parents are fully informed about their participation.

**Parents** need to:
- ensure they are in receipt of regular information (eg fixtures list) relating to their child's involvement in inter-school competition
- keep the school informed about their child's existing or changed medical needs or special circumstances.

**Governors** should:
- be familiar with their health-and-safety obligations and that of the LA in safeguarding the well-being of pupils
- be well informed about their school's involvement in inter-school activities
- establish agreed systems for approval in accordance with school and LA policies.

**Preparation** requires:
- the completion of appropriate risk assessments
- that participating pupils are well prepared and briefed for the planned activity, ensuring the physical/emotional maturity of the pupils and that they are suitably challenging
- that any catering arrangements comply with sound hygiene requirements
- that pupils are suitably equipped for any adverse environmental/weather conditions.

**Programming** should require that:
- pupils are not overextended in terms of activity and/or match scheduling
- start and finish times are strictly adhered to, wherever possible.

**Supervision** requires that:
- recommended staff:pupil ratios are complied with
- staff are appropriately qualified and experienced to supervise the activity
- child-protection measures are fully implemented.

**Procedures** should ensure:
- policy and guidelines for the safe conduct of inter-school activities are made accessible to all supervisory staff, particularly relating to approval, travel arrangements, medical information and emergency procedures.

**Facilities** should offer:
- hazard-free playing, changing and working areas
- sufficient space allocation for safe participation.

**The journey** involves:
- confirming the competence of the driver and roadworthiness of the transport used
- registration and subsequent head counts of participating pupils
- clearly understood procedures for disembarkation and dispersal.

**Equipment** should be:
- regularly checked and inspected
- compliant with national and European safety standards, where required
- compatible with the recommendations of the appropriate body.

# Appendix 2l: Safe Practice in Workforce Planning Poster

**Head teachers** should:

- make clear the circumstances in which support staff may work in school
- inform parents (and the employer if necessary) that support staff will teach PESS
- ensure conditions of employment, insurance, disclosure and pre-employment requirements are clarified and checked
- confirm the support staff's suitability to work with children
- establish that the support staff's confidence and competence are appropriate to the demands of the pupils, the activities and the requirements of the curriculum
- ensure adequate risk assessment of the contribution the support staff will make
- check whether the school/LA policy allows support staff to lead groups off site
- provide for continuing professional development (CPD) of all support staff
- designate a teacher to supervise and direct the work of support staff.

**Support staff** need to:

- have undertaken suitable professional development relevant to the activities they are being asked to supervise and how pupils learn
- have full access to a completed risk assessment of the activity and preferably have contributed to its completion
- be aware of and understand the relevant sections of *Safe Practice 2008*
- fully meet the statutory requirements relating to safeguarding children and young adults
- be clear as to their role and level of responsibility
- be able to manage the group/class and the activity effectively in terms of behaviour, progress and safety.

**Teachers** need to have:

- undertaken appropriate monitoring to ensure support staff are competent to effectively supervise designated activity
- involved support staff in activity planning and agreed health-and-safety procedures
- clearly communicated to support staff intended learning outcomes and pupil capabilities, including provision to be made for special needs
- ensured a contingency plan is in place, should support staff not be available.

**People**

**Organisation**

**Confidence and Competence**

*Support Staff in PESS*

**Acceptable Risk**

**Context**

**The agency** should:

- establish a clear and detailed service level agreement/contract for services with the school
- make effective pre-employment checks on their staff
- provide adequate and appropriate insurance cover
- check the confidence and competence in relation to the demands of the pupils, the activities to be taught and the requirements of the curriculum
- ensure its staff have experience of working with the designated age groups
- maintain consistent standards
- confirm a suitable risk assessment has been completed, including all travel, supervision and emergency arrangements.

**Preparation:**

- Schemes of work and session plans have been agreed by the teacher and support staff.
- Activity-specific risk assessments have been shared.
- Pupils are informed about planned teaching arrangements.
- Assessment strategies are established and roles and responsibilities in the process clearly understood.

**Teaching:**

- Staff:pupil ratios reflect national and local guidance, taking note of national governing body advice, where appropriate.
- Activity is suitably differentiated and pitched to accommodate pupil need, aspiration and competence.
- Safe changing procedures are implemented.
- Approaches to teaching and learning are consistently supportive and inclusive while seeking to challenge and extend pupils, whatever their level of ability.

**Procedures:**

- Parents have been fully informed about teaching arrangements involving the activity and the intended role of support staff to supervise physical activity.
- Emergency and post-accident procedures have been clearly communicated to all staff leading physical activity.
- Insurance arrangements are unambiguous and verified, where necessary.
- Policies relating to clothing, behaviour and non-participation are in place and consistently applied.

**Facilities:**

- Equipment is designed for, and is compatible with, the age and developmental stage of the participating pupils.
- Equipment is checked before usage and maintained in good condition.
- Working areas are safe and secure.
- Wearing of protective equipment/clothing is in line with regulation and local policies.

'Support staff' include volunteers, paid coaches, agency coaches and school staff other than qualified teachers.

# Appendix 2J: Safe Practice for Swimming Poster

**People**

**Pupils should:**
- be informed about standard procedures and made aware of notices on the first visit and reminded throughout the programme
- be encouraged to carry out good hygiene practice
- share in assessment and management of risk at their own level of understanding.

**Preparation** requires:
- a school risk assessment based on the people/context/organisation model
- an emergency action plan shared and understood by all involved
- a shared scheme of work that meets the needs of all pupils
- all staff to carry a whistle.

**Organisation**

**Planning and teaching:**
- Appropriate supervision should always be provided in changing areas and on poolside.
- Assessment and recording procedures should be clearly understood by all staff; the teacher remains accountable for the overall learning outcomes of the pupils.
- Non-swimmers remain in designated shallow-water area unless taught via deep-water method using sufficient and appropriate buoyancy aids.
- Group sizes should reflect the competence of pupils.
- All pupils should remain in view at all times.
- Systems should be in place to ensure satisfactory pool clearance at the end of a session.
- Diving should only take place where the water depth meets specified requirements.

**Safe Practice**

*Swimming*

◄ ►

**Appropriate challenge**

**Context**

**School/pool staff/swimming teachers** need to:
- be suitably confident, qualified and experienced
- have a sound knowledge of pupils
- know and understand roles and responsibilities
- maintain effective communication with all involved
- have access to professional development opportunities.

**The pool/facility** should provide:
- clear signposting of pool depths and potential hazards
- clear marking of the designated working area
- an appropriate safe changing space
- a range of accessible rescue aids
- water clarity to see the bottom of the pool at all times.

**Equipment:**
- Rescue aids readily accessible.
- Goggles only worn in exceptional circumstances. In this instance, pupils should be taught to put them on and remove them safely.
- Swimwear should be appropriate.
- Personal effects removed or made safe.
- Adequate range and amount of teaching equipment to be readily accessible.

**Procedures** should involve:
- regular communication between school, pool and swimming teacher
- registration and head count of group before, during and following session
- emergency procedures, signals and equipment being known and understood by everyone involved
- staff walking round pool at end of lesson to check pool is clear.

## Appendix 2K: Risk-assessment Form

School: ................................................     Work area: ................................................

| Aspects to Consider | Risk Rating | Satisfactory? (tick ✓) | | Who is Affected? | Is Further Action Required? (Control measure – action required to reduce risk to acceptable level) | | |
| --- | --- | --- | --- | --- | --- | --- | --- |
| Only list actual hazards | Low (L) Medium (M) High (H) | Yes | No | Pupils (P) School staff (S) Visitors (V) | What? | Who? | Completed? |
| **People**   • Staff:   • Pupils: | | | | | | | |
| **Context**   • Facility:   • Procedures:   • Equipment:   • Transport: | | | | | | | |

| Aspects to Consider | Risk Rating | Satisfactory? (tick ✓) | | Who is Affected? | Is Further Action Required? (Control measure – action required to reduce risk to acceptable level) | | |
| --- | --- | --- | --- | --- | --- | --- | --- |
| Only list actual hazards | Low (L) Medium (M) High (H) | Yes | No | Pupils (P) School staff (S) Visitors (V) | What? | Who? | Completed? |
| O r g a n i s a t i o n<br>• Class organisation:<br>• Teaching style:<br>• Preparation:<br>• Progression:<br>• Emergency action: | | | | | | | |

Signed:   Head teacher ...........................................................   ...............

Subject leader ...........................................................

Date of assessment: ...........................................................

Review 1 ...............   ...............  (date and initial)
Review 2 ...............   ...............  (date and initial)
Review 3 ...............   ...............  (date and initial)

## Appendix 3A: Developing a Policy Statement and Guidelines for Workforce Planning in PESS

> See pages 37–40 in afPE's *Safe Practice in Physical Education and School Sport 2008 Edition* for general notes.

This framework is based on the health-and-safety policy and guidelines framework in *Appendix 9: Framework for a Policy and Guidelines on Health and Safety in PESS* as workforce planning includes extensive health-and-safety issues.

## Introduction

### Purpose (of the workforce planning guidelines in PESS):

- to offer PESS within a well-managed, safe and educational context
- to establish common codes of practice for all adults teaching pupils
- to provide common administrative procedures
- to ensure that statutory and local requirements are followed and other national guidelines, such as codes of practice, are considered.

### Rationale (for workforce planning in PESS):

- to enable pupils to participate in PESS that provides appropriate challenge, with acceptable risk
- to utilise a broad range of expertise in the delivery of physical-education programmes.

### Context (for workforce planning in PESS):

- delivering high-quality outcomes and provision in physical education
- fulfilling the requirements of the National Curriculum for physical education
- providing an environment that is safe for the activity
- ensuring adequately taught activities
- taking pupils through progressive stages of learning and challenge appropriate to their ability and confidence
- the effective management of support staff contributing to the physical-education programme.

# Guidelines

Consideration should be given to the inclusion of the following in your guidelines on the deployment of support staff.

Page references in brackets relate to the afPE 2008 edition of *Safe Practice in Physical Education and School Sport*, where the topic is discussed. Other guidance may be obtained from:

- *The Education (Specified Work and Registration) (England) Regulations 2003, Statutory Instrument 2003/1663, HMSO* (www.legislation.hmso.gov.uk/si/si2003/20031663.htm)

- baalpe (2005) *Workforce Reform: Essential Safe Practice in Physical Education and School Sport*. Leeds: Coachwise Business Solutions.

- DfES (2007) *Time for Standards: Guidance accompanying the Section 133 Regulations issued under the Education Act 2002*. Nottingham: DfES (www.teachernet.gov.uk/wholeschool/remodelling)

- Workforce Agreement Monitoring Group (WAMG) (2004) 'Guidance for Schools on Higher Level Teaching Assistant (HLTA) Roles for School Support Staff', www.teachernet.gov.uk/_doc/7172/HLTA%20Guidance.pdf

- Whitlam, P. (2004) *Case Law in Physical Education and School Sport: A Guide to Good Practice*. Leeds: Coachwise Business Solutions. ISBN: 978-1-902523-77-4.

- Whitlam, P. (2006) 'The Safe Organisation of Inter-school Fixtures and Area Sports Events', www.afpe.org.uk/public/downloads/interschoolcomp_jun06.pdf

The list below is not definitive. Reference should be made also to local authority (LA) guidelines and your school policy on workforce planning.

## People

### a. Staff:

- Conditions of service – employee, contractor, volunteer, agency coach

- Pre-employment checks – identity, references, qualifications, CRB disclosure (pages 31, 59, 313)

- Qualifications and competence for teaching physical education (pages 31–36, 38, 204)

- Management and monitoring of support staff, volunteers and coaches (pages 313–318)

- Supervision of support staff – direct or distant – circumstances (pages 31–36).

## Context

### a. Facilities:

- Ensure support staff are familiar with the location, routines and use of:

  - storerooms (pages 103–110)

  - work areas (pages 85–93, 103–110, 166, 184).

### b. Equipment:

- Ensure support staff are familiar with the checking, maintenance, use and movement of equipment (pages 85–93, 167)

- Use of mats (pages 90–91, 152).

## c. Procedures:

- Inform parents that support staff will assume responsibility for pupils (pages 39, 318).

- Inform, educate and monitor support staff, as relevant to the particular circumstances, in the application of:

  - accident procedures (pages 10, 49–54, 332–335, 339–342)

  - accident report forms (pages 52–53, 336–338)

  - behaviour, discipline and referral

  - clothing (pages 81, 99–102, 185, 189)

  - codes of conduct (pages 17, 209, 356)

  - contact with, and physical support for, pupils (page 186)

  - contingency plans (page 218)

  - digital imagery (pages 61–63)

  - footwear (pages 101, 168)

  - inter-school matches and sports events (pages 47, 123–131, 356–358)

  - jewellery, body piercing and personal effects (pages 99–100)

  - higher-risk activities (page 15 and relevant sections of Part 2: pages 135–286)

  - parental consent (pages 17, 330)

  - personal protection (pages 95–98)

  - religious and cultural issues (pages 81–84)

  - risk assessment (pages 23–30,  37–39, 103, 208, 296–309)

  - safeguarding children (pages 20, 55–71)

  - safety education (pages 10, 11, 21, 29, 35, 38, 39, 43, 48, 53, 68, 79, 83, 93, 98, 102, 109, 117, 122, 130, 142, 148, 149, 151, 153, 159, 163, 177, 187, 192, 201, 211, 239, 245, 247, 249, 252, 253, 256, 258, 260, 272, 276, 277, 284)

  - specific school procedures (eg notes, issues due to premises etc)

  - transporting pupils (pages 11, 111–117, 297)

  - weather conditions (pages 97, 211, 213, 220).

## Organisation

### a. Preparation:

- Provision of relevant detail in relation to schemes/units of work (pages 10, 38)

- Provision of/support for/monitoring of session planning (page 315).

### b. Teaching and class management:

- Contribution or responsibility for assessment

- Staff participation in games (pages 10, 17)

- Supervision of pupils (page 38 and relevant sections of Part 2 – pages 135–286)

- Teaching group sizes (page 38 and relevant sections of Part 2 – pages 135–286)

- Teaching and learning strategies

- Violent play (pages 19–20).

312

## Appendix 3B: Best-practice Guidance on the Effective Use of Individual and Agency Coaches in PESS

Where the term 'school' is used, this includes school sport partnerships, community learning partnerships and others working on behalf of the school. Where the term 'lesson' is used, this includes sessions delivered before school, during lunchtime and after school.

Extensive guidance exists on the employment, deployment and management of coaches in PESS, such as that provided by the Department for Children, Schools and Families (DCSF), NSPCC Child Protection in Sport Unit (CPSU) and the Association for Physical Education (afPE). However, best practice is not always evident in schools. This brief checklist was created by a group of afPE members during a workshop at the 2007 conference as support for head teachers and others in schools who manage the employment and work of coaches.

**Head teachers and other managers of coaching support staff are strongly advised to follow the guidelines below.**

---

### 1. Safe Recruitment

a. Arrange a face-to-face interview with all coaches to confirm their identity using original documents (passport, driving licence, recent service provider bill confirming current home address).

b. Check CRB enhanced disclosure. See original; decide if portability applies and is acceptable; check with original responsible authority and establish whether additional information is on the CRB form. If so, require a new certificate from the coach to access the additional information. If no response is received to enquiry or information is held, a new disclosure certificate is essential.

c. Check qualifications. See originals; accept Level 2 award as normal baseline qualification for each activity the coach is expected to teach, diverting from this standard only if the coach is observed prior to acceptance and demonstrates exceptional coaching qualities and is working towards a Level 2 qualification; refer to the HLTA standards for your baseline (www.hlta.gov.uk). Alternatively, check the criteria given in *The Effective Use of Coaches*, (afPE, 2006) (www.afpe.org/healthandsafety).

d. Check training undertaken and experience of working with children and young people (eg child protection workshops).

e. Explore motivations to work with children and attitudes towards children and young people.

f. Check reference(s). Investigate any gaps in coaching employment and any conditional comments in the reference.

g. Check with relevant national governing body (NGB) that coach is currently licensed to coach (qualification cannot be rescinded, but NGB licence to coach can be if any poor practice or abuse issues have arisen).

h. Ensure correct employment status and employment rights are known to the coach. Provide written summary/include in contract, as appropriate.

i. Ensure the coach is fully aware of insurance provision and what aspects he/she needs to provide for him/herself (according to employment status) re:

  - employer's liability (compulsory) – legal liability for injuries to employees (permanent/temporary/contracted for services) arising in course of employment

---

- public liability (essential) – legal responsibility for 'third-party' claims against the activities of the individual/group and legal occupation of premises

- professional liability (desirable) – legal cover against claims for breaches of professional duty by employees acting in the scope of their employment (eg giving poor professional advice)

- hirer's liability (desirable) – covers individuals or agencies who hire premises against any liability for injury to others or damage to the property while using it

- libel and slander insurance (optional) – cover against claims for defamation (eg libellous material in publications)

- personal injury – accidental bodily injury or deliberate assault (desirable) – arranged by the individual or the employer

- miscellaneous – a variety of types of insurance, such as travel (compulsory or required) or motor insurance (compulsory – minimum of third party) – check personal exclusions and excesses the individual carries.

j. Set out a clearly defined role, identifying any limits of responsibility, lines of supervision, management and communication, specialist expertise needed (eg children with individual special needs) and ensure he/she is appropriately qualified/experienced to undertake the role.

k. Determine an agreed period of probation and monitor the coach's performance and attitude closely during this period.

l. If an agency coach, check that all of above have been addressed by the agency or by the school before the coach begins work.

m. Agree appropriate induction package that must be fulfilled.

---

**2. Induction**

a. Head teacher or his/her representative to present coach with a summary of relevant school policies and procedures, including risk assessments, emergency evacuation, referral and incentives, behaviour management, first aid, child-protection procedures and something about the ethos of the school – how staff work with children and young people (such as looking for success in young people, rewarding achievement).

b. Identified member of staff to manage induction into school procedures who will:

- arrange meeting with SENCO (and class teacher[s] as appropriate) or other nominated personnel (eg school sport coordinator) for specific information about pupils

- monitor and assess competence of the coach through observations and discussions with pupils and other staff

- determine the coach's role in contributing to the overall assessment of pupils.

314

### 3. Qualifications, Experience and Qualities Necessary for Coach to Work Alone

a. Level 2 award is normal baseline qualification for each activity the coach is expected to teach. Divert from this standard only if the coach is observed prior to acceptance, demonstrates exceptional coaching qualities and is working towards a Level 2 qualification.

b. Check previous experience in working with small/large groups.

c. Check behaviour-management skills.

d. Check:

- quality of relationships – the way the coach cares for and respects pupils, is an appropriate role model and promotes the ethos of the school

- developing knowledge of the pupils – their levels of confidence, ability, individual needs, medical needs and behaviour

- pupil management – how they match pupils' confidence, strength and ability in pair and group tasks, maximise participation, have strategies for effective pupil control and motivation, apply the school's standard procedures and routines (eg child protection, emergency action, jewellery, handling and carrying of equipment)

- knowledge of the activities – appropriate level of expertise to enable learning to take place in the activities being delivered, use of suitable space for the group, differentiated equipment, differentiated practice, evident progression and application of rules

- observation and analytical skills – providing a safe working and learning environment, ability to identify faults and establish strategies for improvement.

### 4. Day-to-day Management of Coach

a. Check that the coach has received a summary of school and subject procedures and understands what is required (including clear guidelines in relation to handover of responsibility at the start and end of lessons/sessions).

b. Ensure the coach receives relevant information on pupils/groups (eg illness, family bereavement, behavioural issues).

c. Monitor promptness.

d. Establish regular review and evaluation of the coach's work.

e. Determine who assesses pupils' work.

f. Ensure the coach is supported, valued and accepted as a member of staff.

g. Monitor dialogue and the relationship between class teacher and coach.

### 5. Monitoring Quality and Effectiveness

a. Ensure the direct monitoring of the coach for agreed period – use criteria set out in section 3 above.

b. Set up continual indirect monitoring to ensure pupils make progress and enjoy lessons/sessions.

c. Ensure pupils are engaged in consistent high-quality, challenging and stimulating activities that support them to achieve their potential, not just activities that keep them 'busy, happy and good' pupils who do not demonstrate high quality – see *High Quality Physical Education* (DfES, 2003).

**6. Identification and Provision of Continuing Professional Development (CPD)**

a. Evaluate the coach's abilities against HLTA standards.

b. Arrange attendance on afPE/sports coach UK ASL induction course.

c. Agree essential qualifications and desirable qualifications – plan and provide for personal development programme beyond NGB coach qualifications to enable coach to proceed from emerging to established, and advanced rating.

**7. Dealing with Inadequate Performance by the Coach**

a. Proactively monitor the coach's work as set out in 5.

b. Where performance is inadequate and poses a health-and-safety risk to the pupils or has the potential to impact on their welfare, intervene immediately; where performance is technically inadequate, review situation with coach after the lesson.

c. Agree and provide supportive CPD to improve inadequate aspects of performance.

d. Monitor for improvement.

e. Where little or no improvement occurs, terminate short-term contract or initiate competency procedures if longer-term contract.

f. Where necessary, terminate longer-term contract where competence does not improve.

**Appendix 3C: Potential Roles and Responsibilities when Support Staff Lead School Groups Off Site**

| The Head Teacher Should: | The Subject Leader/Class Teacher Should: | The Support Staff Should: |
|---|---|---|
| • check whether the local authority (LA) guidance and school policies allow support staff to take a lead role in escorting classes off site without a teacher being present<br>• designate a qualified teacher to supervise and direct the work of the support staff<br>• ensure a clear learning experience is established, around which the visit is planned<br>• check any LA/school insurance, disclosure or qualification requirements are met<br>• meet any required adult:pupil ratios<br>• ensure contingency plans exist in the event of an emergency<br>• ensure a **risk assessment** is carried out to check the support staff have a clear understanding of their role(s) and have appropriate:<br>  ■ confidence to lead the activity<br>  ■ leadership skills<br>  ■ organisational skills<br>  ■ control and discipline<br>  ■ communication skills, with the staff and pupils<br>  ■ competence/expertise/ experience and/or valid qualifications to match the demands of the pupils and the activity or activities to be delivered and the ability to fulfil the tasks delegated to them<br>  ■ knowledge of the limits of their role and responsibility | • establish a clear purpose for the learning experience within any relevant scheme of work/essential off-site outcomes<br>• brief on, summarise or provide necessary documentation relating to school procedures and standards, such as that relating to safeguarding children, physical contact (supporting) in PESS, accident and emergency procedures, rewards and sanctions, confidentiality, referral<br>• provide any relevant schemes/units of work<br>• provide lesson plans or ensure joint planning opportunities or monitor any prepared planning provided by the support staff<br>• be the first point of contact with pupils' parents<br>• ensure clear roles and responsibilities are allocated to each individual adult escorting the group<br>• check that any large groups are subdivided, with each child designated to the care of a nominated adult<br>• ensure all support staff carry a list of the group and emergency contact information, should it be needed | • be clear as to the role and level of responsibility they are assuming<br>• tell the head teacher/ designated teacher if they lack the confidence to lead the group off site or be involved in the specific activity (eg if they have a fear of water if asked to escort a group to a swimming pool)<br>• feel able to request support relating to safety and learning<br>• understand the purpose of the learning experience<br>• have adequate knowledge of the group and individual propensities in terms of behaviour, discipline, attention and safety<br>• subdivide the group, allocating the supervision of specific children to specific support staff for the duration of the event, and ensure each child knows and recognises the adult to whom he/she is designated<br>• be deployed throughout the group to ensure safety and effective management (eg at different positions on a coach or walking a group along a road)<br>• regularly count the number in the group (eg leaving the school gate, onto the coach, after crossing any roads, on arrival, into the work area, during the session, at the end of the session, commencing the return journey, completion of the return journey) |

| The Head Teacher Should: | The Subject Leader/Class Teacher Should: | The Support Staff Should: |
| --- | --- | --- |
| ■ knowledge of the school's emergency procedures<br>• confirm the support staff's suitability to work with children and clarify any child-protection requirements<br>• check all support staff apply the school's ethos, procedures and standards appropriately<br>• monitor that individual and/or joint planning of the work with a designated teacher occurs regularly<br>• provide appropriate professional development opportunities for school support staff<br>• inform parents that support staff are taking their children off site instead of a teacher<br>• maintain sufficient expertise in the area to make the required professional judgements<br>• ensure regular communication between him/herself, class teacher and support staff. | • ensure the support staff have the facility to contact school or a designated teacher in an emergency<br>• instruct the support staff to communicate relevant information about the group to other adults assuming some responsibility for any of the group (eg the number in the group is given to a specialist swimming teacher or lifeguard as the group enters the poolside)<br>• check the support staff's level of competency, compatible with safe and effective practice<br>• check the support staff's understanding of first-aid management<br>• ensure effective and regular communication between the class teacher and the support staff about the event<br>• be familiar with the event risk assessment<br>• evaluate the event with the support staff as soon as possible after its conclusion<br>• regularly and systematically monitor and review the quality of provision by the support staff. | • check that the work area (eg pool, field, beach, museum) is clear of any obvious hazards that could harm the pupils and apply ongoing risk assessment at all times<br>• exhibit good discipline and control at all times<br>• regularly change their supervisory/observation position<br>• constantly scan the group and work area<br>• intervene where concerns become apparent<br>• inform any specialist staff (eg swimming teacher, lifeguard, outdoor-centre staff) of numbers in the group, illnesses, abilities and other relevant group information<br>• carry emergency contact information and group lists at all times<br>• have planned how to deal with any illness that arise during the event – who administers first aid, who manages the rest of the group, who goes to hospital with a child if necessary<br>• know and apply any contingency plan in the event of accident, condition of work area or inclement weather<br>• evaluate the event with other accompanying adults and the head teacher/designated teacher after the event. |

# Appendix four
## Pupils with Special Educational Needs (SEN)

a4

## Introduction

This appendix sets out to offer some information on the more predominant SEN encountered in schools. It also offers links to some of the many possible websites where information is available on the areas listed in this appendix. Typically, these websites offer details on the special need or medical condition, a section on frequently asked questions (FAQs) and some points of contact where further information and/or support can be accessed, possibly both nationally and locally. Neither the information nor the websites should be seen as exclusive. Rather, they provide one starting point for seeking additional help and advice. Similar websites exist for conditions not discussed here. Clearly, those working with children and young people need to access appropriate advice from parents, medical staff, local authority (LA) staff etc on carrying out risk assessments and preparing personal healthcare plans when developing and implementing a suitable programme of physical activity. These risk assessments and healthcare plans should be regularly reviewed and amended as necessary.

Three websites that offer a useful starting point are listed immediately below; other websites appear throughout the text.

BBC Health
www.bbc.co.uk/health/conditions/

Good To Know
www.goodtoknow.co.uk

Teachernet
www.teachernet.gov.uk/

## Asthma

Asthma is a common ailment and currently over one million children take medication for the condition. The usual symptoms of asthma include:

- coughing

- wheezing

- shortness of breath and tightness in the chest.

Attacks can vary from very mild, which require little or no treatment, to those that are so severe, they require prompt medical support. Generally speaking, exercise is good for people with asthma although, for some, it can bring on the symptoms of asthma. Adults working with children with asthma should ensure that:

- levels of fitness are increased gradually

- the child's inhaler is always available when exercising

- where exercise triggers a child's asthma, they should use their inhaler before they warm up

- they should always warm up and cool down thoroughly

- the area is free of irritants that may trigger the child's asthma

- the child is allowed to stop exercising if symptoms occur and appropriate medical procedures are followed until the child feels well enough to take part.

Asthma UK
www.asthma.org.uk/

## Attention Deficit Hyperactivity Disorder (ADHD)

Children with ADHD find it difficult to pay attention, concentrate and thus find remembering instructions difficult. It is sometimes treated with medication to help pupils focus and understand what is expected of them.

Adults working with children with ADHD should:

- ensure instructions are clear and easy to follow

- encourage pupils and reward their efforts and achievements

- remain consistent in their approach

- carefully risk assess physical activities, ensuring that potentially difficult situations can be well managed.

National Attention Deficit Disorder Information and Support Service
www.addiss.co.uk/

## Autism/Autistic Spectrum Disorder (ASD)/ Asperger's Syndrome

Pupils with autism have difficulties with social communication. They tend to be egocentric in conversation, not realising that they should listen to others as well as make their own points. They do not understand jokes or sarcasm and can interpret phrases literally. Thus, told to 'pull their socks up', they will see this as an instruction, rather than an encouragement to work harder. In addition, such pupils like settled routines and sudden changes to these can cause severe anxiety.

Those working with autistic pupils should:

- speak clearly and give pupils time to understand what is expected of them

- encourage and give prompts where necessary

- apply rules consistently

- prepare pupils as much as possible for the activity they will be doing, such as showing them photographs, sharing plans or seeing demonstrations.

The National Autistic Society
www.autism.org.uk

## Cerebral Palsy

Cerebral palsy is a group of conditions that results from damage to, or failure in the development of, part of the brain. It can affect movement and posture. It can present with a range of difficulties, including perceptual, communication, movement and control, sensory impairment, and short attention span.

Adults working with children with cerebral palsy should:

- link with other professionals (eg physiotherapists) to develop an appropriate motor support programme, including the use of any specialist equipment

- encourage support from peers

- ensure the child understands what is expected of him/her, possibly through the use of demonstration

- praise the child and encourage independence.

Scope
www.scope.org.uk


## Diabetes

Diabetes is a condition in which the amount of glucose (sugar) in the blood is too high because the body cannot use it properly. Having diabetes should not stop a child taking a full part in school activities. Indeed, keeping active is a part of a well-planned response to managing diabetes. Those working with children with diabetes should liaise with their parents and healthcare professionals to understand the individual needs of the children and how they may be addressed.

Adults working with children with diabetes should be aware:

- of the symptoms associated with the onset of hypoglycaemia

- that a child with diabetes may carry with them a bag containing a blood glucose testing kit, food, glucose tablets, drinks etc, which he/she should be allowed to use as and when necessary

- that training programmes should be built up gradually.

Diabetes UK
www.diabetes.org.uk


## Down's Syndrome (Trisomy 21)

Down's syndrome is a congenital condition caused at conception. It arises from a failure in cell division of chromosome 21 (hence Trisomy 21), leading to 47, rather than 46, chromosomes developing. Among other characteristics, those with Down's syndrome can have reduced muscle tone, heart conditions, hearing and vision difficulties, respiratory difficulties and learning difficulties that can impact upon physical activity.

**Note:** All children with Down's syndrome are different and advice should be sought on the exact needs of each individual.

Children with Down's syndrome should not be barred from physical activity. However, they do have a small risk of suffering acute dislocation of the atlantoaxial joint. As a result, should a child with Down's syndrome develop pain behind the ear or elsewhere in the neck, abnormal head posture, deterioration of gait, manipulative skills or bowel and/or bladder control, specialist advice should be sought immediately. Further, some children with Down's syndrome may have a heart condition. Therefore, should a child complain of tiredness, he/she should be allowed to rest or sit out an activity and be monitored until he/she recovers.

In addition, adults working with children with Down's syndrome should:

- use demonstration, sign and gesture to support learning

- offer regular encouragement and praise for efforts

- speak directly to the pupil to reinforce instructions and ensure he/she understands the task

- liaise with other professionals in the development of a healthcare plan.

Down's Syndrome Association
www.downs-syndrome.org.uk

## Dyspraxia

Dyspraxia is an impairment or immaturity in movement, often termed 'clumsy child syndrome'. The degree of difficulty experienced can vary greatly. Difficulties are often found with gross and fine motor skills. In addition, poor balance and difficulties in coordinating body parts can lead to poor performance in sport.

Adults working with pupils with dyspraxia should:

- liaise with physiotherapists and occupational therapists in the preparation of physical-activity programmes; it is worth noting that such programmes are also often of value to other pupils as well

- encourage effort

- encourage support from peers through the use of a 'buddy' system.

The Dyspraxia Foundation
www.dyspraxiafoundation.org.uk

## Epilepsy

The effects of epilepsy vary from person to person. Indeed, it is possible that a child with epilepsy may never have a seizure at school. Thus, whether a child with epilepsy can take part in swimming, physical activities or educational visits should be based on that child's individual circumstances. Advice on this should appear in his/her individual healthcare plan and should be used to risk assess each activity, allowing the child either access to it or an alternative activity. In all cases, the pupil, his/her parents and, where necessary, healthcare professionals should be consulted in the formulation of the individual healthcare plan and associated risk assessment.

Adults working with children with epilepsy should:

- make themselves aware of the precise nature of each child's needs with regard to epilepsy

- make sure arrangements to support a pupil with epilepsy are in place (eg a 'buddy' who should be a strong swimmer or a poolside observer when swimming)

- avoid prolonged underwater swimming or flickering strobe-like lighting, as either may cause the onset of a seizure

- be aware of the appropriate first-aid response, should it be required

- be vigilant wherever such pupils work at a height in gymnastics.

Epilepsy Research UK
www.epilepsyresearch.org.uk

Epilepsy Action
www.epilepsy.org.uk

## Hearing Impairment

There are two main types of hearing loss. There is **conductive hearing loss**, which is a condition where sounds cannot pass through the outer or middle ear. This is often caused by a build-up of fluid, as in the case of glue ear. In most cases, conductive hearing loss is temporary. Such conditions can clear up or require surgery.

The second type of hearing loss is **sensorineural deafness**, which is caused by a problem in the inner ear or auditory nerve. This is likely to be permanent.

Adults working with hearing-impaired pupils should:

- get advice on the exact nature of the loss and how it affects the child

- act appropriately on the advice received

- give the pupil time to understand what is required of him/her

- ensure the pupil can see the teacher and activity clearly

- ensure they have eye contact with the pupil and his/her full attention before starting an activity or explanation

- use gesture to encourage pupils

- regularly check understanding

- be aware of the need for a visual alternative to an auditory signal to stop either due to danger or during a game situation.

National Deaf Children's Society
www.ndcs.org.uk

Royal National Institute for Deaf People
www.rnid.org.uk

## Muscular Dystrophy

Muscular dystrophy relates to a group of conditions characterised by a breakdown of muscle fibres, leading to weak and wasted muscles. Symptoms can appear at any time from birth onwards. Muscular dystrophy exists on a continuum from severely disabling with a marked impact on life expectancy through to a mild disability. It is a progressive condition, though the pace of deterioration will vary from child to child.

Regular exercise is often a key part of the child's physical-management programme. This programme may need to be daily and include swimming or hydrotherapy. Those offering physical activities to pupils with muscular dystrophy should:

- liaise with a physiotherapist and occupational therapist to gain information on how to support the pupil's physical-management programme

- offer encouragement and praise for efforts

- be aware of changes in the child's physical condition and report these to specialist support.

Muscular Dystrophy Campaign
www.muscular-dystrophy.org

## Social, Emotional and Behavioural Difficulties (SEBD)

Pupils who display social, emotional and behavioural difficulties require physical-activity programmes that are carefully planned. While some will cope well with team games, others can become agitated if their team is 'losing' and this can lead to disruption. Such pupils also lack confidence and self-belief and, as a result, can refuse to take part in an activity they are unsure of. Thus, activities are best carried out in small groups with appropriate levels of adult support. These supporting adults should:

- set clear and achievable targets for each activity

- encourage pupils to take part by praising small improvements in performance

- help create a team ethic where all pupils praise each others' efforts

- ensure pupils have the opportunity to cool down and settle at the end of a physical-activity session prior to moving on to their next lesson or activity.

Social, Emotional and Behavioural Difficulties Association
www.sebda.org/

Teachernet
www.teachernet.gov.uk/teachingandlearning/socialandpastoral/sebs1/

## Visual Impairment

Visual impairment exists along a continuum from those who have sufficient vision to manage most school tasks, but may need some specialist support on occasion, through those who have severely restricted vision and may need support with mobility, good lighting and careful positioning to take part in activities, to those who are registered blind and will need specialist support. Such pupils' language usually develops normally and adults should discuss with them the nature of tasks set.

In addition, those working with visually impaired pupils should:

- encourage independence through such things as mobility training (ie ensuring pupils are aware of the layout of the facilities which they are to use)

- modify tasks to allow pupils access to a given task

- encourage peer support

Royal National Institute of Blind People
www.rnib.org.uk

## Model Equipment Inspection/ Maintenance Schedule – Gymnasia, Sports Halls and Fitness Areas

## Procedures

a. The contractor will visit each school annually, during normal school hours, on a predetermined date agreed with the school.

b. Any item of equipment, either static or portable, found to be beyond economical repair will be reported in writing together with an estimate of replacement cost. Any such item will be clearly marked '**not to be used**' and arrangements for its safe disposal agreed with the school.

c. No item requiring workshop attention will be removed without signed authorisation from the school and will be returned to the school within a reasonable period of time at no extra transportation cost to the school.

d. The contractor will have available at the time of the inspection sufficient stocks of replacement items under the terms of the contract.

e. The contractor will complete a full report detailing the work undertaken, countersigned by the school and/or local authority (LA). One copy will be retained by the school/LA and one copy retained by the contractor.

f. Should any work be required that is not covered within the terms and conditions of the contract, the contractor will provide a written quotation detailing all costs involved.

g. All work will be carried out in compliance with BS 1892-1:1986 or European equivalent standard and guaranteed for 12 months from the date of completion.

## Schedule of Requirements

a. All necessary timber repairs, including wall bars, beams and frames (to include sanding and varnishing).

b. Cleaning or recovering of leather and synthetic surfaces.

c. Lubrication of all moving parts.

d. Inspection and maintenance of roof/wall fittings and securing points.

e. Replacement of all component parts, including wires, pull ropes, basketball backboards, rings and hinged frames.

f. Worn or missing rubber covers and feet on portable equipment to be replaced where necessary.

g. Replacement of worn climbing ropes, ladders, hand rings and leather cappings.

h. Repairs to mats, safety mattresses and agility mattresses.

i. Repairs to trampolines and trampettes, including the replacement of springs and cables where necessary up to a total of 12 per item.

j. Maintenance, lubrication and repair to multigyms.

k. Repair to soft play, including restitching and patching.

### Appendix 6A: The Use of Child Car Seats in Cars, Vans and Goods Vehicles – Department of Transport

www.thinkroadsafety.gov.uk/campaigns/childcarseats/childcarseats.htm

**The rules as at January 2008:**

| | Front Seat | Rear Seat | Who is Responsible? |
|---|---|---|---|
| **Driver** | Seat belt **must** be worn if available. | | **Driver** |
| **Child aged up to three years*** | Correct child restraint **must** be used*. | Correct child restraint **must** be used*. If one is not available in a taxi, may travel unrestrained. | **Driver** |
| **Child from third birthday up to 135cm in height (approx 4'5") or 12th birthday, whichever they reach first**** | Correct child restraint **must** be used***. | Where seat belts are fitted, the correct child restraint **must** be used. They must use an adult belt if the correct child restraint is not available:<br><br>• in a licensed taxi/private hire vehicle<br><br>• for a short distance for reasons of unexpected necessity<br><br>• where two occupied child restraints prevent fitment of a third.<br><br>A child aged three or over may travel unrestrained in the rear seat of a vehicle if seat belts are not available. | **Driver** |
| **Child over 135cm (approx 4'5") in height or 12–13 years** | Seat belt **must** be worn if available. | Seat belt **must** be worn if available. | **Driver** |
| **Adult passengers (ie aged 14 years and over)** | Seat belt **must** be worn if available. | Seat belt **must** be worn if available. | **Passenger** |

\* Children aged under three years **must** use the child restraint appropriate for their weight in all cars, vans and other goods vehicles, with the single exception of the rear of taxis. They cannot travel otherwise. This means, for example, that they may not travel in cars, vans or goods vehicles that do not have seat belts installed.

\*\* Examples: A seven-year-old who is 140cm tall is over the height for a child restraint and may use an adult seat belt; a 12-year-old who is 130cm tall is over the age threshold and therefore may use an adult belt.

\*\*\* If no seat belts are fitted in the front, then children under 135cm in height (who are also aged under 12 years) cannot travel in the front.

In **buses and coaches (including minibuses)**, seated passengers aged 14 years and above will have to use seat belts where they are fitted. Regulations requiring children aged three years to 13 years to use seat belts (or child restraints if they are available) in these vehicles will be brought forward as soon as practicable. The regulations will not include any obligation for anyone to provide child restraints in these vehicles.

### Appendix 6B: Minibus Driver's Hours of Work Allowed

Vehicle operators and drivers must assess the likely risk of drivers suffering from fatigue, particularly on long journeys or working days extended by additional activities.

If a driver is going to drive for more than four hours in any one day, then he/she must comply with British domestic rules for driver hours if operating solely within the UK.

## British Domestic Drivers' Hours

| Daily driving | 10 hours on any working day |
|---|---|
| Cumulative or continuous driving | 5½ hours – after this, a break of at least 30 minutes must be taken in which the driver is able to obtain rest refreshment; or 8½ hours' driving, as long as breaks from driving totalling at least 45 minutes are taken during the driving period and the driver is able to obtain rest and refreshment |
| Length of working day | No more than 16 hours between the times of work starting and finishing work (including work other than driving and off-duty periods during the working day) |
| Daily rest periods | 10 hours continuously must be taken between two working days; this can be reduced to 8½ hours up to three times a week |
| Fortnightly rest periods | In any two weeks in a row (Monday–Sunday), there must be at least one period of 24 hours off |

## European Travel and Tachographs

In the EU as a whole, the requirement to fit a tachograph applies to all vehicles with 10 or more seats, including the driver. However, the United Kingdom has made use of a national derogation from these regulations so minibuses with 17 seats and under (including the driver) are exempt from the requirement to fit and use a tachograph within the UK. Any establishment contemplating taking a minibus with 10 or more seats abroad should be aware that the EU driver hours and tachograph rules will apply from the start of the journey in the UK until the final destination.

Under EU rules, any tour that starts or finishes in an EU member state is subject to EU regulations. Other tours between UK and non-EU countries are subject to EU or European Agreement Concerning the Work of Crew of Vehicles Engaged in International Road Transport (AETR) rules. If travelling to a non-EU country, check which rules apply. A record of hours driven must be kept and all vehicles with nine or more seats (excluding the driver) must have a tachograph, as explained in leaflet PCV 375.

A summary of the current EU drivers' hours are as follows:

| | |
|---|---|
| **Maximum daily driving** | Nine hours, extendable to 10 hours on two days in the driving week |
| **Maximum weekly driving** | Six driving periods |
| **Maximum fortnightly driving** | 90 hours |
| **Maximum driving before a break** | 4½ hours |
| **Minimum breaks after driving** | 45 minutes or other breaks of at least 15 minutes each |
| **Minimum daily rest** | 11 hours, reducible to nine hours three times a week; compensation must be given before the end of the following week; alternatively 12 hours if split into two or three periods (one of which must provide at least eight hours of continuous rest) |

## Appendix 6C: Volunteer Driver's Declaration

To: The Head Teacher ................................. School ...............................

I confirm that I am willing to use my own vehicle for transporting pupils to and from inter-school fixtures and other sporting events.

I accept responsibility for maintaining appropriate insurance cover and have checked with my insurance company that pupils carried voluntarily are insured.

I have a current clean, valid driving licence.

I shall ensure that the vehicle is roadworthy in all respects.

I shall ensure that all passengers wear correctly fastened seat belts.

I shall at no time transport a single pupil, other than my own child, as part of any journey. (This section does not apply to any 17/18/19-year-old student transporting his/her peers.)

I agree to the terms and conditions outlined in this declaration and will operate within them.

I have never been interviewed, cautioned or convicted of any offence that would render me unsuitable to work with young people.

I shall at no time transport a pupil or pupils while I am under the influence of alcohol or drugs.

Signed: ..................................................... Date: .......................................

Name and address: ........................................................................................

..............................................................................................................

..............................................................................................................

The school/children's service reserves the right at any time to request copies of any relevant documentation, including vehicle registration or ownership document, MOT certificate, insurance certificate, road tax or driving licence.

Persons regularly transporting children will be asked to provide any disclosure certification required by the school or employer's policy. This is in order to ascertain that they have not been declared unsuitable to work with children and young people.

Drivers should retain a copy of this declaration reminding them of the school's expectations.

(With acknowledgement to Staffordshire County Council Education Department.)

## Appendix 6D: Parental Consent Form for a Pupil to be Transported in Another Adult's Vehicle

Schools may wish to obtain parental permission for pupils to be transported in other adults' cars by the use of a pro forma such as this:

1. There may be occasions in which your child could be transported in the car of another adult associated with the school.

2. The conditions under which other adults agree to provide use of their car are as follows:

   He/she:
   - confirms that he/she is willing to use his/her own vehicle for transporting pupils to and from inter-school fixtures and other sporting events

   - accepts responsibility for maintaining appropriate insurance cover and has checked with his/her insurance company that pupils carried voluntarily are insured

   - has a current clean, valid driving licence

   - shall ensure that the vehicle is roadworthy in all respects

   - shall ensure that all passengers wear correctly fastened seat belts

   - shall at no time transport a single pupil, other than his/her own child, as part of any journey (this section does not apply to any 17/18/19-year-old student transporting his/her peers)

   - agrees to the terms and conditions outlined in this declaration and will operate within them

   - has never been interviewed, cautioned or convicted of any offence that would render him/her unsuitable to work with young people

   - shall at no time transport a pupil or pupils while he/she is under the influence of alcohol or drugs.

3. I give permission for my son/daughter ............................. to be transported in the car of another parent within the requirements explained to me.

Signed: ................................................. Date: .....................................

Name and address: ..............................................................................

..............................................................................................................

..............................................................................................................

(Based on similar forms obtained from the Rugby Football League and Staffordshire County Council Education Department.)

Factors that make spotting less effective include the:

- height of the trampoline

- height of jumping

- advanced nature of the skills being performed

- weight of the trampolinist.

Factors that may compromise the effectiveness of spotting include the spotter's:

- height, weight and fitness

- trampoline experience.

It is difficult to train spotters to be more effective without placing both themselves and the performers at risk.

## General guidance to spotters

a. Pay attention to the trampolinist at all times when spotting. This is essential for personal safety, whether assisting a faller or not.

b. Move out of the way of a falling trampolinist if the spotter feels unsure or unable to assist (ie a trampolinist falling with great momentum). Often, an experienced trampolinist is best placed to make adjustments to minimise the impact of a fall, without placing the spotter at risk.

c. If the coach feels the spotter is capable of assisting a falling performer, a simple explanation and demonstration of assitance should include the following advice:

  - reach as high as possible, to contact the chest or shoulders if possible

  - make contact as early as possible, if this will reduce the momentum of the falling trampolinist

  - only attempt to slow down the performer.

d. Where participants are not competent to act as spotters, it is recommended that they are occupied and kept warm by another coach or assistant coach, doing other relevant activities. In this situation, adults may be trained as spotters, but should there be no spotters available, matting should be provided along the side of the trampoline (1.2m wide). The matting should be at least 25mm thick and of appropriate density and absorbency.

## Appendix 8A: First-aid Qualifications and First-aid Kits: an Explanation of the Health and Safety Executive Approved Code of Practice (HSE ACOP) on First Aid 1997

### First aid at work – a qualified first-aider

First-aiders should be trained to a level recognised by the Health and Safety Executive (HSE). The following subjects should be included in the syllabus for those appointed as first-aiders:

- resuscitation
- treatment and control of bleeding
- treatment of shock
- management of unconscious casualties
- contents of first-aid kits and their use
- purchasing of first-aid supplies
- transport of casualties
- recognition of illness
- treatment of injuries to bones, muscles and joints
- treatment of minor injuries
- treatment of burns and scalds
- eye irrigation
- poisons
- simple record keeping
- personal hygiene in treating wounds – reference to hepatitis B and human immunodeficiency virus (HIV) with regard to first-aiders
- communication and delegation in the event of an emergency.

### Emergency first aid for the appointed person

This course is designed for those companies who have carried out a risk assessment and have decided no first-aider is required, but have identified an appointed person. All organisations, as a minimum requirement, must appoint a person to take charge of first-aid arrangements, including looking after first-aid equipment and facilities and calling the emergency services when required. It is not a requirement that the appointed person takes the emergency-aid course, but it is good professional development.

There should be an appointed person available to take control of all first-aid arrangements at all times when people are at work. The syllabus includes the following topics:

- understand the role of the first-aider, including reference to the use of available equipment and the need for recording incidents and actions

- understand the importance of basic hygiene in first-aid procedures

- assess the situation and circumstances in order to act safely, promptly and effectively in an emergency

- demonstrate how to administer first aid safely, promptly and effectively to a casualty who is unconscious and/or in seizure

- demonstrate how to administer cardiopulmonary resuscitation promptly and effectively

- demonstrate how to administer first aid safely, promptly and effectively to a casualty who is wounded or bleeding and/or in shock

- administer first aid safely, promptly and effectively to a casualty who is choking

- provide first aid for minor injuries.

Additional training should be arranged for adults involved in activities in which specific hazards are possible (eg training on how to treat hypothermia during activities that take place in mountainous areas or in, or on, water).

First-aid qualifications are valid for the period of time specified by the HSE, after which time a refresher course and examination are required to obtain re-certification.

## First-aid kits

First-aid kits should be made of suitable material, designed to protect the contents from damp and dust. They should be clearly identified in accordance with the Safety Signs Regulations 1980 (ie white cross on a green background).

A risk assessment should be carried out to determine the contents of a school's permanent first-aid kit.

Sufficient quantities of each item should always be available in every first-aid kit, with nothing else besides.

Most first-aid kits will include the following items:

- one card providing general first-aid guidance

- 20 individually wrapped, sterile adhesive dressings (assorted sizes) appropriate to the work environment

- two sterile eye pads (with attachment)

- four individually wrapped triangular bandages

- six safety pins

- six medium-sized, individually wrapped, sterile, unmedicated wound dressings (approximately 10cm x 8cm)

- two large, individually wrapped, sterile, unmedicated wound dressings (approximately 13cm x 9cm)

- one pair of sterile disposable gloves.

Sterile first-aid dressings should be packaged in such a way as to allow the user to apply the dressing to a wound without touching the part of the dressing that is to come into direct contact with the wound.

The part of the dressing that comes into contact with the wound should be absorbent. A bandage or other similar fixture should be attached to the dressing to hold it in place. The design and type of dressings available (including adhesive ones) should be appropriate for their intended use.

When mains tap water is not readily available for eye irrigation, at least 900ml of sterile water or sterile normal saline (0.9%) should be provided in sealed disposable containers. Each container should hold at least 300ml and should not be reused once the sterile seal is broken. Eye baths, eye cups or refillable containers should not be used for eye irrigation.

Soap and water, and disposable drying materials, should be provided for first-aid purposes. Alternatively, wrapped, moist cleaning wipes, which are not impregnated with alcohol, may be used.

The contents of first-aid kits should be replenished as soon as possible after use in order to ensure there is always an adequate supply of materials. Items should not be used beyond the expiry date shown on the packets. It is therefore essential that first-aid kits are checked frequently to make sure there are sufficient quantities and that all items are still usable.

If an employee has received additional training in the treatment of specific hazards that require the use of special antidotes or special equipment, these may be stored near the hazard area or may be kept in the first-aid kit.

## Supplementary equipment

The following items may be stored alongside first-aid kits:

a. Blunt-ended stainless-steel scissors (minimum length 12.7cm) – when used, consideration should be given to avoiding cross-contamination.

b. Disposable plastic gloves and aprons, suitable protective equipment and appropriate protection against hypothermia – these should be properly stored and regularly checked to ensure they remain in good condition.

c. Plastic disposable bags for soiled or used first-aid dressings – employers should ensure that systems are in place for the safe disposal of items such as used dressings. They should be contacted for guidance on disposal procedures.

d. Blankets – it is recommended that these are stored in such a way as to keep them free from dust and damp.

e. Suitable carrying equipment for transporting casualties – this is recommended if a school covers a large area or is divided into a number of separate and self-contained working areas.

# Travelling first-aid kits

The contents of travelling first-aid kits should be appropriate for the circumstances in which they are to be used. At least the following items should be included:

- one card providing general first-aid guidance
- six individually wrapped, sterile adhesive dressings
- one large sterile, unmedicated dressing
- two triangular bandages
- two safety pins
- individually wrapped moist cleaning wipes.

School staff undertaking ventures with pupils in remote areas should consider attending a relevant mountain first-aid course, which includes practice in the use of inflatable splints.

# Administering medication

School staff are not legally required to administer medication; this is a voluntary duty. Those who agree to do so should:

- have a clear understanding of their legal responsibilities
- be protected by an effective system of medication management
- be adequately trained to ensure they have the understanding, expertise and confidence required
- be familiar with normal precautions for avoiding infections
- be issued with written confirmation of insurance cover to provide specific medical support.

## Appendix 8B: School Accident Report Form

(This form could supplement the employer's accident report form.)

| Accident details |
| --- |
| Pupil's name ................................ Age yrs .........mts ...... Sex ...... Height m ......cm ...... |
| Pupil's home address ........................................ Tel no. ............................................... |
| Class .......................... No. in class ............ No. of boys ............ No. of girls .................. |
| Teacher in charge ............................................. Other adults of lesson present ..................... |
| Type of lesson ................................................................. Unit no. ...... Lesson no. ...... |
| Nature of injury ...................................................................................................... |
| Approx time of accident .............................................................................................. |
| **Location** <br><br><br><br><br><br><br><br> |
| a. In the space above, draw a plan of the location of the accident showing the position of:<br>  • any apparatus, equipment etc<br>  • the pupil involved in the accident<br>  • any adults present<br>  • two witnesses. |
| b. Give approximate measurements (in metric) to show the relative relationship of the people to apparatus and each other. |
| **Other persons involved**<br>1. Names of any school staff sent to assist at the scene of the accident<br><br>......................................................................................................................<br>2. Name of person who carried out emergency aid<br><br>......................................................................................................................<br>3. Names of witnesses<br><br>...................................................................................................................... |
| Statements obtained from witnesses *(circle appropriate response)*      Yes      No<br>1. Name of person who contacted:<br>  a. ambulance service ...........................................................................................<br>  b. pupil's parents ................................................................................................ |

## Post-accident procedures

**1. Assessment of the nature of the injury determined that the pupil should be treated by:**
*(circle appropriate response)*

   a.  school only       b.  hospital A&E department     c.  pupil's doctor

**2. Treatment at school**

   a.  Name of person who carried out treatment .................................................................

   b.  Brief details of that treatment

**3. Treatment at A&E department**

   a. Approximate time between accident and arrival of ambulance ....................................

   b. Name of paramedic (if possible) ....................................................................................

   c. Who accompanied pupil to hospital?
      *(circle appropriate response)*        Parent      School staff

   d. If school staff, state name ............................................................................................

      i. Did hospital ask member of staff to sanction any action or form of treatment prior to arrival of parents? *(circle appropriate response)*   Yes        No

      ii. If **Yes**, specify action or treatment .......................................................................

   e.  Approximate time parents arrived at hospital .............................................................

   f.  Was pupil admitted to hospital following treatment in A&E?
      *(circle appropriate response)*        Yes        No

## Follow-up procedures

**1. Completion of employer's accident report form**

    a. Form completed by ................................................................................................

    b. Date forwarded to employer ..............................................................................

**Note:** The school is legally obliged to complete and submit the form to the employer or direct to HSE if so determined by the employer as soon as possible after the accident so that the employer can comply with RIDDOR.

**2. Risk assessment**

    a. Risk assessment of the lesson reviewed by ...................................................

    b. Date carried out .................................................................................................

    c. Was a change to procedures recommended? *(circle appropriate response)*   Yes    No

    d. When were these changes implemented? .......................................................

**3. Contact with parents**

    a. Who contacted parents to ascertain pupil's progress? ...............................

    b. How soon after the accident was contact made? ........................................

    c. Brief details of information received ...............................................................

**4. Pupil's return to school**

    a. Date of return to school ....................................................................................

    b. Date of restart of physical education ..............................................................

    c. Any restrictions on pupil's involvement in physical education laid down by medical profession ..............................................................................................

Form completed by ................................................................................................

Signed: ................................................................. Date: ..........................................

**Note:** Schools may choose to attach additional information to this form (eg employer's accident report form, witness statements, risk-assessment form covering activity, photocopy of register covering the four weeks prior to the accident).

## Appendix 8C: Standard Accident Procedures

It is essential that all school staff and pupils are aware of the standard accident procedures (SAP) adopted by their school. This will help to ensure they all respond to an emergency in the same way, thus minimising the time spent between the accident occurring and the injured pupil(s) receiving first aid.

This appendix contains a sample SAP. Please note that it does not attempt to constitute an authoritative legal interpretation of the provisions of any enactment, regulations or common law. That interpretation is exclusively a matter for the courts.

The suggested format for an SAP is illustrated in the three flow charts on pages 340–342:

1 **Red procedure:** for serious accidents that require immediate hospitalisation.
2 **Yellow procedure:** for an accident that can be referred to a doctor, clinic or hospital by transport by parent or school.
3 **Green procedure:** for accidents that can be dealt with in-house.

The red procedure should always be used when:

• there is any doubt about the level or nature of the injury

• concussion occurs as a result of an accident.

## Red accident procedures

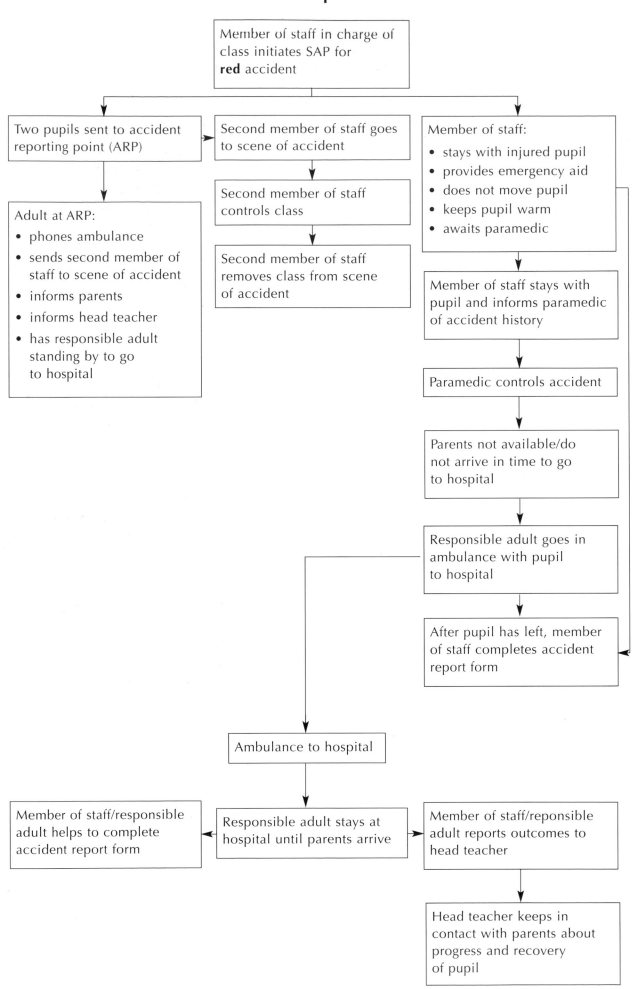

**Member of staff in charge of class initiates SAP for red accident**

**Two pupils sent to accident reporting point (ARP)**

**Second member of staff goes to scene of accident**

**Member of staff:**
- stays with injured pupil
- provides emergency aid
- does not move pupil
- keeps pupil warm
- awaits paramedic

**Adult at ARP:**
- phones ambulance
- sends second member of staff to scene of accident
- informs parents
- informs head teacher
- has responsible adult standing by to go to hospital

**Second member of staff controls class**

**Second member of staff removes class from scene of accident**

**Member of staff stays with pupil and informs paramedic of accident history**

**Paramedic controls accident**

**Parents not available/do not arrive in time to go to hospital**

**Responsible adult goes in ambulance with pupil to hospital**

**After pupil has left, member of staff completes accident report form**

**Ambulance to hospital**

**Member of staff/responsible adult helps to complete accident report form**

**Responsible adult stays at hospital until parents arrive**

**Member of staff/reponsible adult reports outcomes to head teacher**

**Head teacher keeps in contact with parents about progress and recovery of pupil**

340

# Yellow accident procedures

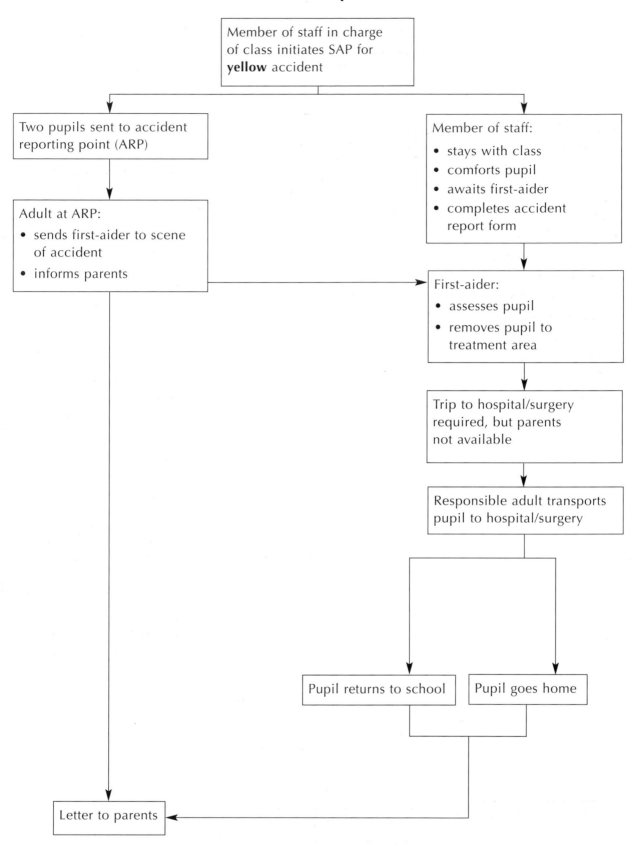

## Green accident procedures

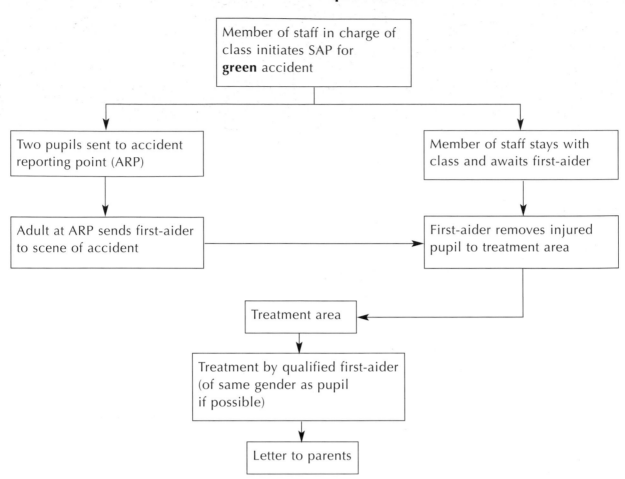

Member of staff in charge of class initiates SAP for **green** accident

Two pupils sent to accident reporting point (ARP)

Member of staff stays with class and awaits first-aider

Adult at ARP sends first-aider to scene of accident

First-aider removes injured pupil to treatment area

Treatment area

Treatment by qualified first-aider (of same gender as pupil if possible)

Letter to parents

342

# Appendix nine

## Framework for a Policy and Guidelines on Health and Safety in PESS

a9

See pages 37–40 in afPE's *Safe Practice in Physical Education and School Sport 2008 Edition* for general notes.

## Introduction/Policy Statement

**Purpose (of the risk-management guidelines in PESS):**

- to offer PESS within a well-managed, safe and educational context

- to establish common codes of practice for staff and pupils

- to provide common administrative procedures

- to ensure statutory and local requirements are followed and other national guidelines, such as codes of practice, are considered.

**Rationale (for teaching risk management in PESS):**

- to enable pupils to participate in PESS that provides appropriate challenge, with acceptable risk

- to educate pupils about risk management in order for them to participate independently in physical activity later in life

- to fulfil the requirements of the National Curriculum for physical education.

**Context (for teaching risk management in PESS):**

- an environment that is safe for the activity

- adequately supervised activities

- using regular and approved practice

- taking pupils through progressive stages of learning and challenge

- building a system of advice and the practice of warning

- using equipment only for the purpose it was intended for

- providing basic care in the event of an accident

- based on forethought and sound preparation.

# Guidelines

Consideration should be given to the inclusion of the following in your school guidelines. Page references in brackets relate to afPE's *Safe Practice in Physical Education and School Sport 2008 Edition* where the topic is discussed.

This list is not definitive. Reference should be made also to local authority (LA) guidelines and your school safety policy.

## People

### a. Pupils

- Dealing with disability discrimination (pages 18, 289)
- Pupils with special needs (pages 73–80, 301, 319–324)
- Pupils with medical needs (pages 73–80, 125, 319–324)
- Ratios (pages 38, 203–262, 265)

### b. Staff

- Qualifications and competence for teaching physical education (pages 31–36, 38, 204)
- Support staff, volunteers and coaches (pages 31–36, 38, 73–80, 313–316)

## Context

### a. Facilities

- Storerooms (pages 103–110)
- Work areas (pages 85–93, 103–110, 166, 184)

### b. Equipment

- Checking, maintenance, use and movement of equipment (pages 85–93, 167)
- Clothing (pages 81, 99–102, 185, 189)
- Footwear (pages 101, 168)
- Jewellery, body piercing and personal effects (pages 99–100)
- Personal protection (pages 95–98)
- Use of mats (pages 90–91, 152)

### c. Procedures

- Accident procedures (pages 10, 49–54, 332–335, 339–342)
- Accident report forms (pages 52–53, 336–338)
- Codes of conduct (pages 17, 209, 356)
- Contingency plans (page 218)
- Digital imagery (pages 61–63)
- Higher-risk activities (page 15 and relevant sections of Part 2 – pages 135–286)
- HIV and Aids (page 52)
- Insurance (pages 45–48)
- Inter-school matches and sports events (pages 47, 123–131, 356–358)
- Parental consent (pages 17, 330)

## Organisation

### a. Preparation

### b. Progression

### c. Teaching and class management

# Appendix ten

### List of Central Council for Physical Recreation (CCPR) Member Organisations Relevant to Schools with Website Details

| Organisation | Web Address |
| --- | --- |
| Air Training Corps Sports Council | www.aircadets.org |
| Amateur Boxing Association of England Limited | www.abae.co.uk |
| Amateur Rowing Association | www.ara-rowing.org |
| Amateur Swimming Association | www.britishswimming.org |
| Army Cadet Force Association | www.armycadets.com |
| Army Sport Control Board | www.army.mod.uk/sportandadventure/army%5Fsports%5Fcontrol%5Fboard/ |
| Association for Physical Education | www.afpe.org.uk |
| Association of British Riding Schools | www.abrs-info.org |
| Association of School and College Leaders | www.ascl.org.uk |
| Association of Teachers and Lecturers | www.atl.org.uk |
| Badminton England | www.badmintonengland.co.uk |
| BaseballSoftballUK | www.baseballsoftballuk.com |
| Be-Active Foundation Limited | www.be-active.co.uk |
| Bowls England | www.bowlsengland.com |
| Boys' Brigade | www.boys-brigade.org.uk |
| British Aikido Board | www.bab.org.uk |
| British Amateur Rugby League Association | www.barla.org.uk |
| British American Football Association | www.BAFA.org.uk |
| British Association of Sport and Exercise Medicine | www.basem.co.uk |

| | |
|---|---|
| British Association of Sport and Exercise Sciences | www.bases.org.uk |
| British Association of Teachers of Dancing | www.batd.co.uk |
| British Blind Sport | www.britishblindsport.org.uk |
| British Boxing Board of Control | www.bbbofc.com |
| British Canoe Union | www.bcu.org.uk |
| British Caving Association | www.british-caving.org.uk |
| British Cheerleading Association | www.cheerleading.org.uk |
| British Colleges Sport | www.britishcollegessport.org |
| British Crown Green Bowling Association | www.bowls.org |
| British Cycling Federation | www.britishcycling.org.uk |
| British Dance Council | www.british-dance-council.org |
| British Dragon Boat Racing Association | www.dragonboat.org.uk |
| British Dressage | www.britishdressage.co.uk |
| British Equestrian Federation | www.bef.co.uk |
| British Equestrian Vaulting | www.vaulting.org.uk |
| British Eventing | www.britisheventing.com |
| British Fencing Association | www.britishfencing.com |
| British Gliding Association | www.gliding.co.uk |
| British Gymnastics | www.british-gymnastics.org |
| British Handball Association | www.britishhandball.com |
| British Horse Society | www.bhs.org.uk |
| British Judo Association | www.britishjudo.org.uk |
| British Ju-Jitsu Association | www.bjjagb.com |

| British Kite Flying Association | www.bkfa.org.uk |
|---|---|
| British Kitesurfing Association | www.kitesurfing.org |
| British Long Distance Swimming Association | www.bldsa.org.uk |
| British Mountaineering Council | www.thebmc.co.uk |
| British Orienteering Federation | www.britishorienteering.org.uk |
| British Parachute Association | www.bpa.org.uk |
| British Paralympic Association | www.paralympics.org.uk |
| British Schools' Tennis Association | www.bsta.org.uk |
| British Show Jumping Association | www.bsja.co.uk |
| British Ski Club for the Disabled | www.bscd.org.uk |
| British Sub-Aqua Club | www.bsac.com |
| British Surfing Association | www.britsurf.co.uk |
| British Table Tennis Association for Disabled People | www.guide-information.org.uk/search_index_detail.lasso?RecID=G5219 |
| British Taekwondo Control Board | www.btcb.org |
| British Tenpin Bowling Association | www.btba.org.uk |
| British Triathlon Association | www.britishtriathlon.org |
| British Universities Sports Association | www.busa.org.uk |
| British Water Ski | www.britishwaterski.co.uk |
| British Weight Lifters' Association | www.bwla.com |
| British Wheel of Yoga | www.bwy.org.uk |
| British Wrestling | www.britishwrestling.org |
| BSES Expeditions | www.bses.org.uk |
| Byways and Bridleways Trust | www.bbtrust.org.uk |
| Canoe-Camping Club | www.canoecampingclub.co.uk |
| Chief Leisure Officers Association | www.cloa.org.uk |
| Church Lads' and Church Girls' Brigade | www.clcgb.org.uk |

| | |
|---|---|
| College of Chinese Physical Culture | www.ccpc.ac.uk |
| Croquet Association | www.croquet.org.uk |
| Cycling Time Trials | www.cyclingtimetrials.org.uk |
| Cyclists' Touring Club | www.ctc.org.uk |
| Dolmetsch Historical Dance Society | www.dhds.org.uk |
| Duke of Edinburgh's Award | www.theaward.org |
| England and Wales Cricket Board | www.ecb.co.uk |
| England Basketball | www.englandbasketball.co.uk |
| England Fencing | www.englandfencing.co.uk |
| England Hockey | www.englandhockey.co.uk |
| England Netball | www.englandnetball.co.uk |
| England Squash | www.englandsquash.com |
| English Amateur Dancesport Association | www.englishdancesport.org.uk |
| English Bowling Federation | www.fedbowls.co.uk |
| English Chess Federation | www.englishchess.org.uk |
| English Federation of Disability Sport | www.efds.co.uk |
| English Folk Dance and Song Society | www.efdss.org |
| English Golf Union | www.englishgolfunion.org |
| English Ice Hockey Association | www.eiha.co.uk |
| English Indoor Bowling Association | www.eiba.co.uk |
| English Lacrosse Association | www.englishlacrosse.co.uk |
| English Petanque Association | www.englishpetanque.org.uk |
| English Schools' Athletic Association | www.esaa.net |
| English Schools' Football Association | www.esfa.co.uk |

| English Short Mat Bowling Association | www.esmba.com |
|---|---|
| English Table Tennis Association | www.etta.co.uk |
| English Women's Indoor Bowling Association | www.ewiba.com |
| Exercise Movement and Dance Partnership | www.emdp.org |
| Federation of Yorkshire Sport | www.yorkshiresport.org.uk |
| Fields in Trust | www.fieldsintrust.org |
| Fitness League | www.thefitnessleague.com |
| Football Association | www.theFA.com |
| Football Foundation | www.footballfoundation.org.uk |
| Forest School Camps | www.fsc.org.uk |
| Girlguiding UK | www.girlguiding.org.uk |
| Girls' Venture Corps Air Cadets | www.gvcac.org.uk |
| Golf Foundation | www.golf-foundation.org |
| Grand National Archery Society | www.gnas.org |
| Great Britain Diving Federation | www.diving-gbdf.com |
| Great Britain Wheelchair Basketball Association | www.gbwba.org.uk |
| Guild of Professional Teachers of Dancing | www.gptd.co.uk |
| Headmasters' Conference | www.bedmod.co.uk |
| Ice Hockey Players Association | www.ihpa.co.uk |
| Ice Hockey UK | www.icehockeyuk.co.uk |
| IMBA UK | www.imba-uk.com |
| Imperial Society of Teachers of Dancing | www.istd.org |
| Inland Waterways Association | www.waterways.org.uk |
| Institute for Outdoor Learning | www.outdoor-learning.org |
| Institute for Sport, Parks and Leisure | www.ispal.org.uk |

| | |
|---|---|
| Institute of Groundsmanship | www.iog.org |
| Institute of Sport and Recreation Management | www.isrm.co.uk |
| International Dance Teachers Association | www.idta.co.uk |
| Jewish Lads' and Girls' Brigade | www.jlgb.org |
| Keep Fit Association | www.keepfit.org.uk |
| Laban Guild for Movement and Dance | www.labanguild.org |
| Ladies' Golf Union | www.lgu.org |
| Language of Dance Centre | www.lodc.org |
| Lawn Tennis Association | www.lta.org.uk |
| Local Government Association | www.lga.gov.uk |
| London Federation of Sport and Recreation | www.london-fed-sport.org.uk |
| Long Distance Walkers Association Ltd | www.ldwa.org.uk |
| Margaret Morris Movement | www.margaretmorrismovement.com |
| Medau Society | www.medau.org.uk |
| Mencap Sport | www.mencap.org.uk/sport |
| Mini-Basketball England | www.mini-basketball.org.uk |
| Model Yachting Association | www.mya-uk.org.uk |
| Modern Pentathlon Association of Great Britain | www.mpagb.org.uk |
| Mountain Leader Training England | www.mlte.org |
| National Association of Clubs for Young People | www.clubsforyoungpeople.org.uk |
| National Association of Fisheries and Angling Consultatives | www.nafac.co.uk |
| National Association of Karate and Martial Art Schools | www.nakmas.org.uk |
| National Association of Schoolmasters and Union of Women Teachers | www.nasuwt.org.uk |
| National Association of Teachers of Dancing | www.natd.org.uk |

| | |
|---|---|
| National Confederation of Parent Teacher Associations | www.ncpta.org.uk |
| National Council for School Sport | www.ncss.org.uk |
| National Council for Voluntary Organisations | www.ncvo-vol.org.uk |
| National County Sports Partnership Network | www.durhamsport.com |
| National Federation of Anglers | www.nfadirect.com |
| National Federation of Sea Anglers | www.nfsa.org.uk |
| National Ice Skating Association UK Ltd | www.iceskating.org.uk |
| National Rifle Association | www.nra.org.uk |
| National Roller Hockey Association | www.nrha.co.uk |
| National Rounders Association | www.nra-rounders.co.uk |
| National School Sailing Association | www.nssa.org.uk |
| National Small-Bore Rifle Association | www.nsra.co.uk |
| National Stoolball Association | www.stoolball.co.uk |
| National Union of Teachers | www.teachers.org.uk |
| North East Federation of Sport and Recreation | www.bsta.org.uk |
| Northern Counties Dance Teachers' Association Ltd | www.ncdta.com |
| Northern Ireland Sports Forum | www.nisf.net |
| Open Spaces Society | www.oss.org.uk |
| Police Sport UK | www.policesportuk.com |
| Pony Club | www.pcuk.org |
| Professional Association of Teachers | www.pat.org.uk |
| Professional Cricketers' Association | www.thepca.co.uk |
| Professional Golfers' Association | www.pga.org.uk |
| RAF Sports Board | www.raf.mod.uk |

| | |
|---|---|
| Ramblers' Association | www.ramblers.org.uk |
| Register of Exercise Professionals | www.exerciseregister.org |
| River and Lake Swimming Association | www.river-swimming.co.uk |
| Royal Academy of Dance | www.rad.org.uk |
| Royal Life Saving Society | www.lifesavers.org.uk |
| Royal Scottish Country Dance Society | www.rscds.org |
| Royal Yachting Association | www.rya.org.uk |
| Rugby Football League | www.therfl.co.uk |
| Rugby Football Union | www.rfu.com |
| Rugby Football Union for Women | www.rfu.com |
| Salmon and Trout Association | www.salmon-trout.org |
| Scottish Equestrian Association | www.conscia.co.uk |
| Scottish Sports Association | www.scottishsportsassociation.org.uk |
| Scout Association | www.scouts.org.uk |
| Sea Cadet Association | www.ms-sc.org |
| Snowsport England | www.snowsportengland.org.uk |
| Snowsport GB | www.snowsportgb.com |
| Society for International Folk Dancing | www.sifd.org |
| Sports and Recreation Trusts Association | www.sporta.org |
| Sports Leaders UK | www.sportsleaders.org |
| Sports Officials UK (SOUK) | www.sportsofficialsuk.com |
| Sports Volunteering North West Limited | www.sportsvolunteeringnw.org |
| SportsAid | www.sportsaid.org.uk |
| sports coach UK | www.sportscoachuk.org |
| St John Ambulance Cadets | www.sja.org.uk/young_people/cadets |

| | |
|---|---|
| Sub Aqua Association | www.saa.org.uk |
| Supporters Direct | www.supporters-direct.org |
| Surf Life Saving Association of Great Britain | www.surflifesaving.org.uk |
| Swimming Teachers' Association | www.sta.co.uk |
| Tall Ships Youth Trust | www.tallships.org |
| Tchoukball Association of Great Britain | www.tagb.org.uk |
| Tennis and Rackets Association | www.tennisandrackets.com |
| Tennis Foundation | www.tennisfoundation.org.uk |
| Torch Trophy Trust | www.ccpr.org.uk |
| Trail Riders Fellowship | www.trf.org.uk |
| UK Alliance | www.ukadance.co.uk |
| UK Athletics | www.ukathletics.net |
| UK Deaf Sport | www.ukdeafsport.org.uk |
| UK Sports Association for People with Learning Disabilities | www.uksportsassociation.org |
| United Kingdom Cheerleading Association | www.abc-ukca.co.uk |
| University and College Sport | www.ucsport.net |
| Volleyball England | www.volleyballengland.org |
| Welsh Sports Association | www.welshsports.org.uk |
| WheelPower | www.wheelpower.org.uk |
| Women's Sport and Fitness Foundation | www.wsff.org.uk |
| Woodcraft Folk | www.woodcraft.org.uk |
| Young Explorers' Trust | www.theyet.org |

# Appendix eleven
Health and Safety – Managing a Sports Event – Some Issues Identified

To be read in conjunction with any school or local authority (LA) educational visits documentation. Local requirements may set out issues additional to those listed here.

| Aspect | Away Match | Day Festival (in addition to aspects listed in the previous column) | Tour (in addition to aspects listed in the TWO previous columns) |
|---|---|---|---|
| **Pre-event** | • Head teacher (HT) aware?<br>• School policies/procedures known and applied?<br>• Consent forms required and, if so, obtained?<br>• Parents aware of itinerary, programme, particular needs and conditions, insurance provision, emergency contact system, venue address?<br>• Staffing – roles and responsibilities/ratio/expertise/group management/knowledge of group?<br>• Group register available?<br>• Medical backgrounds known?<br>• General risk assessment made and requirements followed?<br>• Reciprocal arrangements with host school clarified/known?<br>• Other 'what ifs'/contingency planning thought through?<br>• School's crisis-management plan requirements built in to risk assessment and planning? | • Governors' approval needed?<br>• Additional staffing needed to cover supervision/officiating etc?<br>• Group issues clarified – age, ability, behaviour, selection?<br>• 'Telephone tree' (cascading communication system to convey messages/delays back to parents) completed?<br>• Pre-visit made to venue?<br>• Risk assessment made if possible?<br>• First aid – provided by host? | • LA/governors' approval needed and all requirements met?<br>• Paperwork checked (eg passports/additional insurance if needed)?<br>• Injections/medications required prior to and during tour?<br>• Pupil code of conduct needs to be developed from basic school visit requirements (eg communication/mountain code/country code/safety on water)?<br>• Parents have copy of itinerary, contact details etc?<br>• Leadership skills evident?<br>• Additional staffing requirements identified (eg residential/adventure activities/city tour/swimming involved)?<br>• Implications of taking non-school staff considered and adjustments made?<br>• Safeguarding issues checked (eg host families)?<br>• Pupils adequately prepared for tour? |
| **Assembly** | • Continuous duty of care? If not, clarity re ending/beginning etc?<br>• Register/head count in?<br>• Kit/footwear check?<br>• Medication etc check?<br>• Emergency contact information to hand?<br>• Pupils know and apply code of conduct?<br>• Mobile phone to hand in case of emergency? | • Pupils and parents know time to meet, what to do if miss coach etc? | |

| Aspect | Away Match | Day Festival (in addition to aspects listed in the previous column) | Tour (in addition to aspects listed in the TWO previous columns) |
|---|---|---|---|
| **Journey** | • Coach/minibus/taxi/cars – LA/school/legal requirements met?<br>• First-aid kit/appointed person/who can drive/supervise and drive/where do staff sit/additional supervision or drivers needed/basic vehicle check made?<br>• Safe embarkation point?<br>• Register?<br>• Head count before leaving?<br>• Emergency action plan?<br>• Delays etc?<br>• Illness on journey?<br>• Safe disembarkation point? | • Additional drivers needed?<br>• Management of breaks in journey (eg motorway service areas)?<br>• Head count after any break in journey? | • Package tour conditions?<br>• Implications of foreign law, standards, health, language?<br>• International driving requirements?<br>• Supervision at airport/terminals etc?<br>• Information to be carried by pupils in case of dislocation from main group? |
| **Venue/competition** | • Venue risk assessment – by home team?<br>• Any group or activity management issues (eg one staff with two teams/officiating and supervising)?<br>• Acceptable behaviour assured?<br>• Periodic head counts necessary?<br>• Equality in size/experience/confidence?<br>• Kit and footwear appropriate to weather/playing surface?<br>• Personal effects?<br>• Personal protection – pads/helmets/mouth guards etc?<br>• First-aid cover/reciprocal arrangements with host confirmed?<br>• Competent/qualified officials?<br>• Facility/equipment checked before use as part of host school risk assessment?<br>• Emergency action plan – hospital/rest of team/staff illness/communication?<br>• Weather issues – sun protection/rehydration/storms/other seasonal considerations? | • Programme allows sufficient rest/recovery periods?<br>• Total playing time?<br>• Provision of refreshments?<br>• Contingency plan in case of early completion/abandonment of programme (see telephone tree)?<br>• Has consent been granted/is it necessary for any photography that may be involved?<br>• Sunshade/rain cover available?<br>• Change of clothes needed?<br>• Supervision appropriate? | • Itinerary?<br>• Security of accommodation?<br>• Home care abroad safeguarding requirements/standards/different attitude?<br>• Misuse of camera mobile phones?<br>• Pupil code of conduct applied?<br>• Additional insurance needed?<br>• Down/free-time issues?<br>• Policy on pupil use of mobile phones?<br>• Pupils have accessible point of contact in host country?<br>• Reciprocal arrangements clarified if hosted by another school/group? |

| | | |
|---|---|---|
| **Return journey** | • Head count?<br>• Safe embarkation/disembarkation?<br>• Dispersal point(s)?<br>• Parents aware?<br>• Strategy if parents delayed?<br>• Journey delayed – breakdown/traffic etc?<br>• Anticipated dispersal time communicated? | • Numbers checked after any break in journey?<br>• Supervision arrangements known if public transport/ferry/airport etc involved?<br>• Information to be carried by pupils in case of dislocation from main group? |
| **Event evaluation** | • Any near misses/incidents to review?<br>• Injuries recorded and outcome followed up?<br>• Any improvements for next event?<br>• Any feedback necessary to HT/subject leader/staff/pupils/parents?<br>• Any adjustments to risk assessment? Formally recorded to inform future planning? | |

It is good practice for schools to agree a code of conduct with parents and pupils before pupils participate in educational visits. Acceptance of a code will provide party leaders with the necessary authority to carry out their responsibilities. The agreed code of conduct should be formalised and sent to parents, with the consent and medical forms, for them and their child to sign. Suggested items for inclusion in the code of conduct are listed below.

All pupils should:

a.  observe normal school rules

b.  cooperate fully with leaders at all times

c.  fulfil any tasks or duties set prior to and during the visit

d.  participate fully in all activities and sessions during the visit

e.  be punctual at all times

f.  not leave group sessions or accommodation without permission

g.  always return to the meeting point or accommodation at agreed times

h.  be in groups of not less than three pupils if granted indirectly supervised time

i.  avoid behaviour which may inconvenience others

j.  be considerate to others at all times

k.  respect all requests made by school staff and accompanying adults

l.  behave at all times in a manner that reflects positively on themselves, the party and the school

m. abide by the laws, rules and regulations of the countries and places visited

n.  comply with customs and duty-free regulations

o.  not purchase or consume alcohol, tobacco products or purchase dangerous articles such as explosives and knives

p.  consult with school staff if in doubt about any issues

q.  accept that a full written report of any misconduct will be forwarded to the educational visits coordinator/head teacher and their parents.

# Appendix thirteen a13

## Sample Consent Form for the Use of Digital Imagery in School

*Digital imagery may be used in a number of school activities. The following sample letter does not specifically refer to physical education and should be seen as a means of obtaining parental consent for the use of digital imagery in all school-related activities.*

Dear Parent

Digital imagery is an exciting new medium, which can motivate and inspire pupils. Although the associated risks are minimal, schools have a duty of care towards pupils.

*(school name)* recognises the need to ensure the welfare and safety of all young people. In accordance with our child-protection policy, we will not permit photographs, videos or other images of pupils to be taken without the consent of the parents and pupils involved.

*(school name)* has policies relating to the use of photographs and videos. Copies can be obtained from *(named person)*.

*(school name)* will take all necessary steps to ensure that any images produced are used solely for the purposes for which they are intended. Photographs may be used in our printed publications for display around the school, as teaching resources within the curriculum and on the internal school website. Video clips may also be used as teaching aids within the curriculum and for staff training and educational purposes at both local and national level. At no time will the images be sold or made available for wider publication without further parental approval.

Please complete, sign and return this form to *(named person)* at *(school name)*.

Name of child: ...............................................................................................

Name of parent: ...............................................................................................

Address: ...........................................................................................................

.........................................................................................................................

.........................................................................................................................

.........................................................................................................................

I consent to *(school name)* photographing and videoing my child as described above.

Signature: .......................................................................................................

Date: ...............................................................................................................

Queries regarding this form should be addressed to *(school name and address)*.

# Index

364